Sociology

Introductory Readings

Third Edition

Sociology

Introductory Readings

Third Edition

Edited by Anthony Giddens
and Philip W. Sutton

Polity

Copyright © this collection and editorial summaries Polity Press
2010

First published in 2010 by Polity Press

Polity Press
65 Bridge Street
Cambridge CB2 1UR, UK

Polity Press
350 Main Street
Malden, MA 02148, USA

ISBN-13: 978-0-7456-4883-5 (hardback)
ISBN-13: 978-0-7456-4884-2 (paperback)

A catalogue record for this book is available from the British
Library.

Typeset in 10 on 12.5 pt Galliard
by Toppan Best-set Premedia Limited
Printed and bound in Great Britain by Clays Ltd, St Ives plc

The publisher has used its best endeavours to ensure that the
URLs for external websites referred to in this book are correct
and active at the time of going to press. However, the publisher
has no responsibility for the websites and can make no
guarantee that a site will remain live or that the content is or
will remain appropriate.

Every effort has been made to trace all copyright holders, but if
any have been inadvertently overlooked the publisher will be
pleased to include any necessary credits in any subsequent
reprint or edition.

For further information on Polity, visit our website:
www.politybooks.com

Contents

Acknowledgements

We are grateful to the following for permission to reproduce copyright material:

Oxford University Press for material from *The Sociological Imagination* by C. Wright Mills, copyright © 2000 [1959]. By permission of Oxford University Press, Inc., pp. 3–11; Polity Press for material from *Social Theory and Modern Sociology* by Anthony Giddens, copyright © 1987; Palgrave Macmillan for material from *Foundations of Sociology: Towards a Better Understanding of the Human World* by Richard Jenkins, published 2002, Palgrave Macmillan, reproduced with permission of Palgrave Macmillan, pp. 15–22; Palgrave Macmillan for material from *The Division of Labour in Society*, by Emile Durkheim, translated by W. D. Halls, published 1984, Macmillan Publishers Ltd, reproduced with permission of Palgrave Macmillan, pp. 38–39, 60–61, 83–85, 337–40; Wiley-Blackwell for material from *Theorizing Patriarchy* by Sylvia Walby copyright © 1994 Blackwell Publishers. Reproduced with permission of Blackwell Publishing Ltd, pp. 20–24, 178–82, 200–201; Taylor & Francis Group LLC for material from *Intimations of Postmodernity* by Zygmunt Bauman, copyright © 1992 Routledge. Reproduced by permission of Taylor & Francis Books UK, pp. vii–x, 187–8; Polity Press for material from *The Consequences of Modernity* by Anthony Giddens, copyright © 1996, pp. 10, 137–9, 151–4; Oxford University Press for material from *Social Research Methods*, 3rd Edition by Alan Bryman, copyright © 2008. By permission of Alan Bryman and Oxford University Press, Inc, pp. 588–96, 611, 624; Polity Press for material from

The Survey Methods Workbook by Alan Buckingham and Peter Saunders, copyright © 2004, pp. 11–16, 19–22; Sage for material from *Using Biographical Methods in Social Research* by Barbara Merrill and Linden West. Reproduced by permission of Sage Publications, London, Los Angeles, New Delhi and Singapore copyright © 2009, pp. 1–7, 10–12; Oxford University Press for material from *Body and Soul: Notebooks of an Apprentice Boxer* by Loïc Wacquant, copyright © 2004. By permission of Oxford University Press, Inc., pp. 3–9; The Free Press for material from *The Sociology of Georg Simmel* translated and edited by Kurt H. Wolff. Reprinted and edited with the permission of The Free Press, a Division of Simon & Schuster, Inc. Copyright © 1950 by The Free Press. Copyright renewed © 1978 by The Free Press. All rights reserved, pp. 409–16; Janklow & Nesbit Associates for material from *The Conscience of the Eye: The Design and Social Life of Cities* by Richard Sennett. Copyright © 1991 by Richard Sennett. Reprinted by permission of the author; Princeton University Press for material from *The Global City: New York, London, Tokyo*, Second edition by Saskia Sassen copyright © 1991 Princeton University Press. Reprinted by Princeton University Press, pp. xix, 3–8; Rowman & Littlefield Publishing Group for material from *Sociological Theory and the Environment: Classical Foundations, Contemporary Insights* edited by Riley E. Dunlap, Frederick H. Buttel, Peter Dickens and August Gijswijt copyright © Rowman & Littlefield, 2002, pp. 332–6, 344–5; Polity Press for material from *The Politics of Climate Change* by Anthony Giddens, copyright © 2009, pp. 1–4, 11–13, 68–72; Taylor & Francis Group LLC for material from *The Protestant Ethic and the Spirit of Capitalism*, by Max Weber 1930 [1904–5], translated by Talcott Parsons copyright © 2005 Routledge. Reproduced by permission of Taylor & Francis Books UK, pp. xxxi–xxxv, 116, 122–4; Taylor & Francis Group LLC for material from *The Elementary Forms of the Religious Life* by Emile Durkheim, translated by Joseph Ward Swain, 1976 [1915], George Allen and Unwin Ltd, copyright © Routledge. Reproduced by permission of Taylor & Francis Books UK, pp. 43–7, 416–20, 427–8; Taylor & Francis Group LLC for material from *Between Sex and Power: Family in the World, 1900–2000* by Göran Therborn, copyright © 2004 Routledge. Reproduced by permission of Taylor & Francis Books UK, pp. 1–2, 8–12, 295–6; New Society Publishers for material from *Dumbing Us Down: The Hidden Curriculum of Compulsory Schooling* by John Taylor Gatto, copyright © 2005 New Society Publishers, pp. 1–11; Council on Foreign Relations, Inc. for material from 'Offshoring: The Next Industrial Revolution?' by Alan S. Blinder. Reprinted by permission of *Foreign Affairs*, Issue 85(2) March/April 2006. Copyright © 2006 by the Council on Foreign Relations, Inc. www.ForeignAffairs.com, pp. 113–14, 118–28; Taylor & Francis Group LLC for material from *Stratification: Social Division and Inequality* by Wendy Bottero, copyright © 2004 Routledge. Reproduced by permission of Taylor & Francis Books UK, pp. 3–8, 248–9; The Random House Group Ltd for material from *The Second Sex* by Simone de Beauvoir, translated by H. M. Parshley. Reproduced by permission of The Random House Group Ltd. A new translation by Sheila Malovany-Chevallier and Constance Borde will be published by Jonathan Cape 2009, pp. 13–21, 734; Taylor & Francis Group LLC for material from *Black Feminist Thought: Knowledge, Consciousness, and the Politics of Empowerment*, Revised edition by Patricia Hill-Collins copyright © 2000 Routledge. Reproduced by permission of Taylor & Francis Books UK, pp. 4–6, 18, 22–3, 284–5, 290; Polity Press for material from *Class and Stratification*, 3rd Edition by Rosemary Crompton, copyright © 2008, pp. 2–5, 79–82, 88–9; Polity Press for material from *Exploring Disability* by Colin Barnes, Geof Mercer and Tom Shakespeare, copyright © 1999, pp. 20–4, 27–31, 37–8; Palgrave Macmillan for material from *The Life Course: A Sociological Introduction* by Stephen J. Hunt, published 2005 Palgrave Macmillan, reproduced with permission of Palgrave Macmillan, pp. 10–11, 16–17, 21–2, 30–1; Polity Press for material from *Making Sexual History* by Jeffrey Weeks, copyright © 1999, pp. 128–33, 137–9; Polity Press for material from *The Normal Chaos of Love* by Ulrich Beck and Elisabeth Beck-Gernsheim, translated by Mark Ritter, Jane Wiebel, copyright © Polity Press 1995, pp. 11–13, 45–6, 51–6, 59–61; Open University Press for material from *Ageism* by Bill Bytheway, 1994. Reproduced with the kind permission of Open University Press. All rights reserved, pp. 6–10, 13–14, 124–5; Wiley-Blackwell for material from *The Loneliness of the Dying* by Norbert Elias, translated by Edmund Jephcott copyright © 1985 Blackwell Publishers. Reproduced with permission of Blackwell Publishing Ltd, pp. 2–4, 8, 68–9, 88–91; Penguin Books Ltd for material from *The Presentation of Self in Everyday Life* by Erving Goffman (Allen Lane The Penguin Press, 1980) copyright © Erving Goffman, 1959, pp. 26–7, 109–18; Interlink Publishing Group, Inc. for material from *Reel Bad Arabs: How Hollywood Vilifies a People* by Jack G. Shaheen, published by Olive Branch Press, an imprint of Interlink Publishing Group, Inc. Text copyright © Jack G. Shaheen, 2001. Reprinted by permission, pp. 1–5, 10–11, 16–22, 34–5; Polity Press for material from *The Internet and Society* by James Slevin, copyright © 2000, pp. 44–54; The MIT Press for material from *The Virtual Community, revised edition: Homesteading on the Electronic Frontier* by Howard Rheingold, excerpts from pp. xv–xviii, xxx–xxxii, 347–8, 360–1, © 2000 Massachusetts Institute of Technology, by permission of The MIT Press; Sage for material from *Medical Power and Social Knowledge* by Bryan S. Turner. Reproduced by permission of Sage Publications, London, Los Angeles,

New Delhi and Singapore copyright © 1995, pp. 37–9, 42–5, 51–4; Palgrave Macmillan for material from *What Makes Women Sick: Gender and the Political Economy of Health* by Lesley Doyal, published 1995, Macmillan Press, reproduced with permission of Palgrave Macmillan, pp. 3–4, 9–11, 14–18; Polity Press for material from *Health and Illness* by Mike Bury, copyright © 2005, pp. 68–72, 103–5, 117–18; Marion Boyars Publishers for material from *Limits to Medicine* by Ivan Illich copyright © 1975 Marion Boyars, London. Reproduced with permission, pp. 13–17, 27–35; Sage for material from *The Body and Social Theory* by Chris Shilling. Reproduced by permission of Sage Publications, London, Los Angeles, New Delhi and Singapore copyright © 1993, pp. 19–23, 29–39; The Free Press for material from *The Rules of Sociological Method* by Emile Durkheim, translated by Sarah A. Solovay and John H. Mueller. Edited by George E. G. Catlin. Reprinted and edited with the permission of The Free Press, a Division of Simon & Schuster, Inc. Copyright © 1938 by George E. G. Catlin. Copyright renewed © 1976 by Sarah A. Solovay, John H. Mueller, George E. G. Catlin. All rights reserved, pp. 65–70; The Free Press for material from *Social Theory and Social Structure* by Robert K. Merton. Reprinted and edited with the permission of The Free Press, a Division of Simon & Schuster, Inc. Copyright © 1949, 1957 by The Free Press. Copyright renewed © 1977, 1985 by Robert K. Merton. All rights reserved, pp. 136–41, 144–6; Penguin Books Ltd for material from *Discipline and Punish: The Birth of Prison* by Michel Foucault translated by Alan Sheridan (first published as *Surveiller et punir: Naissance de la prison* by Éditions Gallimard 1975, Allen Lane 1975) copyright © Alan Sheridan, 1977, pp. 3–8, 14–17; John Braithwaite for material from 'Restorative Justice and a Better Future', reproduced from 'Restorative Justice and a Better Future' by John Braithwaite, *Dalhousie Law Review*, Spring 1996, 76:1, pp. 9–32 copyright © John Braithwaite, reproduced with permission; Polity Press for material from *Cybercrime: The Transformation of Crime in the Information Age* by David S. Wall, copyright © 2007, pp. 1–4, 10–11, 17–19; Palgrave Macmillan for material from *Power: A Radical View*, Second edition by Steven Lukes published 2005, Palgrave Macmillan, reproduced with permission of Palgrave Macmillan, pp. 1, 14–22, 25–9, 58–9; Polity Press for material from *New and Old Wars: Organized Violence in a Global Era*, 2nd Edition by Mary Kaldor copyright © 2006, pp. 1–4, 150, 169–70, 193–4; Rowman & Littlefield Publishing Group for material from *The Social Movement Society: Contentious Politics for a New Century* edited by David S. Meyer and Sidney Tarrow copyright © Rowman & Littlefield, 1998, pp. 4–6, 18–24; Orion Publishing Group Ltd for material from *The New Terrorism: Fanaticism and the Arms of Mass Destruction* by Walter Laqueur copyright © Orion Publishing Group Ltd 2001, pp. 3–7, 40–5, 265–7; and Princeton University Press for material from *The Global Commonwealth of Citizens: Toward Cosmopolitan Democracy* by Daniele Archibugi, 2008, Princeton University Press. Reprinted by Princeton University Press, pp. 3–10, 114–19.

Extract 4 is taken from *The Communist Manifesto* by Karl Marx and Friedrich Engels (Harmondsworth: Penguin Books, 1983 [1848], pp. 79–87); extract 12 is taken from *Historical Sociology* by Philip Abrams (Shepton Mallet: Open Books Ltd, 1982, pp. 1–4, 7–8, 16–17); extract 35 is taken from 'Throwing Like a Girl: A Phenomenology of Feminine Body Comportment, Motility and Spatiality', in Jeffner Allen and Iris Marion Young (eds) *The Thinking Muse: Feminism and Modern French Philosophy* (Bloomington: Indiana University Press, 1989, pp. 55–8, 65–7).

In some instances we have been unable to trace the owners of copyright material and we would appreciate any information that would enable us to do so.

Introduction – The Sociological Perspective

This new Reader replaces the previous edition, which was last published in 2001. However, it is a significantly different book this time. Firstly, it contains fewer readings, selected as representative of key issues and subjects. Secondly, the material is organized into ten key themes reflecting the development of sociology's central concerns since the classical founders: Marx, Durkheim and Weber. Thirdly, the Reader tries to strike a productive balance between the older and classical work and more contemporary research that reflects the present state of the art. Fourthly, we have provided stronger and more effective summary essays for each of the themes in order to make this a genuinely student-friendly text. Finally, the impact of globalization will be seen in most of the themes as recognition that the global dimension of modern life is becoming ever more important. One last thing to note is that, with the exception of Anthony Giddens on 'the scope of sociology', all of the readings are new to this edition.

In making these changes we have tried to create a Reader that accurately reflects established and emerging trends in sociology as well as in society at large. For example, environmental issues, the transformation of work, sexualities and romantic love, the impact of the Internet, cybercrimes, shifting patterns of health and illness, terrorism and democratization are all included here. But these are included alongside, not instead of, classical readings on stratification and class conflict, social solidarity, the nature of power, deviance and crime, the social self, the essence of religion and the origins of capitalism. Our aim is to offer a concise yet comprehensive resource that will be useful for both lecturers and students.

The book is designed as a standalone text for introductory level sociology and can be readily used as an accompaniment to any sociology textbook. For those who may already have or use Polity's Giddens and Sutton *Sociology, 7th Edition* (2013), a guide to the relevant chapters and sections in that book is provided alongside recommendations for Further Reading at the end of each themed section. The Further Reading boxes point readers towards some of the relevant works which take further the issues that are introduced here. These are of course only our suggestions and there are many more possibilities.

Sociology remains a vibrant, wide-ranging and exciting academic enterprise in the twenty-first century and one that has to be able to adapt and change quite rapidly in order to keep pace with the similarly fast-moving social world. Today's sociology is very different from that of the 1950s or even 1980s. It is more diverse, both theoretically and in terms of its subject matter. It has incorporated many more areas of social life in more specialized fields of enquiry. The older, staple subjects are still there – education, work, organizations, urban life, inequality, research methods, families and religion. But these now compete for our attention with new subjects such as globalization, global warming, cybercrime, disability, the body, death and dying, virtual communities and terrorism. Reflecting on these lists is enough to suggest why sociology cannot stand still and has to continually reinvent itself. Can we really expect theories devised to understand late-nineteenth-century societies to help us to understand and explain how virtual identities operate, why new forms of terrorism are emerging or what may be the consequences of global warming? At the very least they would need to be updated and modified, but in all likelihood we will need to be theoretically creative if sociology is to fulfil its promise of helping people to grasp the contours and direction of the social world they have created together.

This opening section contains three readings which set out answers to the question, what is sociology? It is very easy to give a simple answer, sociology is the study of human societies. However, in order to grasp all that the discipline has to offer, we need something rather more informative than this. Hence these three readings discuss the relationship between individual experience and social structures, scientific work and commonsense knowledge, the natural and social sciences and what sociology may actually be used for.

One of the most widely adopted accounts of the sociological perspective is C. Wright-Mills's book, *The Sociological Imagination* (1959). Although this is clearly quite old, its central message remains remarkably contemporary. Wright-Mills argues that sociology is the discipline which combines an interest in the personal troubles of individuals with public issues of concern to everyone. In Reading 1, this approach is explained with several examples as illustrations. When people divorce, the consequences for the individuals concerned can be traumatic. The divorcing couple may face emotional distress

for quite some time and may ultimately change their attitudes towards marriage and the family. For children, divorce can be a devastating and incomprehensible experience and as adults, many reflect that seeing their parents permanently separate was *the* worst time of their lives.

However, rising divorce rates in society as a whole is a public issue that demands social policy changes and government attention. Is there enough marriage counselling available? Are family courts equipped to cope with rising rates? Should child benefits be increased to ensure women with children do not fall into poverty? Do we need new agencies to deal with the financial implications (such as the Child Support Agency in the UK)? There are even wider social issues too. How do rising divorce rates affect decisions to marry? Are young people delaying marriage or giving up on it altogether? Is the social stigma previously attached to divorce now being eroded? Are people remarrying in large numbers and, if so, does that mean marriage retains its popularity? What is the experience of stepfamilies and exactly how do they differ from conventional families? As Wright-Mills says, the job of sociologists is to bring together the personal trouble of divorce with the public issues raised by rising divorce rates. In doing so, we should be able to provide reliable evidence for policy-makers as well as helping people to understand better their own situation.

In Reading 2, Anthony Giddens argues that sociology is an inherently controversial discipline, one that has a subversive character. This is because sociology demands a sceptical approach to commonsense and taken-for-granted ideas and beliefs. Often, sociological research shows that these are at best partial and at worst, just plain wrong. For Giddens though, this is a positive benefit as it allows the discipline to keep pace with the fast-changing modern world. This doesn't mean that sociology is not scientific, just that the kind of systematic study engaged in by sociologists does not result in the same kind of knowledge that the natural sciences generate. After all, natural processes operate on a very different timescale to social life. It is also clear that good sociology can be found in micro studies of small-scale interactions, mid-range studies of social institutions and in large-scale analyses of globalization and very long-term social change.

If sociology brings together public and private issues and its enquiries are enormously wide and varied in scope, then what is sociology actually used for? Richard Jenkins in Reading 3 provides some answers, though not all sociologists would agree with these. Jenkins makes the point that previous generations had a very clear view of the use of sociology. It was a discipline that aimed to make the world a better place. Many sociologists today would agree and this desire certainly motivates students to study sociology. However, Jenkins thinks, *as an academic discipline*, sociology is *not* inevitably about improving the human world. Sociological knowledge can be used for both good and ill depending upon who makes use of it and in what ways. This may not be a popular conclusion, but it is one which reflects the situation we find ourselves in today, when the dark side of science has been exposed and ideas of inevitable progress in the modern age now seem threadbare after the massive loss of life in two world wars and recent episodes of mass killing, genocide and ethnic hatred which many thought were things of the past. In this context, perhaps a less certain and more circumspect view of sociology's role is warranted.[1]

NOTE

1. Editors' note: An ellipsis in square brackets has been used whenever material from the original has been omitted. Where a paragraph or more has been omitted, a line space appears above and below [. . .].

1. Private Troubles, Public Issues

C. Wright Mills

The promise

Nowadays men often feel that their private lives are a series of traps. They sense that within their everyday worlds, they cannot overcome their troubles, and in this feeling, they are often quite correct: what ordinary men are directly aware of and what they try to do are bounded by the private orbits in which they live; their visions and their powers are limited to the close-up scenes of job, family, neighbourhood; in other milieux, they move vicariously and remain spectators. And the more aware they become, however vaguely, of ambitions and of threats which transcend their immediate locales, the more trapped they seem to feel.

Underlying this sense of being trapped are seemingly impersonal changes in the very structure of continent-wide societies. The facts of contemporary history are also facts about the success and the failure of individual men and women. When a society is industrialized, a peasant becomes a worker; a feudal lord is liquidated or becomes a businessman. When classes rise or fall, a man is employed or unemployed; when the rate of investment goes up or down, a man takes new heart or goes broke. When wars happen, an insurance salesman becomes a rocket launcher; a store clerk, a radar man; a wife lives alone; a child grows up without a father. Neither the life of an individual nor the history of a society can be understood without understanding both.

Yet men do not usually define the troubles they endure in terms of historical change and institutional contradiction. The well-being they enjoy, they do not usually impute to the big ups and downs of the societies in which they live. Seldom aware of the intricate connection between the patterns of their own lives and the course of world history, ordinary men do not usually know what this connection means for the kinds of men they are becoming and for the kinds of history-making in which they might take part. They do not possess the quality of mind essential to grasp the interplay of man and society, of biography and history, of self and world. They cannot cope with their personal troubles in such ways as to control the structural transformations that usually lie behind them.

Surely it is no wonder. In what period have so many men been so totally exposed at so fast a pace to such earthquakes of change? That Americans have not known such catastrophic changes as have the men and women of other societies is due to historical facts that are now quickly becoming 'merely history': the history that now affects every man is world history. Within this scene and this period, in the course of a single generation, one sixth of mankind is transformed from all that is feudal and backward into all that is modern, advanced and fearful. Political colonies are freed; new and less visible forms of imperialism installed. Revolutions occur; men feel the intimate grip of new kinds of authority. Totalitarian societies rise, and are smashed to bits – or succeed fabulously. After two centuries of ascendancy, capitalism is shown up as only one way to make society into an industrial apparatus. After two centuries of hope, even formal democracy is restricted to a quite small portion of mankind. Everywhere in the underdeveloped world, ancient ways of life are broken up and vague expectations become urgent demands. Everywhere in the overdeveloped world, the means of authority and of violence become total in scope and bureaucratic in form. Humanity itself now lies before us, the supernation at either pole concentrating its most coordinated and massive efforts upon the preparation of the Third World War.

The very shaping of history now outpaces the ability of men to orient themselves in accordance with cherished values. And which values? Even when they do not panic, men often sense that older ways of feeling and thinking have collapsed and that newer beginnings are ambiguous to the point of moral stasis. Is it any wonder that ordinary men feel they cannot cope with the larger worlds with which they are so suddenly confronted? That they cannot understand the meaning of their epoch for their own lives? That – in defence of selfhood – they become morally insensible, trying to remain altogether private men? Is it any wonder that they come to be possessed by a sense of the trap?

It is not only information that they need – in this Age of Fact, information often dominates their attention and overwhelms their capacities to assimilate it. It is not only the skills of reason that they need – although their struggles to acquire these often exhaust their limited moral energy.

What they need, and what they feel they need, is a quality of mind that will help them to use information and to develop reason in order to achieve lucid summations of what is going on in the world and of what may be happening within themselves. It is this quality, I am going to contend, that journalists and scholars, artists and publics, scientists and editors are coming to expect of what may be called the sociological imagination.

1

The sociological imagination enables its possessor to understand the larger historical scene in terms of its meaning for the inner life and the external

career of a variety of individuals. It enables him to take into account how individuals, in the welter of their daily experience, often become falsely conscious of their social positions. Within that welter the framework of modern society is sought, and within that framework the psychologies of a variety of men and women are formulated. By such means the personal uneasiness of individuals is focused upon explicit troubles and the indifference of publics is transformed into involvement with public issues.

The first fruit of this imagination – and the first lessons of the social science that embodies it – is the idea that the individual can understand his own experience and gauge his own fate only by locating himself within his period, that he can know his own chances in life only by becoming aware of those of all individuals in his circumstances. In many ways it is a terrible lesson; in many ways a magnificent one. We do not know the limits of man's capacities for supreme effort or willing degradation, for agony or glee, for pleasurable brutality or the sweetness of reason. But in our time we have come to know that the limits of 'human nature' are frighteningly broad. We have come to know that every individual lives, from one generation to the next, in some society; that he lives out a biography, and that he lives it out within some historical sequence. By the fact of his living he contributes, however minutely, to the shaping of this society and to the course of its history, even as he is made by society and by its historical push and shove.

The sociological imagination enables us to grasp history and biography and the relations between the two within society. That is its task and its promise. [. . .]

No social study that does not come back to the problems of biography, of history, and of their intersections within a society, has completed its intellectual journey. Whatever the specific problems of the classic social analysts, however limited or however broad the features of social reality they have examined, those who have been imaginatively aware of the promise of their work have consistently asked three sorts of questions:

(1) What is the structure of this particular society as a whole? What are its essential components, and how are they related to one another? How does it differ from other varieties of social order? Within it, what is the meaning of any particular feature for its continuance and for its change?

(2) Where does this society stand in human history? What are the mechanics by which it is changing? What is its place within and its meaning for the development of humanity as a whole? How does any particular feature we are examining affect, and how is it affected by, the historical period in which it moves? And this period – what are its essential features? How does it differ from other periods? What are its characteristic ways of history-making?

(3) What varieties of men and women now prevail in this society and in this period? And what varieties are coming to prevail? In what ways are they selected and formed, liberated and repressed, made sensitive and blunted? What kinds of 'human nature' are revealed in the conduct and character we observe in this society in this period? And what is the meaning for 'human nature' of each and every feature of the society we are examining?

[. . .]

2

Perhaps the most fruitful distinction with which the sociological imagination works is between 'the personal troubles of milieu' and 'the public issues of social structure'. This distinction is an essential tool of the sociological imagination and a feature of all classic work in social science.

Troubles occur within the character of the individual and within the range of his immediate relations with others; they have to do with his self and with those limited areas of social life of which he is directly and personally aware. Accordingly, the statement and the resolution of troubles prop-

erly lie within the individual as a biographical entity and within the scope of his immediate milieu – the social setting that is directly open to his personal experience and to some extent his willful activity. A trouble is a private matter: values cherished by an individual are felt by him to be threatened.

Issues have to do with matters that transcend these local environments of the individual and the range of his inner life. They have to do with the organization of many such milieux into the institutions of a historical society as a whole, with the ways in which various milieux overlap and interpenetrate to form the larger structure of social and historical life. An issue is a public matter: some value cherished by publics is felt to be threatened. Often there is a debate about what the value really is and about what it is that really threatens it. This debate is often without focus if only because it is the very nature of an issue, unlike even widespread trouble, that it cannot very well be defined in terms of the immediate and everyday environments of ordinary men. An issue, in fact, often involves a crisis in institutional arrangements, and often too it involves what Marxists call 'contradictions' or 'antagonisms'.

In these terms, consider unemployment. When, in a city of 100,000, only one man is unemployed, that *is* his personal trouble, and for its relief we properly look to the character of the man, his skills, and his immediate opportunities. But when in a nation of 50 million employees, 15 million men are unemployed, that is an issue, and we may not hope to find its solution within the range of opportunities open to any one individual. The very structure of opportunities has collapsed. Both the correct statement of the problem and the range of possible solutions require us to consider the economic and political institutions of the society, and not merely the personal situation and character of a scatter of individuals.

Consider war. The personal problem of war, when it occurs, may be how to survive it or how to die in it with honour; how to make money out of it; how to climb into the higher safety of the military apparatus; or how to contribute to the war's termination. In short, according to one's values, to find a set of milieux and within it to survive the war or make one's death in it meaningful. But the structural issues of war have to do with its causes; with what types of men it throws up into command; with its effects upon economic and political, family and religious institutions, with the unorganized irresponsibility of a world of nation-states.

Consider marriage. Inside a marriage a man and a woman may experience personal troubles, but when the divorce rate during the first four years of marriage is 250 out of every 1,000 attempts, this is an indication of a structural issue having to do with the institutions of marriage and the family and other institutions that bear upon them.

Or consider the metropolis – the horrible, beautiful, ugly, magnificent sprawl of the great city. For many upper-class people, the personal solution to 'the problem of the city' is to have an apartment with private garage under it in the heart of the city, and forty miles out, a house by Henry Hill, garden by Garrett Eckbo, on a hundred acres of private land. In these two controlled environments – with a small staff at each end and a private helicopter connection – most people could solve many of the problems of personal milieux caused by the facts of the city. But all this, however splendid, does not solve the public issues that the structural fact of the city poses. What should be done with this wonderful monstrosity? Break it all up into scattered units, combining residence and work? Refurbish it as it stands? Or, after evacuation, dynamite it and build new cities according to new plans in new places? What should those plans be? And who is

to decide and to accomplish whatever choice is made? These are structural issues; to confront them and to solve them requires us to consider political and economic issues that affect innumerable milieux.

In so far as an economy is so arranged that slumps occur, the problem of unemployment becomes incapable of personal solution. In so far as war is inherent in the nation-state system and in the uneven industrialization of the world, the ordinary individual in his restricted milieu will be powerless – with or without psychiatric aid – to solve the troubles this system or lack of system imposes upon him. In so far as the family as an institution turns women into darling little slaves and men into their chief providers and unweaned dependants, the problem of a satisfactory marriage remains incapable of purely private solution. In so far as the overdeveloped megalopolis and the overdeveloped automobile are built-in features of the overdeveloped society, the issues of urban living will not he solved by personal ingenuity and private wealth.

What we experience in various and specific milieux, I have noted, is often caused by structural changes. Accordingly, to understand the changes of many personal milieux we are required to look beyond them. And the number and variety of such structural changes increase as the institutions within which we live become more embracing and more intricately connected with one another. To be aware of the idea of social structure and to use it with sensibility is to be capable of tracing such linkages among a great variety of milieux. To be able to do that is to possess the sociological imagination.

2. The Scope of Sociology

Anthony Giddens

Sociology is a subject with a curiously mixed reputation. On the one hand, it is associated by many people with the fomenting of rebellion, a stimulus to revolt. Even though they may have only a vague notion of what topics are studied in sociology, they somehow associate sociology with subversion, with the shrill demands of unkempt student militants. On the other hand, quite a different view of the subject is often entertained – perhaps more commonly than the first – by individuals who have had some direct acquaintance with it in schools and universities. This is that in fact it is rather a dull and uninstructive enterprise, which far from propelling its students towards the barricades is more likely to bore them to death with platitudes. Sociology, in this guise, assumes the dry mantle of a science, but not one that proves as enlightening as the natural sciences upon which its practitioners wish to model it.

I think that those who have taken the second reaction to sociology have a good deal of right on their side. Sociology has been conceived of by many of its proponents – even the bulk of them – in such a way that commonplace assertions are disguised in a pseudo-scientific language. The conception that sociology belongs to the natural sciences, and hence should slavishly try to copy their procedures and objectives, is a mistaken one. Its lay critics, in some considerable degree at least, are quite correct to be sceptical of the attainments of sociology thus presented.

My intention in this [discussion] will be to associate sociology with the first type of view rather than the second. By this I do not mean to connect sociology with a sort of irrational lashing-out at all that most of the population hold to be good and proper ways of behaviour. But I do want to defend the view that sociology, understood in the manner in which I shall describe it, necessarily has a subversive quality. Its subversive or critical character, however [. . .], does not carry with it (or should not do so) the implication that it is an intellectually disreputable enterprise. On the contrary, it is exactly because sociology deals with problems of such pressing interest to us all (or should do so), problems which are the objects of major controversies and conflicts in society itself, that it has this character. However kempt or otherwise student radicals, or any other radicals, may be, there do exist broad connections between the impulses that stir them to action and a sociological awareness. This is not [. . .] because sociologists directly preach revolt; it is because the study of sociology, appropriately understood, [. . .] demonstrates how fundamental are the social questions that have to be faced in today's world. Everyone is to some extent aware of these questions, but the study of sociology helps bring them into much sharper focus. Sociology cannot remain a purely academic subject, if 'academic' means a disinterested and remote scholarly pursuit, followed solely within the enclosed walls of the university.

Sociology is not a subject that comes neatly gift-wrapped, making no demands except that its contents be unpacked. Like all the social sciences – under which label one can also include, among other disciplines, anthropology, economics and history – sociology is an inherently controversial endeavour. That is to say, it is characterized by continuing disputes about its very nature. But this is not a weakness, although it has seemed such to many of those who call themselves professional 'sociologists', and also to many others on the outside, who are distressed that there are numerous vying conceptions of how the subject matter of sociology should be approached or analysed. Those who are upset by the persistent character of sociological debates, and a frequent lack of consensus about how to resolve them, usually feel that this is a sign of the immaturity of the subject. They want sociology to be like a natural science, and to generate a similar apparatus of universal laws to those which they see natural science as having discovered and validated. But [. . .] it is a mistake to suppose that sociology should be modelled too closely on the natural sciences, or to imagine that a natural science of society is either feasible or desirable. To say this, I should emphasize, does not mean that the methods and objectives of the natural sciences are wholly irrelevant to the study of human social behaviour. Sociology deals with a factually observable subject matter, depends upon empirical research, and involves attempts to formulate theories and generalizations that will make sense of facts. But human beings are not the same as material objects in nature; studying our own behaviour is necessarily entirely different in some very important ways from studying natural phenomena.

The development of sociology, and its current concerns, have to be grasped in the context of changes that have created the modern world. We live in an age of massive social transformation. In the space of only something like two centuries a sweeping set of social changes, which have hastened rather than lessened their pace today, have occurred. These changes, emanating originally from Western Europe, are now global in their impact. They have all but totally dissolved the forms of social organization in which humankind had lived for thousands of years of its previous history. Their core is to be found in what some have described as the 'two great revolutions' of eighteenth- and nineteenth-century Europe. The first is the French revolution of 1789, both a

specific set of events and a symbol of political transformations in our era. For the 1789 revolution was quite different from rebellions of previous times. Peasants had sometimes rebelled against their feudal masters, for example, but generally in an attempt to remove specific individuals from power, or to secure reductions in prices or taxes. In the French revolution (to which we can bracket, with some reservations, the anti-colonial revolution in North America in 1776) for the first time in history there took place the overall dissolution of a social order by a movement guided by purely secular ideals – universal liberty and equality. If the ideals of the revolutionaries have scarcely been fully realized even now, they created a climate of political change that has proved one of the dynamic forces of contemporary history. There are few states in the world today that are not proclaimed by their rulers to be 'democracies', whatever their actual political complexion may be. This is something altogether novel in human history. It is true that there have been other republics, most especially those of Classical Greece and Rome. But these were themselves rare instances; and in each case those who formed the 'citizens' were a minority of the population, the majority of whom were slaves or others without the prerogatives of the select groups of citizenry.

The second 'great revolution' was the so-called 'industrial revolution', usually traced to Britain in the late eighteenth century, and spreading in the nineteenth century throughout Western Europe and the United States. The industrial revolution is sometimes presented merely as a set of technical innovations: especially the harnessing of steam power to manufacturing production and the introduction of novel forms of machinery activated by such sources of power. But these technical inventions were only part of a very much broader set of social and economic changes. The most important of these was the migration of the mass of the labour force from the land into the constantly expanding sectors of industrial work, a process which also eventually led to the widespread mechanization of agrarian production.

This same process promoted an expansion of cities upon a scale again previously unwitnessed in history. [. . .]

Sociology came into being as those caught up in the initial series of changes brought about by the 'two great revolutions' in Europe sought to understand the conditions of their emergence, and their likely consequences. Of course, no field of study can be exactly pinpointed in terms of its origins. We can quite readily trace direct continuities from writers in the middle of the eighteenth century through to later periods of social thought. The climate of ideas involved in the formation of sociology in some part, in fact, helped give rise to the twin processes of revolution.

How should 'sociology' be defined? Let me begin with a banality. Sociology is concerned with the study of human societies. Now the notion of society can be formulated in only a very general way. For under the general category of 'societies' we want to include not only the industrialized countries, but large agrarian imperial states (such as the Roman Empire, or traditional China), and, at the other end of the scale, small tribal communities that may comprise only a tiny number of individuals.

A society is a cluster, or system, of institutionalized modes of conduct. To speak of 'institutionalized' forms of social conduct is to refer to modes of belief and behaviour that occur and recur – or, as the terminology of modern social theory would have it, are socially reproduced – across long spans of time and space. Language is an excellent example of such a form of institutionalized activity, or institution, since it is so fundamental to social life. All of us speak languages which none of us, as individuals, created, although we all use language creatively. But many other aspects of social life may be institutionalized: that is, become commonly adopted practices which persist in recognizably similar form across the generations. Hence we can speak of economic institutions, political institutions and so on. Such a use of the concept 'institution', it should be pointed out, differs from the way in which the term is often employed in ordinary language, as a loose synonym for 'group' or 'collectivity' – as when, say, a prison or hospital is referred to as an 'institution'.

These considerations help to indicate how 'society' should be understood, but we cannot leave matters there. As an object of study, 'society' is shared by sociology and the other social sciences. The distinctive feature of sociology lies in its overriding concern with those forms of society that have emerged in the wake of the 'two great revolutions'. Such forms of society include those that are industrially advanced – the economically developed countries of the West, Japan and Eastern Europe – but also in the twentieth century a range of other societies stretched across the world. [. . .]

In the light of these remarks, a definition can be offered of the subject as follows. *Sociology is a social science, having as its main focus the study of the social institutions brought into being by the industrial transformations of the past two or three centuries.* It is important to stress that there are no precisely defined divisions between sociology and other fields of intellectual endeavour in the social sciences. Neither is it desirable that there should be. Some questions of social theory, to do with how human behaviour and institutions should be conceptualized, are the shared concern of the social sciences as a whole. The different 'areas' of human behaviour that are covered by the various social sciences form an intellectual division of labour which can be justified in only a very general way. Anthropology, for example, is concerned [. . .] with the 'simpler' societies: tribal societies, chiefdoms and agrarian states. But either these have been dissolved altogether by the profound social changes that have swept through the world, or they are in the process of becoming incorporated within modern industrial states. The subject matter of economics, to take another instance, is the production and distribution of material goods. However, economic institutions are plainly always connected with other institutions in social systems, which both influence and are influenced by them. Finally, history, as the study of the continual distancing of past and present, is the source material of the whole of the social sciences. [. . .]

Although this type of standpoint has been very pervasive in sociology, it is one I reject. To speak of sociology, and of other subjects like anthropology or economics, as 'social sciences' is to stress that they involve the systematic study of an empirical subject matter. The terminology is not confusing so long as we see that sociology and other social sciences differ from the natural sciences in two essential respects:

(1)   We cannot approach society, or 'social facts', as we do objects or events in the natural world, because societies only exist in so far as they are created and re-created in our own actions as human beings. In social theory, we cannot treat human activities as though they were determined by causes in the same way as natural events are. We have to grasp what I would call the double involvement of individuals and institutions: we create society at the same time as we are created by it. [. . .]

(2)   It follows from this that the practical implications of sociology are not directly parallel to the technological uses of science, and cannot be.

3. What is Sociology For?

Richard Jenkins

There are many views about what sociology is and what its business should be, all of them bound up with questions about the nature of its subject matter. Apart from the vague 'study of society' which is probably the most common fall-back position, sociology can be defined in a number of complementary ways. At its most basic it is the study of patterns in human behaviour. Among other things this means that sociology pays particular attention to established relationships between humans; which is why the study of institutions and how they work has always been fundamental to the sociological enterprise. Sociology has, however, always been as interested in individuals as in collectivities. It is particularly concerned with the many ways in which individuals are influenced by human factors outside their immediate environment or control. Finally, sociology has always been concerned with the shared ways in which human beings interpret their lives, with meaning.

What connects all of these is that sociology is the study of the recurrent or regular aspects of human behaviour. Wishing one neighbour a good morning and ignoring another is not, as a one-off occurrence, sociologically interesting. Do it every day, and, as an established relationship of inclusion and exclusion, it becomes so. If this can be connected to wider patterns of behaviour – for example, if the neighbour that you ignore is a member of a different ethnic group than both you and the neighbour that you greet – its sociological interest increases. Similarly, the fact that one woman is elected to an otherwise all-male legislature isn't necessarily sociologically significant. However, that women members come, over time, to number in their tens, scores or hundreds, certainly is.

However we define sociology's subject matter, there will be many different perspectives on it. There are those for whom the fundamental building blocks of sociological analysis can only be individuals, others for whom they must be collectivities. Some sociologists believe we can establish the causes of human behaviour and its patterns, others insist that all we can do is interpret what people do. While some adopt a detached and apparently disinterested perspective on the human world, others think that sociology should be actively oriented towards intervention. Some base their understanding of the human world on numbers and quantity, others focus on in-depth description. There are many different – apparently exclusive, if not mutually antagonistic – theoretical schools, each with its own model of the discipline and its subject matter.

The picture becomes more complex again if we consider the many substantive specialisms, which can give every appearance of intellectual autonomy. There are sociologies of health and illness, religion and ritual, inequality and stratification, economic activity, kinship and the family, deviance, socialization and education, culture, everyday life and interaction, organizations, politics, and gender relations, to mention only a few. Lastly, to muddy the waters even further, national sociologies – defined generically or otherwise – have their own intellectual histories and distinctive styles and concerns, the importance of which shouldn't be overlooked.

Sociologists are, in other words, a diverse crew. Some critics might go so far as to suggest that sociologists are indisciplined to the point of not being a discipline at all. I wouldn't agree. That sociology – even in its narrowest definition – is a broad church, short on articles of faith or consensus about its practices, seems to me to be a good rather than a bad thing, and it is certainly not my intention to suggest that this situation should change. Precisely because of the heterogeneity of its subject matter, the human world, sociology's greatest strength may well be its pluralism. And precisely because sociology is such a broad communion some minimal common ground seems to be vital. [. . .]

The roots of sociology

As conventionally defined by the titles of university departments and degrees, sociology began as the study of the modern world. Auguste Comte first coined the word 'sociology' in 1838, to describe an emergent intellectual field that was seeking to understand better a world that, particularly in Europe and North America, was experiencing transformation at a rate and to an extent that appeared to be unprecedented. New ideas and vocabularies were needed for a dramatically new situation. That new situation was the coming-together of a number of closely connected developments, each of which continues to resonate globally at the beginning of the twenty-first century. These included:

- the runaway triumph of capitalism as the dominant way of organizing production and distribution;
- the massive impact of industrialization and mechanization on humanity's productive powers and its capacities to transform the physical environment;
- the rationalization of collective activities, most obviously the bureaucratization of administration, production, law and finance;
- the increasing number and size of cities;
- the flight from the land and the decay of long-

established agrarian social systems and small-scale rural communities;
- the secularization of the moral universe which attended organized religion's decline and the growing authority of rationalism and science;
- the proliferation of nominally democratic systems of government, particularly as constituted in concepts of individual citizenship rights and responsibilities;
- the emergence of new lines of social differentiation and conflict, in particular social class;
- the increasing size, prosperity and autonomy of the bourgeoisie, and the development of materialist individualism;
- the widespread migration, whether voluntary or forced, of unprecedented numbers of people, made possible by mechanized forms of transport, and bringing together in new locations peoples from an enormous diversity of origins; and
- the imposition of metropolitan, national cultures on peripheral populations, through the expansion of effective rule within their territories by nation-states, and the direct or indirect colonization of all available spaces by global empires.

These developments, feeding off each other and given added force by their simultaneity, were seismic. They called sociology into existence, and provided it with the two intimately related tasks that have been its minimum unifying purpose ever since: to understand social change, and to fathom the relationship between the individual and the collective.

[. . .]

The uses of sociology

Examining the discipline's roots allows us to be clearer about sociology's usefulness. Sociology is not in any necessary sense about making the world a better place, or improving the lot of humankind. While there is nothing to prevent sociology contributing to either, both logic and whatever shaky lessons history can offer insist that a better understanding of that world and the human condition – leaving aside for the moment the question of what 'better' might mean in this context – may, in principle, be used for good or ill (supposing that the difference between the two is clear).

This is not necessarily the mainstream sociological view. Comte and many subsequent sociologists – naturally enough, given the intellectual climate of the times – expected sociology to become the 'science of society'. Some sociologists, of whom John Goldthorpe is an example, still aspire to this goal, albeit in moderate versions.[1] [...] Throughout the nineteenth century and for most of the twentieth, progress and science were assumed to travel hand-in-hand. Marx, ever the optimist, certainly thought so. The only point in understanding the world was, after all, to change it, and for the better.[2] In this vein, sociology's contribution to improving the world has long been axiomatic, albeit vague, for most of its practitioners, At the beginning of the twenty-first century, however, even a mildly critical take on progress and the transformative power of knowledge encourages a humbled view of the possibilities. We don't have to embrace postmodern relativism to be sceptical about progress or to acknowledge the unintended dire consequences

of science (any more than scepticism demands that we turn our backs on everything that has changed for the uncontroversial better).

[...]

The greatest relevance of Marx's work to sociology's founders, particularly Weber, may have been as a whetstone on which to hone many of their ideas. Their legacies, the great sociological traditions of functionalism, the action framework, and symbolic interactionism, overlap with Marx here and there, but Marxist sociology as such was largely a child of the 1950s and 1960s, a product of affluence and widening access to higher education. Serious political radicalism – which in recent sociology means feminism rather than Marxism, anyway – has historically been the sociological exception rather than the rule. It remains so today.

NOTES

1. J. H. Goldthorpe, *On Sociology: Numbers, Narratives and the Integration of Research and Theory* (Oxford: Oxford University Press, 2000) pp. 4–6.
2. See M. Weber, *The Protestant Ethic and the Spirit of Capitalism*, 2nd edn (London: George Allen & Unwin, 1976) p. 182.

Further Reading

There are many introductory sociology texts, but you could begin with Steve Bruce's (2000) *Sociology: A Very Short Introduction* (Oxford: Oxford University Press) which is self-explanatory. Zygmunt Bauman and Tim May's (2001) *Thinking Sociologically* (Oxford: Blackwell) is an excellent account of what sociology has to offer and is enlightening in itself. If you are looking for something rather more challenging, then Richard Kilminster's (2001) *The Sociological Revolution: From the Enlightenment to the Global Age* (London: Routledge) is a stimulating argument that the development of sociology introduced a genuine revolution in human knowledge that is not yet fully appreciated.

Giddens and Sutton *Sociology 7th Edition* (2013)

Chapter 1 reviews the material covered in this section and pages 72–86 of Chapter 3 should also be useful.

Part 1   Theories of Society

Sociology is a product of the eighteenth-century French and industrial revolutions, which marked the end of medieval social relations and the onset of a new, technologically advanced age of modernity. But how did this huge transformation come about and was it permanent? Where are industrialization and urbanization taking us in the future? What are the consequences for community life of large-scale migration from rural villages to urban towns and expanding cities? Trying to answer such major questions was the task of the early sociologists. But to do so, it was not enough just to collect a mass of evidence and data. What was needed were theories – logically related statements which interpret and explain the available data and evidence – enabling a deeper understanding of society and social change. This section focuses on the developed industrial societies, illustrating sociological theorizing with a mix of classical and contemporary theories. These are not exhaustive though, so the Further Reading includes general theory texts for readers to follow up their own particular interests.

In Reading 4, Karl Marx sets out his grand theory of social change based on an essentially simple idea, that all societies contain a fundamental conflict of interest which drives them forward. Marx saw this as a series of class conflicts between property owners and non-owners which could only be resolved by the revolutionary transformation of existing social relations. Industrial capitalism was just the latest version, which simplified and made more explicit the class conflict between workers and capitalists. Using the analogy of a sorcerer making use of spells to conjure up wondrous modern inventions, Marx shows how capitalism radically transformed human beings' relationship to the natural world. And though capitalist modernity offers apparently limitless opportunities for some, this is only at the expense of poverty and exploitation for many more. Marx argued that in the long term, capitalism would give way to another mode of production – communism – that eliminated class conflicts altogether. So far, this forecast has failed to materialize.

With industrialization came a wider and more intense division of labour as factory work came to be broken down into smaller repetitive tasks requiring less skill. The process of industrial production also spread geographically creating increasingly global levels of interdependence. The consequences of an expanding division of labour are discussed by Emile Durkheim in Reading 5. Like many other commentators at the time, Durkheim saw industrialization as radically changing the older pattern of social relations. He described this as a shift away from unthinking, habitual forms of 'mechanical' solidarity, towards an 'organic' solidarity rooted in the interdependencies created by the division of labour. And though the latter was certainly much less personal and emotionally fulfilling for individuals, it was actually a more solid and systematic type of human interdependence that was capable of joining together the activities of people in geographically diverse communities and societies.

If Marx showed us that modernity is built on class-based exploitation, feminist activists and writers demonstrated forcibly that gender inequality had not been eliminated either as men were the main beneficiaries of modern society's benefits. Early campaigners for women's rights explored the basic problem of unequal rights for men and women, particularly in the field of politics and political participation. Such campaigns led, eventually, to the inclusion of women in elections and political life. By the 1960s and 1970s, so-called 'second wave' feminism pushed for equal rights in all spheres of society, which suffered from male dominance or patriarchy. Popularizing the slogan, 'the personal is political', feminists produced a stringent critique of the notion that domestic arrangements, housework, child-rearing and intimate relations were outside of politics and were merely a matter for individuals. Feminist researchers studied families and households, shining a light into the exploitative nature of heterosexual marriage and personal relations. In Reading 6, Sylvia Walby explains how some of the major social changes since the 1970s have transformed patriarchal arrangements in the modern world. Although personal relations remain in many ways unequal, Walby argues that the very success of feminism in gaining a measure of equality at work, in politics and in changing attitudes has shifted the gender conflict into the whole of society. As she caustically comments, 'women now have the whole of society in which to roam and be exploited'. Just because women have made progress in some areas of society does not mean that gender inequality has ended.

Until the mid-1980s, most sociologists tended to assume that although modern societies are characterized by continual change and movement, their underlying principles remained more or less the same. The application of science to production, steady social progress towards equality, secularization and the displacement of religious thinking – these trends looked set to continue into the future. But from the mid-1980s into the 1990s, a new intellectual trend labelled 'postmodernism' challenged all of these assumptions. Postmodern thinkers pointed out the negative side of scientific 'progress' such as massive environmental damage, the devaluing of small-scale local knowledge and the creation of high consequence risks such as that of a nuclear war. Postmodernists also applied this approach to the social sciences. How arrogant and disturbing that psychologists and sociologists should produce knowledge which could be used to survey, police and control the majority of human beings. In Reading 7, Zygmunt Bauman describes the postmodern mentality as one which criticizes and deconstructs modern phenomena, but is incapable of providing anything constructive to replace them. This is because the very act of construction and building poses threats to individual freedom. Bauman argues that postmodernity is not just a state of mind, but also a condition of society in which experts and authorities are losing their position alongside the slow erosion of the nation state. In that case what is needed is a sociology of postmodernity, so we may better understand its consequences.

Of course, not all sociologists accept the thesis of a shift to postmodernity and in recent years there has been a plethora of theories focusing on a single key aspect of contemporary societies such as risk, social movements, knowledge and information production or globalization. What these theories have in common is the basic premise that, as Jurgen Habermas has argued, modernity remains essentially an unfinished project. We are not entering a postmodern society. In

Reading 8, Anthony Giddens takes issue with postmodern theorists, arguing that rather than marking the end of the modern age, the present period really represents the intensification of modernity and its spread to all corners of the globe. However, this spreading of modern modes of life brings with it new uncertainties, concerns and more global-scale problems. In a sense, says Giddens, people have come to feel that modern life is rather like riding a very large truck – a juggernaut – while realizing that no single authority is able to control its direction. A very unsettling experience indeed! The juggernaut continues to career down the highway at breakneck speed as its passengers try to work out how best to point it in a positive direction. Sociological theory has to try to map out the terrain to help us work out where we are heading.

4. Human History as Class Conflict

Karl Marx

1. Bourgeois and proletarians[1]

The history of all hitherto existing society[2] is the history of class struggles.

Freeman and slave, patrician and plebeian, lord and serf, guild-masters[3] and journeyman, in a word, oppressor and oppressed, stood in constant opposition to one another; carried on an uninterrupted, now hidden, now open fight, a fight that each time ended, either in a revolutionary reconstitution of society at large, or in the common ruin of the contending classes.

In the earlier epochs of history, we find almost everywhere a complicated arrangement of society into various orders, a manifold gradation of social rank. In ancient Rome we have patricians, knights, plebeians, slaves; in the Middle Ages, feudal lords, vassals, guild-masters, journeymen, apprentices, serfs; in almost all of these classes, again, subordinate gradations.

The modern bourgeois society that has sprouted from the ruins of feudal society has not done away with class antagonisms. It has but established new classes, new conditions of oppression, new forms of struggle in place of the old ones.

Our epoch, the epoch of the bourgeoisie, possesses, however, this distinctive feature: it has simplified the class antagonisms. Society as a whole is more and more splitting up into two great hostile camps, into two great classes directly facing each other: bourgeoisie and proletariat.

From the serfs of the Middle Ages sprang the chartered burghers of the earliest towns. From these burgesses the first elements of the bourgeoisie were developed.

The discovery of America, the rounding of the Cape, opened up fresh ground for the rising bourgeoisie. The East Indian and Chinese markets, the colonization of America, trade with the colonies, the increase in the means of exchange and in commodities generally, gave to commerce, to navigation, to industry, an impulse never before known, and thereby, to the revolutionary element in the tottering feudal society, a rapid development.

The feudal system of industry, under which industrial production was monopolized by closed guilds, now no longer sufficed for the growing wants of the new markets. The manufacturing system took its place. The guild-masters were pushed on one side by the manufacturing middle class; division of labour between the different corporate guilds vanished in the face of division of labour in each single workshop.

Meantime the markets kept ever growing, the demand ever rising. Even manufacture no longer sufficed. Thereupon, steam and machinery revolutionized industrial production. The place of manufacture was taken by the giant, modern industry, the place of the industrial middle class, by industrial millionaires, the leaders of whole industrial armies, the modern bourgeois.

Modern industry has established the world market, for which the discovery of America paved the way. This market has given an immense development to commerce, to navigation, to communication by land. This development has, in its turn, reacted on the extension of industry; and in proportion as industry, commerce, navigation, railways extended, in the same proportion the bourgeoisie developed, increased its capital, and pushed into the background every class handed down from the Middle Ages.

We see, therefore, how the modern bourgeoisie is itself the product of a long course of development, of a series of revolutions in the modes of production and of exchange.

[. . .]

The bourgeoisie, historically, has played a most revolutionary part.

The bourgeoisie, wherever it has got the upper hand, has put an end to all feudal, patriarchal, idyllic relations. It has pitilessly torn asunder the motley feudal ties that bound man to his 'natural superiors', and has left remaining no other nexus between man and man than naked self-interest, than callous 'cash payment'. It has drowned the most heavenly ecstasies of religious fervour, of chivalrous enthusiasm, of philistine sentimentalism, in the icy water of egotistical calculation. It has resolved personal worth into exchange value, and in place of the numberless indefeasible chartered freedoms, has set up that single, unconscionable freedom – free trade, in one word, for exploitation, veiled by religious and political illusions, it has substituted naked, shameless, direct, brutal exploitation.

The bourgeoisie has stripped of its halo every occupation hitherto honoured and looked up to with reverent awe. It has converted the physician, the lawyer, the priest, the poet, the man of science, into its paid wage labourers.

The bourgeoisie has torn away from the family its sentimental veil, and has reduced the family relation to a mere money relation.

The bourgeoisie has disclosed how it came to pass that the brutal display of vigour in the Middle Ages, which reactionists so much admire, found its fitting complement in the most slothful indolence. It has been the first to show what man's activity can bring about. It has accomplished wonders far surpassing Egyptian pyramids, Roman aqueducts, and Gothic cathedrals; it has conducted expeditions that put in the shade all former exoduses of nations and crusades.

The bourgeoisie cannot exist without constantly revolutionizing the instruments of production, and thereby the relations of production, and with them the whole relations of society. Conservation of the old modes of production in unaltered form, was, on the contrary, the first condition of existence for all earlier industrial classes. Constant revolutionizing of production, uninterrupted disturbance of all social conditions, everlasting uncertainty and agitation distinguish the bourgeois epoch from all earlier ones. All fixed, fast-frozen relations, with their train of ancient and venerable prejudices and opinions, are swept away, all new-formed ones become antiquated before they can ossify. All that is solid melts into air, all that is holy is profaned, and man is at last compelled to face with sober senses, his real conditions of life, and his relations with his kind.

The need of a constantly expanding market for its products chases the bourgeoisie over the whole surface of the globe. It must nestle everywhere, settle everywhere, establish connections everywhere.

The bourgeoisie has through its exploitation of the world market given a cosmopolitan character to production and consumption in every country. To the great chagrin of reactionists, it has drawn from under the feet of industry the national ground on which it stood. All old-established national industries have been destroyed or are daily being destroyed. They are dislodged by new industries, whose introduction becomes a life and death question for all civilized nations, by industries that no longer work up indigenous raw material, but raw material drawn from the remotest zones; industries whose products are consumed, not only at home, but in every quarter of the globe. In place of the old wants, satisfied by the productions of the country, we find new wants, requiring for their satisfaction the products of distant lands and climes. In place of the old local and national seclusion and self-sufficiency, we have intercourse in every direction; universal interdependence of nations. And as in material, so also in intellectual production. The intellectual creations of individual nations become common property. National one-sidedness and narrow-mindedness become more and more impossible, and from the numerous national and local literatures, there arises a world literature.

The bourgeoisie, by the rapid improvement of all instruments of production, by the immensely facilitated means of communication, draws all, even the most barbarian, nations into civilization. The cheap prices of its commodities are the heavy artillery with which it batters down all Chinese walls, with which it forces the barbarians' intensely obstinate hatred of foreigners to capitulate. It compels all nations, on pain of extinction, to adopt the bourgeois mode of production; it compels them to introduce what it calls civilization into their midst, i.e., to become bourgeois themselves. In one word, it creates a world after its own image.

The bourgeoisie has subjected the country to the rule of the towns. It has created enormous cities, has greatly increased the urban population as compared with the rural, and has thus rescued a considerable part of the population from the idiocy of rural life. Just as it has made the country dependent on the towns, so it has made barbarian and semi-barbarian countries dependent on the civilized ones, nations of peasants on nations of bourgeois, the East on the West.

The bourgeoisie keeps more and more doing away with the scattered state of the population, of the means of production, and of property. It has agglomerated population, centralized means of production, and has concentrated property in a few hands. The necessary consequence of this was political centralization. Independent, or but loosely connected provinces, with separate interests, laws, governments and systems of taxation, became lumped together into one nation, with one government, one code of laws, one national class interest, one frontier and one customs tariff.

The bourgeoisie, during its rule of scarce one hundred years, has created more massive and more colossal productive forces than have all preceding generations together. Subjection of nature's forces to man, machinery, application of chemistry to industry and agriculture, steam navigation, railways, electric telegraphs, clearing of whole continents for cultivation, canalization of rivers, whole populations conjured out of the ground – what earlier century had even a presentiment that such productive forces slumbered in the lap of social labour?

We see then: the means of production and of exchange, on whose foundation the bourgeoisie built itself up, were generated in feudal society. At a certain stage in the development of these means of production and of exchange, the conditions under which feudal society produced and exchanged, the feudal organization of agriculture and manufacturing industry, in one word, the feudal relations of property became no longer compatible with the already developed productive forces; they became so many fetters. They had to be burst asunder; they were burst asunder.

Into their place stepped free competition, accompanied by a social and political constitution adapted to it, and by the economical and political sway of the bourgeois class.

A similar movement is going on before our own eyes. Modern bourgeois society with its relations of production, of exchange and of property, a society that has conjured up such gigantic means of production and of exchange, is like the sorcerer, who is no longer able to control the powers of the nether world whom he has called up by his spells. [. . .]

The weapons with which the bourgeoisie felled feudalism to the ground are now turned against the bourgeoisie itself.

But not only has the bourgeoisie forged the weapons that bring death to itself; it has also called into existence the men who are to wield those weapons – the modern working class – the proletarians.

In proportion as the bourgeoisie, i.e., capital, is developed, in the same proportion is the proletariat, the modern working class, developed – a class of labourers, who live only so long as they find work, and who find work only so long as their labour increases capital. These labourers, who must sell themselves piecemeal, are a commodity, like every other article of commerce, and are consequently exposed to all the vicissitudes of competition, to all the fluctuations of the market.

NOTES

1. By bourgeoisie is meant the class of modern capitalists, owners of the means of social production and employers of wage labour. By proletariat, the class of modern wage labourers who, having no means of production of their own, are reduced to selling their labour power in order to live [Engels].
2. That is, all *written* history. In 1847, the prehistory of society, the social organization existing previous to recorded history, was all but unknown. Since then, Haxthausen discovered common ownership of land in Russia, Maurer proved it to be the social foundation from which all Teutonic races started in history, and by and by village communities were found to be, or to have been the primitive form of society everywhere from India to Ireland. The inner organization of this primitive communistic society was laid bare, in its typical form, by Morgan's crowning discovery of the true nature of the *gens* and its relation to the *tribe*. With the dissolution of these primeval communities society begins to be differentiated into separate and finally antagonistic classes. I have attempted to retrace this process of dissolution in: *Der Ursprung der Familie, des Privateigentums und des Staats* (*The Origin of the Family, Private Property and the State*) [Engels].
3. Guild-master, that is, a full member of a guild, a master within, not a head of a guild [Engels].

5. From Mechanical to Organic Solidarity

Emile Durkheim

The totality of beliefs and sentiments common to the average members of a society forms a determinate system with a life of its own. It can be termed the collective or common consciousness. Undoubtedly the substratum of this consciousness does not consist of a single organ. By definition it is diffused over society as a whole, but nonetheless possesses specific characteristics that make it a distinctive reality. In fact it is independent of the particular conditions in which individuals find themselves. Individuals pass on, but it abides. It is the same in north and south, in large towns and in small, and in different professions. Likewise it does not change with every generation but, on the contrary, links successive generations to one another. Thus it is something totally different from the consciousnesses of individuals, although it is only realized in individuals. It is the psychological type of society, one which has its properties, conditions for existence and mode of development, just as individual types do, but in a different fashion. For this reason it has the right to be designated by a special term. It is true that the one we have employed above is not without ambiguity. Since the terms 'collective' and 'social' are often taken as synonyms, one is inclined to believe that the collective consciousness is the entire social consciousness, that is, co-terminous with the psychological life of society, whereas, particularly in higher societies, it constitutes only a very limited part of it. Those functions that are judicial, governmental, scientific or industrial – in short, all the specific functions – appertain to the psychological order, since they consist of systems of representation and action.

However, they clearly lie outside the common consciousness. To avoid a confusion[1] that has occurred it would perhaps be best to invent a technical expression which would specifically designate the sum total of social similarities. However, since the use of a new term, when it is not absolutely necessary, is not without its disadvantages, we shall retain the more generally used expression, 'collective (or common) consciousness', but always keeping in mind the restricted sense in which we are employing it.

[. . .]

In fact we all know that a social cohesion exists whose cause can be traced to a certain conformity of each individual consciousness to a common type, which is none other than the psychological type of society. Indeed under these conditions all members of the group are not only individually attracted to one another because they resemble one another, but they are also linked to what is the condition for the existence of this collective type, that is, to the society that they form by coming together. Not only do fellow-citizens like one another, seeking one another out in preference to foreigners, but they love their country. They wish for it what they would wish for themselves, they care that it should be lasting and prosperous, because without it a whole area of their psychological life would fail to function smoothly. Conversely, society insists upon its citizens displaying all these basic resemblances because it is a condition for its own cohesion. Two consciousnesses exist within us: the one comprises only states that are personal to each one of us, characteristic of us as individuals, whilst the other comprises states that are common to the whole of society.[2] The former represents only our individual personality, which it constitutes; the latter represents the collective type and consequently the society without which it would not exist. When it is an element of the latter determining our behaviour, we do not act with an eye to our own personal interest, but are pursuing collective ends. Now, although distinct, these two consciousnesses are linked to each other, since in the end they constitute only one entity, for both have one and the same organic basis. Thus they are solidly joined together. This gives rise to a solidarity *sui generis* which, deriving from resemblances, binds the individual directly to society. In the next chapter we shall be better able to demonstrate why we propose to term this solidarity mechanical. It does not consist merely in a general, indeterminate attachment of the individual to the group, but is also one that concerts their detailed actions. Indeed, since such collective motives are the same everywhere, they produce everywhere the same effects. Consequently, whenever they are brought into play all wills spontaneously move as one in the same direction.

[...]

We shall identify only two kinds of positive solidarity, distinguished by the following characteristics:

(1)   The first kind links the individual directly to society without any intermediary. With the second kind he depends upon society because he depends upon the parts that go to constitute it.

(2)   In the two cases, society is not viewed from the same perspective. In the first, the term is used to denote a more or less organized society composed of beliefs and sentiments common to all the members of the group: this is the collective type. On the contrary, in the second case the society to which we are solidly joined is a system of different and special functions united by definite relationships. Moreover, these two societies are really one. They are two facets of one and the same reality, but which nonetheless need to be distinguished from each other.

(3)   From this second difference there arises another which will serve to allow us to characterize and delineate the features of these two kinds of solidarity.

The first kind can only be strong to the extent that the ideas and tendencies common to all members of the society exceed in number and intensity those that appertain personally to each one of those members. The greater this excess, the more active this kind of society is. Now what constitutes our personality is that which each one of us possesses that is peculiar and characteristic, what distinguishes it from others. This solidarity can therefore only increase in inverse relationship to the personality. As we have said, there is in the consciousness of each one of us two consciousnesses: one that we share in common with our group in its entirety, which is consequently not ourselves, but society living and acting within us; the other that, on the contrary, represents us alone in what is personal and distinctive about us, what makes us an individual.[3] The solidarity that derives from similarities is at its *maximum* when the collective consciousness completely envelops our total consciousness, coinciding with it at every point. At that moment our individuality is zero. That individuality cannot arise until the community fills us less completely. Here there are two opposing forces, the one centripetal, the other centrifugal, which cannot increase at the same time. We cannot ourselves develop simultaneously in two so opposing directions. If we have a strong inclination to think and act for ourselves we cannot be strongly inclined to think and act like other people. If the ideal is to create for ourselves a special, personal image, this cannot mean to be like everyone else. Moreover, at the very moment when this solidarity exerts its effect, our personality, it may be said by definition, disappears, for we are no longer ourselves, but a collective being.

The social molecules that can only cohere in this one manner cannot therefore move as a unit save in so far as they lack any movement of their own, as do the molecules of inorganic bodies. This is why we suggest that this kind of solidarity should be called mechanical. The word does not mean that the solidarity is produced by mechanical and artificial means. We only use this term for it by analogy with the cohesion that links together the elements of raw materials, in contrast to that which encompasses the unity of living organisms. What finally justifies the use of this term is the fact that the bond that thus unites the individual with society is completely analogous to that which links the thing to the person. The individual consciousness, considered from this viewpoint, is simply a dependency of the collective type, and follows all its motions, just as the object possessed follows those which its owner imposes upon it. In societies where this solidarity is highly developed the individual, as we shall see later, does not belong to himself; life is literally a thing at the disposal of society. Thus, in these same social types, personal rights are still not yet distinguished from 'real' rights.

The situation is entirely different in the case of solidarity that brings about the division of labour. Whereas the other solidarity implies that individuals resemble one another, the latter assumes that they are different from one another. The former type is only possible in so far as the individual personality is absorbed into the collective personality; the latter is only possible if each one of us has a sphere of action that is peculiarly our own, and consequently a personality. Thus the collective consciousness leaves uncovered a part of the individual consciousness, so that there may be established in it those special functions that it cannot regulate. The more extensive this free area is, the stronger the cohesion that arises from this solidarity. Indeed, on the one hand each one of us depends more intimately upon society the more labour is divided up, and on the other, the activity of each one of us is correspondingly more specialized, the more personal it is. Doubtless, however circumscribed that activity may be, it is never completely original. Even in the exercise of our profession we conform to usages and practices that are common to us all within our corporation. Yet even in this case, the burden that we bear is in a different way less heavy than when the whole of society bears down upon us, and this leaves much more room for the free play of our initiative. Here, then, the individuality of the whole grows at the same time as that of the parts. Society becomes more effective in moving in concert, at the same time as each of its elements has more movements that are peculiarly its own. This solidarity resembles that observed in the higher animals. In fact each organ has its own special characteristics and autonomy, yet the greater the unity of the organism, the more marked the individualization of the parts. Using this analogy, we propose to call 'organic' the solidarity that is due to the division of labour.

[...]

Between the different types of society coexisting on earth there are too many intellectual and moral divergences to be able to live in a spirit of brotherhood in the same society. Yet what is possible is that societies of the same species should come together, and it is indeed in this direction that our society appears to be going. We have seen already that there is tending to form, above European peoples, in a spontaneous fashion, a European society that has even now some feeling of its own identity and the beginnings of an organization. If the formation of one single human society is for ever ruled out – and this has, however, not yet been demonstrated[4] – at least the formation of larger societies will draw us continually closer to that goal. Moreover, these facts do not at all contradict the definition we have given of morality. If we cling to humanity and ought to continue to do so, it is because it is a society in the process of realizing itself in this way, one to which we are solidly bound.[5]

Yet we know that more extensive societies cannot be formed without the development of the division of labour. Without a greater specialization of functions not only could they not sustain their equilibrium, but the increase in the number of elements in competition would also automatically suffice to bring about that state. Even more would this be the case, for an increase in volume does not generally occur without an increase in population density. Thus we may formulate the following proposition: the ideal of human brotherhood cannot be realized unless the division of labour progresses. We must choose: either we must abandon our dream, if we refuse to limit our individual activity any further; or we can pursue the consummation of our dream, but only on the condition just stated.

[...]

It has been rightly stated[6] that morality – and this must include both theory and the practice of ethics – is in the throes of an appalling crisis. What we have expounded can help us to understand the causes and nature of this sickness. Over a very short space of time very profound changes have occurred in the structure of our societies. They have liberated themselves from the segmentary model with a speed and in proportions without precedent in history. Thus the morality corresponding to this type of society has lost influence, but without its successor developing quickly enough to occupy the space left vacant in our consciousness. Our beliefs have been disturbed. Tradition has lost its sway. Individual judgement has thrown off the yoke of the collective judgement. On the other hand, the functions that have been disrupted in this period of trial have had no time to adjust to one another. The new life that all of a sudden has arisen has not been able to organize itself thoroughly. Above all, it has not been organized so as to satisfy the need for justice that has been aroused even more passionately in our hearts. If this is so, the remedy for the ill is nevertheless not to seek to revive traditions and practices that no longer correspond to present-day social conditions, and that could only subsist in a life that would be artificial, one only of appearance. We need to put a stop to this anomie, and to find ways of harmonious co-operation between those organs that still clash discordantly together. We need to introduce into their relationships a greater justice by diminishing those external inequalities that are the source of our ills. Our disease is therefore not, as occasionally we appear to believe, of an intellectual order, but linked to deeper causes. We are not suffering because we no longer know on what theoretical idea should be sustained the morality we have practised up to now. The cause is that certain elements of this morality have been irretrievably undermined, and the morality we require is only in the process of taking shape. Our anxiety does not arise because the criticism of scientists has demolished the traditional explanation handed down to us regarding our duties. Consequently it is not a new philosophical system that will ever be capable of dispelling that anxiety. Rather is it because certain of these duties no longer being grounded on reality, a loosening of ties has occurred that can only stop when a new discipline has become established and consolidated itself. In short, our first duty at the present time is to fashion a morality for ourselves. Such a task cannot be improvised in the silence of the study. It can arise only of its own volition, gradually, and under the pressure of internal causes that render it necessary.

NOTES

1. Such a confusion is not without its dangers. Thus it is occasionally asked whether the individual consciousness varies with the collective consciousness. Everything depends on the meaning assigned to the term. If it represents social similarities, the variation, as will be seen, is one of inverse relationship. If it designates the entire psychological life of society, the relationship is direct. Hence the need to draw a distinction.

2. In order to simplify our exposition we assume that the individual belongs to only one society. In fact we form a part of several groups and there exist in us several collective consciousnesses; but this complication does not in any way change the relationship we are establishing.

3. Nevertheless, these two consciousnesses are not regions of ourselves that are 'geographically' distinct, for they interpenetrate each other at every point.

4. There is nothing that demonstrates that the intellectual and moral diversity of societies is destined to continue. The ever greater expansion of higher societies, whereby the absorption or elimination of less advanced societies occurs, is tending in any case to lessen that diversity.

5. Thus the duties we have towards society do not take precedence over those we have towards our country. For the latter is the sole society that is at present realized of which we form part. The other is hardly more than a *desideratum*, whose realization is not even certain.

6. Cf. Beaussire, *Les principes de la morale*, introduction.

6. Structuring Patriarchal Societies

Sylvia Walby

I shall define patriarchy as a system of social structures and practices in which men dominate, oppress and exploit women.

The use of the term social structure is important here, since it clearly implies rejection both of biological determinism, and the notion that every individual man is in a dominant position and every woman in a subordinate one.

Patriarchy needs to be conceptualized at different levels of abstraction. At the most abstract level it exists as a system of social relations. In contemporary Britain this is present in articulation with capitalism, and with racism. However, I do not wish to imply that it is homologous in internal structure with capitalism. At a less abstract level patriarchy is composed of six structures: the patriarchal mode of production, patriarchal relations in paid work, patriarchal relations in the state, male violence, patriarchal relations in sexuality, and patriarchal relations in cultural institutions. More concretely, in relation to each of the structures, it is possible to identify sets of patriarchal practices which are less deeply sedimented. Structures are emergent properties of practices. Any specific empirical instance will embody the effects, not only of patriarchal structures, but also of capitalism and racism.

The six structures have causal effects upon each other, both reinforcing and blocking, but are relatively autonomous. The specification of several rather than simply one base is necessary in order to avoid reductionism and essentialism. The presence of only one base, for instance, reproduction for Firestone (1974) and rape for Brownmiller (1976), is the reason for their difficulty with historical change and cultural variation. It is not necessary to go to the other extreme of denying significant social structures to overcome the charge of essentialism, as some of the postmodernist post-structuralists have done. The six identified are real, deep structures and necessary to capture the variation in gender relations in Westernized societies.

Patriarchal production relations in the household are my first structure. It is through these that women's household labour is expropriated by their husbands or cohabitees. The woman may receive her maintenance in exchange for her labour, especially when she is not also engaged in waged labour. Housewives are the producing class, while husbands are the expropriating class.

The second patriarchal structure within the economic level is that of patriarchal relations within paid work. A complex of forms of patriarchal closure within waged labour exclude women from the better forms of work and segregate them into the worse jobs which are deemed to be less skilled.

The state is patriarchal as well as being capitalist and racist. While being a site of struggle and not a monolithic entity, the state has a systematic bias towards patriarchal interests in its policies and actions.

Male violence constitutes a further structure, despite its apparently individualistic and diverse form. It is behaviour routinely experienced by women from men, with standard effects upon the actions of most women. Male violence against women is systematically condoned and legitimated by the state's refusal to intervene against it except in exceptional instances, though the practices of rape, wife beating, sexual harassment, etc., are too decentralized in their practice to be part of the state itself.

Patriarchal relations in sexuality constitute a fifth structure. Compulsory heterosexuality and the sexual double standard are two of the key forms of this structure.

Patriarchal cultural institutions completes the array of structures. These are significant for the generation of a variety of gender-differentiated forms of subjectivity. This structure is composed of a set of institutions which create the representation of women within a patriarchal gaze in a variety of arenas, such as religions, education and the media.

[. . .]

I want to argue that there have been changes not only in the degree of patriarchy but also in its form. Britain has seen a movement from a private to a public form of patriarchy over the last century.

I am distinguishing two main forms of patriarchy, private and public. Private patriarchy is based upon household production as the main site of women's oppression. Public patriarchy is based principally in public sites such as employment and the state. The household does not cease to be a patriarchal structure in the public form, but it is no longer the chief site. In private patriarchy the

expropriation of women's labour takes place primarily by individual patriarchs within the household, while in the public form it is a more collective appropriation. In private patriarchy the principle patriarchal strategy is exclusionary; in the public it is segregationist and subordinating.

The change from private to public patriarchy involves a change both in the relations between the structures and within the structures. In the private form household production is the dominant structure; in the public form it is replaced by employment and the state. In each form all the remaining patriarchal structures are present – there is simply a change in which are dominant. There is also a change in the institutional forms of patriarchy, with the replacement of a primarily individual form of appropriation of women by a collective one. This takes place within each of the six patriarchal structures. (See table 1.1.)

[. . .]

I am distinguishing between two forms of patriarchy: private and public. They differ on a variety of levels: firstly, in terms of the relations between the structures and, secondly, in the institutional form of each structure. Further, they are differentiated by the main form of patriarchal strategy: exclusionary in private patriarchy and segregationist in public patriarchy. Private patriarchy is based upon household production, with a patriarch

Table 1.1 Private and public patriarchy

Form of patriarchy	Private	Public
Dominant structure	Household production	Employment/State
Wider patriarchal structures	Employment	Household production
	State	Sexuality
	Sexuality	Violence
	Violence	Culture
	Culture	
Period	C19th	C20th
Mode of expropriation	Individual	Collective
Patriarchal strategy	Exclusionary	Segregationist

controlling women individually and directly in the relatively private sphere of the home. Public patriarchy is based on structures other than the household, although this may still be a significant patriarchal site. Rather, institutions conventionally regarded as part of the public domain are central in the maintenance of patriarchy.

In private patriarchy it is a man in his position as husband or father who is the direct oppressor and beneficiary, individually and directly, of the subordination of women. This does not mean that household production is the sole patriarchal structure. Indeed it is importantly maintained by the active exclusion of women from public arenas by other structures. The exclusion of women from these other spheres could not be perpetuated without patriarchal activity at these levels.

Public patriarchy is a form in which women have access to both public and private arenas. They are not barred from the public arenas, but are nonetheless subordinated within them. The expropriation of women is performed more collectively than by individual patriarchs. The household may remain a site of patriarchal oppression, but it is no longer the main place where women are present.

In each type of patriarchy the six structures are present, but the relationship between them, and their relative significance, is different. For instance, I am not arguing that in private patriarchy the only significant site is that of the household. In the different forms there are different relations between the structures to maintain the system of patriarchy.

In the private system of patriarchy the exploitation of women in the household is maintained by their non-admission to the public sphere. In a sense the term 'private' for this form of patriarchy might be misleading, in that it is the exclusion from the public which is the central causal mechanism. Patriarchal relations outside the household are crucial in shaping patriarchal relations within it. However, the effect is to make women's experience of patriarchy privatized, and the immediate beneficiaries are also located there.

In the public form of patriarchy the exploitation of women takes place at all levels, but women are not formally excluded from any. In each institution women are disadvantaged.

The second aspect of the difference between private and public patriarchy is in the institutional form of each of the structures. This is a movement from an individual to a more collective form of appropriation of women. There has also been a shift in patriarchal strategy from exclusionary to segregationist and subordinating.

I have traced the movement from private to public patriarchy within each of the six patriarchal structures during the course of this book. Within paid work there was a shift from an exclusionary strategy to a segregationist one, which was a movement from attempting to exclude women from paid work to accepting their presence but confining them to jobs which were segregated from and graded lower than those of men. In the household there was a reduction in the confinement of women to this sphere over a lifetime and a shift in the main locus of control over reproduction. The major cultural institutions ceased to exclude women, while subordinating women within them. Sexual controls over women significantly shifted from the specific control of a husband to that of a broader public arena; women were no longer excluded from sexual relations to the same extent, but subordinated within them. Women's exclusion from the state was replaced by their subordination within it.

Private and public patriarchy in British history

Recent British history has seen a movement towards the private model, and then a movement away to the public form. The height of the private form was to be found in the mid-nineteenth century in the middle classes. Many scholars have argued that there was an intensification in the domestic ideology and the extent to which middle-class women were confined to the private sphere of the home (Davidoff and Hall, 1987; Gilman, 1966; Pinchbeck, 1930; Schreiner, 1918;

Tilly and Scott, 1978). There were extremely strong sanctions against non-marital sexuality for such women. They did not work in public, only in their own households, and were excluded from the public sphere of the state, lacking citizenship rights such as suffrage and, if married, ability to own property. Violence against wives by husbands was condoned as legitimate chastisement 'so long as the rod was no thicker than a man's thumb'. Cultural institutions, such as the church, supported the notion that a woman's place was in the home.

There were some limits and contradictions to this private model of patriarchy, but they do not destroy the general case. For instance, it was applied to middle-class women to a much greater extent than working-class women, although there were attempts to extend it (for instance the legislation which banned women from working down the mines and restricted their factory employment).

The contemporary form of patriarchy is of a more public kind, and the trend is still in this direction. Women have entered the public sphere, yet are subordinated there. Most women of all social classes engage in paid work. Simultaneously, there is a considerable wages gap between men and women and extensive occupational segregation. The sanctions on non-marital sexuality, while still present to a greater degree for women than for men, are much less severe. At the same time the circulation of sadistic pornographic images has increased. Marriages can be, and increasingly are, legally dissolved. While women are thereby freed from marriages which are especially oppressive, they still remain responsible for child care after divorce, thus continuing the demands upon their labour started in marriage. This is now done under circumstances of increased poverty. Women have citizenship rights which are formally the same as those of men, but they form only a tiny proportion of the elected representatives, and a tiny proportion of the political agenda is around women's concerns. Violence against wives, while tolerated, is not quite as legitimate as it once was, since it can now be used as grounds

for divorce, and minimal welfare provision is available to those who flee; however, few legal penalties await the vast majority of men who are violent against women. Cultural institutions increasingly allow women's active participation, but usually in an inferior way.

Women have entered the public sphere, but not on equal terms. They are now present in the paid workplace, the state and public cultural institutions. But they are subordinated within them. Further, their subordination, in the domestic division of labour, sexual practices, and as receivers of male violence, continues.

The private and public forms of patriarchy constitute a continuum rather than a rigid dichotomy. The trend towards a more public form has been continuing despite the economic recession which some expected to stop the entry of women into paid work, and despite the development of the New Right. We do not yet see its full development. We should expect the movement into paid work to continue, especially given the increase in the number of young women gaining educational qualifications, the reduced expectancy that a husband is for life, and the slow, but steady, removal of barriers to women's participation in paid work. The private form of patriarchy which existed among the middle classes in the nineteenth century did not reach the full limits of that model. We can see its further development in Islamic populations (especially among the upper classes – the lower classes in the countryside could not afford for women not to work outside the home).

Within Britain itself we see different degrees of public and private patriarchy among different ethnic groups. Afro-Caribbeans are closer to the public form, Muslim Asians to the private form, with whites in the middle. Afro-Caribbean women have the highest rates of participation in paid work and the highest rates of female-headed households of the three groups. Muslim Asian women have the lowest rates of paid work, and have the most intense forms of male-headed families (Brown, 1984). Whites appear to be moving towards the Afro-Caribbean pattern.

The two main forms of patriarchy I have identified are useful for conceptualizing major changes in gender relations in Britain in the last couple of centuries. In order to grasp the major differences in the forms of patriarchy between various countries in the industrialized world it is further necessary to divide the public form of patriarchy into two: one founded on the labour market and the other on the state as the basis of bringing women into the public sphere. At one end of the continuum we have the countries of Eastern Europe, where the state has played a major role in this, at the other we have the USA, in which the market has played an equivalent role. In the middle we have the countries of Western Europe, in which the state, in its capacity especially as a welfare state, has been of intermediate significance.

The development of the typology beyond a simple duality to one where one of the elements is again divided is based on the introduction of the level of the state as a new element. In Eastern Europe, and to a lesser extent in Western Europe, the state has taken on some of the tasks which were previously performed by women privately in the household and organized them collectively (even if they are still largely performed by women). This is the case for care of children, the sick and the old. There is clearly a major difference between Western and Eastern Europe in the extent of state activity, but the differences between Western Europe and the USA are also striking in this regard (although the existence of a massive state education system in the USA should preclude comparative statements of an absolute kind). Thus the contemporary USA may be seen to have a labour-market-based form of public patriarchy, Eastern Europe a state-based form of public patriarchy, and Western Europe a mixed state/labour-market-form of public patriarchy. In each of these areas this represents a change from a previous form of private patriarchy.

The variation is caused by the difference in state policy which itself is an outcome of the various struggles between opposing forces on both gender and class issues. In eastern Europe the seizure of the state by forces which were

radical on both class and gender issues is central, even if that radicalism had very significant limits. The development of the welfare state in Western Europe is usually considered to be the outcome of a compromise in the struggle between capital and labour. I think this should further be regarded also to be the outcome of gendered political forces, since an alliance between feminism and the labour movement was key to the development of such policies.

[. . .]

Patriarchy comes in more than one form; each form can be found to different degrees. British history over the last century or so has seen a shift to a more intense form of private patriarchy and then a dramatic reversal of this with a move towards public patriarchy. This latter shift was a result of the successes of first-wave feminism against the background of an expanding capitalist economy. It took its form in the context of the international economy, and various specific forms in different ethnic groups. The British form of public patriarchy involves the market as well as the state, while there is a different sub-type of public patriarchy in Eastern Europe in which the state plays a more central part in comparison with the market.

The major historical changes are different for gender relations from those of capitalist class relations. Gender and class have independent historical dynamics, although of course they do have effects upon each other. The rise of capitalism transformed class relations, changing the very classes which constituted society. This historical shift did not have such dramatic effects upon gender relations: men remained the dominant gender; all six patriarchal structures continued across this period; only a minor shift in the relative significance of public and private sites of patriarchy occurred. The trajectory towards an intensified private form of patriarchy, which can be identified as far back as the seventeenth century (Charles and Duffin, 1985; Clark, 1919), accelerated.

Gender relations are not static, and a developed concept of patriarchy is the best way of theorizing the changes. The idea of patriarchy does not necessarily give rise to fixed, ahistoric analysis.

Women are not passive victims of oppressive structures. They have struggled to change both their immediate circumstances and the wider social structures. First-wave feminism is a much more important historical force than is usually considered. This major feminist push changed the course of history. However, it did not lead to an elimination of all the forms of inequality between men and women which it sought to eradicate. In some ways early feminists won their goals, and their successes were considerable. However, in response, patriarchy changed in form, incorporating some of the hard-won changes into new traps for women.

The form of patriarchy in contemporary Britain is public rather than private. Women are no longer restricted to the domestic hearth, but have the whole society in which to roam and be exploited.

REFERENCES

Brown, Colin (1984), *Black and White Britain: the third PSI survey* (London: Heinemann).

Brownmiller, Susan (1976), *Against Our Will: men, women and rape* (Harmondsworth: Penguin).

Charles, Lindsey and Duffin, Lorna (eds) (1985), *Women and Work in Pre-Industrial England* (London: Croom Helm).

Clark, Alice (1919), *Working Life of Women in the Seventeenth Century* (London: Routledge and Kegan Paul; reprinted 1982).

Davidoff, Leonore and Hall, Catherine (1987), *Family Fortunes: men and women of the English middle class 1780–1850* (London: Hutchinson).

Firestone, Shulamith (1974), *The Dialectic of Sex: the case for feminist revolution* (New York: Morrow).

Gilman, Charlotte Perkins (1966), *Women and Economics: a study of the economic relation between men and women as a factor in social evolution* (New York: Harper Torchbooks).

Pinchbeck, Ivy (1930), *Women Workers and the Industrial Revolution, 1750–1850* (London: Virago; reprinted 1981).

Schreiner, Olive (1918), *Woman and Labour* (London: Fisher Unwin).

Tilly, Louise and Scott, Joan (1978), *Women, Work and Family* (New York: Holt, Reinhart and Winston).

7. Intimations of Postmodernity

Zygmunt Bauman

The re-enchantment of the world, or, how can one narrate postmodernity?

Postmodernity means many different things to many different people. It may mean a building that arrogantly flaunts the 'orders' prescribing what fits what and what should be kept strictly out to preserve the functional logic of steel, glass and concrete. It means a work of imagination that defies the difference between painting and sculpture, styles and genres, gallery and the street, art and everything else. It means a life that looks suspiciously like a TV serial, and a docudrama that ignores your worry about setting apart fantasy from what 'really happened'. It means licence to do whatever one may fancy and advice not to take anything you or the others do too seriously. It means the speed with which things change and the pace with which moods succeed each other so that they have no time to ossify into things. It means attention drawn in all directions at once so that it cannot stop on anything for long and nothing gets a really close look, it means a shopping mall overflowing with goods whose major use is the joy of purchasing there; and existence that feels like a life-long confinement to the shopping mall. It means the exhilarating freedom to pursue anything and the mind-boggling uncertainty as to what is worth pursuing and in the name of what one should pursue it.

Postmodernity is all these things and many others. But it is also – perhaps more than anything else – *a state of mind*. More precisely – a state of those minds who have the habit (or is it a compulsion?) to reflect upon themselves, to search their own contents and report what they found: the state of mind of philosophers, social thinkers, artists – all those people on whom we rely when we are in a pensive mood or just pause for a moment to find out whence we are moving or being moved.

This is a state of mind marked above all by its all-deriding, all-eroding, all-dissolving *destructiveness*. It seems sometimes that postmodern mind is a critique caught at the moment of its ultimate triumph: a critique that finds it ever more difficult to go on being critical just because it has destroyed everything it used to be critical about; with it, off went the very urgency of being critical. There is nothing left to be opposed to. [. . .] How ridiculous it seems to try to change the direction of history when no powers give an inkling that they wish to give history direction. How empty seems the effort to show that what passes for truth is false when nothing has the courage and the stamina to declare itself as truth for everybody and for all time. How farcical it seems to fight for genuine art when one can no more drop anything incidentally without the dropped object being proclaimed art. How quixotic to debunk the distortion in the representation of reality once no reality claims to be more real than its representation. How idle it seems to exhort people to go there rather than somewhere else in a world in which everything goes.

The postmodern state of mind is the radical (though certainly unexpected and in all probability undesired) victory of modern (that is, inherently critical, restless, unsatisfied, insatiable) culture over the modern society it aimed to improve through throwing it wide open to its own potential. Many little victorious battles added up to a victorious war. One after another, hurdles have been taken apart, ramparts crushed and locks broken in the incessant, stubborn work of emancipation. At each moment a particular constraint, an especially painful prohibition was under attack. In the end, a *universal dismantling of power-supported structures* has been the result. No new and improved order has emerged, however, from beneath the debris of the old and unwanted one. Postmodernity (and in this it differs from modernist culture of which it is the rightful issue and legatee) does not seek to substitute one truth for another, one standard of beauty for another, one life ideal for another. Instead, it splits the truth, the standards and the ideal into already deconstructed and about to be deconstructed. It denies in advance the right of all and any revelation to slip into the place vacated by the deconstructed/discredited rules. It braces itself for a life without truths, standards and ideals. It is often blamed for not being positive enough, for not being positive at all, for not wishing to be positive and for pooh-poohing positivity as such, for sniffing a knife of unfreedom under any cloak of saintly righteousness or just placid self-confidence. The postmodern mind seems to condemn everything, propose nothing. Demolition is the only job the postmodern mind seems to be good at. Destruction is the only construction it recognizes. Demolition of coercive constraints and mental blocks is for it the ultimate purpose and the end of emancipatory effort; truth and goodness, says Rorty, will take care of themselves once we have taken proper care of freedom.

[. . .]

All in all, postmodernity can be seen as restoring to the world what modernity, presumptuously, had taken away; as a *re-enchantment* of the world that modernity tried hard to *dis-enchant*. It is the modern artifice that has been dismantled; the modern conceit of meaning-legislating reason that has been exposed, condemned and put to shame. It is that artifice and that reason, the reason of the artifice, that stands accused in the court of postmodernity.

The war against mystery and magic was for modernity the war of liberation leading to the declaration of reason's independence. It was the declaration of hostilities that made the unprocessed, pristine world into the enemy. As is the case with all genocide, the world of nature (as distinct from the house of culture modernity set out to build) had to be beheaded and thus deprived of autonomous will and power of resistance. At stake in the war was the right to initiative and the authorship of action, the right to pronounce on meanings, to construe narratives. To win the stakes, to win all of them and to win them for good, the world had to be *de-spiritualized*, de-animated: denied the opacity of the *subject*.

[. . .]

I propose that:

1 The term *postmodernity* renders accurately the defining traits of the social condition that emerged throughout the affluent countries of Europe and of European descent in the course of the twentieth century, and took its present shape in the second half of that century. The term is accurate as it draws attention to the continuity and discontinuity as two faces of the intricate relationship between the present social condition and the formation that preceded and gestated it. It brings into relief the intimate, genetic bond that ties the new, postmodern social condition to *modernity* – the social formation that emerged in the same part of the world in the course of the seventeenth century, and took its final shape, later to be sedimented in the sociological models of modern society (or models of society created by modern sociology), during the nineteenth century; while at the same time indicating the passing of certain crucial characteristics in whose absence one can no longer adequately describe the social condition as modern in the sense given to the concept by orthodox (modern) social theory.

2 Postmodernity may be interpreted as fully developed modernity taking a full measure of the anticipated consequences of its historical work; as modernity that acknowledged the effects it was producing throughout its history, yet producing inadvertently, rarely conscious of its own responsibility, by default rather than design, as by-products often perceived as waste. Postmodernity may be conceived of as modernity conscious of its true nature – *modernity for itself*. The most conspicuous features of the postmodern condition: institutionalized pluralism, variety, contingency and ambivalence – have all been turned out by modern society in ever increasing volumes; yet they were seen as signs of failure rather than success, as evidence of the unsufficiency of efforts so far, at a time when the institutions of modernity, faithfully replicated by the modern mentality, struggled for *universality, homogeneity, monotony* and *clarity*. The postmodern condition can be therefore described, on the one hand, as modernity emancipated from false consciousness; on the other, as a new type of social condition marked by the overt institutionalization of the characteristics which modernity – in its designs and managerial practices – set about to eliminate and, failing that, tried to conceal.

3 The twin differences that set the postmodern condition apart from modern society are profound and seminal enough to justify (indeed, to call for) a separate sociological theory of postmodernity that would break decisively with the concepts and metaphors of the models of modernity and lift itself out of the mental frame in which they had been conceived. This need arises from the fact that (their notorious disagreements notwithstanding), the extant models of modernity articulated a shared vision of modern history as *a movement with a direction* – and differed solely in the selection of the ultimate destination or the organizing principle of the process, be it universalization, rationalization or systemization. None of those principles can be upheld (at least not in the radical form typical of the orthodox social theory) in the light of postmodern experience. Neither can the very master-metaphor that underlies them be sustained: that of the process with a pointer.

4 Postmodernity is not a transitory departure from the 'normal state' of modernity; neither is it a diseased state of modernity, an ailment likely to be rectified, a case of 'modernity in crisis'. It is, instead, a self-reproducing, pragmatically self-sustainable and logically self-contained social condition defined by *distinctive features of its own*. A theory of postmodernity therefore cannot be a modified theory of modernity, a theory of modernity with a set of negative markers. An adequate theory of postmodernity may be constructed only in a cognitive space organized by a different set of assumptions; it needs its own vocabulary. The degree of emancipation from the concepts and issues spawned by the discourse of modernity ought to serve as a measure of the adequacy of such a theory.

8. Riding the Juggernaut of Modernity

Anthony Giddens

The world in which we live today is a fraught and dangerous one. This has served to do more than simply blunt or force us to qualify the assumption that the emergence of modernity would lead to the formation of a happier and more secure social order. Loss of a belief in 'progress', of course, is one of the factors that underlies the dissolution of 'narratives' of history. Yet there is much more at stake here than the conclusion that history 'goes nowhere'. We have to develop an institutional analysis of the double-edged character of modernity. In so doing, we must make good some of the limitations of the classical sociological perspectives, limitations that have continued to affect sociological thought in the present day.

[. . .]

Two images of what it feels like to live in the world of modernity have dominated the socio-logical literature, yet both of them seem less than adequate. One is that of Weber, according to which the bonds of rationality are drawn tighter and tighter, imprisoning us in a featureless cage of bureaucratic routine. Among the three major founders of modern sociology, Weber saw most clearly the significance of expertise in modern social development and used it to outline a phe-nomenology of modernity. Everyday experience, according to Weber, retains its colour and spon-taneity, but only on the perimeter of the 'steel-hard' cage of bureaucratic rationality. The image has a great deal of power and has, of course, fea-tured strongly in fictional literature in the twen-tieth century as well as in more directly sociological

discussions. There are many contexts of modern institutions which are marked by bureaucratic fixity. But they are far from all-pervasive, and even in the core settings of its application, namely, large-scale organizations, Weber's characteriza-tion of bureaucracy is inadequate. Rather than tending inevitably towards rigidity, organizations produce areas of autonomy and spontaneity – which are actually often less easy to achieve in smaller groups. We owe this counterinsight to Durkheim, as well as to subsequent empirical study of organizations. The closed climate of opinion within some small groups and the modes of direct sanction available to its members fix the horizons of action much more narrowly and firmly than in larger organizational settings.

The second is the image of Marx – and of many others, whether they regard themselves as Marxist or not. According to this portrayal, modernity is seen as a monster. More limpidly perhaps than any of his contemporaries, Marx perceived how shattering the impact of modernity would be, and how irreversible. At the same time, modernity was for Marx what Habermas has aptly called an 'unfinished project.' The monster can be tamed, since what human beings have created they can always subject to their own control. Capitalism, simply, is an irrational way to run the modern world, because it substitutes the whims of the market for the controlled fulfilment of human need.

For these images I suggest we should substi-tute that of the juggernaut[1] – a runaway engine of enormous power which, collectively as human beings, we can drive to some extent but which also threatens to rush out of our control and which could rend itself asunder. The juggernaut crushes those who resist it, and while it sometimes seems to have a steady path, there are times when it veers away erratically in directions we cannot foresee. The ride is by no means wholly unpleasant or unrewarding; it can often be exhilarating and charged with hopeful anticipation. But, so long as the institutions of modernity endure, we shall never be able to control completely either the path or the pace of the journey. In turn, we shall never be able to feel entirely secure, because the terrain across which it runs is fraught with risks of high consequence. Feelings of ontological security and existential anxiety will coexist in ambivalence.

The juggernaut of modernity is not all of one piece, and here the imagery lapses, as does any talk of a single path which it runs. It is not an engine made up of integrated machinery, but one in which there is a tensionful, contradictory, push-and-pull of different influences. Any attempt to capture the experience of modernity must begin from this view, which derives ultimately from the dialectics of space and time, as expressed in the time-space constitution of modern institutions.

[. . .]

How far can we – where 'we' means humanity as a whole – harness the juggernaut, or at least direct it in such a way as to minimize the dangers and maximize the opportunities which modernity offers to us? Why, in any case, do we currently live in such a runaway world, so different from that which the Enlightenment thinkers anticipated? Why has the generalizing of 'sweet reason' not produced a world subject to our prediction and control?

Several factors suggest themselves, none of which, however, have anything to do with the idea that we no longer have any viable methods of sustaining knowledge claims in the sense of Lyotard and others. The first might be termed *design faults*. Modernity is inseparable from the abstract systems that provide for the disembedding of social relations across space and time and span both socialized nature and the social universe. Perhaps too many of these suffer from design faults which, when they lead systems to go wrong, send us spinning away from our projected paths of development? Now plainly we can apply a notion of design faults to social as well as natural systems, where the former are established with definite 'ends in view'. Any organization can in principle be assessed in terms of how far it effectively reaches certain goals or provides certain services. Any aspect of socialized nature can in principle be evaluated in terms of how far it meets particular human needs and produces no unwanted end results. In both contexts, design faults are undoubtedly very common. In the case of systems depending upon socialized nature, there seems no reason, again in principle, why design faults should not be eradicated. The situation in respect of social systems is more complicated and difficult, as we shall see.

A second factor is what we might call *operator failure*. Any abstract system, no matter how well designed it is, can fail to work as it is supposed to do because those who operate it make mistakes. This also applies both to social and natural systems. Unlike design faults, operator failure appears to be ineradicable. Good design can make the possibility of operator failure very low, and so can rigorous training and discipline; but so long as human beings are involved, the risk must be there. In the case of the Chernobyl incident, the root cause of the disaster was a mistake made in the operating of the emergency shutdown systems. Mathematical calculations of risk, such as the risks of human mortality attaching to competing methods of generating power, can be carried out about the working of physical systems. But the element of operator failure cannot effectively be incorporated into such calculations.

However, neither design faults nor operator failure are the most important elements producing the erratic character of modernity. The two most significant influences are those referred to briefly earlier: *unintended consequences* and the *reflexivity* or *circularity of social knowledge*. Design faults and operator failure clearly fall within the category of unintended consequences, but the category includes much more. No matter how well a system is designed and no matter how efficient its operators, the consequences of its introduction and functioning, in the contexts of the operation of other systems and of human activity in general, cannot be wholly predicted. One reason for this is the complexity of systems and actions that make up world society. But even if it were conceivable – as in practice it is not – that the world (human action and the physical environment) could become a single design system, unintended consequences would persist.

The reason for this is the circularity of social knowledge, which affects in the first instance the social rather than the natural world. In conditions of modernity, the social world can never form a stable environment in terms of the input of new knowledge about its character and functioning. New knowledge (concepts, theories, findings) does not simply render the social world more transparent, but alters its nature, spinning it off in novel directions. The impact of this phenomenon is fundamental to the juggernaut-like quality of modernity and affects socialized nature as well as social institutions themselves. For although knowledge about the natural world does not affect the world in a direct way, the circularity of social knowledge incorporates elements of nature via the technological components of abstract systems.

For all these reasons, we cannot seize 'history' and bend it readily to our collective purposes. Even though we ourselves produce and reproduce it in our actions, we cannot control social life

completely. Moreover, the factors just mentioned presume homogeneity of interest and purpose, something which one certainly cannot take for granted as regards humanity overall. The two other influences referred to previously, differential power and the roles of values, are also important. The world is 'one' in some senses, but radically riven by inequalities of power in others. And one of the most characteristic features of modernity is the discovery that the development of empirical knowledge does not in and of itself allow us to decide between different value positions.

Utopian realism

Yet none of this means that we should, or that we can, give up in our attempts to steer the juggernaut. The minimizing of high-consequence risks transcends all values and all exclusionary divisions of power. 'History' is not on our side, has no teleology, and supplies us with no guarantees. But the heavily counterfactual nature of future-oriented thought, an essential element of the reflexivity of modernity, has positive as well as negative implications. For we can envisage alternative futures whose very propagation might help them be realized.

NOTE

1. The term comes from the Hindi *Jagannāth*, 'lord of the world', and is a title of Krishna; an idol of this deity was taken each year through the streets on a huge car, which followers are said to have thrown themselves under, to be crushed beneath the wheels.

Theme 1 – Further Reading

An excellent, comprehensive textbook is George Ritzer's (2010) *Sociological Theory* (McGraw-Hill), now into its eighth edition. For classical sociological theory, Kenneth Morrison's (2006) *Marx, Durkheim, Weber: Formations of Modern Thought* (London: Sage) is very good and contains a handy glossary of key concepts. For contemporary theories, Rob Stones's (2007) *Key Sociological Thinkers* (Basingstoke: Palgrave Macmillan) covers a wide range. To get a better sense of the broad sweep of changes in sociological theories, try Alan Swingewood (2000) *A Short History of Sociological Thought* (Basingstoke: Palgrave Macmillan).

<u>Giddens and Sutton *Sociology* 7th *Edition* (2013)</u>

The obvious place to start is with Chapter 3 on theories and perspectives, though theoretical debates are scattered across the whole book. Specific sections that link with this theme can be found in Chapter 5 on environment, pages 185–97; Chapter 10 on families, pages 420–7; Chapter 12 on social class, pages 485–91; Chapter 14 on inequality, pages 594–602; Chapter 15 on gender inequality, pages 651–8; Chapter 17 on religion, pages 723–8 and Chapter 18 on the mass media.

Part 2 Research Methods

Research studies in sociology range from small-scale interactions to long-term shifts in the structure of societies, taking in everything in between. The techniques and methods adopted by researchers are extremely diverse and any suggestion of a uniform or single method in sociology is unrealistic given the discipline's wide-ranging subject matter. This is not a weakness but a strength as it means that good sociology always begins from a research problem in the real world and from there, sociologists explore the most appropriate methods or techniques which allow them to carry out the study. This is something of an ideal situation however, and it is clear that the sociologist's view of the nature of the social world (its ontology) does shape their decision of how it can best be studied. Of course, many sociologists have their own preference in the selection of research methods and these tend to reflect the kinds of issues and subjects they deal with.

Probably the most common preference is for either quantitative or qualitative research methods. In some cases, qualitative researchers object to the very principle of trying to measure meaningful human action, while quantitative researchers view qualitative methods as too subjective to provide the basis for a social *science*. In recent years, however, many sociologists have seen worthwhile benefits in combining quantitative and qualitative methods in the same study, not least the possibility to enhance the validity of

their findings. In Reading 9, Alan Bryman explores the quantitative–qualitative divide, pointing out that some of the apparent differences between quantitative and qualitative methods are not as real or insurmountable as previously thought. For instance, some of the more recent qualitative software packages enable qualitative data to be systematically categorized, measured and analysed, while ostensibly quantitative survey work is often based around qualitative, semi-structured interview schedules. Bryman outlines some of the main arguments in favour of breaking down the quantitative–qualitative divide in favour of what are now described as 'mixed methods' approaches, which are becoming more popular at present.

One well-used research method in sociology is the survey approach. Social surveys have long been the staple of sociological training and survey research has proved extremely useful in showing patterns in social life. If we want to know what proportion of working women work part-time or what effect working part-time has on their attitude towards the household division of labour, then the survey method still remains the best method for the task. Even in areas where qualitative strategies appear to offer more appropriate methods, such as feminist research aiming to gain insights into women's experience, survey research is still useful as it allows us to ask further questions about the extent to which such personal experiences are likely to be shared. Alan Buckingham and

Peter Saunders tell us what surveys are and where we might make use of them (Reading 10). But they also analyse the apparent links between surveys and positivism, pointing out that British sociology has been less than enthusiastic in its use of quantitative methods, partly perhaps because of the stigma that has become attached to positivism. However, Buckingham and Saunders argue that many researchers who use survey methods would not consider themselves 'positivist' and that the philosophical case against positivism can be distinguished from technical issues of the survey method. This careful dissection of some of the main debates on survey methods and staunch defence of them in the face of criticisms makes us think logically about the connections between methodology and methods.

One of the more popular new methods in sociology is biographical research, which aims to get to grips with the way individual lives are actually lived in differing social and historical contexts. Biographical research includes oral histories, long-term interviews, interpreting personal diaries and other techniques which allow sociologists to gain access to the thoughts, feelings and actions of individuals. In Reading 11, Barbara Merrill and Linden West give a good example of how biographies can help us to connect individual lives with the wider social, economic and political changes they live through. Using their own personal biographies, Merrill and West also go one stage further in bringing themselves within the research frame. It is this aspect that has proved to be most controversial as it erodes the division between researchers and their subject(s). Some have found this particularly uncomfortable as, they argue, it runs the risk of compromising the sociologist's necessary detachment or objectivity both during the research process and in reporting findings. Nonetheless, biographical research has made very rapid progress into the mainstream of research methods,

especially among a new generation of sociologists.

The study of social change is fundamental to the sociological enterprise and is a common theme in the work of the classical sociologists. When did Western economies become capitalistic? What similarities are there in the French, Russian and Chinese revolutions? Where is globalization taking us in the future? Such grand questions demand that sociologists make use of historical research methods. In Reading 12, Philip Abrams explains that sociology and history are closely related and can learn from each other. Historians can better understand the patterns that emerge in long-term social change, while sociologists can begin to appreciate the value of interpreting a wider variety of sources of information. Indeed, Abrams contends that 'historical sociology' is not a special type of sociology reserved for the study of long-term social change, but is, or should be, at the centre of all sociological work. Focusing on the concept of 'process' or the continuous creation and reproduction of social structures through myriad social actions, this view of sociology is not too far removed from C. Wright-Mills's linking of the personal and the public realms in Reading 1.

Our final reading illustrates the value of participant observation in uncovering previously hidden social worlds. Participant observation makes extraordinary demands on the researcher who is charged with immersing themselves into a world which is alien to their experience, while at the same time, maintaining enough detachment to collect data and report their findings without distortion. In Reading 13, Loïc Wacquant's account of how he became involved in a boxing gym in order to understand its attractions for young men in poor neighbourhoods is a type of participant observation, but with a twist. In the process of spending long periods of time among boxers, Wacquant himself boxed in competitive bouts and, as he says in the piece here, this makes his research method 'observant participation' rather than mere participant observation. Needless to say, the majority of professional sociologists would not go as far as Wacquant in the quest for knowledge! But the question is would they have been able to provide the same intimate understanding of the small details of life in the gym by remaining relatively aloof?

9. Quantitative vs. Qualitative Methods?

Alan Bryman

With this book structured so far around the distinction between quantitative and qualitative research, it might appear perverse to raise at this stage the prospect that the distinction might be overblown. The distinction has been employed so far for two main reasons.

- There *are* differences between quantitative and qualitative research in terms of research strategy, and many researchers and writers on research methodology perceive this to be the case.
- It is a useful means of organizing research methods and approaches to data analysis.

However, while epistemological and ontological commitments may be associated with certain research methods – such as the often cited links between a natural science epistemology (in particular, positivism) and social survey research, or between an interpretivist epistemology (for example, phenomenology) and qualitative interviewing – the connections are not deterministic. In other words, while qualitative interviews may often reveal a predisposition towards or a reflection of an interpretivist and constructionist position, this is not always the case. [. . .] This means that the connections [. . .] between epistemology and ontology, on the one hand, and research method, on the other, are best thought of as tendencies rather than as definitive connections. Such connections were implied by the suggestion that within each of the two research strategies – quantitative and qualitative – there is a distinctive mix of epistemology, ontology and research methods [. . .]. However, we cannot say that the use of a structured interview or self-completion questionnaire *necessarily* implies a commitment to a natural scientific model or that ethnographic research *must* mean an interpretivist epistemology. We should not be surprised at this: after all, quantitative research teaches us that it is rarely the case that we find perfect associations between variables. We should not be surprised, therefore, that the practice of social research similarly lacks absolute determinism.

Research methods are much more free-floating than is sometimes supposed. A method of data collection like participant observation can be employed in such a way that it is in tune with the tenets of constructionism, but equally it can be used in a manner that reveals an objectivist orientation. Also, it is easy to under-emphasize the significance of practical considerations in the way in which social research is conducted [. . .]. Conducting a study of drug dealers by mail questionnaire may not be totally impossible, but it is unlikely to succeed in terms of yielding valid answers to questions.

[. . .]

Quantitative research and interpretivism

Qualitative research would seem to have a monopoly of the ability to study meaning. Its proponents essentially claim that it is only through qualitative research that the world can be studied through the eyes of the people who are studied. As Platt (1981: 87) observes, this contention seems rather at odds with the widespread study of attitudes in social surveys based on interviews and question-naires. In fact, it would seem that quantitative researchers frequently address meanings. An example is the well-known concept of 'orientation to work' associated with the *Affluent Worker* research in the 1960s, which sought to uncover the nature and significance of the meanings that industrial workers bring with them to the work-place (Goldthorpe et al., 1968). Similarly, survey research by Stewart et al., (1980: 112) showed that clerks should not be treated as a unitary cat-egory and that 'the *meaning* of clerical work will not be the same for all engaged in it' (emphasis added).

The widespread inclusion of questions about attitudes in social surveys suggests that quantita-tive researchers are interested in matters of meaning. It might be objected that survey ques-tions do not really tap issues of meaning because they are based on categories devised by the designers of the interview schedule or question-naire. Two points are relevant here. First, in the absence of respondent validation exercises, the notion that qualitative research is more adept at gaining access to the point of view of those being studied than quantitative research is invariably assumed rather than demonstrated. Qualitative researchers frequently claim to have tapped into participants' world views because of, for example, their extensive participation in the daily round of those they study, the length of time they spent in the setting being studied, or the lengthy and intensive interviews conducted. However, the explicit demonstration that interpretative under-standing has been accomplished – for example, through respondent validation [. . .] – is rarely undertaken. Secondly, if the design of attitude questions is based on prior questioning that seeks to bring out the range of possible attitudinal posi-tions on an issue [. . .], attitudinal questions may be better able to gain access to meaning.

Also, as Marsh (1982) has pointed out, the practice in much survey research of asking respon-dents the reasons for their actions implies that quantitative researchers are frequently concerned to uncover issues of meaning. For example, she cites Brown and Harris's (1978) research, which was based on a social survey, on the relationship between critical life events (such as loss of a job, death of husband) and depression. In this research, exploring the meaning of critical life events for respondents was a notable feature of the question-ing. As Marsh (1982: 115) puts it, 'it is the *meaning* that these events have for the subjects that gives them their causal force in provoking an onset' (emphasis added). Examples such as these further point to the possibility that the gulf between quantitative and qualitative research is not as wide as is sometimes supposed.

[. . .]

Behaviour versus meaning

The distinction is sometimes drawn between a focus on behaviour and a focus on meanings. However, quantitative research frequently involves the study of meanings in the form of attitude scales (such as the Likert scaling technique) and other techniques. Qualitative researchers may feel that the tendency for attitude scales to be prefor-mulated and imposed on research participants means that they do not really gain access to mean-ings (see above). The key point being made here is that at the very least quantitative researchers frequently *try* to address meanings. Also, some-what ironically many of the techniques with which quantitative research is associated, most notably social survey research based on questionnaires and interviews, have been shown to relate poorly to people's actual behavior [. . .]. Moreover, looking at the other side of the divide, qualitative research frequently, if not invariably, entails the examina-tion of behaviour in context. Qualitative research-ers often want to interpret people's behaviour in terms of the norms, values and culture of the group or community in question. In other words, quantitative and qualitative researchers are typi-cally interested in both what people do and what they think, but go about the investigation of these areas in different ways. Therefore, the degree to which the behaviour versus meaning contrast coincides with quantitative and qualitative research should not be overstated.

A further related point is that the suggestion that theory and concepts are developed prior to undertaking a study in quantitative research is something of a caricature that is true only up to a point. It reflects a tendency to characterize quantitative research as driven by a theory-testing approach. However, while experimental investigations probably fit this model well, survey-based studies are often more exploratory than this view implies. Although concepts have to be measured, the nature of their interconnections is frequently not specified in advance. Quantitative research is far less driven by a hypothesis-testing strategy than is frequently supposed. As a result, the analysis of quantitative date from social surveys is often more exploratory than is generally appreciated and consequently offers opportunities for the generation of theories and concepts. As one American survey researcher has commented in relation to a large-scale survey be conducted in the 1950s, but which has much relevance today: 'There are so many questions which might be asked, so many correlations which can be run, so many ways in which the findings can be organized, and so few rules or precedents for making these choices that a thousand different studies could come out of the same data' (Davis, 1964: 232).

The common depiction of quantitative research as solely an exercise in testing preformulated ideas falls to appreciate the degree to which findings frequently suggest new departures and theoretical contributions.

[. . .]

Numbers versus words

Even perhaps this most basic element in the distinction between quantitative and qualitative research is not without problems. Qualitative researchers sometimes undertake a limited amount of quantification of their data. Silverman (1984, 1985) has argued that some quantification of

findings from qualitative research can often help to uncover the generality of the phenomena being described. While observing doctor–patient interactions in National Health Service and private oncology clinics, Silverman quantified some of his data in order to bring out the differences between the two types of clinic. Through this exercise he was able to show that patients in private clinics were able to have a greater influence over what went on in the consultations. However, Silverman warns that such quantification should reflect research participants' own ways of understanding their social world.

In any case, it has often been noted that qualitative researchers engage in 'quasi-quantification' through the use of terms like 'many', 'often' and 'some' (see below). All that is happening in cases of the kind described by Silverman is that the researcher is injecting greater precision into such estimates of frequency.

Artificial versus natural

The artificial/natural contrast [. . .] can similarly be criticized. It is often assumed that because much quantitative research employs research instruments that are applied to the people being studied (questionnaires, structured interview schedules, structured observation schedules, and so on), it provides an artificial account of how the social world operates. Qualitative research is often viewed as more naturalistic [. . .]. Ethnographic research in particular would seem to exhibit this quality, because the participant observer studies people in their normal social worlds and contexts – in other words, as they go about normal activities. However, when qualitative research is based on interviews (such as semi- and unstructured interviewing and focus groups), the depiction 'natural' is possibly less applicable. Interviews still have to be arranged and interviewees have to be taken away from activities that they would otherwise be engaged in, even when the interviewing style is of the more conversational kind. We know very little about interviewees' reactions to and feelings about being interviewed. Phoenix (1994) reports on the responses of interviewees to in-depth interviews in connection with two studies – one concerned with mothers under the age of 20 and the other with the social identities of young people. While many of her interviewees apparently quite enjoyed being interviewed, it is equally clear that they were conscious of the fact that they had been engaged in interviews rather than conversations. This is revealed by the tendency in the replies quoted by Phoenix for some of the interviewees to disclose that they were aware that the experience was out of the ordinary. In the study of social identities, one black young woman is reported as saying that she liked the interview and added: 'I had the chance to explain how I feel about certain things and I don't really get the opportunity to do that much.' And another interviewee said it was a 'good interview' and added: 'I have never talked so much about myself for a long time, too busy talking about kids and their problems' (Phoenix, 1994: 61). The interviews were clearly valuable in allowing to surface the perspectives of people whose voices are normally silent, but the point being made here is that the view that the methods associated with qualitative research are naturalistic is to exaggerate the contrast with the supposed artificiality of the research methods associated with quantitative research.

[. . .] Focus group research is often described as more natural than qualitative interviewing because it emulates the way people discuss issues in real life. Natural groupings are often used to emphasize this element. However, whether this is how group participants view the nature of their participation is unclear. In particular, when it is borne in mind that people are sometimes strangers, have to travel to a site where the session takes place, are paid for their trouble, and frequently discuss topics they rarely if ever talk about, it is not hard to take the view that the naturalism of focus groups is assumed rather than demonstrated.

In participant observation, the researcher can be a source of interference that renders the research situation less natural than it might superficially appear to be. Whenever the ethnographer is in an overt role, a certain amount of reactivity is possible – even inevitable. It is difficult to estimate the degree to which the ethnographer represents an intrusive element that has an impact on what is found, but once again the naturalism of such research is often assumed rather than demonstrated, although it is admittedly likely that it will be less artificial than the methods associated with quantitative research. However, when the ethnographer also engages is interviewing (as opposed to casual conversations) the naturalistic quality is likely to be less pronounced.

These observations suggest that there are areas and examples of studies that lead us to question the degree to which the quantitative/qualitative contrast is a rigid one. Once again, this is not to suggest that the contrast is unhelpful, but that we should be wary of assuming that in writing and talking about quantitative and qualitative research we are referring to two absolutely divergent and inconsistent research strategies.

[. . .]

The logic of triangulation

The idea of triangulation [. . .] applied to the present context implies that the results of an investigation employing a method associated with one research strategy are cross-checked against the results of using a method associated with the other research strategy. It is an adaptation of the argument by writers like Webb et al. (1966) that confidence in the findings deriving from a study using a quantitative research strategy can be enhanced by using more than one way of measuring a concept.

An illustration of a study using a triangulation approach is an investigation by Hughes et al. (1997) of the consumption of 'designer drinks' by young people. The term 'designer drinks' is usually applied to a new range of fortified wines and strong white cider that became popular in the UK in the 1990s. The authors used two main research methods:

- a qualitative research method: eight focus groups with fifty-six children and young adults with each discussion lasting around two hours;
- a quantitative research method: a questionnaire administered in two parts to a multistage cluster sample of 824 12–17 year olds. The first part was conducted by interview and the second, which sought to elicit more sensitive information, was self-administered.

The overall tenor of the results of the combined use of the two research strategies was mutually reinforcing. The qualitative findings showed differences in attitudes towards designer drinks and other forms of alcoholic drink among young people of different ages: the youngest (12–13) tended to adopt a generally experimental approach; the 14 and 15 year olds thought of drinking as a means of having fun and losing inhibitions and felt that designer drinks met their needs well; the oldest group (16 and 17 year olds) were mainly concerned to appear mature and to establish relationships with the opposite sex, and tended to think of designer drinks as immature as they were mainly associated in this age group's mind as targeted at younger drinkers. These connections with age were confirmed by the quantitative evidence, which also corroborated the suggestion from the qualitative evidence that the designer drinks were largely associated with a desire to get drunk.

In this research, two features are worth noting: the use of a triangulation strategy seems to have been planned by the researchers and the two sets of results were broadly consistent. However, researchers may carry out multi-strategy research for other purposes, but in the course of doing so discover that they have generated quantitative and qualitative findings on related issues, so that they can treat such overlapping findings as a triangulation exercise. Whether planned or unplanned, when a triangulation exercise is undertaken the possibility of a failure to corroborate findings always exists. This raises the issue of what approach should be taken to inconsistent results. One approach is to treat one set of results as definitive,

as Newby did in connection with his research on Suffolk farm workers. Newby (1977: 127) wrote that, when his survey and participant observation findings were inconsistent, he 'instinctively trusted the latter'. The greater richness and depth of participant observation findings, coupled with the ethnographer's greater proximity to the people studied, frequently inspire greater confidence in such data. However, simply and often arbitrarily favouring one set of findings over another is not an ideal approach to reconciling conflicting findings deriving from a triangulation exercise.

[. . .]

There can be little doubt that multi-strategy research is becoming far more common than when I first started writing about it (Bryman, 1988). Two particularly significant factors in prompting this development are:

- a growing preparedness to think of research methods as techniques of data collection or analysis that are not as encumbered by epistemological and ontological baggage as is sometimes supposed, and
- a softening in the attitude towards quantitative research among feminist researchers, who had previously been highly resistant to its use [. . .].

Other factors are doubtlessly relevant, but these two developments do seem especially significant. An example of the operation of these factors can be found in an area of research that has been mentioned on several occasions in this book and that has predominantly been studied using qualitative research methods (in particular focus groups [. . .]) the study of audience reception of media and cultural texts. Some researchers in this area have called for a rethinking of the field's attitude to quantitative research. Some of the studies [. . .] are focus group studies of audience reception. This method, along with other qualitative methods (e.g. Ang, 1985), has been the main data-collection approach employed in this field. Yet lingering unease among some practitioners of qualitative research in this area, particularly regarding issues to do with reliability and generalizability of findings, has led to some calls for a consideration of the possible use of quantitative research in tandem with qualitative methods (e.g. Schrøder, 1999). However, it is important to realize that multi-strategy research is not intrinsically superior to mono-method or mono-strategy research. It is tempting to think that multi-strategy research is more or less inevitably superior to research that relies on a single method on the grounds that more and more varied findings are inevitably 'a good thing'. However, four points must be borne in mind.

- Multi-strategy research, like mono-method research, must be competently designed and conducted. Poorly conducted research will yield suspect findings no matter how many methods are employed.
- Just like mono-method or mono-strategy research, multi-strategy research must be appropriate to the research questions or research area with which you are concerned. There is no point collecting more data simply on the basis that 'more is better'. Multi-strategy research has to be dovetailed to research questions just as all research methods must be. It is, after all, likely to consume considerably more time and financial resources than research relying on just one method.
- Any research project has limited resources. Employing multi-strategy research may dilute the research effort in any area, since resources would need to be spread.
- By no means all researchers have the skills and training to carry out both quantitative and qualitative research, so that their 'trained incapacities' may act as a barrier to integration (Reiss, 1968: 351). However, there is a growing recognition of the potential of multi-strategy research, so that this point probably carries less weight than it did when Reiss was writing.

In other words, multi-strategy research should not be considered as an approach that is univer-

sally applicable or as a panacea. It may provide a better understanding of a phenomenon than if just one method had been used. It may also frequently enhance our confidence in our own or others' findings, for example, when a triangulation exercise has been conducted. It may even improve our chances of access to settings to which we might otherwise be excluded. Milkman (1997: 192), for example, has suggested in the context of her research on a General Motors factory that the promise that she 'would produce "hard", quantitative data through survey research was what secured [her] access', even though she had no experience in this method. But the general point remains, that multi-strategy research, while offering great potential in many instances, is subject to similar constraints and considerations as research relying on a single method or research strategy.

REFERENCES

Ang, I. (1985), *Watching Dallas: Soap Opera and the Melodramatic Imagination* (London: Methuen).

Brown, G. W. and Harris, T. W. (1978), *The Social Origins of Depression: A Study of Psychiatric Disorder in Women* (London: Tavistock).

Bryman, A. (1988), *Quantity and Quality in Social Research* (London: Routledge).

Davis, J. A. (1964), 'Great Books and Small Groups: An Informal History of a National Survey', in P. Hammond (ed.), *Sociologists at Work* (New York: Basic Books).

Goldthorpe, J. H., Lockwood, D., Bechhofer, F. and Platt, J. (1968), *The Affluent Worker: Industrial Attitudes and Behaviour* (Cambridge: Cambridge University Press).

Hughes, K., MacKintosh, A. M., Hastings, G., Wheeler, C., Watson, J. and Inglis, J. (1997), 'Young People, Alcohol, and Designer Drinks: A Quantitative and Qualitative Study', *British Medical Journal*, 314: 414–18.

Newby, H. (1977), 'In the Field: Reflections on the Study of Suffolk Farm Workers', in C. Bell and H. Newby (eds.), *Doing Sociological Research* (London: Allen & Unwin).

Marsh, C. (1982), *The Survey Method: The Contribution of Surveys to Sociological Explanation* (London: Allen & Unwin).

Milkman, R. (1997), *Farewell to the Factory: Auto Workers in the Late Twentieth Century* (Berkeley and Los Angeles: University of California Press).

Phoenix, A. (1994), 'Practising Feminist Research: The Intersection of Gender and "Race" in the Research Process', in M. Maynard and J. Purvis (eds), *Researching Women's Lives from a Feminist Perspective* (London: Taylor & Francis).

Platt, J. (1981), 'The Social Construction of "Positivism" and its Significance in British Sociology, 1950–80', in P. Abrams, R. Deem, J. Finch and P. Rock (eds), *Practice and Progress: British Sociology 1950–1980* (London: George Allen & Unwin).

Reiss, A. J. (1968), 'Stuff and Nonsense about Social Surveys and Participant Observation', in H. S. Becker, B. Geer, D. Riesman and R. S. Weiss (eds), *Institutions and the Person: Papers in Memory of Everett C. Hughes* (Chicago: Aldine).

Schrøder, K. C. (1999), 'The Best of Both Worlds? Media Audience Research between Rival Paradigms', in P. Alasuutari (ed.), *Rethinking the Media Audience* (London: Sage).

Silverman, D. (1984), 'Going Private: Ceremonial Forms in a Private Oncology Clinic', *Sociology*, 18: 191–204.

Silverman, D. (1985), *Qualitative Methodology and Sociology: Describing the Social World* (Aldershot: Gower).

Stewart, S., Prandy, K. and Blackburn, R. M. (1980), *Social Stratification and Occupations* (London: Macmillan).

Webb, E. J., Campbell, D. T., Schwartz, R. D. and Sechrest, L. (1966), *Unobtrusive Measures: Nonreactive Measures in the Social Sciences* (Chicago: Rand McNally).

10. What is a Social Survey?

Alan Buckingham & Peter Saunders

This book introduces you to one of the major research techniques of the social sciences – the social survey. This is an approach to research which has often been criticized in British sociology. It is not unusual to come across sociologists who refuse to have anything to do with surveys and quantitative data, and relatively few have ever carried out a survey or got involved in the statistical analysis of data.

> ### British sociology's antipathy to quantitative methods
>
> In the early 1980s, Frank Bechhofer published a report which claimed that many sociologists felt a 'profound distaste and contempt' for quantitative methods of research. He later demonstrated this with an analysis of articles published in four of Britain's leading sociology journals, in which he showed that two-thirds contained no quantitative data at all, and that only 16 per cent used any serious statistics. He concluded that 'the majority of the profession' in Britain was 'unable to read huge portions of the research literature'.
>
> *Frank Bechhofer, 'Quantitative research in British sociology', Sociology, vol. 30 (1996), pp. 583–91*

This antipathy to survey methods can get passed on from one generation of sociologists to the next. Teachers tell their students that quanti-

tative research involves mindless 'number-crunching', or that questionnaire surveys are superficial and 'empiricist', and students accept these claims, for many have a fear of numbers and need little encouragement to stay away from all the tables, graphs and percentages found in this sort of research.

Early in our study of sociology, therefore, many of us are put off this approach to social research even before we have learned what it involves. This is a pity, for it means we miss out on a potentially powerful and exciting research tool. Like all research techniques, survey methods have their problems, but we hope to demonstrate to you that these are not so severe as to rule out their use.

> ### Empiricism and positivism
>
> Empiricism is the philosophical tradition which believes that (a) the world consists of objects, (b) these objects have their own characteristics and properties which exist irrespective of what we think they are like, and (c) our knowledge of these objects is developed through direct experience of them. Positivism is a variant of empiricism. Positivists endorse empiricists' belief that there is a real world of objects that we can know only through experience, but they add to this some additional rules about how such knowledge is to be achieved. We shall outline the basic principles of positivist sociology a little later in this chapter.

What is a social survey?

A social survey is a method of gathering information about a specified group of people (a 'population') by asking them questions.

- Sometimes every member of the target group will be included in a survey, but more often, a *sample* of people is selected from the group, and their answers are taken to be representative of everybody in the group. For example, in our Smoking Survey, just 334 adults were interviewed out of a total target population of around quarter of a million in Brighton.
- Survey questions are usually standardized, so that everybody is asked about the same things in the same way. This does not mean that everybody is asked exactly the same questions (in our survey, for example, there would be little point in asking non-smokers how many cigarettes they smoke per day), but questions are worded in the same way for all respondents, and are asked in the same order. These questions are put together in the form of a *questionnaire* which may be administered by an interviewer or which may be completed by participants themselves.
- Information is collected on any or all of the 'three A's' – people's *attributes*, their *attitudes* and their *actions*. Surveys typically gather information on personal attributes (such as people's sex, age or occupation), on their attitudes and values (such as whether they favour restrictions on smoking), and on their activities and behaviour (such as whether they smoke).
- Surveys are not usually interested in what any one individual has to say, but are rather aimed at *generalizing* about groups or whole populations. Results are usually produced in number form, as *statistics* – so many per cent do this, so many per cent think that, and so on.

A social survey, therefore, can be defined as *a technique for gathering statistical information about the attributes, attitudes or actions of a population by administering standardized questions to some or all of its members.*

What are surveys used for?

Social surveys usually aim to do one or both of two things:

- They try to *discover facts about a population* (e.g. we might want to know how many people smoke, how many smokers would like to give up smoking, and so on). We can call this *descriptive research*, for the aim is to describe a social phenomenon, and to measure its incidence in a population.
- Surveys may also try to find *evidence about some of the likely causes of people's behaviour or attitudes* (e.g. Why have so many adolescent girls taken up smoking in recent years? Does cigarette advertising encourage people to smoke?). This can be referred to as *analytical or explanatory research*, for it aims to explain why people think or act as they do by identifying likely causal influences on their attitudes and behaviour.

Descriptive surveys may be almost completely atheoretical. This is often the case in market research where the aim is to find out whether people like a product, or which product they prefer to buy, but there is no attempt to analyse *why* certain groups chose one product over another.

Analytical surveys, on the other hand, are driven by theoretical questions. Here the aim is to collect evidence which supports or contradicts some *hypothesis* about the causes of people's behaviour or attitudes. This normally means collecting information which will enable us to *compare* one group's answers against another.

Hypotheses

Hypotheses are statements about what our theoretical propositions lead us to expect to find. They enable theories to be tested by predicting patterns of observations that should occur. Hypotheses therefore predict patterns of association in observed data as a means for testing causal theories.

We should not exaggerate the distinction between descriptive and analytical surveys, for the difference between them may not be very sharp in practice:

- Many surveys set out *both* to discover facts, *and* to test some causal propositions. The same survey might be interested in discovering how many people smoke (a descriptive question) and why smokers took up cigarettes in the first place (an analytical one).
- Descriptive surveys can be used to help us *develop* theories and hypotheses that we can then go out to test in later analytical research.

Problems of method and problems of methodology

Sociologists who are sceptical about the use of survey methods doubt whether they should be used to describe facts or to test theories, for they reject the idea that survey researchers can simply go out and 'gather facts' in the way that we have been suggesting.

To understand what is at issue here, it will help to distinguish problems of *method* from problems of *methodology*.

- Problems of method are *technical* problems to do with whether research tools are used properly.
- Problems of methodology are more *philosophical* and relate to whether it is possible or advisable to use such tools in the first place.

Most critics of social surveys and quantitative data analysis see the problem as one of methodology rather than method. They are not really interested in whether a survey has been carried out 'well' or 'badly' – they are more concerned to demonstrate that the research should not have been carried out in this way at all.

> ### Methods and methodology
>
> 'The term "methods" is normally reserved for the technology of research, the actual tools by which data are gathered and analysed, while "methodology" refers to the logic or philosophy underlying particular methods.'
>
> John Hughes, *Sociological Analysis: Methods of Discovery* (London: Nelson, 1976), p. 6

Technical problems of *method*

Technical problems of survey method concern the quality of the information that we gather in surveys. For example:

- Do our sampling techniques really give us a group of respondents whose answers represent the whole population from whom they are drawn?
- Do our questions get at the kind of information we want?
- Do our interviewing techniques unwittingly introduce a bias into the information that we gather?

When critics raise these sorts of concerns, they are worrying about the possibility that the facts that we gather in our surveys might be distorted, and that the empirical tests that we apply to our theories might in some way be inadequate. While such concerns must be taken seriously, there are procedures we can learn and rules we can follow to minimize these technical problems. We shall see in later chapters how to ensure that samples are likely to be representative, that interviews are not unduly biased, that measures are appropriate, and so on.

Philosophical problems of *methodology*

Such reassurances are unlikely to impress those critics for whom the problem is more philosophical than technical. Their concern is not that surveys might gather 'inaccurate information'; it is rather that survey researchers make a fundamental *epistemological* error when they assume that they can use these research techniques to go out and 'collect facts' in the first place.

> ## Epistemology
>
> Epistemology is that branch of philosophy which concerns itself with claims to knowledge. In other words, epistemology asks: 'How can we claim to know that something is true or false?'

The philosophical case against survey methods attacks on two fronts:

- It queries the way surveys claim to *collect information*, for it rejects the notion that 'facts' can simply be observed and recorded by survey researchers.
- It questions the way information is *analysed* once it has been collected, for it rejects all attempts to express social reality in the form of numbers and percentages.

Both lines of attack derive from the same philosophical source – namely, the *rejection of positivism* which swept through Western sociology in the 1960s and which has left its mark ever since. This philosophical attack on positivism resulted in the widespread rejection of the basic principles and assumptions on which quantitative techniques are based. We can always refine our tools, but there is not much we can do if the tools are rejected as being inappropriate for the job.

[...]

Do you have to be a positivist if you want to do a survey?

There is no necessary correspondence between the use of quantitative survey techniques and a commitment to positivist philosophy:

- It is possible to be a positivist but to use other methods of research and analysis than social surveys – experimental and observational methods, for example, can be perfectly consistent with the basic rules of positivism;
- It is also possible to use survey techniques without endorsing all aspects of positivist philosophy. Indeed, most sociologists who carry out surveys or use statistical data would probably deny that they are 'positivists'.

Nevertheless, there is a connection between positivism, social surveys, and the use of statistics to analyse social phenomena. Most quantitative sociologists today are much more cautious than Comte and Durkheim were about the possibilities of measuring facts and testing theories – but that does not mean they think it cannot be done. We are just more aware today of the philosophical problems that we have to grapple with.

> ## Reluctant positivists
>
> 'Much of sociology remains gently positivist at heart . . . a model of sociology which believes in a world external to the sociologist, which needs to be experienced in a systematic way. When a sociologist presents an account of his [sic] work, he is usually implicitly saying "the external world is like this: if you in the audience study it in the same way as I have done you will come to the same conclusions." '
>
> *Geoff Payne, Robert Dingwall, Judy Payne and Mick Carter, Sociology and Social Research (London: Routledge & Kegan Paul, 1981), p. 56*

The (mildly) positivist assumptions on which survey research is based

Leszek Kolakowski (in *Positivist Philosophy, Penguin, 1972*) helpfully isolates the four key principles that define positivist philosophy:

- *Phenomenalism* The insistence that scientific knowledge has to be grounded in sensory experience of *phenomena*, or 'things'. If we cannot see, touch, smell, taste or hear something, either directly or indirectly, then we cannot study it scientifically.
- *Nominalism* The assertion that concepts are only labels for things and can never tell us more than can be gathered from experience. Labelling a group of people as 'working class', for example, does not itself tell us anything more than we already know about them – it just helps us classify them.
- *Unity of scientific method* The claim that all science should follow the same method of accumulating knowledge through direct observation and rigorous testing of theories against factual evidence.
- *Value freedom* The recognition that science cannot make ethical judgements about good and bad, right and wrong, because such evaluations cannot be justified with reference to knowledge based in experience.

Each of these principles is reflected to some degree in the assumptions on which quantitative survey methods operate.

1 *The phenomenalist assumption in survey methods: Facts exist prior to, and independently of, research, and can be discovered by asking questions and recording answers systematically.*

Survey researchers typically talk of 'gathering evidence' or 'collecting data'. This implies that the data – the factual evidence – exist 'out there' in the population, and that the task is to identify, classify and measure them accurately.

Strictly speaking, of course, the data do not 'exist' until we get people to answer our questions, and survey researchers understand this. But this approach to social research does assume that there are facts to be known about people's behaviour, attitudes and characteristics, and that these facts – 'phenomena' – have an existence before we ask our questions. It is in this sense that social survey research is 'phenomenalist', for it is premised on the belief that facts exist outside of the research process and can be discovered by it – even though this may not be as straightforward as classical empiricists seemed to imagine.

2 *The nominalist assumption in survey methods: Theories guide the questions we ask, and theories can be tested against the evidence we find, but the facts themselves stand independently of the theories we may hold.*

Survey researchers know that the way they collect facts about people will be guided by their theoretical interests and concerns. The way they frame their questions, classify people's answers and analyse their results will inevitably reflect their theoretical starting point. They nevertheless insist that none of this *determines* what they find – their concepts and theories give shape to their research, but they do not blind them to evidence that they did not expect to find, nor do they reveal facts that are not there.

The crucial role that theory plays in research derives from the deductive logic on which quantitative data analysis is based – we start out from theory, but we use factual evidence to test our theoretical generalizations. The assumption we make when we do a survey is that our theory guides what we are looking for, but that facts about people's lives determine what we find.

[. . .]

3 *The 'unity of science' assumption in survey methods: Survey data consist of responses to questions which can be analysed, in much the same way as observations in any other science are analysed, by means of statistical comparison.*

When positivists insist that social science and natural science share the same method, they do not mean that they share the same techniques of investigation. Sociologists do not sit in laboratories heating up families in test tubes or dissecting social classes under a microscope. What they mean is that the *logic* of investigation (the 'methodology') is the same – that in social science as in natural science, we gather facts and we use them to test our theories.

All social scientists are aware that, unlike natural science (which studies *objects*), they are dealing with human *subjects*. While objects simply react to stimuli, human subjects initiate action – human behaviour is *motivated*. This means that if you want to know what 'causes' us to act in certain ways, you need to know something about the way we are thinking, and no natural science technique of observation is ever going to tell you that.

This difference between the unthinking objects of the natural world and the thinking subjects who inhabit the social world opens up research strategies to social scientists which cannot be used in the natural sciences. In particular, we can use *empathy* to understand how people may be thinking and feeling, and hence to develop plausible insights into why they are behaving as they are. There is obviously no equivalent to this in the natural sciences where we can only ever analyse data from the outside looking in.

Most survey researchers acknowledge all this, and they therefore reject a strong version of the positivist postulate of the 'unity of science'. However, the fact that we can use empathic methods in the social sciences does not rule out the use of other, more observational methods such as surveys, provided they are appropriate to the kind of information we are trying to gather. Indeed, we might decide to use empathy to develop hypotheses which can then be tested using survey methods. The stand-off between so-called 'quantitative' and 'qualitative' approaches in sociology is a false dilemma – we can use both.

4 *The assumption of value freedom in survey methods: The collection of facts is distinct from their evaluation, and the survey itself should be unbiased.*

The principle of 'value freedom' is that the results of research cannot be used to demonstrate the superiority of any particular ethical or political argument. The reason is that you cannot logically derive an 'ought' statement from an 'is' statement – knowing what the world is like (facts) cannot tell you what it 'should' be like (values).

Suppose, for example, that our research shows that young people are encouraged by advertising to start smoking. Such a finding cannot justify us concluding that cigarette advertising should 'therefore' be banned. This is because the fact that advertising influences people to start smoking cannot tell us whether protecting the health of young people is more or less important than, say, protecting the rights of free speech (which are curtailed by any ban on advertising). The research finding helps *inform* the ethical debate, but it can in no way help to resolve it.

Many social researchers do use their results to try to bring about changes in public policy, and surveys are sometimes commissioned in the hope that they will produce evidence that will help one cause rather than another. But good survey researchers will always insist that if their results do not come out as hoped, the findings should still be published and should not be altered or censored. The facts, in the end, must prevail over one's personal values.

The research process itself is also assumed to be objective and impartial. In particular, it is assumed that there is nothing about the way that data are collected in a survey, or about the way they are subsequently analysed, that favours or discriminates against any group or interest in society. The survey is simply a tool, and as such it carries no bias.

11. Researching Individual Lives

Barbara Merrill & Linden West

We are all, it seems, biographers now and want to tell our stories. The genre is pervasive throughout our culture. A glance in most bookshops will reveal the extent to which biography and autobiography serve as prime vehicles for self and social exploration, or maybe self promotion. This is an age of biography, and telling stories seems ubiquitous in popular culture: we consume the stories of celebrities, are fascinated by stories on reality TV, and are constantly intrigued by wartime narratives, as witnessed by various series being repeated on television (Goodley et al., 2004). Gossip and celebrity magazines, fun-based websites, podcasts, blogs, biopics (film) and biodramas (theatre) are all sites for biographical expression and experiment, by ordinary people as well as celebrities. New biographies of celebrities appear, it seems, almost daily. Jerry Springer, the American chat show host, is using television to explore his own story and family history – including of grandmothers murdered in the Holocaust – as part of wrestling with questions of identity. Oprah Winfrey has helped create an intimate confessional as well as controversial form of media communication, which, among other things, is said to have allowed gays, transsexuals and transgender people to tell their stories. We are all, as stated, biographers now or encouraged to be so.

Very serious writers are using a biographical approach in diverse, even surprising contexts. The universe, for example, has a recent biography, as have a number of cities (Ackroyd, 2000; Gribbin, 2007). Peter Ackroyd has employed the biographical form to weave greater understanding and connections between apparently disparate aspects of London's history. The genre allows him, he says, to do this: 'if the history of London poverty is beside a history of London madness, then the connections may provide more significant information than any orthodox historiographical survey' (Ackroyd, 2000: 2). Connecting disparate social phenomena and personal experience and weaving understanding between them in new and sometimes surprising ways characterizes, as we will illustrate, a great deal of biographical research.

Biographical methods have claimed an increasing place in academic research and are alive and well (if sometimes marginal and contested) in various academic disciplines such as literature, history, sociology, anthropology, social policy and education, as well as in feminist and minority studies (Smith, 1998). There is a mushrooming of PhD and Masters programmes, dedicated research centres and conferences which, in various ways, are concerned with researching lives and the stories people tell about them. The words used to describe such methods can vary – autobiography, auto-ethnography, personal history, oral history or life story, as well as narrative, for instance – yet as Norman Denzin (1989) has observed, there are many similarities (if also differences of emphasis). There can, for instance, be shared interest in the changing experiences and viewpoints of people in their daily lives, what they consider important, and how to make sense of what they say about their pasts, presents and futures, and the meanings they give to these in the stories they tell. There can be sensitivity towards the uniqueness yet also the similarities of lives and stories, like the snowflakes referred to above. Biography enables us to discern patterns but also distinctiveness in lives. The relationship between the particular and general, uniqueness and commonality, is in fact a central issue in biographical research.

The pervasive interest in biography may be understood by reference to living in a postmodern culture in which intergenerational continuities have weakened and a new politics of identity and representation has emerged among diverse groups. Women and men, gay and lesbian, black and white, young and old, may increasingly seek to live lives in different ways from parents or grandparents and doing biographical work has been one means to this end. The self and experience become a sort of reflexive life project, a focus for reworking who we are, and communicating this to others and for challenging, perhaps, some of the dominant stories told about people like us in the wider culture. Such a phenomenon can also be understood by reference to profound economic and cultural change over the last few decades, including the rise of feminism. These processes have provided more opportunities for self-definition (in the interplay of the global and local via mass communication technologies and in the celebration of diverse lifestyles, for example). Yet this historical moment, as commentators like Anthony Giddens and Ulrich Beck have observed, seems riddled with paradox: new opportunities for self-definition co-exist with deep-seated anxieties and existential doubt about our capacity to cope. The biographical imperative, at all levels, may be fuelled by the necessity to compose a life and make meaning in a more fragmented, individualized and unpredictable culture where inherited templates can be redundant and the nature of the life-course increasingly uncertain in a globalizing world.

[. . .]

Barbara

Barbara's interest in using biographical approaches is rooted in her own life history. As a sociologist,

Barbara writes, working in adult education, I am interested in researching the stories and experiences of adults who decide to return to learning later in their lives, in community, further or higher education. In particular, I am interested in looking at marginalized groups of adult learners whose life histories have been shaped by inequalities of class, gender and race. The latter have been central concerns throughout my life. Being female and working class, I soon became aware of class and later gender discrimination and inequalities in society through my own experiences and those of my family. Later, as a teacher in a multicultural comprehensive school, I became very conscious of the pervasiveness of racism in society through the lives of the black pupils.

My life experiences of being female and working class drew me towards Marxist and feminist politics at the age of 17 in the early 1970s. Studying sociology at school and university enabled me to articulate, understand and politicize my life experiences. Like many young people at that time, I was optimistic that the injustices of capitalism could be challenged and that through collective political action society could be changed. It was a belief in the importance of subjectivity in building agency and in overcoming the determinism of structural forces. This is probably one reason why, in relation to the biographical research I undertake, I am interested in the dynamic of structure and agency in people's lives.

However, despite my political awareness as an undergraduate student at the University of Warwick from 1973 until 1976, I felt overwhelmed by the middle-class culture and the privileged lives of the majority of its students, and the culture of the institution. This led to feelings of not always belonging – of being an outsider – despite enjoying my academic studies and having a circle of friends, as well as being involved in political groups. My confidence was occasionally undermined despite this political background and sociological knowledge.

My first experience of doing biographical research was in the mid-1980s when I was studying part-time for a Master of Philosophy degree in the Sociology Department at the University of Warwick, while also teaching at a school. The topic of my research was racism in schools and involved interviewing black pupils and getting them to talk about their life experiences. Looking back on my first encounters with life history interviews, my approach was not embedded in any particular theoretical underpinning. It was more about taking the plunge and engaging with people in what may have been a naive way. Luckily, all the pupils were willing to talk and talk intimately about how racism affected their own and their family's daily lives. What struck me was how articulate they were in discussing personal and political issues of racism and what they felt about other pupils, teachers and the school. They illustrated how powerful biographical approaches could be in understanding everyday lives.

Later, I made a career change from teaching 14–18 year olds to teaching adults at the University of Warwick. I entered academia feeling excited about the opportunity to undertake research but also experienced some trepidation. Echoing my earlier time as an undergraduate student, I was concerned about whether or not I would be good enough to work in the academic world. It was hinted to me that if I wanted to remain at Warwick I would need to obtain a PhD. My biography helped me to choose an area of study. I, therefore, became interested in how working-class adult students who had been out of the education system for a long time coped with the middle-class environment of a 'traditional', although relatively young university like Warwick. I reflected back on my pupils at the school where I had taught because many of them had been alienated by the middle-class and white school system and, as a result, left school having underachieved. Did the adult students at Warwick share similar life experiences? If so, why had they chosen to return to learn and why at this moment in their lives?

Here was my second encounter with using biographical approaches. However, this time I was part of a research team and environment. Although the focus was on mature women students, I also interviewed male adult students to explore differ-

ences and similarities. The process confirmed my belief in the value of the life history in enabling the social science researcher to gain an in-depth understanding of social life as well as revealing how past lives impact upon the present. The stories were often painful but also filled with resilience in a determination to juggle lives and struggle on in order to get degrees. Such narratives illustrated how education could be empowering and change lives for the better.

Furthermore, my own biography was implicated in developing a particular orientation in research: employing life histories to examine collective experiences and possibilities for change in people's lives. My family life history also led me to be aware that in using biographical research, we have to remember that there are stories which some people never tell or reveal only partially, because, perhaps, they are simply too painful or even traumatic.

My father had a story which he never really shared because of painful memories. The untold story affected the life of my family as a whole. My father was a British prisoner of war at Auschwitz III camp (E715) – the fact that there were such prisoners is not well known. Auschwitz III (Monowitz) was located near the IG Farben chemical factory where British prisoners of war, alongside Jews and others, were used as forced labour in the factory. They were witnesses to many atrocities committed against Jews and others. The camp was the target for a bombing raid by the Americans. It was a Sunday, I subsequently discovered – their day off – and they were playing football. My father survived but friends were killed. He spoke a little about these events but not in detail: it was too painful. After my parents' deaths, I found out more about his story by seeing a picture of him at Auschwitz in a British war veteran's magazine, as well as in documentary evidence in a letter from another British prisoner there. More recently, I have found reference to him in a book about the experiences of British prisoners of war at Auschwitz. It refers to an episode, which I did not know about, whereby he and a friend attempted an escape during an air raid in 1944. I talked to his sister and visited Auschwitz with two friends. The site of Auschwitz III could not be visited at the time, nor was it easy to find out much detail about the camp, but I want to go back in the near future to complete an aspect of my life history. Biographies, and researching others' lives, can affect us in profound, interconnected ways.

[. . .]

A question of terms and cross-cultural perspectives

We need to make clear that our use of the term biographical method denotes research which utilizes individual stories or other personal documents to understand lives within a social, psychological and/or historical frame. One of the problems is the bewildering use of different labels such as life history, narrative, life writing, autobiographical and auto/biographical research [. . .]. We employ 'biographical' as a convenient term to encompass research that can have different labels.

[. . .]

Biographical research has academic critics too. Some historians question the biographical turn as a sort of retreat into 'fine, meaningless detail', which obscures the big picture and important social policy questions (Fieldhouse, 1996: 119). Researchers get lost, in this view, in the detailed description of lives, even in a narcissistic way perhaps, without helping people understand how society works or how it can be changed for the better. A different criticism comes from certain 'post-structuralist' perspectives, influenced by, among others, the work of the French philosopher Michel Foucault (1979a, 1979b). Foucault conceived human subjectivity as forged in the play of various power–knowledge formations: human beings become positioned by language in ways they may only be dimly aware of, if at all.

Focusing on biographies risks missing a bigger point about how power permeates knowledge and

knowing at every level. Power works to control, not least in what has been termed our confessional society. At earlier times, the body was regulated but now it is the soul that is the target, via technologies of the self, expressed in a range of psychological, medical and professional practices. Power, in this view, circulates in and regulates subjectivities, which includes the stories people tell, whether to Oprah Winfrey or researchers. Mention should also be made, however, that Foucault and other post-structuralists have inspired various biographical researchers, including in feminist collective biography, where attempts are made to articulate the discourses through which selves and bodies may be shaped. This can challenge the tendency to think of the individual who exists independently of discourse as well as of time and place (Davies and Gannon, 2006).

We believe that biographical methods offer rich rewards in making sense of self and others in social and historical contexts but that such research raises many questions, which researchers – new or experienced – must consider. In fact, a major reason for writing the book is to share our work, and what has inspired it but also some of the insights we have gained into diverse theoretical, interpretative and practical challenges, and about the relationship between the stories people tell and the realities they purport to represent: between 'realists' at one end of the spectrum and some post-structuralists, at another. Can we in truth talk about reality at all? There is also a question about the nature and status of theory in biographical research. This is considered essential by biographical researchers, yet with a note of caution: that its development should be grounded in an engagement with real people and their complex experience and stories. Overly abstract theorizing tends to be treated with suspicion.

At another level, there are questions about how to do interviews and what makes for good or rich interview material. (Our main interest is the biographical interview, given its central place in social research, but there are many other ways of doing biographical research, using diaries, letters, autobiographies and memorabilia of various kinds. There can be visual biographies, using photography and video. Interviews can be combined with these other sources of evidence.) How should we conduct interviews and what might be meant by a good interview and why? How should we transcribe interviews as well as interpret and code the material? How then to employ the material in our writing or other forms of representation: how do we balance quotations with our interpretations, for instance? Crucially, what of the ethics of biographical research, given that we may engage with difficult, emotionally charged and potentially vulnerable aspects of people's lives? [. . .] Is there a danger of voyeurism, of being over intrusive, or of meddling with people's souls? Finally, what makes such research valid and on what terms? Such questions – both theoretical as well as practical – inform our writing.

[. . .] We favour, under the influence of feminism, more collaborative approaches to research, including interviewing as well as interpretation. We tend, because of our own backgrounds and values, towards working with marginalized peoples or at least to challenging dominant orthodoxies. We favour interdisciplinarity as well as engaging with our own role in the construction of the other's story. And we think it possible to build a convincing sense of the realities of others' lives, of what it is like to be in someone else's shoes, albeit necessitating reflexive understanding of how we, and other influences, may shape the other's story.

REFERENCES

Ackroyd, P. (2000) *London: The Biography*. London: Chatto and Windus.

Davies, B. and Gannon, S. (2006) *Doing Collective Biography*. Maidenhead: Open University Press.

Denzin, N. D. (1989) *The Research Act*. Englewood Cliffs, NJ: Prentice Hall.

Fieldhouse, R. (1996) 'Mythmaking and Mortmain: A Response', *Studies in the Education of Adults* 28(1): 117–20.

Foucault, M. (1979a) 'What is an Author?', *Screen* 20: 13–35.

Foucault, M. (1979b) *The History of Sexuality, Vol. 1*. London: Allen Lane.

Goodley, D., Lawthorn, R., Clough, P., and Moore, M. (2004) *Researching Life Stories: Method, Theory and Analyses in a Biographical Age*. London: Routledge Falmer.

Gribbin, J. (2007) *The Universe: A Biography*. London: Allen Lane.

Smith, L. (1998) 'Biographical Methods', in N. K. Denzin and Y. S. Lincoln (eds) *Strategies of Qualitative Enquiry*. Thousand Oaks, CA: Sage.

12. Sociology's Historical Imagination

Philip Abrams

Try asking serious questions about the contemporary world and see if you can do without historical answers. Whether it is a matter of conflict in the Middle East or in Northern Ireland, or racism in urban ghettoes, of poverty and social problems on the Clyde or the Tyne, or of the fall of governments in Italy or Chile, we tend to assume that an adequate answer, one that satisfactorily explains whatever it is that puzzles us, will be one that is couched in historical terms. This appeal to history is not a natural human inclination but it has become almost natural to the modern western mind. The idea that 'in my beginning is my end', that the present needs to be understood as a product of the past, is one we have come to take for granted. And in taking it for granted we achieve, perhaps unconsciously, an important sociological insight. For it is indeed not the 'problem families' living in west Newcastle or south Chicago today who explain the concentration of social ills in those areas, but the long-term workings of housing markets and job markets of which those families are the present victims. It is not the intransigence of the present governments of Israel or Syria that explains the persistent risk of war in Palestine, but the meaning and depth of that intransigence in the setting of centuries of cultural and religious struggle, imperialism and mistrust. It is not the incompetence or opportunism of contemporary Italian politicians that accounts for Italy's endless crisis of government, but the problems resulting from attempts throughout the past century to make a unified nation state but of a deeply divided and fragmented society. Insofar as we reject explanations of the present that deal with the present, insofar as we turn to history for more satisfactory explanations, we are turning towards a deeper and more realistic understanding. And we are also turning towards sociology.

Sociological explanation is necessarily historical. Historical sociology is thus not some special kind of sociology; rather, it is the essence of the discipline. All varieties of sociology stress the so-called 'two-sidedness of' the social world, presenting it as a world of which we are both the creators and the creatures, both makers and prisoners; a world which our actions construct and a world that powerfully constrains us. The distinctive quality of the social world for the sociologist is, accordingly, its *facticity* – the way in which society is experienced by individuals as a fact-like system, external, given, coercive, even while individuals are busy making and re-making it through their own imagination, communication and action. Thus the central issue for sociological analysis can be said, by Berger and Luckmann (1967), to be the resolution of the 'awesome paradox' discovered in turn by each of the founding fathers of sociology: 'how is it possible that human activity should produce a world of things?' And increasingly sociologists have come to affirm the wisdom of their founding fathers in concluding that there is only one way in which that paradox can be resolved: namely, historically. The two-sidedness of society, the fact that social action is both something we choose to do and something we have to do, is inseparably bound up with the further fact that whatever reality society has is an historical reality, a reality in time. When we refer to the two-sidedness of society we are refer-ring to the ways in which, in time, actions become institutions and institutions are in turn changed by action. Taking and selling prisoners becomes the institution of slavery. Offering one's services to a soldier in return for his protection becomes feudalism. Organizing the control of an enlarged labour force on the basis of standardized rules becomes bureaucracy. And slavery, feudalism and bureaucracy become the fixed, external settings in which struggles for prosperity or survival or freedom are then pursued. By substituting cash payments for labour services the lord and peasant jointly embark on the dismantling of the feudal order their great-grandparents had constructed.

In both its aspects, then, the social world is essentially historical. Process is the link between action and structure. The idea of process and the study of process are the tools to unlock Berger and Luckmann's 'awesome paradox'. What we choose to do and what we have to do are shaped by the historically given possibilities among which we find ourselves. But history is not a force in its own right any more than society is. Rather, as the French historical sociologist Roland Mousnier puts it (1973: 145): 'History has no direction of its own accord, for it is shaped by the will of men and the choices they make. Yet with every second that passes, men are making their choice by their behaviour.' And how we behave now – whether we throw a bomb or go on a peace march, whether we protest about inequality or thrive on it – is very largely a matter of what previous experience has made possible and meaningful for us. The conscientious exam candidate and the truant are both dominated by the historically established weight of the institutions of education; the meaning of their activity derives from the reality of those institutions. We can construct new worlds but only on the basis and within the framework of what our predecessors have constructed for us. On that basis and within that framework the content of our activity may re-make or un-make the institutions that surround us. This shaping of action by structure and transforming of structure by action both occur as processes in time. It is by

seizing on that idea that history and sociology merge and that sociology becomes capable of answering our urgent questions about why the world is as it is; about why particular men and women make the particular choices they do and why they succeed or fail in their projects.

In this sense historical sociology has always been a core element of sociology as a whole. The idea of process is crucial to the way sociological work is done. But sociology became historical in more specific ways, too. As a distinct way of thought sociology came into being in the face of momentous historical changes and from the first was shaped by the experience of those changes. By the 1840s, when systematic social analysis first became widespread in Europe, it was a common feeling that the pace and range of change associ-ated with the political and industrial revolutions of the previous two generations had left the social world an incomprehensible chaos in which only the fact of change itself was certain. In the words of the poet Lamartine 'the world had jumbled its catalogue' (cited in Burrow, 1966: 94). Faced with the prospect of intellectual and social anarchy the early sociologists sought an ordered under-standing of the processes of social change and above all of the changes involved in the transition to industrialism. Marx, Weber and Durkheim, the three founding fathers whose influence is greatest today, all made the nature of the transition to industrialism the basic organizing concern of their work and sought through understanding that par-ticular transition to move to a larger understand-ing of social process, or history, in general. So, too, did their contemporaries Comte, Spencer and Hobhouse. All were sharply aware of living in a world that was changing dramatically from year to year and in which the relationships between the changes people wanted and the changes that actually occurred were mysterious, frustrating and obscure. Why did the pursuit of wealth seem to generate poverty on an unprecedented scale? Why did the triumph of the principles of liberty and equality appear to go hand in hand with mon-strous new forms of oppression? Was what was happening to social relationships in the course of industrialization a matter of chance, of choice or of necessity? How far was industrialism an unavoidable destiny? Which of its characteristics could be altered by human action, and how. Such questions could be answered in many different ways. What the early sociologists agreed about was that these were the important questions to ask. The transition to industrialism compelled the imagination. From the analysis of that transition one could move to a more general but no less historical sociology.

[. . .]

We have three types of concern which can be said to constitute historical sociology. First, the specific concern with the transition to industrialism – to which we might add a concern that has emerged in recent years about what industrialism in its turn is turning into. Second, a concern to trace the pattern of freedom and constraint involved in the careers of life-histories of individuals in the immediate personal worlds of everyday social life – families, hospitals, churches, workplaces. And third, the underlying insistence that what sociology is ultimately about is the relation of the individual as an agent with purposes, expectations and motives to society as a constraining environment of institutions, values and norms – and that that relationship is one which has its real existence not in some abstract world of concepts, theories and jargon but in the immediate world of history, of sequences of action and reaction in time. By contrast, theories about the relation of past, present and future which rule out the need for detailed examination of the action of individuals on social structure and vice versa by proposing laws and stages of evolution and development with a necessity of their own may be dismissed as something less than serious sociology. (I am not going to digress here to discuss evolutionary and developmentalist arguments in detail; definitive criticisms of them can be found in the works of Popper (1959), Nisbet (1969) and Hirst (1976).) And by the same token it should be clear that what is being advocated when we speak of histori-

cal sociology as the central element of sociology as a whole is a great deal more than a request for more 'historical background'. Most sociology books do have a chapter or so setting out the historical background of whatever is going to be discussed in the body of the book. Such chapters typically give an account of 'significant' events which provide the context for present experience – thus, slavery is often presented as part of the background to the contemporary situation of blacks in the United States of America, or the development of contraceptive techniques as an important background factor in understanding the modern family. But too often the rest of the analysis is quite a-historical – the black ghetto is not treated as something that is constantly being constructed and coped with; the modern family is not analysed as something that people receive and transform in the course of living their personal relationships. Doing justice to the reality of history is not a matter of noting the way in which the past provides a background to the present; it is a matter of treating what people do in the present as a struggle to create a future *out of* the past, of seeing that the past is not just the womb of the present but the only raw material out of which the present can be constructed.

[. . .]

Historical sociology is not, then, a matter of imposing grand schemes of evolutionary development on the relationship of the past to the present. Nor is it merely a matter of recognizing the historical background to the present. It is the attempt to understand the relationship of personal activity and experience on the one hand and social organization on the other as something that is continuously constructed in time. It makes the continuous process of construction the focal concern of social analysis. That process may be studied in many different contexts: in personal biographies and careers; in the rise and fall of whole civilizations; in the setting of particular events such as a revolution or an election, or of particular developments such as the making of the welfare state or the formation of the working class. The particular context to which sociologists have chosen to pay most attention is the one I have called the transition to industrialism. But in the end historical sociology is more a matter of how one interprets the world than of what bit of it one chooses to study. And on that basis one can say firstly, that there is no necessary difference between the sociologist and the historian, and secondly that sociology which takes itself seriously must be historical sociology. As C. Wright Mills (1959) put it, the whole 'intellectual promise' of the discipline is 'to enable men . . . to become aware of historical structures and of their own place within them'.

REFERENCES

Berger, P. and Luckmann, T. (1967) *The Social Construction of Reality*. London: Allen Lane.

Burrow, J. (1966) *Evolution and Society*. Cambridge: Cambridge University Press.

Hirst, P. Q. (1976) *Social Evolution and Sociological Categories*. London: Allen & Unwin.

Mills, C. W. (1959) *The Sociological Imagination*. New York: Oxford University Press.

Mousnier, R. (1973) *Social Hierarchies*. London: Croom Helm.

Nisbet, R. (1969) *Social Change and History*. New York: Oxford University Press.

Popper, K. (1959) *The Poverty of Historicism*. London: Routledge & Kegan Paul.

13. Participant Observation / Observant Participation

Loïc Wacquant

In August 1988, following a combination of chance circumstances,[1] I enrolled in a boxing gym in a neighborhood of Chicago's black ghetto. I had never practiced that sport or even considered trying it. Aside from the superficial notions and stereotyped images that everyone can gain of boxing through the media, movies, and literature,[2] I had never had any contact with the pugilistic world. I thus found myself in the situation of the perfect novice.

For three years I trained alongside local boxers, both amateur and professional, at the rate of three to six sessions a week, assiduously applying myself to every phase of their rigorous preparation, from shadowboxing in front of mirrors to sparring in the ring. Much to my own surprise, and to the surprise of those close to me, I gradually got taken in by the game, to the point where I ended up spending all my afternoons at the Woodlawn gym and "gloving up" with the professionals from the club on a regular basis, before climbing through the ropes for my first official fight in the Chicago Golden Gloves. In the intoxication of immersion, I even thought for a while of aborting my academic career to "turn pro" and thereby remain with my friends from the gym and its coach, DeeDee Armour, who had become a second father for me.[3]

Following in their wake, I attended some thirty tournaments and boxing "cards" held in various nightclubs, movie theaters, and sports arenas in the city and its suburbs, in the capacity of gym-mate and fan, sparring partner and confidant, "cornerman" and photographer, which earned me access to all the stages and backstages of the theater of bruising. I also accompanied the boxers from my gym "on the road," going to fights organized in other Midwestern towns and in the glittering (but seedy) casinos of Atlantic City. And I gradually absorbed the categories of pugilistic judgment under DeeDee's guidance, gabbing endlessly with him at the gym and dissecting fights on television at his place at night, the two of us sitting side by side on his bed in the kitchen of his little apartment.

The friendship and trust accorded to me by the regulars of Woodlawn were such that I was able not only to blend in among them in the gym but also to accompany them in their everyday peregrinations outside of it, in search of a job or an apartment, hunting for bargains in ghetto stores, in their hassles with their wives, the local welfare office, or the police, as well as cruising with their "homies" from the fearsome housing projects nearby. My ring colleagues allowed me to share in their joys and sorrows, their dreams and their setbacks, their picnics, evenings out dancing, and family excursions. They took me with them to pray in their churches, to get a "fade" at their barber shop, to play pool in their favorite tavern, to listen to rap until I had gotten my fill of it, and even to applaud Minister Louis Farrakhan at a political-religious meeting of the Nation of Islam – where I found myself the only European non-believer among ten thousand entranced African-American faithful. I lived through three funerals, two weddings,[4] four births, and a baptism with them, and I witnessed, at their side, with unfathomable sadness, the closing of the Woodlawn gym, condemned in February 1992 and razed a year later as part of an urban "renewal" operation.

Nightly after each training session I consigned my notes to my field notebooks for several hours, initially to help me overcome a profound feeling of awkwardness and physical unease, a feeling no doubt exacerbated by the fact of being the only white member of a gym frequented exclusively by black athletes at the time of my entry. Together with the observations, pictures, and recordings made at the fights in which members of my gym performed, these notes provide the materials for the texts that follow.[5]

From the outset it was clear that, to have any chance of escaping from the preconstructed object of collective mythology, a sociology of boxing has to renounce the facile recourse to the *prefabricated exoticism* of the public and publicized side of the institution – the fights, great or small, the heroism of the social ascent of the excluded ("Marvelous Marvin Hagler: From Ghetto to Glory," eloquently proclaimed a poster taped onto one of the walls of the Woodlawn Boys Club), the exceptional lives and careers of champions. It must instead grasp boxing through its least known and least spectacular side: the drab and obsessive routine of the gym workout, of the endless and thankless preparation, inseparably physical and moral, that preludes the all-too-brief appearances in the limelight, the minute and mundane rites of daily life in the gym that produce and reproduce the belief feeding this very peculiar corporeal, material, and symbolic economy that is the pugilistic world. In short, to avoid the excess knowledge of spontaneous sociology that the evocation of fights never fails to conjure, one must not step into the ring by proxy with the extra-ordinary figure of the "champ" but "hit the bags" alongside anonymous boxers in their habitual setting of the gym.

The other virtue of an approach based on participant observation (which, in this case, is better characterized as an "observant participation") in a run-of-the-mill gym is that the materials thus produced do not suffer from the "ecological fallacy" that affects most available studies and accounts of the Manly art. Thus none of the statements reported here were expressly solicited, and the behaviors described are those of the boxer in his "natural habitat,"[6] not the dramatized and highly codified (re)presentation that he likes to give of himself in public, and that journalistic reports and novels retranslate and magnify according to their specific canons.

Breaking with the moralizing discourse – that indifferently feeds both celebration and denigration – produced by the "gaze from afar" of an outside observer standing at a distance from or above the specific universe, this book seeks to suggest how boxing "makes sense" as soon as one takes pains to get close enough to it to grasp it *with one's body*, in a quasi-experimental situation. It is for this reason composed of three texts of deliberately disparate statuses and styles, which juxtapose sociological analysis, ethnographic description, and literary evocation in order to convey at once percept and concept, the hidden determinations and the lived experiences, the external factors and the internal sensations that intermingle to make the boxer's world. In short, the book aims to *display and demonstrate* in the same move the social and sensual logic that informs boxing as a bodily craft in the contemporary black American ghetto.

The first text unravels the skein of the troubled relations tying the street to the ring and deciphers the inculcation of the Manly art as a work of gymnic, perceptual, emotional, and mental conversion effected in a practical and collective mode, on the basis of an implicit and mimetic pedagogy that patiently recalibrates all the parameters of the boxer's existence one by one. It is based on an article written during the summer of 1989, a year after I joined the Woodlawn club, when getting my nose broken during a sparring session had forced me into a period of inactivity propitious to a reflexive return on my novitiate in progress.[7] I had to resist the temptation to totally revise this early writing effort, as to a more comprehensive analysis of the "manufacturing" of the boxer which is the theme of another book-in-progress,[8] especially by investing in it all the results of subsequent works that grew out of two additional years of intensive immersion. I strove instead to enrich the data, to deepen the backdrop, and to clarify the original analyses while preserving their overall economy. For it seemed to me that the empirical lacunae and analytic semi-naïvety of this text by an apprentice sociologist had in its favor an ethnographic freshness and a candor of tone that might help the reader to better slip into the skin of the boxer.

The second part of this book, first drafted in 1993 and then revised and completed seven years later with the help of audio and video tapes recorded at the time, describes in minute detail the day leading to a boxing "card" at a tavern in a working-class neighborhood of Chicago's far South Side, from the preparations for the official weigh-in early in the morning at the gym until the return from the postfight festivities late in the night. The unity of time, place, and action makes it possible to set into relief the mutual interweaving of the social ingredients and networks that the first text necessarily had to separate: interest and desire, affection and exploitation, the masculine and the feminine, the sacred and the profane, abstinence and jouissance, the routine and the unexpected, the virile code of honor and the brutal dictates of material constraints.

The third part of this book is, if I may be permitted an expression that borders on the oxymoronic, a "sociological novella." Written at the request of Michel Le Bris for a special issue of the French literary journal *Gulliver* devoted to "Writing Sports,"[9] it follows step-by-step the author's preparation for and performance at the 1990 Chicago Golden Gloves, the biggest amateur tournament in the Midwest, in a narrative mode that aims to erase the traces of the work of sociological construction (to the point where Le Bris thought, wrongly, that he was warranted to characterize it in his preface as a "narrative, all sociology suspended") while preserving the insights and results of that work.[10] The blending of these genres ordinarily kept safely segregated, sociology, ethnography (in the strict sense of the term), and novella, aims to enable the reader to better

grasp pugilistic things "in the concrete, as they are" and to see boxers in motion, "as in mechanics one sees masses and systems, or as in the sea we see octopi and anemones. We catch sight of numbers of men, of mobile forces, and which float through their environment and their sentiments."[11]

In closing, it is instructive to point out the main factors that made this research possible, the most decisive of which was no doubt the "opportunistic" character of my insertion.[12] In point of fact, I did not enter the boxing club with the express aim of dissecting the pugilistic world. My original intention was to use the gym as a "window" onto the ghetto so as to observe the social strategies of young men in the neighborhood – my initial object of study – and it was not until after sixteen months of assiduous attendance, and after I had been inducted as a bona fide member of the inner circle of the Boys Club, that I decided, with the approval of those concerned, to make the craft of the boxer an object of study in its own right. There is no doubt that I would never have been able to gain the trust and to benefit from the collaboration of the Woodlawn regulars if I had joined the gym with the explicit and avowed aim of studying it, for that very intention would have irrevocably modified my status and role within the social and symbolic system under consideration.

NOTES

1. This combination was set off by my friend Olivier Hermine, to whom I am forever grateful for having taken me to the Woodlawn Boys Club. I would like to thank Pierre Bourdieu for having supported me from the outset in an enterprise which, because it requires putting one's physical person on the line, could not have been brought to fruition without constant moral sustenance. His encouragement, his advice, and his visit to the Boys Club helped me in my moments of doubt (and exhaustion) find the strength to persist in my investigations. My gratitude

also goes to all those colleagues, relatives and friends too numerous to be named here, who succored, stimulated, and comforted me during and after this research: they know who they are and what I owe them. Thanks are due also to Thierry Discepolo for the boundless energy and patience with which he worked on the production of the original French manuscript. Finally it goes without saying that this book would not exist without the generosity and fraternal trust of my 'gym buddies' from Woodlawn and of our mentor, DeeDee: I hope that they will see in it the sign of my eternal esteem and affection.

2. To keep to the great names of contemporary US literature, Arthur Krystal ('Ifs, Ands, Butts: The Literary Sensibility at Ringside,' *Harper's* 274 (June 1987): 63–67) mentions among others Ernest Hemingway, Jack London, Dashiell Hammeett, Nelson Algren, James Farrell, Ring Lardner, Norman Mailer, and Ralph Ellison, joined lately by one of very few women, novelist Joyce Carol Oates, to whom we owe the beautiful *On Boxing* (Garden City, NY: Doubleday, 1987).

3. As is attested by this note, among many others of the same ilk, written in my field notebook in August 1990: "Today I had such a ball being in the gym, talking and laughing with DeeDee and Curtis, sitting in the back room and just *living and breathing* there, among them, soaking up the atmosphere of the gym like a human sponge, that I was suddenly suffocated by a wave of anguish at the idea of having to leave soon for Harvard, where I had just been elected at the Society of Fellows. I feel so much pleasure simply *participating* that observation becomes secondary and, frankly, I'm at the point where I tell myself that I'd gladly give up my studies and my research and all the rest to be able to stay here and box, to remain 'one of the boys.' I know that's completely crazy and surely unrealistic but,

at this very moment, I find the idea of migrating to Harvard, of going to present a paper at the ASA (American Sociological Association) meetings, of writing articles, reading books, attending lectures, and participating in the *tutti frutti* of academe totally devoid of meaning and downright depressing, so dreary and dead compared to the pure and vivacious carnal joy that this goddamn gym provides me (you've got to see the scenes between DeeDee and Curtis, they're worthy of Marcel Pagnol) that I would like to quit everything, drop out, to stay in Chicago. It's really crazy. PB [Pierre Bourdieu] was saying the other day that he's afraid that I'm 'letting myself be seduced by my object' but, boy, *if he only knew*: I'm already way beyond seduction!"

4. One will find an ethnography of the matrimonial festivities of Anthony and Mark in my article, "Un mariage dans le ghetto," *Actes de la recherche en sciences sociales* 113 (June 1996): 63–84.

5. These ethnographic observations made day-to-day in and around the gym were complemented and triangulated at the end of the research journey by the systematic collection of the life stories of the main members of the Woodlawn Boys Club, over one hundred in-depth interviews with professional pugilists then active in Illinois as well as with their trainers and managers, and by the dissection of the "native" literature (specialized magazines and newsletters, biographies and autobiographies) and its scholarly derivatives (literary and historiographical writings). I also trained in three other professional gyms in Chicago and visited another dozen clubs in the United States and in Europe over a period of four years. After my departure from Chicago, I was a member of boxing gyms in Boston, New York City, and Oakland, California.

6. On the ecological fallacy, read Aaron Cicourel, "Interviews, Surveys, and the Problem of Ecological Validity," *The Amer-*

ican Sociologist 17, 1 (February 1982), 11–20, and the kindred methodological remarks of Howard Becker, "Studying Practioners of Vice and Crime," in *Pathways to Data*, ed. William Habenstein (Chicago: Aldine, 1970), 31–49.

7. Loïc Wacquant, "Corps et âme: notes ethnographiques d'un apprenti-boxeur," *Actes de la recherche en sciences sociales* 80 (November 1989), 33–67. It was in writing this article that I understood to what extent the gym constitutes a "strategic research site" (as Robert Merton would say) and decided to make the craft of the boxer a second object of study, parallel to my investigations of social life in the ghetto.

8. *The Passion of the Pugilist* will address in a more in-depth manner, among other topics, the dialectic of desire and domination in the social genesis of the boxer's vocation, the structure and functioning of the pugilistic economy, the work of the trainer as virile mothering, native beliefs about sex and women, and confrontation in the ring as a homoerotic ritual of masculinization.

9. Loïc Wacquant, " 'Busy' Louie aux Golden Gloves," *Gulliver* 6 (April–June 1991), 12–33.

10. This text furthermore poses in practical terms the question of writing in the social sciences and of the difference between sociology and fiction, a question that has much preoccupied anthropologists over the last decade, since, shortly after its publication, this article earned me the offer by a leading Parisian publishing house of a contract for . . . my "novel."

11. Marcel Mauss, "Essai sur le don. Forme et raisons de l'échange dans les sociétés archaïques," in *Sociologie et anthropologie* (Paris: Presses Universitaires de Prance. 1950, orig. 1925), 276, my translation. *The Gift* (New York: Norton, 1990), 80.

12. Jeffrey M. Riemer, "Varieties of Opportunistic Research," *Urban Life* 4, 5 (January 1977): 467–77.

Theme 2 – Further Reading

Alan Bryman's (2012) *Social Research Methods*, 4th Edition (Oxford: Oxford University Press) is a popular student textbook and Judith Bell's (2010) *Doing Your Research Project: A Guide for First-time Researchers in Education, Health and Social Science*, 5th Edition (Buckingham: Open University Press) would be a useful accompaniment for introductory level sociology. Victor Jupp (2006) *The SAGE Dictionary of Social Research Methods* (London: Sage) is also a useful book which helps to clarify an often difficult terminology.

Giddens and Sutton *Sociology 7th Edition* (2013)

Chapter 2 provides a good grounding in research methods, covering the main issues. Other places that deal with methodological issues are Chapter 8 on social interactions, pages 302–9; Chapter 12 on measuring stratification and class, pages 491–6 and 511–8; Chapter 13 on poverty, pages 531–42; Chapter 14 on inequality, pages 570–81; Chapter 15 on sexuality, pages 627–33; Chapter 17 on secularization, pages 728–36 and Chapter 21 on crime patterns, pages 938–41.

Part 3 Natural and Urban Environments

The emergence and rapid growth of modern cities and urban environments during the late nineteenth and early twentieth centuries fascinated many sociologists and divided opinion. While some, like the German sociologist Ferdinand Tönnies saw urbanization as destroying longstanding community-based ways of life, tilting the balance of social life away from community towards looser associations of people, others focused on the liberating new opportunities opening up in the modern city. In truth, life in urban environments remains a complex mixture of pros and cons – more freedom and independence, but with the constant threat of this tipping over into social isolation and loneliness. As David Riesman once argued, paradoxically the place we often experience the most extreme feelings of loneliness is in the midst of an urban crowd of people who we do not, and never will, really know.

In Reading 14, German sociologist Georg Simmel explores some of the ways in which city dwellers adapt to cope with life in the modern metropolis. Cities overload the senses with stimuli from all directions – shops and window displays, dense populations, bright lights, signals and signs, vehicle movements, a cacophony of noise and a multitude of smells – all of which combine to make the city an exciting place but also one that drains our energy. Simmel argues that the only way to survive all this is to find ways of effectively blocking some of it out and thus preserve our psychic energy. In *The Metropolis and Mental Life* (1903) Simmel drew on his own experience of Berlin, a city that was still expanding and, by twenty-first-century standards, was relatively small. However, the sociological insights within this essay still speak to our urban condition today.

While Simmel's main interest was how the individual coped with city life, later studies moved on to examine the layout and structure of urban environments. Most notably, in the 1920s and 1930s, the Chicago School of Sociology developed a model of urban development and change known as 'urban ecology', due to its analogy with natural ecosystems. The Chicago School researchers studied the way that particular social groups tend to become concentrated in different areas of cities alongside the spatial distribution of functions epitomized by the creation of business and financial districts in the heart of the city. This research programme has been very significant. However, one aspect of city living that has perhaps not received so much attention in sociology is the effect of the built environment itself on urban life. In Reading 15, Richard Sennett examines the impact of the urban architectural landscape on our sense of well-being. For Sennett, the architectural forms of the modern city appear designed to discourage routine social contacts, separating and dividing rather than offering opportunities for interaction. The disjunction between our personal, inner experience and the outer world of 'things' serves to blunt our senses and severely limit the human experience. His solution is to find ways of reinvigorating our visual appreciation of the city's diverse social life.

Since the Berlin of Simmel's time, the modern city discussed by Sennett has continued to expand to the point at which some cities can now legitimately be described as 'world cities'. That is, they play a crucial role in the world economy and globalization. In Reading 16, Saskia Sassen describes the idea of the global city using London, New York and Tokyo to tease out some of the ways that the global city has become central to contemporary globalization processes.

Since the 1980s, interest in the human impact on the natural environment has gradually and somewhat hesitantly entered sociology. Given the discipline's mistrust of biological explanations of human affairs, it took sociologists some time to appreciate just how significant the environmental issues emerging from within green movements might be. Today there is little doubt that global climate change, biodiversity loss, ozone depletion and many more problems are not simply matters for natural scientists. Environmental problems are both caused (in part) by and have deleterious consequences for human societies, and sociologists can no longer ignore them. Hence, this section includes two readings which show that sociological theorizing will need to accommodate nature–society relations and be able to inform policy-makers on how environmental issues can best be approached.

Humans do not just inhabit urban environments, but natural environments too and in spite of the many positive aspects of city living, as many early commentators and sociologists recognized, there are negatives too. Since the 1970s, some of the strongest voices of criticism against cities have come from within the environmental or green movement based on the deleterious impact of urban life and urbanization on the natural environment. American social critic and environmental campaigner Murray Bookchin saw cities as huge, energy-using, waste-generating monsters. Anyone who has flown over a large city with its millions of lights or visited a landfill site should be able to appreciate this assessment. For many environmentalists the city represents all that is wrong with modernity. And though sociologists have always been interested in studying urban life, they have largely ignored the impact of human societies on the natural environment. Because of this, the classical theories may have less to offer an environmentally conscious sociology. In Reading 17, self-styled 'environmental sociologist' Riley E. Dunlap argues that the environmental crisis represented by global climate change, biodiversity loss and other major problems, demands that sociology shift from an anthropocentric or human-centredness, towards a new 'ecological paradigm' which rejects the assumption that human societies are somehow exempt from the natural limits to which all other species are subject. In fact, Catton and Dunlap coined the phrase the New Ecological Paradigm or NEP for short, as early as the 1970s. In this piece, Dunlap reflects on what progress has been made in moving sociology in this direction.

For those sociologists who ultimately reject such a radical transformation of their discipline, environmental issues and problems still present a major challenge. In particular, the growing scientific consensus is that, not only is global warming a reality, but its causes include a significant anthropogenic (human-created) element. The potentially disastrous medium- to long-term consequences of global warming surely demand the attention of sociologists and policy-makers, but Anthony Giddens (in Reading 18) argues forcefully that, surprisingly, we still do not have a proper politics of climate change. Turning away from the radical green proposal for adopting a precautionary principle to development and the more widely accepted idea of sustainable development, Giddens proposes instead that we should work towards more sophisticated risk analysis and a refocusing on economic development in those parts of the world where it is urgently needed.

14. Individuality in the Modern City

Georg Simmel

The deepest problems of modern life derive from the claim of the individual to preserve the autonomy and individuality of his existence in the face of overwhelming social forces, of historical heritage, of external culture, and of the technique of life. The fight with nature which primitive man has to wage for his *bodily* existence attains in this modern form its latest transformation. The eighteenth century called upon man to free himself of all the historical bonds in the state and in religion, in morals and in economics. Man's nature, originally good and common to all, should develop unhampered. In addition to more liberty, the nineteenth century demanded the functional specialization of man and his work; this specialization makes one individual incomparable to another, and each of them indispensable to the highest possible extent. However, this specialization makes each man the more directly dependent upon the supplementary activities of all others. Nietzsche sees the full development of the individual conditioned by the most ruthless struggle of individuals; socialism believes in the suppression of all competition for the same reason. Be that as it may, in all these positions the same basic motive is at work: the person resists to being leveled down and worn out by a social-technological mechanism. An inquiry into the inner meaning of specifically modern life and its products, into the soul of the cultural body, so to speak, must seek to solve the equation which structures like the metropolis set up between the individual and the super-individual contents of life. Such an inquiry must answer the question of how the personality accommodates itself in the adjustments to external forces. This will be my task today.

The psychological basis of the metropolitan type of individuality consists in the *intensification of nervous stimulation* which results from the swift and uninterrupted change of outer and inner stimuli. Man is a differentiating creature. His mind is stimulated by the difference between a momentary impression and the one which preceded it. Lasting impressions, impressions which differ only slightly from one another, impressions which take a regular and habitual course and show regular and habitual contrasts – all these use up, so to speak, less consciousness than does the rapid crowding of changing images, the sharp discontinuity in the grasp of a single glance, and the unexpectedness of onrushing impressions. These are the psychological conditions which the metropolis creates. With each crossing of the street, with the tempo and multiplicity of economic, occupational and social life, the city sets up a deep contrast with small town and rural life with reference to the sensory foundations of psychic life. The metropolis exacts from man as a discriminating creature a different amount of consciousness than does rural life. Here the rhythm of life and sensory mental imagery flows more slowly, more habitually, and more evenly. Precisely in this connection the sophisticated character of metropolitan psychic life becomes understandable – as over against small town life which rests more upon deeply felt and emotional relationships. [. . .]

The metropolis has always been the seat of the money economy. Here the multiplicity and concentration of economic exchange gives an importance to the means of exchange which the scantiness of rural commerce would not have allowed. Money economy and the dominance of the intellect are intrinsically connected. They share a matter-of-fact attitude in dealing with men and with things; and, in this attitude, a formal justice is often coupled with an inconsiderate hardness. The intellectually sophisticated person is indifferent to all genuine individuality, because relationships and reactions result from it which cannot be exhausted with logical operations. In the same manner, the individuality of phenomena is not commensurate with the pecuniary principle. Money is concerned only with what is common to all: it asks for the exchange value, it reduces all quality and individuality to the question: How much? All intimate emotional relations between persons are founded in their individuality, whereas in rational relations man is reckoned with like a number, like an element which is in itself indifferent. Only the objective measurable achievement is of interest.

[...]

There is perhaps no psychic phenomenon which has been so unconditionally reserved to the metropolis as has the blasé attitude. The blasé attitude results first from the rapidly changing and closely pressed contrasting stimulations of the nerves. From this, the enhancement of metropolitan intellectuality, also, seems originally to stem. Therefore, stupid people who are not intellectually alive in the first place usually are not exactly blasé. A life in boundless pursuit of pleasure makes one blasé because it agitates the nerves to their strongest reactivity for such a long time that they finally cease to react at all. In the same way, through the rapidity and contradictoriness of their changes, more harmless impressions force such violent responses, tearing the nerves so brutally hither and thither that their last reserves of strength are spent, and if one remains in the same milieu they have no time to gather new strength. An incapacity thus emerges to react to new sensa-

tions with the appropriate energy. This constitutes that blasé attitude which, in fact, every metropolitan child shows when compared with children of quieter and less changeable milieus.

This physiological source of the metropolitan blasé attitude is joined by another source which flows from the money economy. The essence of the blasé attitude consists in the blunting of discrimination. This does not mean that the objects are not perceived, as is the case with the half-wit, but rather that the meaning and differing values of things and thereby the things themselves, are experienced as insubstantial. They appear to the blasé person in an evenly flat and gray tone; no one object deserves preference over any other. This mood is the faithful subjective reflection of the completely internalized money economy. By being the equivalent to all the manifold things in one and the same way, money becomes the most frightful leveler. For money expresses all qualitative differences of things in terms of "how much?" Money, with all its colorlessness and indifference, becomes the common denominator of all values; irreparably it hollows out the core of things, their individuality, their specific value, and their incomparability. All things float with equal specific gravity in the constantly moving stream of money. All things lie on the same level and differ from one another only in the size of the area which they cover. In the individual case this coloration, or rather discoloration, of things through their money equivalence may be unnoticeably minute. However, through the relations of the rich to the objects to be had for money, perhaps even through the total character which the mentality of the contemporary public everywhere imparts to these objects, the exclusively pecuniary evaluation of objects has become quite considerable. The large cities, the main seats of the money exchange, bring the purchasability of things to the fore much more impressively than do smaller localities. That is why cities are also the genuine locale of the blasé attitude. In the blasé attitude the concentration of men and things stimulate the nervous system of the individual to its highest achievement so that it attains its peak. Through the mere quantitative intensification of the same conditioning factors this achievement is transformed into its opposite and appears in the peculiar adjustment of the blasé attitude. In this phenomenon the nerves find in the refusal to react to their stimulation the last possibility of accommodating to the contents and forms of metropolitan life. The self-preservation of certain personalities is bought at the price of devaluing the whole objective world, a devaluation which in the end unavoidably drags one's own personality down into a feeling of the same worthlessness.

Whereas the subject of this form of existence has to come to terms with it entirely for himself, his self-preservation in the face of the large city demands from him a no less negative behavior of a social nature. This mental attitude of metropolitans toward one another we may designate, from a formal point of view, as reserve. If so many inner reactions were responses to the continuous external contacts with innumerable people as are those in the small town, where one knows almost everybody one meets and where one has a positive relation to almost everyone, one would be completely atomized internally and come to an unimaginable psychic state. Partly this psychological fact, partly the right to distrust which men have in the face of the touch-and-go elements of metropolitan life, necessitates our reserve. As a result of this reserve we frequently do not even know by sight those who have been our neighbors for years. And it is this reserve which in the eyes of the small-town people makes us appear to be cold and heartless. Indeed, if I do not deceive myself, the inner aspect of this outer reserve is not only indifference but, more often than we are aware, it is a slight aversion, a mutual strangeness and repulsion, which will break into hatred and fight at the moment of a closer contact, however caused. The whole inner organization of such an extensive communicative life rests upon an extremely varied hierarchy of sympathies, indifferences, and aversions of the briefest as well as of the most permanent nature. The sphere of indifference in this hierarchy is not as large as might appear on the surface. Our psychic activity still responds to almost every impression of somebody else with a somewhat distinct feeling. The unconscious, fluid and changing character of this impression seems to result in a state of indifference. Actually this indifference would be just as unnatural as the diffusion of indiscriminate mutual suggestion would be unbearable. From both these typical dangers of the metropolis, indifference and indiscriminate suggestibility, antipathy protects us. A latent antipathy and the preparatory stage of practical antagonism effect the distances and aversions without which this mode of life could not at all be led. The extent and the mixture of this style of life, the rhythm of its emergence and disappearance, the forms in which it is satisfied – all these, with the unifying motives in the narrower sense, form the inseparable whole of the metropolitan style of life. What appears in the metropolitan style of life directly as dissociation is in reality only one of its elemental forms of socialization.

15. Creating Humane Cities

Richard Sennett

The ancient Greek could use his or her eyes to see the complexities of life. The temples, markets, playing fields, meeting places, walls, public statuary, and paintings of the ancient city represented the culture's values in religion, politics, and family life. It would be difficult to know where in particular to go in modern London or New York to experience, say, remorse. Or were modern architects asked to design spaces that better promote democracy, they would lay down their pens; there is no modern design equivalent to the ancient assembly. Nor is it easy to conceive of places that teach the moral dimensions of sexual desire, as the Greeks learned in their gymnasiums – modern places, that is, filled with other people, a crowd of other people, rather than the near silence of the bedroom or the solitude of the psychiatrist's couch. As materials for culture, the stones of the modern city seem badly laid by planners and architects, in that the shopping mall, the parking lot, the apartment house elevator do not suggest in their form the complexities of how people might live. What once were the experiences of places appear now as floating mental operations.

We could never recover the Greek past, even if we wished and we would not wish to; their city was founded on massive slavery. But the clarity with which they could literally see the fullness of life raises at least the question of why we cannot see as fully, a question this book attempts to answer.

One difference between the Greek past and the present is that whereas the ancients could use their eyes in the city to think about political, religious, and erotic experiences, modern culture suffers from a divide between the inside and the outside. It is a divide between subjective experience and worldly experience, self and city. Moreover, our culture is marked by hard struggle whenever people seek to make inner life concrete. This sets us off not just from our own origins but also from non-European cultures nearer in time whose masks, dances, ceremonials, shrines, sacred grounds, and cosmologies connect subjective life to physical things.

This divide between inner, subjective experience and outer, physical life expresses in fact a great fear which our civilization has refused to admit, much less to reckon. The spaces full of people in the modern city are either spaces limited to and carefully orchestrating consumption, like the shopping mall, or spaces limited to and carefully orchestrating the experience of tourism. This reduction and trivializing of the city as a stage of life is no accident. Beyond all the economic and demographic reasons for the neutralized city there exists a profound, indeed, "spiritual" reason why people are willing to tolerate such a bland scene for their lives. The way cities look reflects a great, unreckoned fear of exposure. "Exposure" more connotes the likelihood of being hurt than of being stimulated. The fear of exposure is in one way a militarized conception of everyday experience, as though attack-and-defense is as apt a model of subjective life as it is of warfare. What is characteristic of our city-building is to wall off the differences between people, assuming that these differences are more likely to be mutually threatening than mutually stimulating. What we make in the urban realm are therefore bland, neutralizing spaces, spaces which remove the threat of social contact: street walls faced in sheets of plate glass, highways that cut off poor neighborhoods from the rest of the city, dormitory housing developments.

In this book I shall try to show how fear of exposure came about, how the wall between inner and outer life was built. The wall arose in part from our religious history: Christianity set Western culture upon the course that built a wall between the inner and outer experience. The shadows cast by that wall continue to darken secular society. Moreover, attempts to unify the inner and outer dimensions simply by tearing down the wall, making the inner and outer one organic whole, have not proved successful; unity can be gained only at the price of complexity.

The exposed, outer life of the city cannot be simply a reflection of inner life. Exposure occurs in crowds and among strangers. The cultural problem of the modern city is how to make this impersonal milieu speak, how to relieve its current blandness, its neutrality, whose origin can be traced back to the belief that the outside world of things is unreal. Our urban problem is how to revive the reality of the outside as a dimension of human experience.

[. . .] A city ought to be a school for learning how to lead a centered life. Through exposure to others, we might learn how to weigh what is important and what is not. We need to see differences on the streets or in other people neither as threats nor as sentimental invitations, rather as necessary visions. They are necessary for us to learn how to navigate life with balance, both individually and collectively.

This might seem a matter simply of reflecting upon what we see, of reckoning our places in the midst of others. But for the Greeks, to balance oneself one had to act as well as to look. The result of caring about what one sees is the desire to make something. The Greeks called this desire *poiesis*, from which we derive the English word "poetry," but their word was broader than one art in scope. The balanced person wants to make

a speech, a battle, love, as well as a poem with the same qualities of grace and poise. As a result of his or her own engagement in making or doing things carefully, *sophrosyne* and *poiesis* were intimately related. While I do not go so far as to consider "the city as a work of art," as does Donald Olsen in a book of that title, the impulse behind his title seems to me right. To care about what one sees in the world leads to mobilizing one's creative powers. In the modern city, these creative powers ought to take on a particular and humane form, turning people outward. Our culture is in need of an art of exposure; this art will not make us one another's victims, rather more balanced adults, capable of coping with and learning from complexity.

[. . .]

Since I've lived in New York I've liked walking, avoiding subways or taxis whenever I can. These days I usually walk from my apartment in Greenwich Village up to midtown on the East Side to eat, an amble of about three miles. There are plenty of restaurants in the Village but none quite like those just above the United Nations, in the side streets of the Fifties. They are French, but not fashionable; food is still prepared with butter and lard and cream, the patrons are bulky and comfortable, the menu seldom changes. The restaurants are in the ground floors of townhouses, and most are done up alike; a bar in front leading to a long room lined with banquettes of red plush or red leather; Sunday-painter oil paintings of provincial France hang in gold frames on the walls above the banquettes; a kitchen is tucked in the back. People say New York is an unfriendly city, and I suppose any one of these restaurants could be cited in evidence. The waiters, Italians or Frenchmen in late middle age, lack that air of reassuring familiarity tourists like. But the restaurants are filled with people seemingly quite content to be left alone, many regular, solitary clients as well as couples speaking quietly.

To reach the French restaurants I have to pass from my house through a drug preserve just to the east of Washington Square. Ten years ago junkie used to sell to junkie in the square and these blocks east to Third Avenue. In the morning stoned men lay on park benches, or in doorways; they slept immobile under the influence of the drugs, sometimes having spread newspapers out on the pavements as mattresses. It was then the sort of scene that might have attracted Baudelaire's spleen: in a prose poem of 1851 the poet wrote of a poisoned group of workers:

This languishing and pining population . . . who feel a purple and impetuous blood coursing through their veins, and who cast a long, sorrow-laden look at the sunlight and shadows of the great parks . . .[1]

The dulled heroin addicts now are gone, replaced by addict-dealers in cocaine. The cocaine dealers are never still, their arms are jerky, they pace and pace; in their electric nervousness, they radiate more danger than the old stoned men.

In Baudelaire's Paris, misery and wealth were inextricable; everywhere he walked he encountered aggressive beggars and spontaneous fights, his lapels were grabbed by men selling watches while his pockets were picked by men stealing them. These disorders stimulated his muse. The civilized man must, somehow, take into account pain he can do nothing about. But now that accounting does not occur. Baudelaire's inflamed poetic voice no longer conjures an observer's impression of the woe of drugs, for the sight of these human beings whose bodies are short-circuiting on cocaine, while disturbing, is not too disturbing, if I also keep moving.

Along Third Avenue, abruptly above Fourteenth Street, there appear six blocks or so of white brick apartment houses built in the 1950s and 1960s on the edges of the Gramercy Park area; the people who live here are buyers for department stores, women who began in New York as secretaries and may or may not have become something more but kept at their jobs. Until very recently, seldom would one see in an American city, drinking casually in bars alone or dining quietly with one another, these women of a certain age, women who do not attempt to disguise the crowsfeet at the edge of the eyes; for

generations the blocks here have been their shelter. It is a neighborhood also of single bald men, in commerce and sales, not at the top but walking confidently enough to the delis and tobacco stands lining Third Avenue. All the food sold in shops here is sold in small cans and single portions; it is possible in the Korean groceries to buy half a lettuce.

"By 'modernity,'" Baudelaire wrote, "I mean the ephemeral, the fugitive, the contingent, the half of art whose other half is the eternal and the immutable."[2] Gramercy Park is a community of refugees, like so many other places in New York, but here there are refugees from the family. These are ephemeral lives, one might say, their daily round consisting of little bits of business, of shopping after work, of watering plants and feeding cats in the evening. Most of the imagery of anomie, isolation, and estrangement of the nineteenth century assumed that solitude was an urban affliction. The image of a mass of solitary, middle-aged people living in characterless apartment buildings still might conjure a pathetic picture. Yet there are lots of people on the street in this swath of Third Avenue at all hours; though hardly fashionable, these blocks skirting Gramercy Park are in the companionable spirit of Constantin Guys. There is nothing sublime in this solitude; it seems to enhance the ordinary business of life.

Unfortunately, in a few minutes of walking this scene too has disappeared, and now my walk takes an unexpected turn. The middle Twenties between Third and Lexington is the equestrian center of New York, where several stores sell saddles and Western apparel. The clientele is varied: polo players from the lusher suburbs, Argentines, people who ride in Central Park, and then another group, more delicate connoisseurs of harnesses, crops, and saddles. The middle Twenties play host as well to a group of bars that cater to these leather fetishists, bars in run-down townhouses with no signs and blacked-out windows. What makes the middle Twenties distinct is that all the customers in the leather shops are served alike – rudely. Saddles and whips are sold by harassed salesmen, wrapped by clerks ostentatiously bored. Nor do the horsey matrons seem to care much where the men with careful eyes take their purchases, no curiosity about the blacked-out windows from behind which ooze the smells of beer, leather, and urine. A city of differences and of fragments of life that do not connect: in such a city the obsessed are set free.

My walk takes me along a diverse street, but its differences evoke something other than the vivid scenes in which Baudelaire's *flâneur* becomes profoundly engaged.

[. . .]

The smell of urine is perfumed if only I keep walking. In the upper Twenties along Lexington Avenue bags of spices lie in ranks within the shops run by Indians and Pakistanis; when the doors are open in spring and fall, the combined scents waft out to the street, but like most of the ethnic enclaves in New York these sensuous sights and smells are not beacons to the outside world. In the Indian shops few of the bags of spices are identified by labels. This brilliantly simple expedient discourages all but the most intrepid of tourists who, upon asking for an explanation of the mysterious bags, will be smilingly informed by perfectly polite shopkeepers that one is "hot spice" or another an "imported ingredient." The shop owners stand in their doorways in summer, making jokes or comments – could it possibly be about us? – which are met by their neighbors with the faintest parting of the lips, the slight smile that acknowledges more, and perhaps condemns more, than a loud laugh.

New York should be the ideal city of exposure to the outside. It grasps the imagination because it is a city of differences par excellence, a city collecting its population from all over the world. Yet it is here that the passion of the Parisian poet – that desire for enhancement of stimulation and release from self – seems contravened. By walking in the middle of New York one is immersed in the differences of this most diverse of cities, but precisely because the scenes are disengaged they

seem unlikely to offer themselves as significant encounters in the sense of a vivid stimulus, a telling moment of talking or touching or connection. The leather fetishist and spice merchant are protected by disengagement; the admirable women who have made lives for themselves near Gramercy Park are also disengaged, not those needy sort of Americans who feel they must tell you the entire story of their lives in the next five minutes; the junkies doing business are seldom in a mood to chat. All the more is this true – more largely – of the races, who live segregated lives close together, and of social classes, who mix but do not socialize.

Nor are the chameleon virtues of the Chicago urbanists much in evidence: people do not take on the colors of their surroundings, the light-hued colors of otherness. A walk in New York reveals instead that difference from and indifference to others are a related, unhappy pair. The eye sees differences to which it reacts with indifference. I, too, feel no curiosity to know what is problematic in the life of a drug dealer; I am too polite to intrude upon the solitude of a middle-aged woman, or to violate the privacy of another man's sexual obsessions. When I do reach out, harmlessly, the spice merchant pushes me away with his irony.

This reaction of disengagement when immersed in difference is the result of the forces that have created a disjunction between inner and outer life. These forces have annihilated the humane value of complexity, even in a city where differences are an overwhelming sociological fact. Sheer exposure to difference is no corrective to the Christian ills of inwardness. There is withdrawal and fear of exposure, as though all differences are potentially as explosive as those between a drug dealer and an ordinary citizen. There is neutralization: if something begins to disturb or touch me, I need only keep walking to stop feeling. Moreover, I suffer from abundance, the promised remedy of the Enlightenment. My senses are flooded by images, but the difference in value between one image and another becomes as fleeting as my own movement; difference becomes a mere parade of variety. This display of difference on the street obeys the same visual logic, moreover, that ruled the construction of the first modern interiors. These scenes are sequential and linear displays of differences, like the rooms in a railroad flat. Linear, sequential distinctions are no more arousing outside than they were inside. A New York street resembles the studio of a painter who has assembled in it all the paints, books of other artists, and sketches he will need for a grand triptych that will crown his career; then the painter has unaccountably left town.

Which brings us again to power. The last lap of my walk passes through Murray Hill. The townhouses here are dirty limestone or brownstone; the apartment buildings have no imposing entrance lobbies. There is a uniform of unfashion in Murray Hill: elderly women in black silk dresses and equally elderly men sporting pencil-thin mustaches and malacca canes, their clothes visibly decades old. This is a quarter of the old elite in New York.

The quarter likes to depict itself as a dying neighborhood – aristocracy buried by the loud men, civility crushed in the hands of people who have the temerity of their vigor. In one way the manners of Murray Hill simply mirror those of the spice merchants five blocks south – the same self-effacement and strategic discretion; a dealer in turmeric and the senior vice president of a bank are at least brothers in silence. But old money/power reveals a further dimension of indifference.

The center of Murray Hill is the Morgan Library, housed in the mansion at Thirty-sixth and Madison of the capitalist whose vigor appalled old New York at the turn of the century. The talk at black-tie dinners here is dull; the Morgan does not glitter. Some few of the men at Morgan Library dinners will go to the Century Association nearby for that sort of exercise, or even farther afield to the Grolier Club. The Century has chamber music concerts and art exhibits and evening lectures; at the Grolier there is bibliophile chat; the dinners at the Morgan evoke the aura of civilized discourse without a taxing expenditure of thought. At the tables set under the library's dark oak beams, dwarfed in the architectural volume of J. P. Morgan's swagger, people speak cozily of children and of their friends' divorces.

Near the Morgan Library is B. Altman's, an enormous store recently closed which was regularly open in the evenings so that people could shop after a day of work. Often one saw women, of the sort who live nearby in Gramercy Park, shopping for sheets there; the sheet-shoppers had clipped the advertisement for a white sale out of the newspaper and still carried it in their unscuffed calf handbags; they were hardworking, thrifty. I have, as I say, often seen them stop after a round of shopping to contemplate these other women in their unfashionable dresses and jewels in old settings, the men in their worn dinner jackets, entering the portals of the Morgan Library, the doors opening and closing by the aid of flunkies within so that those about to dine need not push. There was a moment of hostility on the street, perhaps clouded in the shopper's eyes by her surprise at how shabby are the permanently rich, and then a shrug – her slight shrug of the shoulders.

In one way the negligence of the diners at the Morgan to their circumstances was thus mirrored at its entrance, in this lifting of shoulders, as though between circumstance, place, and person there were only a neutral connection. The shopper shrugged, accepted, and, like me, moved on; life will go on. This oil of the mechanism of indifference is not the machine of power itself. Instead, the display of indifference is how the eye sees power at work in space. In walking the streets where people go about their own business, we are constantly witnessing scenes of submission in which the actors think they are simply keeping to themselves, numbed to the fact that true indifference requires a privileged place in society. Submission passes through power's magic lantern so that the image illuminated on the city's streets does not irritate the eye. Submission appears on the streets as detachment. If what one sees hurts, one can always keep walking.

Now I've sighted the restaurant. The east Forties between Lexington and First avenues is the most neutral area of Manhattan, a forest of tall, dull apartment buildings in and out of which junior diplomats at the United Nations move their children and their chattel as governments at home rise and fall. Office towers each month encroach upon residential towers, a marriage of towers in the sky that blot out the sun on the streets. On the periphery of the city, one can see literally miles of burned-out or abandoned ruins, the buildings often with bricked-up windows or windows covered in sheets of metal behind which, at night, one spies gleams of light. This permissible belt of desolation in so rich a city is like a boast of civic indifference. Near my restaurant in the very center, the buildings, especially at night, have their own derelict, homeless air, the remaining townhouses more like provisional structures than dwellings a hundred years old, as they are so obviously slated for the wrecker's ball.

NOTES

1. Charles Baudelaire, *Spleen de Paris*, trans. Harry Zohn, in Walter Beniamin, *Charles Baudelaire, A Lyric Poet in the Era of High Capitalism* (London: Verso, 1983), p. 74.
2. Charles Baudelaire, *The Painter of Modern Life and Other Essays*, ed. Jonathan Mayne (Cambridge, MA: Da Capo Press, 1986), p. 13.

16. The Global City

Saskia Sassen

When I first chose to use global city (1984) I did so knowingly – it was an attempt to name a difference: the specificity of the global as it gets structured in the contemporary period. I did not chose the obvious alternative, world city, because it had precisely the opposite attribute: it referred to a type of city which we have seen over the centuries (e.g., Braudel 1984; Hall 1966; King 1990), and most probably also in much earlier periods in Asia than in the West (Abu-Lughod 1989; King 1990). In this regard it could be said that most of today's major global cities are also world cities, but that there may well be some global cities today that are not world cities in the full, rich sense of that term. This is partly an empirical question for me; further, as the global economy expands and incorporates additional cities into the various networks, it is quite possible that the answer to that particular question will vary. Thus the fact that Miami has developed global city functions beginning in the late 1980s does not make it a world city in that older, sense of the term.

[. . .]

In the decades after World War II, there was an international regime based on United States dominance in the world economy and the rules for global trade contained in the 1945 Bretton Woods agreement. By the early 1970s, the conditions supporting that regime were disintegrating. The breakdown created a void into which stepped, perhaps in a last burst of national dominance, the large U.S. transnational industrial firms and banks.

In this period of transition, the management of the international economic order was to an inordinate extent run from the headquarters of these firms. By the early 1980s, however, the large U.S. transnational banks faced the massive Third World debt crisis, and U.S. industrial firms experienced sharp market share losses from foreign competition. Yet the international economy did not simply break into fragments. The geography and composition of the global economy changed so as to produce a complex duality: a spatially dispersed, yet globally integrated organization of economic activity.

The point of departure for the present study is that the combination of spatial dispersal and global integration has created a new strategic role for major cities. Beyond their long history as centers for international trade and banking, these cities now function in four new ways: first, as highly concentrated command points in the organization of the world economy; second, as key locations for finance and for specialized service firms, which have replaced manufacturing as the leading economic sectors; third, as sites of production, including the production of innovations, in these leading industries; and fourth, as markets for the products and innovations produced. These changes in the functioning of cities have had a massive impact upon both international economic activity and urban form: cities concentrate control over vast resources, while finance and specialized service industries have restructured the urban social and economic order. Thus a new type of city has appeared. It is the global city. Leading examples now are New York, London, Tokyo,

Frankfurt, and Paris. The first three are the focus of this book.

As I shall show, these three cities have undergone massive and *parallel* changes in their economic base, spatial organization, and social structure. But this parallel development is a puzzle. How could cities with as diverse a history, culture, politics, and economy as New York, London, and Tokyo experience similar transformations concentrated in so brief a period of time? Not examined at length in my study, but important to its theoretical framework, is how transformations in cities ranging from Paris to Frankfurt to Hong Kong and São Paulo have responded to the same dynamic. To understand the puzzle of parallel change in diverse cities requires not simply a point-by-point comparison of New York, London, and Tokyo, but a situating of these cities in a set of global processes. In order to understand why major cities with different histories and cultures have undergone parallel economic and social changes, we need to examine transformations in the world economy. Yet the term *global city* may be reductive and misleading if it suggests that cities are mere outcomes of a global economic machine. They are specific places whose spaces, internal dynamics, and social structure matter; indeed, we may be able to understand the global order only by analyzing why key structures of the world economy are *necessarily* situated in cities.

How does the position of these cities in the world economy today differ from that which they have historically held as centers of banking and trade? When Max Weber analyzed the medieval cities woven together in the Hanseatic League, he conceived their trade as the exchange of surplus production; it was his view that a medieval city could withdraw from external trade and continue to support itself, albeit on a reduced scale. The modern molecule of global cities is nothing like the trade among self-sufficient places in the Hanseatic League, as Weber understood it. The first thesis advanced in this book is that the territorial dispersal of current economic activity creates a need for expanded central control and manage-

ment. In other words, while in principle the territorial decentralization of economic activity in recent years could have been accompanied by a corresponding decentralization in ownership and hence in the appropriation of profits, there has been little movement in that direction. Though large firms have increased their subcontracting to smaller firms, and many national firms in the newly industrializing countries have grown rapidly, this form of growth is ultimately part of a chain.

[. . .]

The character of a global city is shaped by the emerging organization of the financial industry. The accelerated production of innovations and the new importance of a large number of relatively small financial institutions led to a renewed or expanded role for the marketplace in the financial industry in the decade of the 1980s. The marketplace has assumed new strategic and routine economic functions, in comparison to the prior phase, when the large transnational banks dominated the national and international financial market. Insofar as financial "products" can be used internationally, the market has reappeared in a new form in the global economy. New York, London, and Tokyo play roles as production sites for financial instruments and centralized marketplaces for these "products."

A key dynamic running through these various activities and organizing my analysis of the place of global cities in the world economy is their capability for producing global control. By focusing on the production of services and financial innovations, I am seeking to displace the focus of attention from the familiar issues of the power of large corporations over governments and economies, or supracorporate concentration of power through interlocking directorates or organizations, such as the IMF. I want to focus on an aspect that has received less attention, which could be referred to as the *practice* of global control: the work of producing and reproducing the organization and management of a global production system and a global marketplace for finance. My focus is not on power, but on production: the production of those inputs that constitute the capability for global control and the infrastructure of jobs involved in this production.

The power of large corporations is insufficient to explain the capability for global control. Obviously, governments also face an increasingly complex environment in which highly sophisticated machineries of centralized management and control are necessary. Moreover, the high level of specialization and the growing demand for these specialized inputs have created the conditions for a freestanding industry. Now small firms can buy components of global capability, such as management consulting or international legal advice. And so can firms and governments anywhere in the world. While the large corporation is undoubtedly a key agent inducing the development of this capability and is a prime beneficiary, it is not the sole user.

Equally misleading would be an exclusive focus on transnational banks. Up to the end of the 1982 Third World debt crisis, the large transnational banks dominated the financial markets in terms of both volume and the nature of firm transactions. After 1982, this dominance was increasingly challenged by other financial institutions and the innovations they produced. This led to a transformation in the leading components of the financial industry, a proliferation of financial institutions, and the rapid internationalization of financial markets rather than just a few banks. The incorporation of a multiplicity of markets all over the world into a global system fed the growth of the industry after the 1982 debt crisis, while also creating new forms of concentration in a few leading financial centers. Hence, in the case of the financial industry, a focus on the large transnational banks would exclude precisely those sectors of the industry where much of the new growth and production of innovations has occurred; it would leave out an examination of the wide range of activities, firms, and markets that constitute the financial industry since the 1980s.

Thus, there are a number of reasons to focus a study on marketplaces and production sites rather than on the large corporations and banks. Most scholarship on the internationalization of the economy has already focused on the large corporations and transnational banks. To continue to focus on the corporations and banks would mean to limit attention to their formal power, rather than examining the wide array of economic activities, many outside the corporation, needed to produce and reproduce that power. And, in the case of finance, a focus on the large transnational banks would leave out precisely that institutional sector of the industry where the key components of the new growth have been invented and put into circulation. Finally, exclusive focus on corporations and banks leaves out a number of issues about the social, economic, and spatial impact of these activities on the cities that contain them, a major concern in this book and one I return to below.

A third major theme explored in this book concerns the consequences of these developments for the national urban system in each of these countries and for the relationship of the global city to its nation-state. While a few major cities are the sites of production for the new global control capability, a large number of other major cities have lost their role as leading export centers for industrial manufacturing, as a result of the decentralization of this form of production. Cities such as Detroit, Liverpool, Manchester, and now increasingly Nagoya and Osaka have been affected by the decentralization of their key industries at the domestic and international levels. [. . .] This same process has contributed to the growth of service industries that produce the specialized inputs to run global production processes and global markets for inputs and outputs. These industries – international legal and accounting services, management consulting, financial services – are heavily concentrated in cities such as New York, London, and Tokyo. We need to know how this growth alters the relations between the global cities and what were once the leading industrial centers in their nations. Does globalization bring about a triangulation so that New York, for example, now plays a role in the fortunes of Detroit that it did not play when that city was home to most production jobs in one of the leading industries, auto manufacturing? Or, in the case of Japan, we need to ask, for example, if there is a connection between the increasing shift of production out of Toyota City (Nagoya) to off-shore locations (Thailand, South Korea, and the United States) and the development for the first time of a new headquarters for Toyota in Tokyo.

Similarly, there is a question about the relation between such major cities as Chicago, Osaka, and Manchester, once leading industrial centers in the world, and global markets generally. Both Chicago and Osaka were and continue to be important financial centers on the basis of their manufacturing industries. We would want to know if they have lost ground, relatively, in these functions as a result of their decline in the global industrial market, or instead have undergone parallel transformation toward strengthening of service functions. Chicago, for example, was at the heart of a massive agroindustrial complex, a vast regional economy. How has the decline of that regional economic system affected Chicago?

In all these questions, it is a matter of understanding what growth embedded in the international system of producer services and finance has entailed for different levels in the national urban hierarchy. The broader trends – decentralization of plants, offices, and service outlets, along with the expansion of central functions as a consequence of the need to manage such decentralized organization of firms – may well have created conditions contributing to the growth of regional subcenters, minor versions of what New York, London, and Tokyo do on a global and national scale. The extent to which the developments posited for New York, London, and Tokyo are also replicated, perhaps in less accentuated form, in smaller cities, at lower levels of the urban hierarchy, is an open, but important, question.

REFERENCES

Abu-Lughod, Janet L. (1989) *Before European Hegemony: the World System A.D. 1250–1350.* New York and Oxford: Oxford University Press.

Braudel, Fernand. (1984) *The Perspective of the World.* New York: Harper and Row.

Hall, Peter. (1966) *The World Cities.* New York: McGraw-Hill.

King, Anthony D. (1990) *Urbanism, Colonialism, and the World Economy: Culture and Spatial Foundations.* London and New York: Routledge.

17. A New Ecological Paradigm for Sociology

Riley E. Dunlap

Sociology has at least implicitly adopted the assumption that technological development, economic growth, and progress are the normal state of affairs.

Changes in how and where people lived, especially the massive shift toward industrialism and urbanism and away from agriculture, reinforced the notion that modern societies were becoming increasingly independent from their biophysical environments. In fact, life in industrialized societies created the impression that not only was the environment a source of inexhaustible natural resources, but also that humans could manipulate and control that environment to suit their needs.

In addition to the inherently optimistic orientation toward progress that sociology adopted from Western culture, various factors unique to our discipline have strengthened sociologists tendency to ignore the importance of the environment. To establish a new discipline, the founding fathers of sociology asserted the uniqueness of our subject matter and perspectives. Of special importance was Durkheim's emphasis on the "objective reality of social facts" and the irreducibility of such facts to the psychological properties of individuals. A corollary of this sui generis conception of social phenomena was the dictum that the *cause* of a social fact must always be found in other social, as opposed to psychological, facts. The resultant "antireductionism taboo" also legitimated sociological rejection of biological and physical variables as potential explanations of social phenomena (Catton and Dunlap 1980).

When sociology was being founded, efforts to explain social phenomena in terms of biological and physical factors were still common. Because they often suggested that biological conditions such as heredity or physical conditions such as climate were the *primary* determinants of human affairs, proponents of these explanations came to be criticized as biological or geographical "determinists." Encouraged by antireductionism, sociologists have been especially adamant in rejecting these views, to the point that the charge of determinism is now leveled – incorrectly in my view – at those who suggest that biological or environmental factors have *any* degree of influence on human affairs (Benton 1991).

Besides the Durkheimian antireductionism taboo, another major tradition in sociology contributed to our discipline's tendency to ignore the biophysical environment. Inherited from Weber and elaborated by Mead, Cooley, Thomas, and others, this tradition emphasized the importance of understanding the ways in which people define their situations in order to understand their actions. Assuming that "the reality of a situation is in the definition attached to it by the participating actors," this perspective implied "that the physical properties of the situation may be ignored" (Choldin 1978: 353). Physical properties became relevant *only* if they were perceived and defined as relevant by the actors – that is, transformed into "social facts" (see, e.g., Klausner 1971: 41). This "social definition" perspective therefore complemented Durkheim's antireductionism in leading sociologists to ignore the physical environment.[1] [. . .]

The impact of these disciplinary traditions can be summarized as follows: the Durkheimian antireductionism legacy suggested that the physical environment *should* be ignored, while the Weberian legacy suggested that it *could* be ignored, for it was deemed unimportant in social life (Catton and Dunlap 1980; Dunlap and Catton 1983). Should one violate these traditions and suggest that the physical environment *might* be relevant for understanding social behavior, one risked being labeled an "environmental determinist" (Franck 1984). While these strictures were understandable at a time when sociology was still seeking secure disciplinary status, they seemed outmoded by the 1970s. One consequence, for example, is that while for most other disciplines "the environment" refers to our physical surroundings, within sociology it typically refers to social and cultural factors external to the entity being examined.

The Human Exemptionalism Paradigm

As a result of the historical, cultural, and social context in which it developed and the unique traditions it evolved in its quest for disciplinary autonomy, sociology developed a largely implicit set of assumptions about the presumed irrelevance of the physical world for modern industrial societies. While seldom made explicit, these background assumptions influence the way in which sociologists approach their subject matter and practice their craft. As such, they appear to represent a fundamental "paradigm" or "lens" through which most sociologists view the world. [. . .]

Catton and I (1978a; 1978b; 1980) argued that these assumptions are so taken for granted that they are virtually never made explicit; yet, they clearly influence the practice of sociology and, we argued, account for our discipline's slow recognition of the significance of environmental problems. Taken together, they constitute a paradigm that is anthropocentric, technologically optimistic, and profoundly unecological. This paradigm serves to blind sociologists to the significance of environmental problems, for it suggests that humans can solve whatever problems arise and implies that *Homo sapiens* is not subject

to the ecological constraints facing other species. Indeed, the overall image of human societies portrayed by these assumptions is one that emphasizes the "exceptional" nature of our species stemming from our cultural heritage, including language, social organization, and technology. For that reason, we originally labeled them the "Human Exceptionalism Paradigm" (HEP) (Catton and Dunlap 1978a: 42–3). However, we did not wish to deny that *Homo sapiens* is an "exceptional species," but rather that our exceptional characteristics do *not* "exempt" us from ecological principles and constraints. For this reason, we subsequently renamed the HEP the "Human Exemptionalism Paradigm" (Dunlap and Catton 1979: 250).

In arguing that these assumptions constitute a sociological paradigm, Catton and I were following the lead of sociologists like Ritzer (1975: 7) who conceptualized a paradigm broadly as "a fundamental image of the subject matter" and "the broadest unit of consensus" within a discipline. In our view, the HEP created a largely consensual view among mid-twentieth-century sociologists that modern industrial societies could be understood without any consideration of their biophysical base, and therefore that environmental phenomena were irrelevant to our discipline. Although widely used by sociologists in this fashion, others have argued that such a broad conceptualization of paradigm is inconsistent with the intent of Kuhn, its progenitor (see, e.g., Eckberg and Hill 1979). Nonetheless, our conceptualization remains popular within sociology, as witness Warner's recent statement that, "[a] paradigm is a gestalt, a way of seeing the world, a representation, picture or narrative of the fundamental properties of reality" (1997: 193). As we shall see, however, differing interpretations regarding the nature of paradigms and thus their relationship to theories has been a major source of the controversy stimulated by our depiction of the HEP.

In sum, Catton and I argued that our discipline was premised on a set of background assumptions or paradigm that led most sociologists – regardless of their particular *theoretical* orientation (functionalism, Marxism, interactionism, and so on) – to "see" modern societies as being "exempt" from ecological constraints (Catton and Dunlap 1978a: 42). As part of the emphasis on the exceptional characteristics of humans, by the mid-twentieth century most sociologists were totally ignoring the biophysical environment, reflecting the implicit disciplinary consensus that it was irrelevant for understanding societal dynamics. This perspective was nicely captured in an article published in the *American Sociological Review* offering a "sociocultural theory of scarcity" in which the author argued: "If one were to ask for an expression, in a single sentence, of the main accomplishment of the social sciences to date, a fair answer would be the progressive substitution of sociocultural explanations for those stressing the determinative influence of physical nature" (Stanley 1968: 855). In the process, of course, sociologists became "sociocultural determinists"!

Given the grounding of our discipline in such an inherently unecological world-view, one that failed to recognize the ecosystem-dependence of *all* human societies, it is not surprising that sociologists were slow in paying attention to environmental problems when many other disciplines had already begun to take such problems seriously. In fact, writing at the time of the first U.S. "Earth Day," the prominent and progressive sociologist Etzioni argued that "the newly found environmental dangers are being vastly exaggerated" and that "human problems" rather than "environmental problems" should continue to receive top priority (1970: 921).

The HEP not only blinded mainstream sociologists to the importance of environmental problems, but predisposed them to accept the optimism inherent in the DWW by assuming that endless growth and progress were not threatened by resource scarcities or other ecological constraints. For example, in a wide-ranging critique of opposition to nuclear power, the influential American sociologist Nisbet (1979) viewed such opposition as a manifestation of declining "faith in progress" and went on to note that it was loss of such faith – rather than shortages of energy sources – that was the *real* threat to continued progress.

These optimistic tendencies were reinforced by sociologists' habit of seeking the causes of social change solely in terms of social phenomena, rather than acknowledging the possibility that ecological conditions *might* influence modern societies. Thus, Bell, another prominent American sociologist, dismissed the idea of "*physical* limits to growth" by assuring us "that one does not need to worry about ever running out of resources," but did acknowledge the possibility that there might be "*social* limits to growth" (1977: 18). Bell thus issued a quintessential HEP response to the "anomaly" of resource constraints by saying that *if* there were limits to the development of human societies, then they would surely be social rather than physical!

The New Ecological Paradigm

Despite the skepticism of sociologists like Nisbet and Bell and, more importantly, many sectors of society, the evidence of serious environmental problems continued to mount throughout the 1970s and has continued more or less unabated ever since. Evidence of the threats posed by local air and water pollution as well as more dispersed problems such as acid rain and ozone depletion, combined with continued energy shortages and fears of overpopulation, were seen by some sociologists as major anomalies for the HEP (and by many members of society as anomalies for the DWW) because such problems emphasized that the welfare of human societies was dependent on their biophysical environments. This awareness led some environmental sociologists to go beyond examining societal attention to environmental problems and begin analyzing more fundamental aspects of the relations between industrial societies and their environments – such as the crucial causes of environmental degradation and the societal impacts of pollution and resource scarcity (e.g., Schnaiberg 1975).

Studies of societal-environmental interactions involved rejection of the disciplinary tradition of focusing only on "social facts" as explanations of social phenomena and at least tacit rejection of the assumption that modern, industrialized societies are exempt from ecological constraints. Such work led Catton and me to argue that implicit in the emergence of environmental sociology was a set of assumptions that together constituted a worldview or paradigm that clearly challenged the inherently anthropocentric HEP. We originally labeled this alternative paradigm the "New Environmental Paradigm" (NEP) (Catton and Dunlap 1978a), but because is seeks to emphasize the ecological foundation of human societies we quickly relabeled it the "New Ecological Paradigm" (Dunlap and Catton 1979: 250).

[...]

We never intended the NEP to replace or supplant existing sociological theories, but to encourage development of ecologically oriented theories and research. While Catton and I were certainly critical of contemporary "mainstream" sociology for its staunch exemptionalist orientation, we did not mean to suggest that it was useless or irrelevant! Similarly, I now see that neither were we suggesting that theories premised on the exemptionalist paradigm would prove to be totally incommensurable with those that might be developed from the NEP.

Indeed, the *weak* interpretation of our argument is that we were simply calling for sociology to shed the blinders we labeled the "Human Exemptionalism Paradigm" (HEP) in order to recognize the significance of environmental problems. Judged by this criterion, our argument has fared pretty well. First, in ensuing years other scholars have come to compatible conclusions regarding the degree to which sociological traditions have inhibited serious concern with environmental issues (e.g., Giddens 1990; Goldblatt 1996; Redclift and Woodgate 1994). Second, our portrayal of sociology's exemptionalist orientation seems to have resonated with a number of

previously cited colleagues whose efforts to green one or more theoretical perspectives represent (in our view) superb examples of efforts to replace exemptionalism with more ecologically realistic perspectives.

Most important, however, is the growing attention to environmental issues within the larger discipline. While obviously a response to the increased salience of ecological problems and movements in societies around the world, rather than anything that environmental sociologists have written, such attention nonetheless continues to challenge our discipline's exemptionalist orientation. One need only compare current theorizing on modernization, ranging from theories of ecological modernization to reflexive modernization to risk society, with the modernization theories of two or three decades ago (see Hannigan 1995: 9–10) to see the declining credibility of exemptionalism in our discipline.

The *moderate* interpretation of our argument, and the one most consistent with my original goal of legitimating environmental sociology as a distinct area of inquiry by virtue of its focus on environmental variables, is that we were trying to justify incorporation of environmental variables or "nonsocial facts" into sociological analyses – something that our discipline's exemptionalist traditions prohibited. Like Gramling and Freudenburg (1996), I think that this has clearly been accomplished via numerous empirical investigations by environmental sociologists, such as studies of communities' experiences with toxic wastes, minorities' exposure to environmental hazards, patterns of tropical deforestation, and nations' contributions to carbon dioxide emissions (see, e.g., various chapters in Dunlap and Michelson 2002). Indeed, it is becoming common to find articles in sociology journals that employ environmental "variables" in empirical analyses, and this is not only a good indication of the declining strength of traditional "taboos" against sociological consideration of environmental phenomena, but also that a "real" environmental sociology – in the sense that I felt was required to justify creation of a new field as noted in the introduction – has indeed arrived.

For all of these reasons, despite the ambiguity and subsequent confusions surrounding Catton's and my call for replacement of our discipline's exemptionalist orientation with a more ecological one, I am pleased that our effort to define the field of environmental sociology led us to make our argument about the need for a paradigm shift. In important ways, I believe this shift is occurring, as our discipline slowly reacts to such anomalies as growing evidence of the reality of human-induced global environmental change. Phenomena such as ozone depletion and global warming, which have potentially significant consequences for the future welfare of modern, industrialized societies, clearly challenge the notion of human exemptionalism (Dunlap and Catton 1994). For this reason, I am optimistic that a more ecologically sound perspective will continue to gain strength in our discipline.

In sum, the degree to which one sees our discipline's staunch exemptionalist orientation as being challenged by the emergence of a new ecological paradigm clearly depends on one's notion of a paradigm and expectations regarding the nature of paradigm shifts. Nonetheless, it seems clear to me that sociology in general and sociological theory in particular are paying far more attention to the environment nowadays than was the case in the 1970s. The old assumptions that environmental problems are insignificant and that modern industrialized societies are not subject to ecological constraints are becoming more and more untenable, and one no longer finds prominent American sociologists defending these assumptions as was the case in the 1970s.

NOTE

1. This perspective evolved into the "social constructivist" or "constructionist" perspective that developed in areas such as social problems and sociology of science in the 1970s

and eventually gained prominence in the discipline as a whole, and became popular in environmental sociology in the 1990s (see e.g., Yearley, 1991; Hannigan 1995).

REFERENCES

Bell, D. (1977) "Are There 'Social Limits' to Growth?" In *Prospects for Growth: Changing Expectations for the Future*, ed. K. D. Wilson, 13–26. New York: Praeger.

Benton, T. (1991) "Biology and Social Science: Why the Return of the Repressed Should be Given a (Cautious) Welcome." *Sociology* 25: 1–29.

Catton, W. R., Jr., and R. E. Dunlap. (1978a) "Environmental Sociology: A New Paradigm." *The American Sociologist* 13: 41–9.
 (1978b) "Paradigms, Theories, and the Primacy of the HEP-NEP Distinction." *The American Sociologist* 13: 256–9.
 (1980) "A New Ecological Paradigm for Post-exuberant Sociology." *American Behavioral Scientist* 24: 15–47.

Choldin, H. M. (1978) "Social Life and the Physical Environment." In *Handbook of Contemporary Urban Life*, ed. D. Street. San Francisco: Jossey-Bass. 352–84.

Dunlap, R. E., and W. R. Catton Jr. (1979) "Environmental Sociology." *Annual Review of Sociology* 5: 243–73.
 (1983) "What Environmental Sociologists Have in Common (Whether Concerned with 'Built' or 'Natural' Environments)." *Sociological Inquiry* 53: 113–35.
 (1994) "Struggling with Human Exemptionalism: The Rise, Decline and Revitalization of Environmental Sociology." *The American Sociologist* 25: 5–30.

Dunlap, R. E., and W. Michelson. (eds. 2002) *Handbook of Environmental Sociology.* California: Greenwood.

Eckberg, D. L., and L. Hill Jr. (1979) "The Paradigm Concept and Sociology: A Critical Review." *American Sociological Review* 44: 925–37.

Etzioni, A. (1970) "The Wrong Top Priority." *Science* 168 (May): 921.

Franck, K. A. (1984) "Exorcising the Ghost of Physical Determinism." *Environment and Behaviour* 16: 411–35.

Giddens, A. (1990) *The Consequences of Modernity.* Stanford: Stanford University Press.

Goldblatt, D. (1996) *Social Theory and the Environment.* Boulder, Colo.: Westview.

Gramling, R., and W. R. Freudenburg. (1996) "Environmental Sociology: Toward a Paradigm for the 21st Century." *Sociological Spectrum* 16: 347–70.

Hannigan, J. A. (1995) *Environmental Sociology: A Social Constructionist Perspective.* London: Routledge.

Klausner, S. Z. (1971) *On Man in His Environment.* San Francisco: Jossey-Bass.

Nisbet, R. (1979) "The Rape of Progress." *Public Opinion* 2 (June–July): 2–6, 55.

Redclift, M., and G. Woodgate. (1994) "Sociology and the Environment: Discordant Discourse?" In *Social Theory and the Global Environment*, ed. M. Redclift and T. Benton, 51–66. London: Routledge.

Ritzer, G. (1975) *Sociology: A Multiple Paradigm Science.* Boston: Allyn and Bacon.

Schnaiberg, A. (1975) "Social Syntheses of the Societal-Environmental Dialectic: The Role of Distributional Impacts." *Social Science Quarterly* 56: 5–20.

Stanley, M. (1968) "Nature, Culture and Scarcity: Forward to a Theoretical Synthesis." *American Sociological Review* 33: 855–70.

Warner, R. S. (1997) "A Paradigm Is Not a Theory: Reply to Lechner." *The American Journal of Sociology* 103(1):192–198.

Yearley, S. (1991) *The Green Case: A Sociology of Environmental Issues, Arguments and Politics.* London: HarperCollins.

18. A Politics for Global Warming

Anthony Giddens

Almost everyone across the world must have heard the phrase 'climate change' and know at least a bit about what it means. It refers to the fact that the greenhouse gas emissions produced by modern industry are causing the earth's climate to warm up, with potentially devastating consequences for the future. Yet the vast majority are doing very little, if anything at all, to alter their daily habits, even though those habits are the source of the dangers that climate change has in store for us.

It is not as if climate change is creeping up on us unawares. On the contrary, large numbers of books have been written about it and its likely consequences. Serious worries about the warming of the earth's climate were expressed for a quarter of a century or more without making much of an impact. Within the past few years the issue has jumped to the forefront of discussion and debate, not just in this or that country but across the world. Yet, as collective humanity, we are only just beginning to take the steps needed to respond to the threats that we and succeeding generations are confronting. Global warming is a problem unlike any other, however, both because of its scale and because it is mainly about the future. Many have said that to cope with it we will need to mobilize on a level comparable to fighting a war; but in this case there are no enemies to identify and confront. We are dealing with dangers that seem abstract and elusive, however potentially devastating they may be.

No matter how much we are told about the threats, it is hard to face up to them, because they feel somehow unreal – and, in the meantime, there is a life to be lived, with all its pleasures and pressures. The politics of climate change has to cope with what I call 'Giddens's paradox'. It states that, since the dangers posed by global warming aren't tangible, immediate or visible in the course of day-to-day life, however awesome they appear, many will sit on their hands and do nothing of a concrete nature about them. Yet waiting until they become visible and acute before being stirred to serious action will, by definition, be too late.

Giddens's paradox affects almost every aspect of current reactions to climate change. It is the reason why, for many citizens, climate change is a back-of-the-mind issue rather than a front-of-the-mind one. Attitude surveys show that most of the public accept that global warming is a major threat; yet only a few are willing to alter their lives in any significant way as a result. Among elites, climate change lends itself to gestural politics – grandiose-sounding plans largely empty of content.

What social psychologists call 'future discounting' further accentuates Giddens's paradox – more accurately, one could say it is a sub-category of it. People find it hard to give the same level of reality to the future as they do to the present. Thus a small reward offered now will normally be taken in preference to a much larger one offered at some remove. The same principle applies to risks. Why do many young people take up smoking even though they are well aware that, as it now says on cigarette packets, 'smoking kills'? At least part of the reason is that, for a teenager, it is almost impossible to imagine being 40, the age at which the real dangers start to take hold and become life-threatening.

Giddens's paradox is at the centre of a range of other influences that tend to paralyse or inhibit action. Think back to the SUV. In the US, lots of people drive them, partly because, under the presidency of George W. Bush, no attempt was made to impose the taxes on gas-guzzling vehicles that some other countries have levied. The large motor-vehicle companies, not just in America but to some extent elsewhere as well, continued to pour them forth and had a vested interest in so doing. And their sales had a certain justifiable rationale. SUVs are valuable in rough terrain. People who use them in cities often do so because of a sense of style, but also because they offer more protection in accidents than smaller vehicles do. And not all SUV drivers are macho men by any means. Women sometimes drive them, because of the sense of security they provide.

People carry on driving SUVs for other reasons too. There is a high level of agreement among scientists that climate change is real and danger-ous, and that it is caused by human activity. A small minority of scientists, however – the climate change 'sceptics' – dispute these claims, and they get a good deal of attention in the media. Our driver can always say, 'it's not proven, is it?' if anyone were to suggest that he should change his profligate ways. Another response might be: 'I'm not going to change unless others do', and he could point out that some drive even bigger gas-guzzlers, like Bentleys or Ferraris. Yet another reaction could be: 'Nothing that I do, as a single individual, will make any difference'. Or else he could say, 'I'll get round to it sometime', because one shouldn't underestimate the sheer force of habit. I would suggest that even the most sophis-ticated and determined environmentalist – who owns no car at all – struggles with the fact that, under the shadow of future cataclysm, there is a life to be lived within the constraints of the here-and-now.

[. . .]

I want to make the somewhat startling assertion that, at present, *we have no politics of climate change*. In other words, we do not have a devel-oped analysis of the political innovations that have to be made if our aspirations to limit global warming are to become real. It is a strange and indefensible absence, which I have written this book to try to repair. My approach is grounded in realism. There are many who say that coping with climate change is too difficult a problem to be dealt with within the confines of orthodox politics. Up to a point I agree with them, since quite profound changes will be required in our established ways of political thinking. Yet we have to work with the institutions that already exist and in ways that respect parliamentary democracy.

[. . .]

I don't want to sound panglossian. Quite to the contrary – some policies will have to have a hard edge to them; many will be unpopular and actively resisted. Powerful interests often stand in the way of reform and have to be faced down. My point is that even hard-edged constraints, if handled properly, can – and in fact almost always do – generate new opportunities. We can anticipate, and should do our best to encourage, a surge of technological innovation in response to both climate change and energy security. Without such innovation, it is impossible to see how we can break our dependency upon oil, gas and coal, the major sources of environmental pollution. A turn to renewable sources of energy is essential, and it has to be on a very large scale. Yet research shows that technological change can take years to per-colate through the whole economy and society. No quick fix is available to deal with the problems we face – it's going to be a slog, even with the breakthroughs we need, and in fact must have.

The prize is huge. There is another world waiting for us out there if we can find our way to it. It is one where not only climate change has been held at bay, but where oil has lost its capacity to determine the shape of world politics.

Summarizing some of the key themes I discuss in the book, my advice to policy-makers would be as follows:

1 Promote political and economic convergence wherever possible and do so in an active way. It is important, for example, to cultivate an advance guard of entrepreneurs who will maximize the economic advantages of enlightened environmental policy. Work with what I call climate change positives – as has aptly been said, Martin Luther King didn't stir people to action by proclaiming, 'I have a nightmare!' Fear and anxiety are not necessarily good motivators, especially with risks perceived as abstract ones, or dangers that are seen as some way off. Moreover, the risks from climate change, as the public experiences them, constitute only one set of worries among others.

2 Look first and foremost to embed a concern with climate change into people's everyday lives, while recognizing the formidable problems involved in doing so. Indirect means may sometimes be the best way. For instance, the public may be more responsive to a drive for energy efficiency than to warnings about the dangers of climate change. Don't wrangle too much about targets. What matters at this point is the how of climate change policy. Plan ahead, but remember that the short term is the key to the long term. Target-setting can be an excuse for inaction rather than the reverse. Don't place too much faith in carbon markets. The point is not only that their level of likely success at present is difficult to evaluate, but that they can easily become a political cop-out. They sound painless even if they are not. Carbon taxes are the way to go, but they must not be introduced piecemeal. A full-scale audit of the fiscal system is needed.

3 Avoid making political capital out of global warming. The temptation to do so may be great, especially when a government or party is under pressure. If possible, establish an agreement with major party rivals to ensure continuity of climate change policy. Feed a concern with climate change through all branches of government and work to produce consistency in different political areas. It is no good introducing progressive environmental policies and then subverting them through decisions taken elsewhere. Don't neglect issues of social justice. Poorer people are more likely to be affected by the consequences of changes affecting the climate unless policy is specifically directed to countering those influences.

4 Set up detailed risk assessment procedures, stretching into the long term, since the implications of climate change policy are complex. We have to construct a future in which renewable sources will comprise the bulk of energy use. It will be a far-reaching transition indeed, with a whole raft of complex social and economic effects. Cooperate with other countries, regions or cities in an intensive and continuing way, with as wide a global spread as possible. Season policy with a dash of utopian thinking. Why? Because, however it happens, we are working our way towards a form of society that eventually will be quite different from the one in which we live today. We have to chance our arm.

[. . .]

We should discard the precautionary principle and the concept of sustainable development. The first should be replaced by more sophisticated modes of risk analysis, as discussed at many points in the book. The second is something of an oxymoron, and it seems most sensible to disentangle the two component terms again. In the case of 'development', we should focus on the contrast between the developed and developing societies. In so far as the rich countries are concerned, the problems created by affluence have to be put alongside the benefits of economic growth. I shall argue that dealing with these problems proves to be of direct relevance to the politics of climate change.

Below, I propose a list of concepts [. . .] They mostly concern how to analyse and promote climate change policy in the context of political institutions. From the preceding discussion, I take the notions of 'sustainability' and 'the polluter pays'. The other concepts are:

1 The *ensuring state*. I talk about the state a lot in this book, both in the sense of the institutions of government and in the sense of the nation-state, but I don't want readers to get the wrong idea. I don't mean to go back to the old idea of the state as a top-down agency. The state today has to be an 'enabling state': its prime role is to help energize a diversity of groups to reach solutions to collective problems, many such groups operating in a bottom-up fashion. However, the concept of the enabling state isn't strong enough to capture the state's role, which also has to be to deliver outcomes. Nowhere is this principle clearer than in the case of responding to climate change. The ensuring state is a stronger notion. It means that the state is responsible for monitoring public goals and for trying to make sure they are realized in a visible and acceptable fashion.

2 *Political convergence*. This idea refers to the degree to which policies relevant to mitigating climate change overlap positively with other areas of public policy, such that each can be used to gain traction over the other. Political convergence is likely to be crucial to how far we can effectively respond to global warming; being abstract, and concerning mostly future dangers, global warming tends all too easily to give way to more everyday concerns in people's minds. Some of the most important areas of political convergence are energy security and energy planning, technological innovation, lifestyle politics and the downside of affluence, as just discussed. The largest and most promising convergence is between climate change policy and an orientation to welfare going well beyond GDP. For instance, the car is supposed to confer freedom and mobility, but can lead to the opposite – being stuck in traffic jams. Reducing congestion by upgrading public transport and other measures responds to this issue, and is also a positive gain for reducing CO_2 emissions.

3 *Economic convergence*. This notion refers to the overlap between low-carbon technologies, forms of business practice and lifestyles with economic competitiveness. Again, it will have a fundamental impact upon our efforts to contain global warming. Economic convergence has some similarities to what has been called 'ecological modernization' – the idea that environmentally progressive policies often coincide with what is good for the economy and for wider political goals. Ecological modernization has been defined as 'a partnership in which governments, businesses, moderate environmentalists, and scientists co-operate in the restructuring of the capitalist political economy along more environmentally defensible lines'.[1] At the time when it was first mooted, in the mid-1980s, the concept of ecological modernization marked an important step forward in the environmental literature, and a major deviation from green orthodoxy. The authors who introduced it distanced themselves from the pessimism of the 'limits to development' literature, and also from those in the green movement who set themselves against modernity and, to some extent, against science and technology more generally.[2] The basic thesis was that environmental issues (not just climate change) could best be dealt with by being normalized – by drawing them into the existing framework of social economic institutions, rather than contesting those institutions as many greens chose to do. A strong emphasis was placed on the role of science and technology in generating solutions to environmental difficulties, including in coping with the problem of diminishing world resources. However, 'modernization' also included reforming governmental institutions and markets with environmental

goals in mind; and it attributed an important role to civil society groups in keeping both the state and business on the right track. I have no quarrel with any of these emphases and am therefore in general a supporter of the ecological modernization approach. Valid criticisms have been made of it, however, at least in its original formulations. It seemed as though we could have the best of all worlds. Yet while I am strongly in favour of a win–win approach to climate change policy, we must at the same time recognize the compromises that have to be made and the difficult decisions that have to be negotiated. It is also a mistake, as I have said, to assume that growth is an unalloyed benefit, especially in the more developed countries.

4   *Foregrounding.* Given its potentially cataclysmic implications, we need global warming to be a front-of-the-mind issue; however, both in the political sphere and in the minds of citizens, it all too readily becomes a back-of-the-mind one. Foregrounding refers to the use of the various political devices that can be deployed to keep global warming at the core of the political agenda.

5   *Climate change positives.* It won't be possible to mobilize effectively against global warming simply on the basis of the avoidance of future dangers – that is, in a wholly negative way. We will need some more positive goals to aim for. I believe these can come mainly from areas of political and economic convergence. Climate change policy involves thinking in the long term, and it involves an emphasis on the 'durable' rather than the ephemeral. I shall try to show that these concerns overlap significantly with well-being, rather than with sheer economic growth.

6   *Political transcendence.* Responding to climate change must not be seen as a left–right issue. Climate change has to be a question that largely transcends party politics, and about which there is an overall framework of agreement that will endure across changes of government. I have never agreed with the idea that the political centre – where the parties converge – is the antithesis of radicalism. Sometimes overall political agreement is the condition of radical policy-making, and coping with climate change certainly falls into that category.

7   *The percentage principle.* This concept marks the recognition that no course of action (or inaction) is without risks; and that, consequently, there is always a balance of risks and opportunities to be considered in any policy context.

8   *The development imperative.* Poorer countries must have the right to develop economically, even if this process involves a significant growth in greenhouse gas emissions.

9   *Overdevelopment.* In the rich countries, affluence itself produces a range of quite profound social problems. Economic growth correlates with measures of welfare only up to a certain level; after that point, the connection becomes more problematic. Addressing problems of overdevelopment forms a major area of political convergence with policies relevant to controlling climate change.

10 *Proactive adaptation.* Given that climate change will happen whatever we do from now onwards, a politics of adaptation will have to be worked out alongside that of climate change mitigation. We must as far as possible prepare beforehand in a pre-emptive fashion, basing what we do upon risk assessment, with policies evolving as scientific information shifts and matures.

NOTES

1. John Dryzek, *The Politics of the Earth* (Oxford: Oxford University Press, 1997), p. 145.
2. See Arthur Mol and David Sonnenfeld, *Ecological Modernisation Around the World* (London: Cass, 2000).

Theme 3 – Further Reading

On cities and urban sociology, Mike Savage, Alan Warde and Kevin Ward's (2002) *Urban Sociology, Capitalism and Modernity* (Basingstoke: Palgrave Macmillan) is an excellent introduction. Along with this, try Phil Hubbard's (2006) *The City* (London: Routledge) which introduces all the key debates in a readable style. For something rather more challenging, no student of urban sociology should miss Marshall Berman's classic from 1983, *All that is Solid Melts into Air: The Experience of Modernity* (London: Verso) which is an inspiring book. Philip W. Sutton's (2007) *The Environment: A Sociological Introduction* (Cambridge: Polity) is exactly what you would expect it to be. Alan Irwin's (2001) *Sociology and the Environment: A Critical Introduction to Society, Nature and Knowledge* (Cambridge: Polity) makes excellent use of case studies as does John Hannigan's (2006) *Environmental Sociology: A Social Constructionist Perspective, second edition* (London: Routledge), though the latter is rooted in a specifically constructionist approach.

Giddens and Sutton *Sociology 7th Edition* (2013)

Chapters 5 and 6 are designed to complement each other and contain all the major issues. However, you will find relevant material in Chapter 3 on risk and environment, pages 101–4; Chapter 4 on urbanization, pages 117–24; Chapter 14 on population growth, pages 589–94 and Chapter 22 on social movements (including green movements), pages 994–1002.

Part 4 Institutions and Organizations

While some sociologists focus primarily on social structures and others concentrate on individual actions, one way of combining both is to study the social institutions and organizations which help to shape people's lives but are also changed by them over time. Social institutions in modern, industrial societies include the family, religion, education, work and the economy. Organizations are those collective enterprises which exist for specific purposes, such as churches, schools and business corporations. Studying institutions and organizations can often be the key to understanding cultural differences and in a period of rapid globalization, can also help us appreciate the similarities and so-called 'cultural universals' – aspects of social life that are common to most societies.

Many scholars of globalization tend to see the process as an essentially economic one linked to the spread of capitalistic enterprise outwards from the West. It is certainly true that capitalism has expanded across the globe in a relatively short historical period, though the specific form it takes differs according to national and regional contexts. But what exactly is capitalism and when did it begin? Is it the product of simple human greed? Is its success down to the basic self-interestedness of human nature? For the German social scientist Max Weber, capitalism is none of these things. What Weber set out to explain is why this rational form of capitalism originated only in the West. Reading 19 gives a flavour of Weber's classic study of the inti-mate connection between the 'spirit' of capitalism and the ethical dimension of puritan Protestantism. For Weber, the roots of modern capitalism do not lie in human nature or simple greed, but stem from religious adherents' response to certain tenets of their Protestant belief system. Nor is capitalism a relentless quest for material goods and money, rather the 'spirit' of capitalism lies in the rational and systematic pursuit of business success and ever increasing profit.

While Weber's studies of the world religions aimed to grasp the links between economy and society, Emile Durkheim sought answers to fundamental questions – what is religion and what is it for? Religions are incredibly diverse but do they have something essential in common? In Reading 20, Durkheim sets out the logic underpinning his sociological approach to these issues. To get behind all of the confusing, complex and very different belief systems of religion in the world, it is necessary to find a religion that is relatively simple. Such a religion may offer easier access to the fundamental or elementary forms of the religious life itself. Durkheim claimed to find this in the Aboriginal totemic form of religion and proceeded to analyse its beliefs and practices in a sociological way. His conclusion remains both striking and controversial. Religion is necessary and functional for human societies, not because it offers realistic or 'true' answers to the mysteries of the universe, but because it brings together communities of worshippers and constantly re-creates the social bond and thus strengthens social solidarity. Even in a secular world where the traditional religions are no longer dominant, some form of religion is still necessary. The old gods may be dead, but new ones will have to be found.

One social institution that has generated an enormous amount of research in sociology is the family. Initial studies sought to explain what functions the family performs for individuals, groups and society as a whole, culminating in Talcott Parsons's argument that families socialize new members of society, inculcating basic values and stabilizing adult personalities. While this perspective appeared to fit the situation in Western societies of the 1940s and 1950s, a series of developments cast doubt on the validity of the thesis as well as its proposed universal application. The emergence of multicultural societies, a recognition of the diversity of family forms, increasing acceptance of homosexual relationships and feminist research which shone a light on the dark side of family life, such as domestic violence and the sexual abuse of children, combined to render functionalist views of the family outdated. Instead wider historical and cross-cultural studies of family forms were required that were also grounded in solid empirical findings. In Reading 21, Göran Therborn tries to do exactly that. His analysis of families across the world and over time is a bold attempt to grasp both similarity and difference in the organization of the family. In doing so he constructs a productive framework for the cross-cultural study of families and their relationship to the societies in which they are embedded.

Emile Durkheim's election to the first Professorship of Sociology at the Sorbonne in Paris in 1912 is well known, but in fact the title he held was Professor of Education and Sociology. Durkheim saw a close relationship between the two, with sociology helping to produce an educated citizenry for a democratic France. The sociology of education is one of the more established fields of enquiry within the discipline. One of the more provocative findings from several influential research studies is that there exists in schools a 'hidden curriculum', an informal process of learning which is outside of formal classroom lessons. Marxists such as Bowles and Gintis (1976) saw the hidden curriculum as important for capitalism, training young people to accept work discipline and to bow to authority figures. Ivan Illich (1971) offered a similar analysis, pointing out that compulsory schooling dulled the creative energies of young people, binding them into an exploitative society. His solution was radical – the 'deschooling' of society in favour of diverse educational arrangements. Reading 22 follows this line of argument and is all the more forcefully presented as the author was a teacher for more than thirty years. John Taylor Gatto presents an insider's view of schooling in a compulsory education system, pointing out the unwritten aspects of his job. Of course, the broader issue is whether the benefits of the schooling system outweigh its hidden or unstated assumptions.

Our final institution in this section is work. Many, if not most, people assume that the main purpose of education is to make sure students have the skills and abilities needed to find suitable jobs in the formal economy. As illustrated above, this view is of course open to challenge. Nonetheless, work and the making of livings takes up a large part of all our lives. The Industrial Revolution altered work forever, moving people away from agrarian lifestyles and into urban centres with factories, workshops and offices. Since the late 1960s, sociologists have theorized a shift away from manufacturing towards services and in most advanced industrial economies, a majority of people now make their living in education, social and health care, finance and other service occupations. In Reading 23, Alan S. Blinder makes a provocative argument for yet another revolution in work based on the principle of 'offshoring'. He suggests that the very common practice of 'outsourcing' or 'subcontracting' is undergoing a revolutionary change as even service sector work starts to be moved offshore to take advantage of cheaper labour and weaker regulation. A simple example is the transformation of financial services through computerized records enabling overseas call centres to deal with our personal banking needs. But Blinder argues that there are many, many more types of service work which could just as easily be 'offshored' in this way.

The big question this raises is, in the absence of manufacturing and agricultural jobs in the developed societies, just what will the workers of the future actually do to make their livings?

REFERENCES

Bowles, S. and Gintis, H. (1976), *Schooling in Capitalist America* (London: Routledge & Kegan Paul).

Illich, I. (1971), *Deschooling Society* (New York: Harper and Row).

19. The Spirit of Capitalism

Max Weber

The impulse to acquisition, pursuit of gain, of money, of the greatest possible amount of money, has in itself nothing to do with capitalism. This impulse exists and has existed among waiters, physicians, coachmen, artists, prostitutes, dishonest officials, soldiers, nobles, crusaders, gamblers, and beggars. One may say that it has been common to all sorts and conditions of men at all times and in all countries of the earth, wherever the objective possibility of it is or has been given. It should be taught in the kindergarten of cultural history that this naïve idea of capitalism must be given up once and for all. Unlimited greed for gain is not in the least identical with capitalism, and is still less its spirit. Capitalism *may* even be identical with the restraint, or at least a rational tempering, of this irrational impulse. But capitalism is identical with the pursuit of profit, and forever *renewed* profit, by means of continuous, rational, capitalistic enterprise. For it must be so: in a wholly capitalistic order of society, an individual capitalistic enterprise which did not take advantage of its opportunities for profit-making would be doomed to extinction.

[. . .]

In modern times the Occident has developed, in addition to this, a very different form of capitalism which has appeared nowhere else: the rational capitalistic organization of (formally) free labour. Only suggestions of it are found elsewhere. Even the organization of unfree labour reached a considerable degree of rationality only on plantations and to a very limited extent in the *Ergasteria* of antiquity. In the manors, manorial workshops, and domestic industries on estates with serf labour it was probably somewhat less developed. Even real domestic industries with free labour have definitely been proved to have existed in only a few isolated cases outside the Occident. The frequent use of day labourers led in a very few cases – especially State monopolies, which are, however, very different from modern industrial organization – to manufacturing organizations, but never to a rational organization of apprenticeship in the handicrafts like that of our Middle Ages.

Rational industrial organization, attuned to a regular market, and neither to political nor irrationally speculative opportunities for profit, is not, however, the only peculiarity of Western capitalism. The modern rational organization of the capitalistic enterprise would not have been possible without two other important factors in its development: the separation of business from the household, which completely dominates modern economic life, and closely connected with it, rational book-keeping. A spatial separation of places of work from those of residence exists elsewhere, as in the Oriental bazaar and in the *ergasteria* of other cultures. The development of capitalistic associations with their own accounts is also found in the Far East, the Near East, and in antiquity. But compared to the modern independence of business enterprises, those are only small beginnings. The reason for this was particularly that the indispensable requisites for this independence, our rational business book-keeping and our legal separation of corporate from personal property, were entirely lacking, or had only begun to develop.

[. . .]

On the side of the production of private wealth, asceticism condemned both dishonesty and impulsive avarice. What was condemned as covet-ousness, Mammonism, etc., was the pursuit of riches for their own sake. For wealth in itself was a temptation. But here asceticism was the power 'which ever seeks the good but ever creates evil'[1]; what was evil in its sense was possession and its temptations. For, in conformity with the Old Testament and in analogy to the ethical valuation of good works, asceticism looked upon the pursuit of wealth as an end in itself as highly reprehensible; but the attainment of it as a fruit of labour in a calling was a sign of God's blessing. And even more important: the religious valuation of restless, continuous, systematic work in a worldly calling, as the highest means to asceticism, and at the same time the surest and most evident proof of rebirth and genuine faith, must have been the most powerful conceivable lever for the expansion of that attitude toward life which we have here called the spirit of capitalism.[2]

When the limitation of consumption is combined with this release of acquisitive activity, the inevitable practical result is obvious: accumulation of capital through ascetic compulsion to save. The restraints which were imposed upon the consumption of wealth naturally served to increase it by making possible the productive investment of capital. How strong this influence was is not, unfortunately, susceptible of exact statistical demonstration.

[. . .]

One of the fundamental elements of the spirit of modern capitalism, and not only of that but of all modern culture: rational conduct on the basis of the idea of the calling, was born – that is what this discussion has sought to demonstrate – from the spirit of Christian asceticism.

[. . .]

The Puritan wanted to work in a calling; we are forced to do so. For when asceticism was carried out of monastic cells into everyday life, and began to dominate worldly morality, it did its part in building the tremendous cosmos of the modern economic order. This order is now bound to the technical and economic conditions of machine production which today determine the lives of all the individuals who are born into this mechanism, not only those directly concerned with economic acquisition, with irresistible force. Perhaps it will so determine them until the last ton of fossilized coal is burnt. In Baxter's view the care for external goods should only lie on the shoulders of the 'saint like a light cloak, which can be thrown aside at any moment'.[3] But fate decreed that the cloak should become an iron cage.

Since asceticism undertook to remodel the world and to work out its ideals in the world, material goods have gained an increasing and finally an inexorable power over the lives of men as at no previous period in history. Today the spirit of religious asceticism – whether finally, who knows? – has escaped from the cage. But victorious capitalism, since it rests on mechanical foundations, needs its support no longer. The rosy blush of its laughing heir, the Enlightenment, seems also to be irretrievably fading, and the idea of duty in one's calling prowls about in our lives like the ghost of dead religious beliefs. Where the fulfilment of the calling cannot directly be related to the highest spiritual and cultural values, or when, on the other hand, it need not be felt simply as economic compulsion, the individual generally abandons the attempt to justify it at all. In the field of its highest development, in the United States, the pursuit of wealth, stripped of its religious and ethical meaning, tends to become associated with purely mundane passions, which often actually give it the character of sport.[4]

No one knows who will live in this cage in the future, or whether at the end of this tremendous development entirely new prophets will arise, or there will be a great rebirth of old ideas and ideals, or, if neither, mechanized petrification, embellished with a sort of convulsive self-importance. For of the last stage of this cultural development, it might well be truly said: 'Specialists without spirit, sensualists without heart; this nullity imagines that it has attained a level of civilization never before achieved.'

NOTES

1. Adapted by Weber from Faust, Act I. Goethe there depicts Mephistopheles as 'Die Kraft, die stets das Böse will, und stets das Gute schafft.' Translator's Note.

2. It has already been remarked that we cannot here enter into the question of the class relations of these religious movements. In order to see, however, that for example Baxter, of whom we make so much use in this study, did not see things solely as a bourgeois of his time, it will suffice to recall that even for him in the order of the religious value of callings, after the learned professions comes the husband-man, and only then mariners, clothiers, booksellers, tailors, etc. Also, under mariners (characteristically enough) he probably thinks at least as often of fishermen as of shipowners. In this regard several things in the *Talmud* are in a different class. Compare, for instance, in Wünsche, *Babyl Talmud*, II, pp. 20, 21, the sayings of Rabbi Eleasar, which though not unchallenged, all content in effect that business is better than agriculture.

3. Baxter, R. (1829) *The Saints' Everlasting Rest.* London: Fisher, Son and Jackson chap. xii.

4. 'Couldn't the old man be satisfied with his $75,000 a year and rest? No! The frontage of the store must be widened to 400 feet. Why? That beats everything, he says. In the evening when his wife and daughter read together, he wants to go to bed. Sundays he looks at the clock every five minutes to see when the day will be over – what a futile life!' In these terms the son-in-law (who had emigrated from Germany) of the leading dry-goods man of an Ohio city expressed his judgement which would undoubtedly have seemed simply incomprehensible to the old man. A symptom of German lack of energy.

20. The Essence of Religion

Emile Durkheim

The really religious beliefs are always common to a determined group, which makes profession of adhering to them and of practising the rites connected with them. They are not merely received individually by all the members of this group; they are something belonging to the group, and they make its unity. The individuals which compose it feel themselves united to each other by the simple fact that they have a common faith. A society whose members are united by the fact that they think in the same way in regard to the sacred world and its relations with the profane world, and by the fact that they translate these common ideas into common practices, is what is called a Church. In all history, we do not find a single religion without a Church. Sometimes the Church is strictly national, sometimes it passes the frontiers, sometimes it embraces an entire people (Rome, Athens, the Hebrews), sometimes it embraces only a part of them (the Christian societies since the advent of Protestantism), sometimes it is directed by a corps of priests, sometimes it is almost completely devoid of any official directing body.[1] But wherever we observe the religious life, we find that it has a definite group as its foundation. Even the so-called private cults, such as the domestic cult or the cult of a corporation, satisfy this condition; for they are always celebrated by a group, the family or the corporation. Moreover, even these particular religions are ordinarily only special forms of a more general religion which embraces all,[2] these restricted Churches are in reality only chapels of a vaster Church which, by reason of this very extent, merits this name still more.[3]

It is quite another matter with magic. To be sure, the belief in magic is always more or less general, it is very frequently diffused in large masses of the population, and there are even peoples where it has as many adherents as the real religion. But it does not result in binding together those who adhere to it, nor in uniting them into a group leading a common life. *There is no Church of magic.* Between the magician and the individuals who consult him, as between these individuals themselves, there are no lasting bonds which make them members of the same moral community, comparable to that formed by the believers in the same god or the observers of the same cult. The magician has a clientele and not a Church, and it is very possible that his clients have no other relations between each other, or even do not know each other; even the relations which they have with him are generally accidental and transient; they are just like those of a sick man with his physician. The official and public character with which he is sometimes invested changes nothing in this situation; the fact that he works openly does not unite him more regularly or more durably to those who have recourse to his services.

It is true that in certain cases, magicians form societies among themselves; it happens that they assemble more or less periodically to celebrate certain rites in common; it is well known what a place these assemblies of witches hold in European folk-lore. But it is to be remarked that these associations are in no way indispensable to the working of the magic; they are even rare and rather exceptional. The magician has no need of uniting himself to his fellows to practise his art. More frequently, he is a recluse: in general, far from seeking society, he flees it. 'Even in regard to his colleagues, he always keeps his personal independence.'[4] Religion, on the other hand, is inseparable from the idea of a Church. From this point of view, there is an essential difference between magic and religion. But what is especially important is that when these societies of magic are formed, they do not include all the adherents to magic, but only the magicians; the laymen, if they may be so called, that is to say, those for whose profit the rites are celebrated, *in fine*, those who represent the worshippers in the regular cults, are excluded. Now the magician is for magic what the priest is for religion, but a college of priests is not a Church, any more than a religious congregation which should devote itself to some particular saint in the shadow of a cloister, would be a particular cult. A Church is not a fraternity of priests; it is a moral community formed by all the believers in a single faith, laymen as well as priests. But magic lacks any such community.[5]

But if the idea of a Church is made to enter into the definition of religion, does that not exclude the private religions which the individual establishes for himself and celebrates by himself? There is scarcely a society where these are not found. Every Ojibway, as we shall see below, has his own personal *manitou*, which he chooses himself and to which he renders special religious services: the Melanesian of the Banks Islands has his *tamaniu*;[6] the Roman, his *genius*;[7] the Christian, his patron saint and guardian angel, etc. By definition all these cults seem to be independent of all idea of the group. Not only are these individual religions very frequent in history, but nowadays many are asking if they are not destined to be the pre-eminent form of the religious life, and if the day will not come when there will be no other cult than that which each man will freely perform within himself.[8]

But if we leave these speculations in regard to the future aside for the moment, and confine ourselves to religions such as they are at present or have been in the past, it becomes clearly evident that these individual cults are not distinct and autonomous religious systems, but merely aspects of the common religion of the whole Church, or which the individuals are members. The patron saint of the Christian is chosen from the official list of saints recognized by the Catholic Church; there are even canonical rules prescribing how each Catholic should perform this private cult. In the same way, the idea that each man necessarily has a protecting genius is found, under different forms, at the basis of a great number of American religions, as well as of the Roman religion (to cite only these two examples), for, as will be seen later, it is very closely connected with the idea of the soul, and this idea of the soul is not one of those which can be left entirely to individual choice. In a word, it is the Church of which he is a member which teaches the individual what these personal gods are, what their function is, how he should enter into relations with them and how he should honour them. When a methodical analysis is made of the doctrines of any Church whatsoever, sooner or later we come upon those concerning private cults. So these are not two religions of different types, and turned in opposite directions, both are made up of the same ideas and the same principles, here applied to circumstances which are of interest to the group as a whole, there to the life of the individual. This solidarity is even so close that among certain peoples,[9] the ceremonies by which the faithful first enter into communication with their protecting geniuses are mixed with rites whose public character is incontestable, namely the rites of initiation.[10]

There still remain those contemporary aspirations towards a religion which would consist entirely in internal and subjective states, and which would be constructed freely by each of us. But howsoever real these aspirations may be, they cannot affect our definition, for this is to be applied only to facts already realized, and not to uncertain possibilities. One can define religions such as they are, or such as they have been, but not such as they more or less vaguely tend to become. It is possible that this religious individualism is destined to be realized in facts, but before we can say just how far this may be the case, we must first know what religion is, of what elements it is made up, from what causes it results, and what function it fulfils – all questions whose solution cannot be foreseen before the threshold of our study has been passed. It is only at the close of this study that we can attempt to anticipate the future.

Thus we arrive at the following definition: *A religion as a unified system of beliefs and practices relative to sacred things, that is to say, things set apart and forbidden – beliefs and practices which unite, into one single moral community called a Church, all those who adhere to them.* The second element which thus finds a place in our definition is no less essential than the first; for by showing that the idea of religion is inseparable from that of the Church, it makes it clear that religion should be an eminently collective thing.[11]

[. . .]

The theorists who have undertaken to explain religion in rational terms have generally seen in it before all else a system of ideas, corresponding to some determined object. This object has been conceived in a multitude of ways: nature, the infinite, the unknowable, the ideal, etc.; but these differences matter but little. In any case, it was the conceptions and beliefs which were considered as the essential elements of religion. As for the rites, from this point of view they appear to be only an external translation, contingent and material, of these internal states which alone pass as having any intrinsic value. This conception is so commonly held that generally the disputes of which religion is the theme turn about the question whether it can conciliate itself with science or not, that is to say, whether or not there is a place beside our scientific knowledge for another form of thought which would be specifically religious.

But the believers, the men who lead the religious life and have a direct sensation of what it really is, object to this way of regarding it, saying that it does not correspond to their daily experience. In fact, they feel that the real function of religion is not to make us think, to enrich our knowledge, nor to add to the conceptions which we owe to science others of another origin and another character, but rather, it is to make us act, to aid us to live. The believer who has communicated with his god is not merely a man who sees new truths of which the unbeliever is ignorant; he is a man who is *stronger*. He feels within him more force, either to endure the trials of existence, or to conquer them. It is as though he were raised above the miseries of the world, because he is raised above his condition as a mere man; he believes that he is saved from evil, under whatever form he may conceive this evil. The first article in every creed is the belief in salvation by faith. But it is hard to see how a mere idea could have this efficacy. An idea is in reality only a part of ourselves; then how could it confer upon us powers superior to those which we have of our own nature? Howsoever rich it might be in affective virtues, it could add nothing to our natural vitality; for it could only release the motive powers which are within us, neither creating them nor increasing them. From the mere fact that we consider an object worthy of being loved and sought after, it does not follow that we feel ourselves stronger afterwards; it is also necessary that this object set free energies superior to those which we ordinarily have at our command and also that we have some means of making these enter into us and unite themselves to our interior lives. Now for that, it is not enough that we think of them; it is also indispensable that we place ourselves within their sphere of action, and that we set ourselves where we may best feel their influence; in a word, it is necessary that we act, and that we repeat the acts thus necessary every time we feel the need of renewing their effects. From this point of view, it is readily seen how that group of regularly repeated acts which form the cult get their importance. In fact, whoever has really practised a religion knows very well that it is the cult which gives rise to these impressions of joy, of interior peace, of serenity, of enthusiasm which are, for the believer, an experimental proof of his beliefs. The cult is not simply a system of signs by which the faith is outwardly translated; it is a collection of the means by which this is created and recreated periodically. Whether it consists in material acts or mental operations, it is always this which is efficacious.

Our entire study rests upon this postulate that the unanimous sentiment of the believers of all times cannot be purely illusory. Together with a recent apologist of the faith[12] we admit that these religious beliefs rest upon a specific experience whose demonstrative value is, in one sense, not one bit inferior to that of scientific experiments, though different from them. We, too, think that 'a tree is known by its fruits',[13] and that fertility is the best proof of what the roots are worth. But from the fact that a 'religious experience', if we choose to call it this, does exist and that it has a certain foundation – and, by the way, is there any experience which has none? – it does not follow that the reality which is its foundation conforms objectively to the idea which believers have of it. The very fact that the fashion in which it has been conceived has varied infinitely in different times is enough to prove that none of these conceptions express it adequately. If a scientist states it as an axiom that the sensations of heat and light which we feel correspond to some objective cause, he does not conclude that this is what it appears to the senses to be. Likewise, even if the impressions which the faithful feel are not imaginary, still they are in no way privileged intuitions; there is no reason for believing that they inform us better upon the nature of their object than do ordinary sensations upon the nature of bodies and their properties. In order to discover what this object consists of, we must submit them to an examination and elaboration analogous to that which has substituted for the sensuous idea of the world another which is scientific and conceptual.

This is precisely what we have tried to do, and we have seen that this reality, which mythologies have represented under so many different forms, but which is the universal and eternal objective cause of these sensations *sui generis* out of which religious experience is made, is society. We have

shown what moral forces it develops and how it awakens this sentiment of a refuge, of a shield and of a guardian support which attaches the believer to his cult. It is that which raises him outside himself; it is even that which made him. For that which makes a man is the totality of the intellectual property which constitutes civilization, and civilization is the work of society. Thus is explained the preponderating role of the cult in all religions, whichever they may be. This is because society cannot make its influence felt unless it is in action, and it is not in action unless the individuals who compose it are assembled together and act in common. It is by common action that it takes consciousness of itself and realizes its position, it is before all else an active co-operation. The collective ideas and sentiments are even possible only owing to these exterior movements which symbolize them, as we have established. Then it is action which dominates the religious life, because of the mere fact that it is society which is its source.

[. . .]

If religion has given birth to all that is essential in society, it is because the idea of society is the soul of religion.

Religious forces are therefore human forces, moral forces. It is true that since collective sentiments can become conscious of themselves only by fixing themselves upon external objects, they have not been able to take form without adopting some of their characteristics from other things: they have thus acquired a sort of physical nature; in this way they have come to mix themselves with the life of the material world, and then have considered themselves capable of explaining what passes there. But when they are considered only from this point of view and in this role, only their most superficial aspect is seen. In reality, the essential elements of which these collective sentiments are made have been borrowed by the understanding. It ordinarily seems that they should have a human character only when they are conceived under human forms;[14] but even the most impersonal and the most anonymous are nothing else than objectified sentiments.

It is only by regarding religion from this angle that it is possible to see its real significance. If we stick closely to appearances, rites often give the effect of purely manual operations: they are anointings, washings, meals. To consecrate something, it is put in contact with a source of religious energy, just as today a body is put in contact with a source of heat or electricity to warm or electrize it; the two processes employed are not essentially different. Thus understood, religious technique seems to be a sort of mystic mechanics. But these material manoeuvres are only the external envelope under which the mental operations are hidden. Finally, there is no question of exercising a physical constraint upon blind and, incidentally, imaginary forces, but rather of reaching individual consciousnesses, of giving them a direction and of disciplining them. It is sometimes said that inferior religions are materialistic. Such an expression is inexact. All religions, even the crudest, are in a sense spiritualistic: for the powers they put in play are before all spiritual, and also their principal object is to act upon the moral life. Thus it is seen that whatever has been done in the name of religion cannot have been done in vain for it is necessarily the society that did it, and it is humanity that has reaped the fruits.

[. . .]

Thus there is something eternal in religion which is destined to survive all the particular symbols in which religious thought has successively enveloped itself. There can be no society which does not feel the need of upholding and reaffirming at regular intervals the collective sentiments and the collective ideas which make its unity and its personality. Now this moral remaking cannot be achieved except by the means of reunions, assemblies and meetings where the individuals, being closely united to one another, reaffirm in common their common sentiments; hence come ceremonies which do not differ from regular religious ceremonies, either in their object, the

results which they produce, or the processes employed to attain these results. What essential difference is there between an assembly of Christians celebrating the principal dates of the life of Christ, or of Jews remembering the exodus from Egypt or the promulgation of the decalogue, and a reunion of citizens commemorating the promulgation of a new moral or legal system or some great event in the national life?

If we find a little difficulty today in imagining what these feasts and ceremonies of the future could consist in, it is because we are going through a stage of transition and moral mediocrity. The great things of the past which filled our fathers with enthusiasm do not excite the same ardour in us, either because they have come into common usage to such an extent that we are unconscious of them, or else because they no longer answer to our actual aspirations, but as yet there is nothing to replace them. We can no longer impassionate ourselves for the principles in the name of which Christianity recommended to masters that they treat their slaves humanely, and, on the other hand, the idea which it has formed of human equality and fraternity seems to us today to leave too large a place for unjust inequalities. Its pity for the outcast seems to us too Platonic; we desire another which would be more practicable; but as yet we cannot clearly see what it should be nor how it could be realized in facts. In a word, the old gods are growing old or already dead, and others are not yet born. This is what rendered vain the attempt of Comte with the old historic souvenirs artificially revived: it is life itself, and not a dead past which can produce a living cult. But this state of incertitude and confused agitation cannot last for ever. A day will come when our societies will know again those hours of creative effervescence, in the course of which new ideas arise and new formulae are found which serve for a while as a guide to humanity; and when these hours shall have been passed through once, men will spontaneously feel the need of reliving them from time to time in thought, that is to say, of keeping alive their memory by means of celebrations which regularly reproduce their fruits. We have already seen how the French Revolution established a whole cycle of holidays to keep the principles with which it was inspired in a state of perpetual youth. If this institution quickly fell away, it was because the revolutionary faith lasted but a moment, and deceptions and discouragements rapidly succeeded the first moments of enthusiasm. But though the work may have miscarried, it enables us to imagine what might have happened in other conditions; and everything leads us to believe that it will be taken up again sooner or later. There are no gospels which are immortal, but neither is there any reason for believing that humanity is incapable of inventing new ones. As to the question of what symbols this new faith will express itself with, whether they will resemble those of the past or not, and whether or not they will be more adequate for the reality which they seek to translate, that is something which surpasses the human faculty of foresight and which does not appertain to the principal question.

NOTES

1. Undoubtedly it is rare that a ceremony does not have some director at the moment when it is celebrated; even in the most crudely organized societies, there are generally certain men whom the importance or their social position points out to exercise a directing influence over the religious life (for example, the chiefs of the local groups of certain Australian societies). But this attribution of functions is still very uncertain.

2. At Athens, the gods to whom the domestic cult was addressed were only specialized forms of the gods or the city ($Ζεύς\ κτῆσις\ Ζενς\ έρκεî$). In the same way, in the Middle Ages, the patrons of the guilds were saints or the calendar.

3. For the name Church is ordinarily applied only to a group whose common beliefs refer to a circle of more special affairs.

4. Hubert and Mauss, *Théorie Générale de la Magie*, in *Année Sociologique*, vol. VII, p. 18.

5. Robertson Smith has already pointed out that magic is opposed to religion, as the individual to the social (*The Religion of the Semites*, 2nd edn, pp. 264–5). Also, in thus distinguishing magic from religion, we do not mean to establish a break or continuity between them. The frontiers between the two domains are frequently uncertain.

6. Codrington, *Trans. and Proc. Roy. Soc. of Victoria*, XVI, p. 136.

7. Negrioli, *Dei Genii presso i Romani*.

8. This is the conclusion reached by Spencer in his *Ecclesiastical Institutions* (ch. xvi), and by Sabatier in his *Outlines of a Philosophy of Religion, based on Psyonology and History* (tr. by Seed), and by all the school to which he belongs.

9. Notably among numerous Indian tribes of North America.

10. This statement of fact does not touch the question whether exterior and public religion is not merely the development of an interior and personal religion which was the primitive fact, or whether, on the contrary, the second is not the projection of the first into individual consciences. [. . .] For the moment, we confine ourselves to remarking that the individual cult is presented to the observer as an element of, and something dependent upon, the collective cult.

11. It is by this that our present definition is connected to the one we have already proposed in the *Année Sociologique*. In this other work, we defined religious beliefs exclusively by their obligatory character; but, as we shall show, this obligation evidently comes from the fact that these beliefs are the possession of a group which imposes them upon its members. The two definitions are thus in a large part the same. If we have thought it best to propose a new one, it is because the first was too formal, and neglected the contents of the religious representations too much. It will be seen, in the discussions which follow, how

important it is to put this characteristic into evidence at once. Moreover, if their imperative character is really a distinctive trait of religious beliefs, it allows of an infinite number of degrees; consequently there are even cases where it is not easily perceptible. Hence come difficulties and embarrassments which are avoided by substituting for this criterion the one we now employ.

12. William James, *The Varieties of Religious Experience*.
13. Quoted by James, *op. cit.*, p. 20.
14. It is for this reason that Frazer and even Preuss set impersonal religious forces outside of, or at least on the threshold of, religion, to attach them to magic.

21. Families in Global Perspective

Göran Therborn

Sex is a basic driving force of human biology; power is a key feature of human sociology. They are entangled, not worlds apart. Power can be observed in the animal kingdom, while the forms of human sexuality are socially constructed and variable. Both are convertible currencies, and merge into one another. Sex may lead to power, through the conduit of seduction. Power is also a basis for obtaining sex, whether by force or lubricated with money and what it can buy. The family is an enclosure in the open battlefields of sex and power, delimiting the free-for-all by staking out boundaries, between members and non-members, substituting rights and obligations for free trade and perpetual combat. As such, the family is a social institution, the most ancient, the most widespread of institutions.

[. . .]

The family is suspended between sex and power as biological and social forces. But it is, of course, not a safe haven or an escape from power and sex. A family is always an outcome of sexual relations past or current: no sex, no family. But it is a regulator of sexual relations, determining who may, who must, and who must not, have sexual relations with whom. Power relations are inscribed in the rights and obligations of family members. Indeed, it makes good analytical sense to view an institution in terms of an equilibrium, between the pattern of rights and obligations, on one hand, and the distribution of power resources among the members, on the other. This balance or equilibrium is what explains the resilience of

an institutional form, in this case a certain kind of family, once established. Those privileged by it can maintain their status because their resources of control and of sanction match their rights, while those who have few power resources have more duties than rights.

Institutional change is then induced by events or processes which upset a given balance between, on one hand, rights and duties, and on the other, powers and dependencies. Fathers may lose their property, children may get a chance to go to school, women may get opportunities on the labour market, religious traditions may weaken, states or international organizations may intrude into families, curtailing the rights of fathers and husbands, providing rebelling daughters with routes of escape. Or, the forces pushing existing equilibria out of joint may work in the opposite direction: family property – and the control and transmission of it – may become more important, as in China in recent decades; women may be pressured away from the labour market – as has at least been attempted from the Elbe to the Yellow Sea; religious support of the rights of fathers and husbands may become stronger; within living memory French fathers had the right to hand over disobedient children to state penitence.

The privacy of family life has always been linked to societal authority, through institutionalized rights and duties prescribed and proscribed by organized religious bodies, buttressed or licensed by political authorities or directly by state legislation. But the links may be distant and/or tenuous, largely lost in the labyrinths of individual family power structures, or modified by provincial or local customs. A global view of the family will have to catch something of the diversity in which these powerful canons of authority exist.

Each present has its past. The family is an ancient institution, its origins going beyond history. But this is a study of the family from experiences and preoccupations of the turn of the twentieth and twenty-first centuries. While written in a scholarly rather than an opinionated mode and with the perspective of an individual author, this work is, of course, coming out of a period which has seen what Juliet Mitchell (1966) on the barricades, referring to women, called 'the Longest Revolution', and Francis Fukuyama (1999), from the opposite side of the frontline, termed 'The Great Disruption'. It is appearing at a time, when 'heterosexual marriage' is envisaged as 'largely undermined by the rise of the pure relationship and plastic sexuality' (Giddens 1992: 154), and when it apparently makes sense to talk about 'The End of Marriage' (Lewis 2001) or of 'What comes after the family' (Beck-Gernsheim 1998). If all this were true, one might, perhaps at least understand, if not necessarily agree with, the great US economist who compares 'the disaster of the failure of the family system in America to the Irish Potato Famine (Akerlof 1998: 308). We have to face the fact that the 'Western family' is widely seen by writers with loud voices and strong opinions to be in great disorder (Roudinesco 2002).

[. . .]

This book has three main themes, which reflect how the author is trying to make scholarly sense of his time and context. Patriarchy, and the relative rights and duties of parents and children, of men and women, is the first. The 'rule of the father' is here seen more broadly than by Le Play, referring to male family powers, whether of fathers, maternal uncles in matrilineal societies, husbands, or other family members qua males. Its main focus will be on parent–adult child (on other parent–child relations, see Therborn 1993) and

husband–wife relations. Parental power will largely concentrate on the control – degree or absence – of children's marriages and household formation, as a most important aspect of control over the life-course of the next generation, but it will also pay attention to specific intra-family discrimination of daughters, from infanticide or malnutrition and neglect to disinheritance. In this perspective, parental power and control will be taken as manifestations of patriarchy, without singling out or excluding maternal matchmakers and commanding mothers-in-law, as long as they are delegated by or linked to paternal power. Male sexual power without paternal significance will be referred to as phallocracy, which may be taken as a younger brother of patriarchy.

Paternal power is the core meaning of patriarchy, historically and etymologically, and we shall have to take stock of its operation, many times, in many places. It tells us something noteworthy of recent changes in the UK that an influential British feminist theorist in 1990, and throughout eight reprints in the 1990s, could dismiss paternal power as irrelevant at best: 'This inclusion of generation in the definition [of patriarchy] is confusing. It is a contingent element and best omitted' (Walby 1990: 20). With that reservation, the approach to patriarchy in this book owes much to contemporary feminism, and to its critique of twentieth-century masculinist silence on the subject.

Powerful fathers are also husbands, so it seems both logical and practical to extend the notion of patriarchy to the power of husbands. We shall look at their various prerogatives, legal and/or actual: in family decision-making as 'head of the family', in control of their wives' activities and mobility, in polygyny and sexual double standards. We shall also pay attention to the discrimination against daughters and to special sacrifices demanded from women for male sexual reasons, such as the crushing of girls' feet in imperial China, euphemistically called 'foot-binding', or genital mutilation. But patriarchy in this book will not be cut loose from the family and made synonymous with the subordination, discrimination, or social disadvantages of women in general. Gender discrimination and gender inequality should be seen as a broader concept than patriarchy, with the latter's family tradition and historical connotations. A significant erosion, and even disappearance of the latter does not necessarily entail the end of the former, and has not actually done so, as we shall see.

A second main topic of this endeavour concerns the role of marriage, and non-marriage, in regulating sexual behaviour, and sexual bonding in particular. Single living and informal sexual bonding, in cohabitation or otherwise, are not recent inventions. They were widespread in northwestern Europe and in Latin America and the Caribbean at the time of Le Play and Westermarck. The latter also noted, more than a century ago, that 'the proportion of unmarried people has been gradually increasing in Europe' (Westermarck 1903: 541). Historically, marriage rates have actually gone both up and down, and the current North Atlantic rates of non-marriage, extra-marital births, and unmarried cohabitation are by no means unique in modern history, as global analysis will show.

Current customs and debates in Europe, the Americas and Oceania underline that contemporary family sociology cannot neglect the sexual revolution of the 1960 and 1970s. Marriage should be seen, not (only) as an institution *sui generis*, but as a major part of a mutating sociosexual order. We shall pay special attention to the sexual position of adolescents worldwide, as adolescence is the normal entry into that order, in one variant or another.

The third part of the book deals with the past, present and future prospects of fertility and birth control, with their implications for ageing and for geopolitical shifts. It thus relates also to the beginning of population decline in Europe, the rapid ageing of Japan, and the emerging scarcity of children in some parts of the world, following an enormously successful global effort at birth control.

In particular, we shall try to understand the link between, on the one hand, the sexual intimacy of individual couples, and, on the other, the national, continental and inter-continental waves of fertility change. This will take us to issues of politics, social movements, states and supranational organizations; again, we shall have to be very aware of the multi-sided, multi-level politics of patriarchy and of marriage and sexuality as well.

These three themes we shall pursue through a century, from about 1900 to 2000 and beyond. However, tradition did not end in 1900, nor did modernity begin in 1901. Substantial changes of patriarchy had already occurred by 1900, although not as much as Westermarck hoped or Le Play feared, and the origins of collective patterns of birth control can be traced back to the seventeenth century. While generally starting the investigative clock around 1900, the pre-story is not to be interpreted as pre-history, as some kind of 'primordiality'.

The themes of this book cross academic disciplines, and the author has tried to follow the tracks of the former, rather than the boundaries of the latter. The search area is indicated by sociology, law and demography, but tools and experiences of anthropology, history and political science have also been called for, because the task is not just the normative structures of the family institution, but their actual operation and their limits, across the globe and during a century or more.

[. . .]

I have found it useful to distinguish five major and two important interstitial family systems in the modern world. The major ones derive from a specific value system, of religious/philosophical origin, and shaped by the history of the area. The interstitial ones have gained their character from encounters with different value systems. These family systems may be, and will be, sub-divided in various ways, but their number has to be small and their area large, to be practical. The major family systems are those of:

Africa (sub-Saharan)
European (including the New World settlements)
East Asia
South Asia
West Asia/North Africa

Interstitial family systems of global weight are those of:

Southeast Asia, from Sri Lanka to the Philippines and with Indonesia at its centre, where the rigid patriarchies of Confucianism, Islam, and Catholicism were mellowed by Buddhist insouciance in family matters, and by Malay customs.

Creole America, coming out of the American socio-economic history of Christian Europeans running plantations, mines and landed estates with African slaves and servile Indian labour. Alongside the strict patriarchal white high culture, that history developed a particular black, mulatto, mestizo and uprooted Indian family pattern. While most distinctive in the Caribbean, the pattern may be seen throughout the Americas from the Afro-American ghettos of the USA to the Andean peripheries of South America.

Behind the divisions are certain findings which will be demonstrated later, for example that territorial geocultures have a tendency to prevail, in their bearing upon the family features under study, over religious divisions, such as between Muslims, Christians and Animists in Africa, or between Hindus and Muslims in South Asia. Across the areas there are major divides, which sometimes have to be drawn differently for different periods or different purposes. In Africa it is often meaningful to follow a northwest to southeast diagonal, although the continent's ethnic mosaic makes any neat patterning almost impossible. In Europe there is a historical east–west family division along a line from Trieste to St Petersburg, going back to the early Middle Ages, but one may also occasionally find a rationale for a northwest versus the rest, or for a Western Europe versus New World distinction. Whereas in East Asia the first subdivision is clearly between China and Japan, in South Asia the non-political,

non-religious geocultural north–south divide is decisive, bringing the extremely patriarchal north of the Indian Hindu centre together with Muslim Bangladesh and Pakistan, versus a south of both Hindus and Muslims with milder patriarchal manners, by comparison. But within all areas many national pictures will be shown, because of national productions of power as well as because many sources are nationally generated.

[. . .]

All over the world, the institution of the family has changed in the course of the past century. Some changes have been epochal – the erosion of patriarchy, the worldwide establishment of birth control, and some large populations setting out to natural decline. Sex and marriage have changed radically before, and their mutations in the twentieth century do not yet amount to a new global era. But from a provincial European or North American outlook, the sexual revolution and informal coupling are about to take unprecedented dimensions.

While family change has been universal, the starting-point, the timing, the pace, and the amount of change of the three dimensions of family relations studied in this book have differed greatly across the globe. Even within regions changes have varied widely, like patriarchy in Western Europe, marriage in Southeast Asia, or fertility in Latin America and in South Asia. To grasp and to convey one pattern of global secular change, then, is a daunting task.

Figures of change

The concrete overall change pattern is different among our three clusters of variables. The twentieth-century history of patriarchy is basically one of stepwise decline, begun at different points in time across the world. The first breakthrough came in the 1910s, by broadly consensual reform in Scandinavia, by violent revolution in Russia. The late 1940s and early 1950s provided another important ladder of descent, this time centred in East Asia – in Japan under American occupation and in China through Communist Revolution.

The Communist takeover of Eastern Europe meant that the bell tolled for institutionalized patriarchy there too. Without being implemented in the short term, the UN Declaration of Human Rights signalled an important global constitutional victory against patriarchy. Finally the years following upon '1968', in particular the years around 1975 (the International Women's Year), released a worldwide wave against the special powers and privileges of husbands and fathers, with the first breaks coming in Western Europe and North America, but leaving no part of the planet untouched.

Marriage change has the shape of an inverted V in Western Europe and the Americas. That is, referring to marriage frequency which rose towards midcentury, and descended in the last third of it. After the convulsions of colonial conquest and slavery in the Americas, including post-Independence crises in Hispanic America, and of proletarianization in Western Europe, a marital stabilization began in the late nineteenth century, carried by industrialization and economic development, which continued into the post-World War II boom, with some brief conjunctural effects of the world wars and the Depression. Before the end of the unprecedented boom and prosperity, marriage in these regions took a new, downward path, aided by the new economic crisis of Latin America. Scandinavia, with its old flexibility of marriage, has been in the vanguard.

In the rest of the world, the high flat plateau of virtually universal marriage has been basically maintained, until the post-Communist plunge in Eastern Europe. Some big Asian cities and Southern Africa provide recent exceptions, of marital decline. In terms of age, there is a J-shaped age curve of later female marriage, though less clear in sub-Saharan Africa than in North Africa and all over Asia.

Fertility declined in two different international waves, after pioneering mass change in post-revolutionary France and the USA in the early nineteenth century. One, covering all Europe and the European settlements overseas, started after the Depression of the 1870s and ran into the Depression of the 1930s. The other was global and rolled in the last third of the century, at different pace in different parts of the world. In between there was a significant contra-flow of recovered fertility in the first wave countries, and significant oscillations have continued in recent years, for instance in Scandinavia and the United States.

However, with all three variables and their trajectories, there are three common noteworthy features. First, they are all patterned, in timing, pace and amount of change, by the family system. Second, they are temporally uneven, with clearly discernible breaking points, statistical as well as legal, and with periods of no or insignificant change alternating with ones of rapid transformation. Third, often, but not always, they are remarkably synchronized in space, into international or intercontinental waves of change or at least of attempts at change.

On a more abstract, analytical level, this means that family change in the twentieth century has been neither evolutionary nor unilinear.

REFERENCES

Akerlof, G. (1998) 'Men without Children', *The Economic Journal* 108: 287–309.

Beck-Gernsheim, E. (1998) *Was Kommt nach der Familie?* Munich: C.H. Beck.

Fukuyama, F. (1999) *The Great Disruption*, New York: The Free Press.

Giddens, A. (1992) *The Transformation of Intimacy*, Cambridge: Polity Press.

Lewis, J. (2001) *The End of Marriage?*, Cheltenham: Edward Elgar.

Mitchell, J. (1966) 'Women – the Longest Revolution', *New Left Review* 40: 11–37.

Roudinesco, E. (2002) *La Famille en désordre*, Paris: Fayard.

Therborn, G. (1993) 'The politics of childhood', in F. Castles (ed.), *Families of Nations*, Aldershot: Dartmouth.

Walby, S. (1990) *Theorizing Patriarchy*, Oxford: Basil Blackwell.

Westermarck, E. (1903) *The History of Human Marriage* (3rd edn), London: Macmillan.

22. The Hidden Curriculum – A Teacher's View

John Taylor Gatto

Thirty years ago, having nothing better to do with myself at the time, I tried my hand at schoolteaching. The license I have certifies that I am an instructor of English language and English literature, but that isn't what I do at all. I don't teach English; I teach school – and I win awards doing it.

Teaching means different things in different places, but seven lessons are universally taught from Harlem to Hollywood Hills. They constitute a national curriculum you pay for in more ways than you can imagine, so you might as well know what it is. You are at liberty, of course, to regard these lessons any way you like, but believe me when I say I intend no irony in this presentation. These are the things I teach; these are the things you pay me to teach. Make of them what you will.

1. Confusion

A lady named Kathy wrote this to me from Dubois, Indiana, the other day:

What big ideas are important to little kids? Well, the biggest idea I think they need is that what they are learning isn't idiosyncratic – that there is some system to it all and it's not just raining down on them as they helplessly absorb. That's the task, to understand, to make coherent.

Kathy has it wrong. *The first lesson I teach is confusion. Everything* I teach is out of context. I teach the un-relating of everything. I teach disconnections. I teach too much: the orbiting of planets, the law of large numbers, slavery, adjectives, architectural drawing, dance, gymnasium, choral singing, assemblies, surprise guests, fire drills, computer languages, parents' nights, staff-development days, pull-out programs, guidance with strangers my students may never see again, standardized tests, age-segregation unlike anything seen in the outside world . . . What do any of these things have to do with each other?

Even in the best schools a close examination of curriculum and its sequences turns up a lack of coherence, a host of internal contradictions. Fortunately the children have no words to define the panic and anger they feel at *constant violations of natural order and sequence* fobbed off on them as quality in education. The logic of the school-mind is that it is better to leave school with a tool kit of superficial jargon derived from economics, sociology, natural science, and so on than with one genuine enthusiasm. But quality in education entails learning about something in depth. Confusion is thrust upon kids by too many strange adults, each working alone with only the thinnest relationship with each other, pretending, for the most part, to an expertise they do not possess.

[. . .]

I teach the un-relating of everything, an infinite fragmentation the opposite of cohesion; what I do is more related to television programming than to making a scheme of order. In a world where home is only a ghost because both parents work, or because of too many moves or too many job changes or too much ambition, or because something else has left everybody too confused to maintain a family relation, I teach students how to accept confusion as their destiny. That's the first lesson I teach.

2. Class position

The second lesson I teach is class position. I teach that students must stay in the class where they belong. I don't know who decides my kids belong there but that's not my business. The children are numbered so that if any get away they can be returned to the right class. Over the years the variety of ways children are numbered by schools has increased dramatically, until it is hard to see the human beings plainly under the weight of numbers they carry. Numbering children is a big and very profitable undertaking, though what the strategy is designed to accomplish is elusive. I don't even know why parents would, without a fight, allow it to be done to their kids.

In any case, that's not my business. My job is to make them like being locked together with children who bear numbers like their own. Or at least to endure it like good sports. If I do my job well, the kids can't even *imagine* themselves somewhere else because I've shown them how to envy and fear the better classes and how to have contempt for the dumb classes. Under this efficient discipline the class mostly polices itself into good marching order. That's the real lesson of any rigged competition like school. You come to know your place.

In spite of the overall class blueprint that assumes that ninety-nine percent of the kids are in their class to stay, I nevertheless make a public effort to exhort children to higher levels of test success, hinting at eventual transfer from the lower class as a reward. I frequently insinuate the day will come when an employer will hire them on the basis of test scores and grades, even though my own experience is that employers are rightly indifferent to such things. I never lie outright, but I've come to see that truth and schoolteaching are, at bottom, incompatible, just as Socrates said thousands of years ago. The lesson of numbered classes is that everyone has a proper place in the pyramid and that there is no way out of your class except by number magic. Failing that, you must stay where you are put.

3. Indifference

The third lesson I teach is indifference. I teach children not to care too much about anything, even though they want to make it appear that they do. How I do this is very subtle. I do it by demanding that they become totally involved in my lessons, jumping up and down in their seats with anticipation, competing vigorously with each other for my favor. It's heartwarming when they do that; it impresses everyone, even me. When I'm at my best I plan lessons very carefully in order to produce this show of enthusiasm. But when the bell rings I insist they drop whatever it is we have been doing and proceed quickly to the next work station. They must turn on and off like a light switch. Nothing important is ever finished in my class nor in any class I know of. Students never have a complete experience except on the installment pull.

Indeed, the lesson of bells is that no work is worth finishing, so why care too deeply about anything? Years of bells will condition all but the strongest to a world that can no longer offer important work to do. Bells are the secret logic of school time; their logic is inexorable. Bells destroy the past and future, rendering every interval the same as any other, as the abstraction of a map renders every living mountain and river the same, even though they are not. Bells inoculate each undertaking with indifference.

4. Emotional dependency

The fourth lesson I teach is emotional dependency. By stars and red checks, smiles and frowns, prizes, honors, and disgraces, I teach kids to surrender their will to the predestined chain of command. Rights may be granted or withheld by any authority without appeal, because rights do not exist inside a school – not even the right of free speech, as the Supreme Court has ruled – unless school authorities say they do. As a schoolteacher, I intervene in many personal decisions, issuing a pass for those I deem legitimate and initiating a disciplinary confrontation for behavior that threatens my control. Individuality is constantly trying to assert itself among children and teenagers, so my judgments come thick and fast. Individuality is a contradiction of class theory, a curse to all systems of classification.

Here are some common ways in which individuality shows up: children sneak away for a private moment in the toilet on the pretext of moving their bowels, or they steal a private instant in the hallway on the grounds they need water. I know they don't, but I allow them to 'deceive' me because this conditions them to depend on my favors. Sometimes free will appears right in front of me in pockets of children angry, depressed, or happy about things outside my ken; rights in such matters cannot be recognized by schoolteachers, only privileges that can be withdrawn, hostages to good behavior.

5. Intellectual dependency

The fifth lesson I teach is intellectual dependency. Good students wait for a teacher to tell them what to do. This is the most important lesson of them all: we must wait for other people, better trained than ourselves, to make the meanings of our lives. The expert makes all the important choices; only I, the teacher, can determine what my kids must study, or rather, only the people who pay me can make those decisions, which I then enforce. If I'm told that evolution is a fact instead of a theory, I transmit that as ordered, punishing deviants who resist what I have been told to tell them to think. This power to control what children will think lets me separate successful students from failures very easily.

Successful children do the thinking I assign them with a minimum of resistance and a decent show of enthusiasm. Of the millions of things of value to study, I decide what few we have time for. Actually, though, this is decided by my face-

less employers. The choices are theirs – why should I argue? Curiosity has no important place in my work, only conformity.

Bad kids fight this, of course, even though they lack the concepts to know what they are fighting, struggling to make decisions for themselves about what they will learn and when they will learn it. How can we allow that and survive as schoolteachers? Fortunately there are tested procedures to break the will of those who resist; it is more difficult, naturally, if the kids have respectable parents who come to their aid, but that happens less and less in spite of the bad reputation of schools. No middle-class parents I have ever met actually believe that *their* kid's school is one of the bad ones. Not one single parent in many years of teaching. That's amazing, and probably the best testimony to what happens to families when mother and father have been well-schooled themselves, learning the seven lessons.

Good people wait for an expert to tell them what to do. It is hardly an exaggeration to say that our entire economy depends upon this lesson being learned. Think of what might fall apart if children weren't trained to be dependent: the social services could hardly survive – they would vanish, I think, into the recent historical limbo out of which they arose. Counselors and therapists would look on in horror as the supply of psychic invalids vanished. Commercial entertainment of all sorts, including television, would wither as people learned again how to make their own fun. Restaurants, the prepared food industry, and a whole host of other assorted food services would be drastically down-sized if people returned to making their own meals rather than depending on strangers to plant, pick, chop, and cook for them. Much of modern law, medicine, and engineering would go too, as well as the clothing business and schoolteaching, unless a guaranteed supply of helpless people continued to pour out of our schools each year.

Don't be too quick to vote for radical school reform if you want to continue getting a paycheck. We've built a way of life that depends on people doing what they are told because they don't know how to tell *themselves* what to do. It's one of the biggest lessons I teach.

6. Provisional self-esteem

The sixth lesson I teach is provisional self-esteem. If you've ever tried to wrestle into line kids whose parents have convinced them to believe they'll be loved in spite of anything, you know how impossible it is to make self-confident spirits conform. Our world wouldn't survive a flood of confident people very long, so I teach that a kid's self-respect should depend on expert opinion. My kids are constantly evaluated and judged.

A monthly report, impressive in its provision, is sent into a student's home to elicit approval or mark exactly, down to a single percentage point, how dissatisfied with the child a parent should be. The ecology of 'good' schooling depends on perpetuating dissatisfaction, just as the commercial economy depends on the same fertilizer. Although some people might be surprised how little time or reflection goes into making up these mathematical records, the cumulative weight of these objective-seeming documents establishes a profile that compels children to arrive at certain decisions about themselves and their futures based on the casual judgment of strangers. Self-evaluation, the staple of every major philosophical system that ever appeared on the planet, is never considered a factor. The lesson of report cards, grades, and tests is that children should not trust themselves or their parents but should instead rely on the evaluation of certified officials. People need to be told what they are worth.

7. One can't hide

The seventh lesson I teach is that one can't hide. I teach students that they are always watched, that each is under constant surveillance by me and my colleagues. There are no private spaces for children; there is no private time. Class change lasts exactly three hundred seconds to keep promiscuous fraternization at low levels. Students are encouraged to tattle on each other or even to tattle on their own parents. Of course, I encourage parents to file reports about their own child's waywardness too. A family trained to snitch on itself isn't likely to conceal any dangerous secrets.

I assign a type of extended schooling called 'homework,' so that the effect of surveillance, if not the surveillance itself, travels into private households, where students might otherwise use free time to learn something unauthorized from a father or mother, by exploration or by apprenticing to some wise person in the neighborhood. Disloyalty to the idea of schooling is a devil always ready to find work for idle hands.

[. . .]

It is the great triumph of compulsory government monopoly mass schooling that among even the best of my fellow teachers, and among even the best of my students' parents, only a small number can imagine a different way to do things. 'The kids have to know how to read and write, don't they?' 'They have to know how to add and subtract, don't they?' 'They have to learn to follow orders if they ever expect to keep a job.'

23. Work in the Next Industrial Revolution

Alan S. Blinder

In February 2004, when N. Gregory Mankiw, a Harvard professor then serving as chairman of the White House Council of Economic Advisers, caused a national uproar with a 'textbook' statement about trade, economists rushed to his defense. Mankiw was commenting on the phenomenon that has been clumsily dubbed 'offshoring' (or 'offshore outsourcing') – the migration of jobs, but not the people – who perform them, from rich countries to poor ones. Offshoring, Mankiw said, is only 'the latest manifestation of the gains from trade that economists have talked about at least since Adam Smith. More things are tradable than were tradable in the past, and that's a good thing.' Although Democratic and Republican politicians alike excoriated Mankiw for his callous attitude toward American jobs, economists lined up to support his claim that offshoring is simply international business as usual.

Their economics were basically sound: the well-known principle of comparative advantage implies that trade in new kinds of products will bring overall improvements in productivity and well-being. But Mankiw and his defenders underestimated both the importance of offshoring and its disruptive effect on wealthy countries. Sometimes a quantitative change is so large that it brings about qualitative changes, as offshoring likely will. We have so far barely seen the tip of the offshoring iceberg, the eventual dimensions of which may be staggering.

To be sure, the furor over Mankiw's remark was grotesquely out of proportion to the current importance of offshoring, which is still largely a prospective phenomenon. Although there are no reliable national data, fragmentary studies indicate that well under a million service-sector jobs in the United States have been lost to offshoring to date. (A million seems impressive, but in the gigantic and rapidly churning U.S. labor market, a million jobs is less than two weeks' worth of normal gross job losses.) However, constant improvements in technology and global communications virtually guarantee that the future will bring much more offshoring of 'impersonal services' – that is, services that can be delivered electronically over long distances with little or no degradation in quality.

That said, we should not view the coming wave of offshoring as an impending catastrophe. Nor should we try to stop it. The normal gains from trade mean that the world as a whole cannot lose from increases in productivity, and the United States and other industrial countries have not only weathered but also benefited from comparable changes in the past. But in order to do so again, the governments and societies of the developed world must face up to the massive, complex, and multifaceted challenges that offshoring will bring. National data systems, trade policies, educational systems, social welfare programs, and politics all must adapt to new realities. Unfortunately, none of this is happening now.

[. . .]

What sorts of jobs are at risk of being offshored? In the old days, when tradable goods were things that could be put in a box, the key distinction was between manufacturing and nonmanufacturing jobs. Consistent with that, manufacturing workers in the rich countries have grown accustomed to the idea that they compete with foreign labor. But as the domain of tradable services expands, many service workers will also have to accept the new, and not very pleasant, reality that they too must compete with workers in other countries. And there are many more service than manufacturing workers.

Many people blithely assume that the critical labor-market distinction is, and will remain, between highly educated (or highly skilled) people and less-educated (or less-skilled) people – doctors versus call-center operators, for example. The supposed remedy for the rich countries, accordingly, is more education and a general 'upskilling' of the work force. But this view may be mistaken. Other things being equal, education and skills are, of course, good things; education yields higher returns in advanced societies, and more schooling probably makes workers more flexible and more adaptable to change. But the problem with relying on education as the remedy for potential job losses is that 'other things' are not remotely close to equal. The critical divide in the future may instead be between those types of work that are easily deliverable through a wire (or via wireless connections) with little or no diminution in quality and those that are not. And this unconventional divide does not correspond well to traditional distinctions between jobs that require high levels of education and jobs that do not.

A few disparate examples will illustrate just how complex – or, rather, how untraditional – the new divide is. It is unlikely that the services of either taxi drivers or airline pilots will ever be delivered electronically over long distances. The first is a 'bad job' with negligible educational requirements; the second is quite the reverse. On the other hand, typing services (a low-skill job) and security analysis (a high-skill job) are already being delivered electronically from India – albeit on a small scale so far. Most physicians need not fear that their jobs will be moved offshore, but radiologists are beginning to see this happening already. Police officers will not be replaced by electronic monitoring, but some security guards will be. Janitors and crane operators are probably immune to foreign competition; accountants and computer programmers are not. In short, the dividing line between the jobs that produce services that are suitable for electronic delivery (and are thus threatened by offshoring) and those that do not does not correspond to traditional distinctions between high-end and low-end work.

The fraction of service jobs in the United States and other rich countries that can potentially be moved offshore is certain to rise as technology improves and as countries such as China and India continue to modernize, prosper, and educate their work forces. Eventually, the number of service-sector jobs that will be vulnerable to competition from abroad will likely exceed the total number of manufacturing jobs. Thus, coping with foreign competition, currently a concern for only a minority of workers in rich countries, will become a major concern for many more.

There is currently not even a vocabulary, much less any systematic data, to help society come to grips with the coming labor-market reality. So here is some suggested nomenclature. Services that cannot be delivered electronically, or that are notably inferior when so delivered, have one essential characteristic: personal, face-to-face contact is either imperative or highly desirable. Think of the waiter who serves you dinner, the doctor who gives you your annual physical, or the cop on the beat. Now think of any of those tasks being performed by robots controlled from India – not quite the same. But such face-to-face human contact is not necessary in the relationship you have with the telephone operator who arranges your conference call or the clerk who takes your airline reservation over the phone. He or she may be in India already.

The first group of tasks can be called personally delivered services, or simply personal services, and the second group impersonally delivered services, or impersonal services. In the brave new world of globalized electronic commerce, impersonal services have more in common with manufactured goods that can be put in boxes than they do with personal services. Thus, many impersonal services are destined to become tradable and therefore vulnerable to offshoring. By contrast, most personal services have attributes that cannot be transmitted through a wire. Some require face-to-face contact (child care), some are inherently 'high-touch' (nursing), some involve high levels of personal trust (psychotherapy), and some depend on location-specific attributes (lobbying).

However, the dividing line between personal and impersonal services will move over time. As information technology improves, more and more personal services will become impersonal services. No one knows how far this process will go. Forrester Research caused a media stir a few years ago by estimating that 3.3 million U.S. service-sector jobs will move offshore by 2015, a rate of about 300,000 jobs per year. That figure sounds like a lot until you realize that average gross job losses in the U.S. labor market are more than 500,000 in the average week. In fact, given the ample possibilities for technological change in the next decade, 3.3 million seems low. So do the results of a 2003 Berkeley study and a recent McKinsey study, both of which estimated that 11 percent of U.S. jobs are at risk of being offshored. The Berkeley estimate came from tallying up workers in 'occupations where at least some [offshoring] has already taken place or is being planned,' which means the researchers considered only the currently visible tip of the offshoring iceberg. The future will reveal much more.

To obtain a ballpark figure of the number of U.S. jobs threatened by offshoring, consider the composition of the U.S. labor market at the end of 2004. There were 14.3 million manufacturing jobs. The vast majority of those workers produced items that could be put in a box, and so virtually all of their jobs were potentially movable offshore. About 7.6 million Americans worked in construction and mining. Even though these people produced goods, not services, their jobs were not in danger of moving offshore. (You can't hammer a nail over the Internet.) Next, there were 22 million local, state, and federal government jobs. Even though many of these jobs provide impersonal services that need not be delivered face to face, hardly any are candidates for offshoring – for obvious political reasons. Retail trade employed 15.6 million Americans. Most of these jobs require physical presence, although online retailing is increasing its share of the market, making a growing share of retail jobs vulnerable to offshoring as well.

Those are the easy cases. But the classification so far leaves out the majority of private-service jobs – some 73.6 million at the end of 2004. This extremely heterogeneous group breaks down into educational and health services (17.3 million), professional and business services (16.7 million), leisure and hospitality services (12.3 million), financial services (8.1 million), wholesale trade (5.7 million), transportation (4.3 million), information services (3.2 million), utilities (0.6 million), and 'other services' (5.4 million). It is hard to divide such broad job categories into personal and impersonal services, and it is even more difficult to know what possibilities for long-distance electronic delivery the future will bring. Still, it is possible to get a rough sense of which of these jobs may be vulnerable to offshoring.

The health sector is currently about five times as large as the educational sector, and the vast majority of services in the health sector seem destined to be delivered in person for a very long time (if not forever). But there are exceptions, such as radiology. More generally, laboratory tests are already outsourced by most physicians. Why not out of the country rather than just out of town? And with a little imagination, one can envision other medical procedures being performed by doctors who are thousands of miles away. Indeed, some surgery has already been performed by robots controlled by doctors via fiber-optic links.

Educational services are also best delivered face to face, but they are becoming increasingly expensive. Electronic delivery will probably never replace personal contact in K-12 education, which is where the vast majority of the educational jobs are. But college teaching is more vulnerable. As college tuition grows ever more expensive, cheap electronic delivery will start looking more and more sensible, if not imperative.

The range of professional- and business-service jobs includes everything from CEOs and architects to typists and janitors – a heterogeneous lot. That said, in scanning the list of detailed subcategories, it appears that many of these jobs are at least potentially offshorable. For example, future technological developments may dictate how much accounting stays onshore and how much comes to be delivered electronically from countries with much lower wages.

The leisure and hospitality industries seem much safer. If you vacation in Florida, you do not want the beachboy or the maid to be in China. Reservation clerks can be (and are) located anywhere. But on balance, only a few of these jobs can be moved offshore.

Financial services, a sector that includes many highly paid jobs, is another area where the future may look very different from the present. Today, the United States 'onshores' more financial jobs (by selling financial services to foreigners) than it offshores. Perhaps that will remain true for years. But improvements in telecommunications and rising educational levels in countries such as China and, especially, India (where many people speak English) may change the status quo dramatically.

Wholesale trade is much like retail trade, but with a bit less personal contact and thus somewhat greater potential for offshoring. The same holds true for transportation and utilities. Information-service jobs, however, are the quintessential types of jobs that can be delivered electronically with ease. The majority of these jobs are at risk. Finally, the phrase 'other services' is not very informative, but detailed scrutiny of the list (repair and laundry workers appear, for example) reveals that most of these services require personal delivery.

The overall picture defies generalization, but a rough estimate, based on the preceding numbers, is that the total number of current U.S. service-sector jobs that will be susceptible to offshoring in the electronic future is two to three times the total number of current manufacturing jobs (which is about 14 million). That said, large swaths of the U.S. labor market look to be immune. But, of course, no one knows exactly what technological changes the future will bring.

[. . .]

What is to be done about all of this?

[. . .]

In the first place, rich countries such as the United States will have to reorganize the nature of work to exploit their big advantage in nontradable services: that they are close to where the money is. That will mean, in part, specializing more in the delivery of services where personal presence is either imperative or highly beneficial. Thus, the U.S. work force of the future will likely have more divorce lawyers and fewer attorneys who write routine contracts, more internists and fewer radiologists, more salespeople and fewer typists. The market system is very good at making adjustments like these, even massive ones. It has done so before and will do so again. But it takes time and can move in unpredictable ways. Furthermore, massive transformations in the nature of work tend to bring wrenching social changes in their wake.

In the second place, the United States and other rich nations will have to transform their educational systems so as to prepare workers for the jobs that will actually exist in their societies. Basically, that requires training more workers for personal services and fewer for many impersonal services and manufacturing. But what does that mean, concretely, for how children should be educated? Simply providing more education is probably a good thing on balance, especially if a more educated labor force is a more flexible labor force, one that can cope more readily with non-routine tasks and occupational change. However, education is far from a panacea, and the examples given earlier show that the rich countries will retain many jobs that require little education. In the future, how children are educated may prove to be more important than how much. But educational specialists have not even begun to think about this problem. They should start right now.

Contrary to what many have come to believe in recent years, people skills may become more valuable than computer skills. The geeks may not inherit the earth after all – at least not the highly paid geeks in the rich countries. Creativity will be prized. Thomas Friedman has rightly emphasized that it is necessary to steer youth away from tasks that are routine or prone to routinization into work that requires real imagination. Unfortunately, creativity and imagination are notoriously difficult to teach in schools – although, in this respect, the United States does seem to have a leg up on countries such as Germany and Japan. Moreover, it is hard to imagine that truly creative positions will ever constitute anything close to the majority of jobs. What will everyone else do?

[. . .]

Contrary to current thinking, Americans, and residents of other English-speaking countries, should be less concerned about the challenge from China, which comes largely in manufacturing, and more concerned about the challenge from India, which comes in services. India is learning to exploit its already strong comparative advantage in English, and that process will continue. The economists Jagdish Bhagwati, Arvind Panagariya, and T. N. Srinivasan meant to reassure Americans when they wrote, 'Adding 300 million to the pool of skilled workers in India and China will take some decades.' They were probably right. But decades is precisely the time frame that people should be thinking about – and 300 million people is roughly twice the size of the U.S. work force.

Many other effects of the coming industrial transformation are difficult to predict, or even to imagine. Take one possibility: for decades, it has seemed that modern economic life is characterized by the ever more dehumanized workplace parodied by Charlie Chaplin in *Modern Times*. The shift to personal services could well reverse that trend for rich countries – bringing less alienation and greater overall job satisfaction. Alas, the future retains its mystery. But in any case, offshoring will likely prove to be much more than just business as usual.

Theme 4 – Further Reading

Because of the broad content of the readings in this theme, it is only possible to give a brief idea of where to begin your reading on institutions. Hence, on religion, try Grace Davie's (2007) *The Sociology of Religion* (London: Sage). For the family, Graham Allan and Graham Crow's (2001) *Families, Households and Society* (Basingstoke: Palgrave Macmillan) is difficult to better. Rob Moore's (2004) *Education and Society: Issues and Explanations in the Sociology of Education* (Cambridge: Polity) covers this field extremely well and on the subject of work, Keith Grint's (2005) *The Sociology of Work: An Introduction,* 3rd Edition (Cambridge: Polity) is one of the most popular texts among students.

Giddens and Sutton *Sociology 7ᵗʰ Edition* (2013)

Chapter 19 deals with the general subject of organizations, but as this section covers a wide range of institutions, several other chapters can be recommended, namely Chapter 7 on work, Chapter 10 on the family, Chapter 17 on religion, Chapter 18 on the media and Chapter 20 on education. Other sections include Chapter 13 on the welfare state, pages 553–63; Chapter 22 on government, pages 970–7 and Chapter 23 on the nation-state, pages 1018–28.

Part 5 Social Inequalities

The study of social inequality is one of sociology's foundational subjects. With one foot in the French Revolution with its principles of liberty, equality and fraternity and the other in the consequences of industrialization, sociologists took philosophical speculation about a future egalitarian society into the empirical study of existing inequalities and the evaluation of policies designed to mitigate or eliminate them. In particular, the condition of working-class life and urban poverty were among the concerns of early sociologists. Over time, more inequality was uncovered rather than less, as the patterning of social relations came to be mapped in more detail. Social class has taken up the bulk of research into inequality, but gender inequality and inequality based on ethnic groups have occupied many researchers in recent decades. Indeed these three forms are widely seen as the main three types of inequality in societies, though disability and sexual orientation have been identified as sources of discrimination and inequality too.

The terminology used in this area has changed quite a lot over time. *Social inequality* gave way to the more general term *social stratification* with its geological imagery, and the latter was then challenged by the term *social divisions* emphasizing how inequality creates divided societies. The concept of *social exclusion* was then devised to capture the differing ways in which social groups can effectively become 'outsiders' in their own society and in very recent years, social inequality appears to be making a comeback as sociologists have recognized that in spite of all the efforts made over the years to combat disadvantage and exclusion, even the advanced industrial societies remain deeply scarred by clear inequalities. The selected readings in this section are chosen to reflect something of this complex picture.

The basic and most general concept of social stratification is discussed by Wendy Bottero in Reading 24, though it is interesting to note that her book title actually contains three of the concepts discussed above. She suggests that studying stratification means taking an interest in who gets what and why, which is a good place to start the section. Stratification also implies that societies are structured rather like large rock formations with inequality sedimented into the very structure of social relations. Bottero acknowledges this when discussing how inequality comes to be accepted and taken for granted, leading to the reproduction of unequal social relations over long periods of time.

Once it became the subject of feminist research studies, gender inequality is now seen as one of the most enduring forms of social inequality. One of the most influential texts here is Simone de Beauvoir's *The Second Sex*, an excerpt from which is included as Reading 25. De Beauvoir sets out the thesis that gender inequality leads to a society which takes male experience as the norm and is structured accordingly. This makes women appear as a 'second sex', an 'other' compared to male 'normality' legitimizing the dependence of women on men and presenting a severe obstacle to movement towards equal rights. De Beauvoir compares the position of women to that of the exploited industrial working class, an argument taken up by later feminist researchers who investigated family life, housework and childcare, finding that domestic life was only 'a haven in a heartless world' for men. For women, domesticity was the centre of gender inequality, male dominance and exploitation.

A third major type of inequality is that based on 'race' and ethnicity. The concept of race has fallen into disrepute in sociology due to its implication of biologically fixed races with certain behavioural characteristics, which has no basis in scientific research and evidence. Ethnicity is now generally used to refer to the different and unequal experience of social groups with specific cultural attributes such as language, religion and dress codes. In the UK and other European societies, for instance, Black and South Asian groups are over-represented among prison populations, victims of crime and in poor housing stock, but under-represented in the higher paid occupations and higher education. Rather than seeing class, gender and ethnicity as separate from each other, sociologists have come to theorize people's life chances in terms of their position in relation to all three. For example, the life experience of black working-class women is very different from that of white, middle-class men. In Reading 26, Patricia Hill Collins explores this approach through the concept of intersecting inequalities in relation to the USA. Focusing particularly on the lives of black women, she argues in favour of policies aimed at empowering women, which, she suggests, can only be achieved if black feminism can be reinvigorated to create enough pressure for institutional reform and transformation.

In Reading 27, we return to the issue of social class with Rosemary Crompton's review of recent arguments suggesting that the very concept of social class has become irrelevant. Although it is clear that there have been some significant social changes in the industrialized world since the 1970s, including the continuing loss of manufacturing jobs and increasing service sector employment, the rise of consumerism and individualization of identities, a widely reported 'feminization' of the workforce and the breakdown of many cohesive class-based communities, Crompton argues for the continued relevance of class analysis in sociology. Even though people's identification with class may well be competing with other forms of individual identity, for a discipline that aims to understand the structure and dynamics of social life and to explain the persistence of inequality in a globalizing world, the concept of social class remains indispensable.

The section closes with Colin Barnes, Geof Mercer and Tom Shakespeare's account (Reading 28) of 'a tale of two models', the individual and the social models of disability. Prior to the development of the social model from within the disabled people's movement, disability tended to be seen as an individual matter rooted in physical or mental infirmities – a series of personal tragedies. This view fed into a medicalization of disability that led sociologists to believe that the study of disabilities was of, at best, marginal importance for sociology. However, advocates of the social model argued that although *impairments* are very common, disability arises when the institutions and structures of society fail to accommodate people with impairments. In short, disability is *not* a personal tragedy but a consequence of the mal-organization of society. Along with campaigning disabled people's organizations, the social model has helped to shift perceptions of disability from an individual issue requiring medical intervention, to a form of deep-seated social inequality requiring political and policy solutions.

24. What is Social Stratification?

Wendy Bottero

Social stratification is concerned with the patterning of inequality and its enduring consequences on the lives of those who experience it. All of us live within pre-existing relations of unequal power; status or economic resources; and these unequal relations surround and constrain us, providing the context of our interactions, inevitably affecting the choices we make in life, opening some channels of opportunity, and closing off others. This is a condition of social life (individual choice is always limited by the choices of those around us), but stratification is concerned with how some have more freedom and choice than others. Money, power or influence give those who possess them greater control over the external forces which affect us all, and open doors which might otherwise be closed. The point of stratification analysis is to see how such inequalities persist and endure – over lifetimes and between generations. Going to university, for example, opens the door to higher-level, better-paid jobs. So someone who cannot take up a university place because they cannot afford the fees will be affected by this throughout their life, in the sort of career they can get, and in the level of their lifetime earnings. If we start off as unequal, these disadvantages are likely to accumulate and be reinforced over our lifetimes. As the old phrase has it: 'the rich get richer, and the poor get poorer'.

The study of stratification is therefore the study of how inequalities between individuals at any given point in time are reproduced between and across generations As Otis Duncan argues, the difference between *inequality* and *stratification* is that 'social *stratification* refers to the persistence of positions in a hierarchy of inequality, either over the life time of a birth cohort of individuals or, more particularly, between generations' (1968: 681). The notion of *inter-generational transmission* is important here. Inequality in one generation affects inequality in the next. The resources that are available to us growing up as children affect the success of our schooling, and so our eventual occupational careers, and the lifestyles we adopt as adults. However, this means there is also an impact on the *next* generation, since our social position influences the resources to which our children have access, and so their life-chances too. Here the social location of children constrains the choices of their adult lives, and the choices of *their* children, quite independent of their individual efforts. So social stratification also looks at the extent to which advantage (or disadvantage) is handed down from one generation to the next, reproducing the pattern of inequalities between individuals and groups over time.

Stratification analysis looks at how where we *start* in life affects where we *end up*, and the impact of parents' social position on that of their children. However, the persistence of inequality is represented in more ways than inter-generational transmission, since stratification also has an important impact on our *social relations*. Whom we fall in love and settle down with, and the friends and social contacts that we make throughout our life, are all affected by our hierarchical position. This process, called *differential association*, is an essential feature of stratification. People sharing a similar social position, in terms of social class or status group membership, are more likely to interact socially with members of the same group than with members of other groups. So, acquaintances, friends and sexual partners all tend to be chosen much more frequently from within the same group than from without. There are many reasons why this occurs, but all of them result from living within stratified social arrangements. So people may actively seek to exclude certain groups from their social circles, for reasons of prejudice or snobbery, but this is bound up with the uneven levels of prestige, resources and social standing of different groups. However, differential association is not just based on the deliberate exclusion of others. It also happens because people with different social resources (whether economic, social or cultural) tend to travel in different social circles, and have different lifestyles, so they are less likely to bump into those from different social groups and, when they do, they often don't have much in common.

The lives of social unequals are often lived in different places, with different sorts of people, who have different lifestyles, tastes and interests. This is a *consequence* of the impact on stratification of social arrangements, but it also helps to reproduce stratification. If individual and family decisions – about the choice of a partner, the raising of children or the choice of a career – are choices influenced by our (stratified) social location, then such patterned choices help to maintain differences in the outcomes of people's lives. Friends and family are important sources of financial help, useful contacts and social support. They help us to 'get on' in life. But differential association means that disadvantaged people tend to associate with people who are similarly disadvantaged, whilst the privileged likewise draw more of their contacts from the privileged. If two people settling down are both from privileged backgrounds, this will reinforce (rather than dissipate) the pattern of economic privilege in such families. Similarly, if working-class people rarely make friends with upper-middle-class people, their friends will only be able to help them get working-class jobs. Differential association acts as a conservative force on the distribution of opportunities and resources, circulating them within groups rather than across them.

What this means is that the persistence of inequality is not simply a matter of material advantage and disadvantage; along with it goes a range of attitudes, social relationships and styles of life, so the persistence of inequality over time is partly about the continual reproduction of these social relationships and style of life. Because social hierarchy acts as a constraint on all close social relationships, in turn, the patterning of such relationships helps to transmit anti reproduce hierarchy itself.

The stratification space

To understand stratification as a process of enduring, unequal, social relations, we have to think about the nature of the social hierarchies in which people live their lives. Stratified social relations occur when social differences are organized hierarchically along some dimension of inequality. There are many dimensions to inequality, because we value many different resources and attributes (cultural, social and economic) which all serve to stratify our social relations. Unequal social relations occur along lines of prestige, reputation, property, income, occupation, education, skill, gender, race, ethnicity, age, disability and sexuality, to name just a few. And to complicate things, these dimensions of inequality do not straightforwardly map onto each other, but nor are they completely independent. This gives us a series of highly differentiated and stratified social relations which intersect and combine to influence an individual's overall stratification position. Our social position, then, is the product of all our social relations, of our gender, age, race, class, sexuality, and so on. But how do these combine to produce an all-embracing stratification order, an overall space of unequal social relations – and how is this ordering best understood?

As the writer Pierre Bourdieu argues, because of the complex differentiation of social relations, the same experience of the social world can be constructed in different ways . . . according to different principles of vision and division (1985: 726), and this is true for both stratification theorists and the people they study. There are a series of different approaches to stratification, which all picture it differently. Many of these approaches will be examined during the course of this book. However, these approaches can – very schematically – be divided into two main ways of thinking about stratification: *structural* approaches and *relational* or *interaction* approaches. Both of them use the notion of social distance, albeit in contrasting ways. The first sees social distance in terms of the different locations of people within an external structure of stratification. The second sees social distance in terms of social relations of closeness and distance, in which stratification is composed of the patterned nature of these social relations.

Social structure

The term 'social distance' is part of the language of spatial metaphor which has dominated stratification theory (Ossowski 1963: 9). Social distance, for most stratification writers, refers to the relative position of individuals within a structure, and is a metaphor for the degree of separation between groups placed by other criteria (so, the 'distance' between the rich and the poor refers to the extent of their difference economically). One early approach, by Pitirim Sorokin (1927), emphasizes distance within an overall social space, in which an individual's overall location is determined by the values of many coordinates, among them 'family status, the state in which he [sic] is a citizen, his nationality, his religious group, his occupational group, his political party, his economic status, his race, and so on' (1927: 5). Therefore, the level of social distance between individuals depends on how different they arc in terms of various attributes. People from different ethnic backgrounds, and with different religions, would be regarded as 'socially distant' from hach other, whereas people with different ethnic backgrounds, but the same religion (or vice versa),

might be seen as somewhat closer to each other in social space.

> The greater the resemblance of the positions of the different men [*sic*], the nearer they are towards each other in social space. The greater and more numerous are their differences in these respects, the greater is the social distance between them.
>
> (Sorokin 1927: 6)

Because theorists of stratification are interested in the constraining and enduring nature of unequal social relations they have naturally been drawn to *structural* accounts of social behaviour, which usually focus on one main dimension of stratification, whilst recognizing other, complicating, factors. Structural approaches then investigate this dominant dimension of inequality (usually, the economic) as an external structure, which – to a greater or lesser extent – determines people's lives. In this method, the identification of the social structure comes first. The best-known approach of this kind is class analysis, which sees economic inequality as the main dimension of stratification, and so defines a structure of economic positions. Structural approaches see differential association (the impact of hierarchical location on our social relationships) as a key aspect of stratification. However, their method first defines the main dimension of stratification (as a set of classes or status groups) and then investigates patterns of social interaction *between* these groups.

Structural accounts of stratification are much the better known, and have dominated work in the area, with their models of social behaviour proving to be powerful analytical tools. However, in recent years a disillusionment with structural approaches in social analysis more generally has led to a declining interest in stratification. In this bock I argue that these attacks are misguided and dramatically overstate the difficulties of structural analysis. Stratification remains a key force structuring our social experience, and structural approaches still have much to tell us about the nature of these processes. However, certain weaknesses in structural approaches have opened the door to such charges.

There are two related problems. First, there is the problem of how the structure of stratification relates to other dimensions of difference. Usually 'structure' is defined in terms of the valued resource that is seen to be the *most* important in people's lives, and then analysts look at how inequalities in that resource affect social relations. This inevitably separates 'structure' from 'action', since – because there are always other, acknowledged, dimensions of difference – the 'dominant' structural location will only explain *part* of people's social behaviour. Recent attacks have focused on this gap. It is argued that structural accounts are necessarily incomplete explanations, which make exaggerated claims. Second, therefore, structural accounts have been accused of determinism, placing too much emphasis on structural locations (the membership of class or status groups) which cannot explain the diversity of people's lives. Structural accounts, it is claimed, see stratification as a mould into which we must pour our behaviour, whether we wish to or not, denying the freedom, choice and agency of individuals. Recent postmodern accounts of social 'difference' have stressed the hyper-differentiated nature of social relations, arguing that actors can slice up the social order in different ways, in much the same way as stratification theorists. That is, that highly differentiated social relations can be interpreted in different ways. Such accounts have argued that the internal differences within, and across, the categories of structural accounts simply undermine the usefulness of stratification theory altogether.

Relations in social space

However, there is another way of thinking about stratification and social distance, a parallel, less well-known tradition, which is less susceptible to charges of determinism or essentialism, but which still stresses the constraining nature of stratified social relations. Some of these approaches (particularly the work of Pierre Bourdieu) have come into greater prominence as a way of defending stratification analysis from the incursions of post-modernism. In the second tradition – known as relational or interaction approaches – the concept of social distance refers to closeness in social interactions.

According to an interaction notion of social distance, low distances should be assigned between individuals or groups who are likely to be involved in such social interactions as living near each other, seeing each other socially, intermarriage, having friends or relatives in the other group, moving from one group to the other, or merely approving of each other. High distances should be assigned where such social interactions are unlikely.
(McFarland and Brown 1973: 227)

In structural approaches, groups are defined as socially distant if they are very *different* from each other (in terms of class, gender, or race categories), in relational approaches groups are defined as socially distant if they rarely *associate* with each other. Groups can be very different (belonging to different class or racial categories) but can still be socially close if they engage in friendship and sexual partnership on a regular basis. The pattern of social relationships between categories (how similar their social behaviour is) is used to map the relative social distance between all the various categories.

Although they are less well known, relational accounts of social distance have a long history. One early approach, by Bogardus (1925), emphasizes *subjective* social distance, and refers to the social approval for various social groups, as measured by the level of intimacy (neighbourliness, friendship, marriage, and so on) that respondents would find acceptable with individuals from different national, ethnic and religious groups. The urban sociologist Robert E. Park used the concept of social distance to describe the crowded urban neighbourhoods of Chicago in the early twentieth century, where different racial, ethnic and class groups lived in close physical proximity, rubbing up against each other in the normal course of their working and community lives However:

Amongst the dense, diverse and transient populations of large and rapidly growing cities, one could no longer presume social affiliations and relationships from the mere fact of propinquity. People might live alongside each other, cheek by jowl, but the social distance separating them could still be a chasm of class, ethnic, occupational and age differences, a 'mosaic of little worlds that touch but do not interpenetrate'

(Amit and Rapport 2002: 42–43)

These early perspectives have given way to modern accounts which look at the patterning of social relationships to determine the stratification order (Blau 1977: 32). These approaches identify a 'social space of relationships' by empirically mapping relations of proximity. Such approaches use the patterning of actual social relationships (either of relations of intimacy, or through similar relations to cultural lifestyle) to identify the ordered (and stratified) nature of social life. The most famous approach in this tradition, that of Bourdieu (1984 [1979]), argues that people living the same cultural lifestyles occupy the same location in social space. He places groups with similar tastes close to each other in the space, whilst groups with very different tastes are more distant. Bourdieu focuses on lifestyle, but sees lifestyle emerging from processes of social interaction and differential association, since those who interact socially tend to be similar in terms of lifestyle (Prandy 1999: 229). Other approaches, such as that of the Cambridge Stratification Group, have focused more directly on interaction patterns (such as friendship and marriage) (Stewart et al. 1980). The idea behind such approaches is that looking at patterns of intimate social interaction allows us to conceptualize 'social distance' in terms of both the gap that separates people with dissimilar social and cultural relations, and also the proximity of those with similar social and cultural relationships (Bottero and Prandy 2003).

So if the usual approach to stratification is to define a structure of groups and then look at the relations between them, relational approaches reverse this method, and use patterned social relations to determine the nature of the stratification order: differential association is seen as a way of defining distances within a social space. If social interaction occurs frequently between categories they are socially close to one another, if social

interaction is infrequent between them then they are socially distant.

[. . .]

Social advantage – in whatever form – gives those who possess it a considerable head start in weathering the social changes and upheaval that confront successive generations. If you start ahead you tend to stay ahead – whatever life throws at you. This provides support for Bourdieu's contention that the various sources of advantage are readily convertible into each other. Indeed, the persistence of relative inequality has only been possible because of the relative ease with which the more privileged have been able to convert economic holdings into educational and cultural success. It is still the case that economic position can 'insure' against poor educational performance, and numerous studies show that low-achieving children from more privileged backgrounds have much better careers than their less-advantaged peers. So if advantaged children do not do well academically, alternative resources are used to ensure their success. But the link between social background and educational attainment has also strengthened over time. The more advantaged are dramatically more successful in educational terms, and this is true even when we hold measured 'ability' constant. If there has been a loosening of the impact of family background on social position it has not been 'by degrees' – the educational route – since family background has been increasingly significant for educational success (Prandy et al. 2003). Whether it is through living in better areas (with better schools), through the hiring of private tutors, through the choice of private schooling, through the possession of cultural capital, through the more strategic and confident negotiation of the school system, through the mobilization of well-placed social contacts, or through the higher aspirations that privileged parents have for their children, or indeed through all of these factors – the fact remains that it is harder for privileged children to fail than it is for disadvantaged children to succeed. Education has not contributed to increased social mobility, but rather has served as a mechanism for social reproduction.

REFERENCES

Amit, V. and Rapport, N. (2002) *The Trouble with Community*, London: Pluto Press.

Blau, P. (1977) 'A Macrosociological Theory of Social Structure', *American Journal of Sociology*, 83 (1): 26–54.

Bogardus, E. (1925) 'Measuring Social Distance', *Journal of Applied Sociology*, 9: 299–308.

Bottero, W. and Prandy, K. (2003) 'Social Interaction Distance and Stratification', *British Journal of Sociology*, 54 (2): 177–97.

Bourdieu, P. (1984 [1979]) *Distinction: A Social Critique of the Judgement of Taste*, London: Routledge & Kegan Paul.

Bourdieu, P. (1985) 'Social Space and the Genesis of Groups', *Theory and Society*, 14 (6): 723–44.

Duncan, O. (1968) 'Social Stratification and Mobility: Problems in the Measurement of Trend', in E. Sheldon and W. Moore (eds) *Indicators of Change: Concepts and Measurement*, New York: Russell Sage Foundation.

McFarland, D. and Brown, D. (1973) 'Social Distance as a Metric: A Systematic Introduction to Smallest Space Analysis', in E. O. Lauman (ed.) *Bonds of Pluralism*, New York: John Wiley.

Ossowski, S. (1963) *Class Structure in the Social Consciousness*, London: Routledge & Kegan Paul.

Prandy, K. (1999) 'The Social Interaction Approach to the Measurement and Analysis of Social Stratification', *International Journal of Sociology and Social Policy*, 19 (9/10/11): 215–49.

Prandy, K., Unt, M. and Lambert, P. (2003) 'Not by Degrees: Education and Social Reproduction in Twentieth-century Britain', unpublished paper.

Sorokin, P. (1927) *Social Mobility*, New York: Harper & Brothers.

Stewart, A., Prandy, K. and Blackburn, R. M. (1980) *Social Stratification and Occupations*, London: Macmillan Press.

25. Woman – The Second Sex?

Simone de Beauvoir

For a long time I have hesitated to write a book on woman. The subject is irritating, especially to women; and it is not new. Enough ink has been spilled in quarrelling over feminism, and perhaps we should say no more about it. It is still talked about, however, for the voluminous nonsense uttered during the last century seems to have done little to illuminate the problem. After all, is there a problem? And if so, what is it? Are there women, really? Most assuredly the theory of the eternal feminine still has its adherents who will whisper in your ear: 'Even in Russia women still are women'; and other erudite persons – sometimes the very same – say with a sigh: 'Woman is losing her way, woman is lost.' One wonders if women still exist, if they will always exist, whether or not it is desirable that they should, what place they occupy in this world, what their place should be. 'What has become of women?' was asked recently in an ephemeral magazine.

But first we must ask: what is a woman? 'Tota mulier in utero', says one, 'woman is a womb'. But in speaking of certain women, connoisseurs declare that they are not women, although they are equipped with a uterus like the rest. All agree in recognizing the fact that females exist in the human species; today as always they make up about one half of humanity. And yet we are told that femininity is in danger; we are exhorted to be women, remain women, become women. It would appear, then, that every female human being is not necessarily a woman; to be so considered she must share in that mysterious and threatened reality known as femininity. Is this attribute something secreted by the ovaries? Or is it a Platonic essence, a product of the philosophic imagination? Is a rustling petticoat enough to bring it down to earth? Although some women try zealously to incarnate this essence, it is hardly patentable. It is frequently described in vague and dazzling terms that seem to have been borrowed from the vocabulary of the seers, and indeed in the times of St Thomas it was considered an essence as certainly defined as the somniferous virtue of the poppy.

But conceptualism has lost ground. The biological and social sciences no longer admit the existence of unchangeably fixed entities that determine given characteristics, such as those ascribed to woman, the Jew, or the Negro. Science regards any characteristic as a reaction dependent in part upon a *situation*. If today femininity no longer exists, then it never existed. But does the word *woman*, then, have no specific content? This is stoutly affirmed by those who hold to the philosophy of the enlightenment, of rationalism, of nominalism; women, to them, are merely the human beings arbitrarily designated by the word *woman*. Many American women particularly are prepared to think that there is no longer any place for woman as such; if a backward individual still takes herself for a woman, her friends advise her to be psychoanalysed and thus get rid of this obsession. In regard to a work, *Modern Woman: The Lost Sex*, which in other respects has its irritating features, Dorothy Parker has written: 'I cannot be just to books which treat of woman as woman ... My idea is that all of us, men as well as women, should be regarded as human beings.' But nominalism is a rather inadequate doctrine, and the antifeminists have had no trouble in showing that women simply *are* not men. Surely woman is, like man, a human being; but such a declaration is abstract. The fact is that every concrete human being is always a singular, separate individual. To decline to accept such notions as the eternal feminine, the black soul, the Jewish character, is not to deny that Jews, Negroes, women exist today – this denial does not represent a liberation for those concerned, but rather a flight from reality. Some years ago a well-known woman writer refused to permit her portrait to appear in a series of photographs especially devoted to women writers; she wished to be counted among the men. But in order to gain this privilege she made use of her husband's influence! Women who assert that they are men lay claim nonetheless to masculine consideration and respect. I recall also a young Trotskyite standing on a platform at a boisterous meeting and getting ready to use her fists, in spite of her evident fragility. She was denying her feminine weakness; but it was for love of a militant male whose equal she wished to be. The attitude of defiance of many American women proves that they are haunted by a sense of their femininity. In truth, to go for a walk with one's eyes open is enough to demonstrate that humanity is divided into two classes of individuals whose clothes, faces, bodies, smiles, gaits, interests, and occupations are manifestly different. Perhaps these differences are superficial, perhaps they are destined to disappear. What is certain is that they do most obviously exist.

If her functioning as a female is not enough to define woman, if we decline also to explain her through 'the eternal feminine', and if nevertheless we admit, provisionally, that women do exist, then we must face the question 'what is a woman'?

To state the question is, to me, to suggest, at once, a preliminary answer. The fact that I ask it is in itself significant. A man would never set out to write a book on the peculiar situation of the human male. But if I wish to define myself, I must first of all say: 'I am a woman'; on this truth must be based all further discussion. A man never begins by presenting himself as an individual of a certain sex; it goes without saying that he is a man. The terms *masculine* and *feminine* are used symmetrically only as a matter of form, as on legal papers. In actuality the relation of the two sexes is not quite like that of two electrical poles, for man represents both the positive and the neutral, as is indicated by the common use of *man* to designate human beings in general; whereas woman represents only the negative, defined by limiting criteria, without reciprocity. In the midst of an abstract discussion it is vexing to hear a man say: 'You think thus and so because you are a woman'; but I know that my only defence is to reply: 'I think thus and so because it is true,' thereby removing my subjective self from the argument. It would be out of the question to reply: 'And you think the contrary because you are a man', for it is understood that the fact of being a man is no peculiarity. A man is in the right in being a man; it is the woman who is in the wrong. It amounts to this: just as for the ancients there was an absolute vertical with reference to which the oblique was defined, so there is an absolute human type, the masculine. Woman has ovaries, a uterus: these peculiarities imprison her in her subjectivity, circumscribe her within the limits of her own nature. It is often said that she thinks with her glands. Man superbly ignores the fact that his anatomy also includes glands, such as the testicles, and that they secrete hormones. He thinks of his body as a direct and normal connection with the world, which he believes he apprehends objectively, whereas he regards the body of woman as a hindrance, a prison, weighed down by everything peculiar to it. 'The female is a female by virtue of a certain lack of qualities,' said Aristotle; 'we should regard the female nature as afflicted with a natural defectiveness.' And St Thomas for his part pronounced woman to be an 'imperfect man', an 'incidental' being. This is symbolized in Genesis where Eve is depicted as made from what Bossuet called 'a supernumerary bone' of Adam.

Thus humanity is male and man defines woman not in herself but as relative to him; she is not regarded as an autonomous being.

[...]

Now, woman has always been man's dependant, if not his slave; the two sexes have never shared the world in equality. And even today woman is heavily handicapped, though her situation is beginning to change. Almost nowhere is her legal status the same as man's, and frequently it is much to her disadvantage. Even when her rights are legally recognized in the abstract, long-standing custom prevents their full expression in the mores. In the economic sphere men and women can almost be said to make up two castes; other things being equal, the former hold the better jobs, get higher wages, and have more opportunity for success than their new competitors. In industry and politics men have a great many more positions and they monopolize the most important posts. In addition to all this, they enjoy a traditional prestige that the education of children tends in every way to support, for the present enshrines the past – and in the past all history has been made by men. At the present time, when women are beginning to take part in the affairs of the world, it is still a world that belongs to men.

[...]

But is it enough to change laws, institutions, customs, public opinion, and the whole social context, for men and women to become truly equal? 'Women will always be women,' say the sceptics. Other seers prophesy that in casting off their femininity they will not succeed in changing themselves into men and they will become monsters. This would be to admit that the woman of today is a creation of nature; it must be repeated once more that in human society nothing is natural and that woman, like much else, is a product elaborated by civilization. The intervention of others in her destiny is fundamental: if this action took a different direction, it would produce a quite different result. Woman is determined not by her hormones or by mysterious instincts, but by the manner in which her body and her relation to the world are modified through the action of others than herself. The abyss that separates the adolescent boy and girl has been deliberately widened between them since earliest childhood; later on, woman could not be other than what she *was made*, and that past was bound to shadow her for life. If we appreciate its influence, we see clearly that her destiny is not predetermined for all eternity.

We must not believe, certainly, that a change in woman's economic condition alone is enough to transform her, though this factor has been and remains the basic factor in her evolution; but until it has brought about the moral, social, cultural, and other consequences that it promises and requires, the new woman cannot appear. At this moment they have been realized nowhere, in Russia no more than in France or the United States; and this explains why the woman of today is torn between the past and the future. She appears most often as a 'true woman' disguised as a man, and she feels herself as ill at ease in her flesh as in her masculine garb. She must shed her old skin and cut her own new clothes. This she could do only through a social evolution.

[...]

The parallel [...] between women and the proletariat is valid in that neither ever formed a minority or a separate collective unit of mankind. And instead of a single historical event it is in both cases a historical development that explains their status as a class and accounts for the membership of *particular individuals* in that class. But proletarians have not always existed, whereas there have always been women. They are women in virtue of their anatomy and physiology. Throughout history they have always been subordinated to men, and hence their dependency is not the result of a historical event or a social change – it was not something that *occurred*. The reason why otherness in this case seems to be an absolute is in part that it lacks the contingent or incidental nature of historical facts. A condition brought about at a certain time can be abolished at some other time, as the Negroes of Haiti and others have proved: but it might seem that natural condition is beyond the possibility of change. In truth, however, the nature of things is no more immutably given, once for all, than is historical reality. If woman seems to be the inessential which never becomes the essential, it is because she herself fails to bring about this change. Proletarians say 'We'; Negroes also. Regarding themselves as subjects, they transform the bourgeois, the whites, into 'others'. But women do not say 'We', except at some congress of feminists or similar formal demonstration; men say 'women', and women use the same word in referring to themselves. They do not authentically assume a subjective attitude. The proletarians have accomplished the revolution in Russia, the Negroes in Haiti, the Indo-Chinese are battling for it in Indo-China; but the women's effort has never been anything more than a symbolic agitation. They have gained only what men have been willing to grant; they have taken nothing, they have only received.

The reason for this is that women lack concrete means for organizing themselves into a unit which can stand face to face with the correlative unit. They have no past, no history, no religion of their own; and they have no such solidarity of work and interest as that of the proletariat. They are not even promiscuously herded together in the way that creates community feeling among the American Negroes, the ghetto Jews, the workers of Saint-Denis, or the factory hands of Renault. They live dispersed among the males, attached through residence, housework, economic condition, and social standing to certain men – fathers or husbands – more firmly than they are to other women. If they belong to the bourgeoisie, they feel solidarity with men of that class, not with proletarian women; if they are white, their allegiance is to white men, not to Negro women. The proletariat can propose to massacre the ruling class, and a sufficiently fanatical Jew or Negro might dream of getting sole possession of the atomic bomb and making humanity wholly Jewish or black; but woman cannot even dream of exterminating the males. The bond that unites her to her oppressors is not comparable to any other. The division of the sexes is a biological fact, not an event in human history. Male and female stand opposed within a primordial *Mitsein*, and woman has not broken it. The couple is a fundamental unity with its two halves riveted together, and the cleavage of society along the line of sex is impossible. Here is to be found the basic trait of woman: she is the Other in a totality of which the two components are necessary to one another.

26. Intersecting Inequalities

Patricia Hill Collins

The vast majority of African-American women were brought to the United States to work as slaves in a situation of oppression. Oppression describes any unjust situation where, systematically and over a long period of time, one group denies another group access to the resources of society. Race, class, gender, sexuality, nation, age, and ethnicity among others constitute major forms of oppression in the United States. However, the convergence of race, class, and gender oppression characteristic of U.S. slavery shaped all subsequent relationships that women of African descent had within Black American families and communities, with employers, and among one another. It also created the political context for Black women's intellectual work.

African-American women's oppression has encompassed three interdependent dimensions. First, the exploitation of Black women's labor essential to U.S. capitalism – the 'iron pots and kettles' symbolizing Black women's long-standing ghettoization in service occupations – represents the economic dimension of oppression (Davis 1981; Marable 1983; Jones 1985; Amott and Matthaei 1991). Survival for most African-American women has been such an all-consuming activity that most have had few opportunities to do intellectual work as it has been traditionally defined. The drudgery of enslaved African-American women's work and the grinding poverty of 'free' wage labor in the rural South tellingly illustrate the high costs Black women have paid for survival. The millions of impoverished African-American women ghettoized in Philadelphia, Birmingham, Oakland, Detroit, and other U.S. inner cities demonstrate the continuation of these earlier forms of Black women's economic exploitation (Brewer 1993; Omolade 1994).

Second, the political dimension of oppression has denied African-American women the rights and privileges routinely extended to White male citizens (Burnham 1987; Scales-Trent 1989; Berry 1994). Forbidding Black women to vote, excluding, African-Americans and women from public office, and withholding equitable treatment in the criminal justice system all substantiate the political subordination of Black women. Educational institutions have also fostered this pattern of disenfranchisement. Past practices such as denying literacy to slaves and relegating Black women to underfunded, segregated Southern schools worked to ensure that a quality education for Black women remained the exception rather than the rule (Mullings 1997). The large numbers of young Black women in inner cities and impoverished rural areas who continue to leave school before attaining full literacy represent the continued efficacy of the political dimension of Black women's oppression.

Finally, controlling images applied to Black women that originated during the slave era attest to the ideological dimension of U.S. Black women's oppression (King 1973; White 1985; Carby 1987; Morton 1991). Ideology refers to the body of ideas reflecting the interests of a group of people. Within U.S. culture, racist and sexist ideologies permeate the social structure to such a degree that they become hegemonic, namely, seen as natural, normal, and inevitable. In this context, certain assumed qualities that are attached to Black women are used to justify oppression. From the mammies, jezebels, and breeder women of slavery to the smiling Aunt Jemimas on pancake mix boxes, ubiquitous Black prostitutes, and ever-present welfare mothers of contemporary popular culture, negative stereotypes applied to African-American women have been fundamental to Black women's oppression.

Taken together, the supposedly seamless web of economy, polity, and ideology function as a highly effective system of social control designed to keep African-American women in an assigned, subordinate place. This larger system of oppression works to suppress the ideas of Black women intellectuals and to protect elite White male interests and worldviews. Denying African-American women the credentials to become literate certainly excluded most African-American women from positions as scholars, teachers, authors, poets, and critics. Moreover, while Black women historians, writers, and social scientists have long existed, until recently these women have not held leadership positions in universities, professional associations, publishing concerns, broadcast media, and other social institutions of knowledge validation. Black women's exclusion from positions of power within mainstream institutions has led to the elevation of elite White male ideas and interests and the corresponding suppression of Black women's ideas and interests in traditional scholarship (Higginbotham 1989; Morton 1991; Collins 1998, 95–123). Moreover, this historical exclusion means that stereotypical images of Black women permeate popular culture and public policy (Wallace 1990; Lubiano 1992; Jewell 1993).

U.S. and European women's studies have challenged the seemingly hegemonic ideas of elite White men. Ironically, Western feminisms have also suppressed Black women's ideas (duCille 1996, 81–119). Even though Black women intellectuals have long expressed a distinctive African-influenced and feminist sensibility about how race and class intersect in structuring gender, historically we have not been full participants in White feminist organizations (Giddings 1984; Zinn

et al. 1986; Caraway 1991). As a result, African-American, Latino, Native American, and Asian-American women have criticized Western feminisms for being racist and overly concerned with White, middle-class women's issues (Moraga and Anzaldua 1981; Smith 1982; Dill 1983; Davis 1989).

Traditionally, many U.S. White feminist scholars have resisted having Black women as full colleagues. Moreover, this historical suppression of Black women's ideas has had a pronounced influence on feminist theory. One pattern of suppression is that of omission. Theories advanced as being universally applicable to women as a group upon closer examination appear greatly limited by the White, middle-class and Western origins of their proponents. For example, Nancy Chodorow's (1978) work on sex role socialization and Carol Gilligan's (1982) study of the moral development of women both rely heavily on White, middle-class samples. While these two classics made key contributions to feminist theory, they simultaneously promoted the notion of a generic woman who is White and middle class. The absence of Black feminist ideas from these and other studies placed them in a much more tenuous position to challenge the hegemony of mainstream scholarship on behalf of all women.

Another pattern of suppression lies in paying lip service to the need for diversity, but changing little about one's own practice. Currently, some U.S. White women who possess great competence in researching a range of issues acknowledge the need for diversity, yet omit women of color from their work. These women claim that they are unqualified to understand or even speak of 'Black women's experiences' because they themselves are not Black. Others include a few safe hand-picked Black women's voices to avoid criticisms that they are racist. Both examples reflect a basic unwillingness by many U.S. White feminists to alter the paradigms that guide their work.

A more recent pattern of suppression involves incorporating, changing, and thereby depoliticizing Black feminist ideas. The growing popularity of post-modernism in U.S. higher education in the

1990s, especially within literary criticism and cultural studies, fosters a climate where symbolic inclusion often substitutes for bona fide substantive changes. Because interest in Black women's work has reached occult status, suggests Ann duCille (1996), it 'increasingly marginalizes both the black women critics and scholars who excavated the fields in question and their black feminist "daughters" who would further develop those fields' (p. 87). Black feminist critic Barbara Christian (1994), a pioneer in creating Black women's studies in the U.S. academy, queries whether Black feminism can survive the pernicious politics of resegregation. In discussing the politics of a new multiculturalism, Black feminist critic Hazel Carby (1992) expresses dismay at the growing situation of symbolic inclusion, in which the texts of Black women writers are welcome in the multicultural classroom while actual Black women are not.

[. . .]

Using and furthering an interpretive framework or paradigm that has come to be known as race, class, and gender studies constitute a second objective of *Black Feminist Thought*. Rejecting additive models of oppression, race, class, and gender studies have progressed considerably since the 1980s. During that decade, African-American women scholar-activists, among others, called for a new approach to analyzing Black women's experiences. Claiming that such experiences were shaped not just by race, but by gender, social class, and sexuality, works such as *Women, Race and Class* by Angela Davis (1981), 'A Black Feminist Statement' drafted by the Combahee River Collective (1982), and Audre Lorde's (1984) classic volume *Sister Outsider* stand as groundbreaking works that explored interconnections among systems of oppression. Subsequent work aimed to describe different dimensions of this interconnected relationship with terms such as *intersectionality* (Crenshaw 1991) and *matrix of domination*. In this volume, I use and distinguish between both terms in examining how

oppression affects Black women. Intersectionality refers to particular forms of intersecting oppressions, for example, intersections of race and gender, or of sexuality and nation. Intersectional paradigms remind us that oppression cannot be reduced to one fundamental type, and that oppressions work together in producing injustice. In contrast, the matrix of domination refers to how these intersecting oppressions are actually organized. Regardless of the particular intersections involved, structural, disciplinary, hegemonic, and interpersonal domains of power reappear across quite different forms of oppression.

[. . .]

As long as Black women's subordination within intersecting oppressions of race, class, gender, sexuality, and nation persists, Black feminism as an activist response to that oppression will remain needed.

In a similar fashion, the overarching purpose of U.S. Black feminist thought is also to resist oppression, both its practices and the ideas that justify it. If intersecting oppressions did not exist, Black feminist thought and similar oppositional knowledges would be unnecessary. As a critical social theory, Black feminist thought aims to empower African-American women within the context of social injustice sustained by intersecting oppressions. Since Black women cannot be fully empowered unless intersecting oppressions themselves are eliminated, Black feminist thought supports broad principles of social justice that transcend U.S. Black women's particular needs.

Because so much of U.S. Black feminism has been filtered through the prism of the U.S. context, its contours have been greatly affected by the specificity of American multiculturalism (Takaki 1993). In particular, U.S. Black feminist thought and practice respond to a fundamental contradiction of U.S. society. On the one hand, democratic promises of individual freedom, equality under the law, and social justice are made to all American citizens. Yet on the other hand, the reality of differential group treatment based on race, class, gender, sexuality, and citizenship status persists. Groups organized around race, class, and gender in and of themselves are not inherently a problem. However, when African-Americans, poor people, women, and other groups discriminated against see little hope for group-based advancement, this situation constitutes social injustice.

Within this overarching contradiction, U.S. Black women encounter a distinctive set of social practices that accompany our particular history within a unique matrix of domination characterized by intersecting oppressions. Race is far from being the only significant marker of group difference – class, gender, sexuality, religion, and citizenship status all matter greatly in the United States (Andersen and Collins 1998). Yet for African-American women, the effects of institutionalized racism remain visible and palpable. Moreover, the institutionalized racism that African-American women encounter relies heavily on racial segregation and accompanying discriminatory practices designed to deny U.S. Blacks equitable treatment. Despite important strides to desegregate U.S. society since 1970, racial segregation remains deeply entrenched in housing, schooling, and employment (Massey and Denton 1993). For many African-American women, racism is not something that exists in the distance. We encounter racism in everyday situations in workplaces, stores, schools, housing, and daily social interaction (St. Jean and Feagin 1998). Most Black women do not have the opportunity to befriend White women and men as neighbors, nor do their children attend school with White children. Racial segregation remains a fundamental feature of the U.S. social landscape, leaving many African-Americans with the belief that 'the more things change, the more they stay the same' (Collins 1998, 11–43). Overlaying these persisting inequalities is a rhetoric of color blindness designed to render these social inequalities invisible. In a context where many believe that to talk of race fosters racism, equality allegedly lies in treating everyone the same. Yet as Kimberle Crenshaw (1997) points out, 'it is fairly obvious that treating different things the same can generate as much inequality as treating the same things differently' (p. 285).

Although racial segregation is now organized differently than in prior eras (Collins 1998, 11–43), being Black and female in the United States continues to expose African-American women to certain common experiences. U.S. Black women's similar work and family experiences as well as our participation in diverse expressions of African-American culture mean that, overall, U.S. Black women as a group live in a different world from that of people who are not Black and female.

[. . .]

To maintain their power, dominant groups create and maintain a popular system of 'commonsense' ideas that support their right to rule. In the United States, hegemonic ideologies concerning race, class, gender, sexuality, and nation are often so pervasive that it is difficult to conceptualize alternatives to them, let alone ways of resisting the social practices that they justify. For example, despite scant empirical research, beliefs about Black women's sexuality remain deeply held and widespread. Moreover, the sexual politics of Black womanhood reveals how important the controlling images applied to Black women's sexuality have been to the effective operation of domination overall.

School curricula, religious teachings, community cultures, and family histories have long been important social locations for manufacturing ideologies needed to maintain oppression. However, an increasingly important dimension of why hegemonic ideologies concerning race, class, gender, sexuality, and nation remain so deeply entrenched lies, in part, in the growing sophistication of mass media in regulating intersecting oppressions. It is one thing to encounter school curricula that routinely exclude Black women as bona fide subjects of study; religious teachings that preach equality yet are often used to justify Black women's submission to all then; Black community ideologies that counsel Black women to be more 'feminine' so that Black men can reclaim their masculinity;

arid family histories that cover up patterns of physical and emotional abuse that blame Black women for their own victimization. It is quite another to see images of U.S. Black women as 'hoochies' broadcast globally in seemingly infinite variation.

In the United States, one would think that the combination of a better-educated public and scholarship designed to shatter old myths would effectively challenge hegemonic ideologies. As the resurgence of White supremacist organizations with staunch beliefs about Black intellectual and moral inferiority suggest, this has not been the case. Instead, old ideas become recycled in new forms. Yesterday's welfare mother splits into social-class-specific images of the welfare queen and the Black lady. Yesterday's jezebel becomes today's 'hoochie.'

Racist and sexist ideologies, if they are disbelieved, lose their impact. Thus, an important feature of the hegemonic domain of power lies in the need to continually refashion images in order to solicit support for the U.S. matrix of domination. Not just elite group support, but the endorsement of subordinated groups is needed for hegemonic ideologies to function smoothly. Realizing that Black feminist demands for social justice threaten existing power hierarchies, organizations must find ways of appearing to include African-American women – reversing historical patterns of social exclusion associated with institutional discrimination – while disempowering us. Ideas become critical within this effort to absorb and weaken Black women's resistance. Regardless of their placement in social hierarchies, other groups also encounter these pressures. For example, White women are told that they become 'race traitors' if they date Black men, a stigma that in effect asks them to calculate whether the gain of an interracial relationship is worth the loss of White privilege. Similarly, in the current reorganization of U.S. racial ideologies where Vietnamese, Cambodians, and other recent Asian immigrant groups jockey to find a racial identity between the fixed points of Blackness and Whiteness, Asians are encouraged to derogate Blacks.

Taking one's place at the top of the 'minority' ladder certainly provides better treatment than that dished out to the Blacks and Native Americans who are relegated to the bottom. Yet until the category of 'Whiteness' is expanded to reclassify Asians as 'White,' becoming a 'model minority' remains a hollow victory.

The significance of the hegemonic domain of power lies in its ability to shape consciousness via the manipulation of ideas, images, symbols, and ideologies. As Black women's struggles for self-definition suggest, in contexts such as these where ideas matter, reclaiming the 'power of a free mind' constitutes an important area of resistance. Reversing this process whereby intersecting oppressions harness various dimensions of individual subjectivity for their own ends becomes a central purpose of resistance. Thus, the hegemonic domain becomes a critical site for not just fending off hegemonic ideas from dominant culture, but in crafting counter-hegemonic knowledge that fosters changed consciousness. Regardless of the actual social locations where this process occurs – families, community settings, schools, religious institutions, or mass media institutions – the power of reclaiming these spaces for 'thinking and doing not what is expected of us' constitutes an important dimension of Black women's empowerment.

[. . .]

Black women's empowerment involves revitalizing U.S. Black feminism as a social justice project organized around the dual goals of empowering African-American women and fostering social justice in a transnational context Black feminist thought's emphasis on the ongoing interplay between Black women's oppression and Black women's activism presents the matrix of domination and its interrelated domains of power as responsive to human agency. Such thought views the world as a dynamic place where the goal is not merely to survive or to fit in or to cope; rather, it becomes a place where we feel ownership and accountability. The existence of Black feminist thought suggests that there is always choice, and power to act, no matter how bleak the situation may appear to be. Viewing the world as one in the making raises the issue of individual responsibility for bringing about change. It also shows that while individual empowerment is key, only collective action can effectively generate the lasting institutional transformation required for social justice.

REFERENCES

Amott, Teresa L., and Julie Matthaei. 1991. *Race, Gender, and Work: A Multicultural Economic History of Women in the United States*. Boston: South End Press.

Andersen, Margaret L., and Patricia Hill Collins, eds. 1998. *Race, Class, and Gender; An Anthology, Third Edition*. Belmont, CA: Wadsworth Press.

Berry, Mary Frances. [1971] 1994. *Black Resistance, White Law: A History of Constitutional Racism in America*. New York: Penguin.

Brewer, Rose. 1983. 'Theorizing Race, Class and Gender: The New Scholarship of Black Feminist Intellectuals and Black Women's Labor.' In *Theorizing Black Feminisms: The Visionary Pragmatism of Black Women*, ed. Stanlie, M. James and Abena P. A. Busia, 13–30. New York: Routledge.

Burnham, Margaret A. 1987. 'An Impossible Marriage: Slave Law and Family Law.' *Law and Inequality* 5: 187–225.

Caraway, Nancie. 1991. *Segregated Sisterhood: Racism and the Politics of American Feminism*. Knoxville: University of Tennessee Press.

Carby, Hazel. 1987. *Reconstructing Womanhood: The Emergence of the Afro-American Woman Novelist*. New York: Oxford University Press.

Carby, Hazel. 1992. 'The Multicultural Wars.' In *Black Popular Culture*, ed. Michele Wallace and Gina Dent, 187–199. Seattle: Bay Press.

Chodorow, Nancy. 1978. *The Reproduction of Mothering*. Berkeley: University of California Press.

Christian, Barbara. 1994. 'Diminishing Returns: Can Black Feminism(s) Survive The Academy?' In *Multiculturalism: A Critical Reader*, ed. David Theo Goldberg, 168–79. Cambridge: Basil Blackwell.

Collins, Patricia Hill. 1998. *Fighting Words: Black Women and the Search for Justice*. Minneapolis: University of Minnesota Press.

The Combahee River Collective. 1982. 'A Black Feminist Statement.' In *But Some of Us Are Brave*, ed. Gloria T. Hull, Patricia Bell Scott, and Barbara Smith, 13–22. Old Westbury, NY: Feminist Press.

Crenshaw, Kimberle Williams. 1991. 'Mapping the Margins: Intersectionality, Identity Politics, and Violence Against Women of Color.' *Stanford Law Review* 43 (6): 1241–99.

Crenshaw, Kimberle Williams. 1997. 'Color Blindness, History, and the Law.' In *The House That Race Built*, ed. Wahneema Lubiano, 280–88. New York: Pantheon.

Davis, Angela Y. 1981. *Women, Race and Class*. New York: Random House.

Davis, Angela Y. 1989. *Women, Culture, and Politics*. New York: Random House.

Dill, Bonnie Thornton. 1983. 'Race, Class, and Gender: Prospects for an All-Inclusive Sisterhood.' *Feminist Studies* 9 (1): 131–50.

duCille, Ann. 1996. *Skin Trade*. Cambridge, MA: Harvard University Press.

Giddings, Paula. 1984. *When and Where I Enter . . . The Impact of Black Women on Race and Sex in America*. New York: William Morrow.

Gilligan, Carol. 1982. *In A Different Voice: Psychological Theory and Women's Development*. Cambridge, MA: Harvard University Press.

Higginbotham, Evelyn Brooks. 1989. 'Beyond the Sound of Silence: Afro-American Women in History.' *Gender and History* 1 (1): 50–67.

Jewell, K. Sue. 1993. *From Mammy to Miss America and Beyond: Cultural Images and the Shaping of U.S. Social Policy*. New York: Routledge.

Jones, Jacqueline. 1985. *Labor of Love, Labor of Sorrow: Black Women, Work, and the Family from Slavery to the Present*. New York: Basic Books.

King, Mae. 1973. 'The Politics of Sexual Stereotypes.' *Black Scholar* 4 (6–7): 12–23.

Lorde, Audre. 1984. *Sister Outsider*. Trumansberg, NY: Crossing Press.

Lubiano, Wahneema. 1992. 'Black Ladies, Welfare Queens, and State Minstrels: Ideological War by Narrative Means.' In *Race-ing Justice, En-Gendering Power*, ed. Toni Morrison, 323–63. New York: Pantheon.

Marable, Manning. 1983. 'Grounding with My Sisters: Patriarchy and the Exploitation of Black Women.' In *How Capitalism Underdeveloped Black America*, 69–104. Boston: South End Press.

Massey, Douglas S., and Nancy A. Denton. 1993. *American Apartheid: Segregation and the Making of the Underclass*. Cambridge, MA: Harvard University Press.

Moraga, Cherrie, and Gloria Anzaldua, eds. 1981. *This Bridge Called My Back: Writings by Radical Women of Color*. Watertown, MA: Persephone Press.

Morton, Patricia. 1991. *Disfigured Images: The Historical Assault on Afro-American Women*. New York: Praeger.

Mullings, Leith. 1997. *On Our Own Terms: Race, Class, and Gender in the Lives of African American Women*. New York: Routledge.

Omolade, Barbara. 1994. *The Rising Song of African American Women*. New York: Routledge.

Scales-Trent, Judy. 1989. 'Black Women and the Constitution: Finding Our Place, Asserting Our Rights.' *Harvard Civil Rights – Civil Liberties Law Review* 24 (Winter): 9–43.

Smith, Barbara. 1982. 'Racism and Women's Studies.' In *But Some of Us Are Brave*, ed. Gloria T. Hull, Patricia Bell Scott, and Barbara Smith, 157–75. Old Westbury, NY: Feminist Press.

St. Jean, Yannick, and Joe R. Feagin. 1998. *Double Burden: Black Women and Everyday Racism*. Armonk, NY: M. E. Sharpe.

Takaki, Ronald. 1993. *A Different Mirror: A History of Multicultural America*. Boston: Little, Brown.

Wallace, Michele. 1990. *Invisibility Blues: From Pop to Theory*. New York: Verso.

White, Deborah Gray. 1985. *Ar'n't I a Woman? Female Slaves in the Plantation South*. New York: W. W. Norton.

Zinn, Maxine Baca, Lynn Weber Cannon, Elizabeth Higginbotham, and Bonnie Thornton Dill. 1986. 'The Costs of Exclusionary Practices in Women's Studies.' *Signs* 11 (2): 290–303.

27. The Rise, Fall and Rise of Social Class

Rosemary Crompton

The election of a 'New Labour' government in Britain in 1997, after eighteen years of Conservative rule, seemed to offer new possibilities for change and improvement, particularly for those concerned with addressing inequalities. However, although equality-directed New Labour policies (such as reducing child poverty) have been introduced, the New Labourite 'third way' has to a large extent retained the neo-liberal economic policies developed under Thatcherism.

In brief, contemporary neo-liberalism builds on the foundations of nineteenth-century economic liberalism (that is, economic *laissez-faire*), and indeed, the majority of its principles are very similar to this older doctrine.[1] Neo-liberalism claims that society as a whole is best served by maximum market freedom and minimum intervention by the state. Thus the role of government should be limited to security, the defence of the realm and the protection of private property, together with the creation and maintenance of markets. Other functions, including the provision of essential services (such as transport, water, energy and even health and education), are best carried out by private enterprise. The profit motive will ensure rationality in decision-making and thus the 'best' outcome for society as a whole, whilst individual citizens remain free from the oppressive demands of the state.

In Britain (and the United States) the decades after the Second World War had been characterized by social and economic policies (often described as 'Keynesian'[2]) that had sought directly to restrain the impact of 'market forces'. These policies had included restraints on borrowing and lending and the use of taxation, interest rates, etc. to control demand, as well as the regulation of prices and incomes. These policies were redistributive (indeed, up until the 1970s, the extent of material inequalities declined). However, Keynesian policies were increasingly criticized, by neo-liberals, as contributing to economic decline. In Britain, the election of the Conservative government in 1979 marked a decisive shift to neo-liberal policies, and 'the market' was reintroduced as the preferred mechanism of economic and social organization. [. . .] state-owned assets (e.g. gas, electricity, transport, telecommunications) were privatized, wage controls and other labour market 'restrictions' were removed, financial services were deregulated, and 'quasi-markets' introduced in areas of public provision such as education and health.

'New Labour', despite its long period in office, has not substantially reversed these neo-liberal policies. Thus the labour market in Britain remains largely deregulated (although a minimum wage has been established) and the government continues to adopt a 'hands-off' policy as far as business interests, and market forces more generally, are concerned. Indeed, neo-liberal economic policies would seem to be gaining in influence worldwide and are particularly entrenched in the US (Harvey 2005). There has been no real change, therefore, in the broad structuring of economic class inequalities.

Nevertheless, other profound changes *have* taken place. In most 'Western' countries, the structure of employment is in a process of constant transformation. The proportion of those engaged in 'professional and managerial' employ-ment continues to rise (although at a slower rate), and in England and Wales, nearly a third of the adult population were so classified in the 2001 Census. There has been a corresponding decline in the proportion of jobs requiring physical strength and a modicum of intelligence – that is, the 'good' working class jobs (in mining, car assembly and steel-working, for example) once held by men. Technological change means that this kind of labour has increasingly been replaced by machines (or computers). However, many of these kinds of jobs have been 'exported' to coun-tries such as China and India, and in Britain, immigrant labour is increasingly recruited to carry out the jobs at the lower levels of the employment structure. In addition, the nature of jobs is constantly changing – in the 1990s, for example, call centres were considered as a 'new' form of employment; today, they are outsourced overseas.

In all 'Western' countries, women increasingly expect to be in employment for most of their adult lives, even when they have small children. Indeed, in Britain, the greatest growth in employ-ment from the last decade of the twentieth century onwards has been amongst women with children under school age. Women who are well educated and in good jobs tend to enter into partnerships with similar men, and (besides the loss of 'good' working class jobs and increasing wage disparities) this 'assortative mating' is another factor contrib-uting to social polarization, as the gap widens between two-earner households and households in which no adult works at all (Gregg and Wad-sworth 2001).

Despite this process of constant change, however, a number of underlying processes remain the same. Capitalism (and the capitalist state) continues to generate a diverse range of differentially rewarded jobs. Profitability remains a major concern for the capitalist enterprise. Great concentrations of wealth persist – and indeed, are on the increase. At the individual level, people still want to do the best they can for themselves and their families. Thus parents still work around the educational system as far as they can, and 'market'-inspired changes in the education system have increased opportunities for middle-class parents to ensure that their children are placed in aca-demically successful schools (in Britain, social mobility is actually in decline). People still con-stantly compare themselves to others, and eco-nomic and social hierarchies are enduring.

It still makes sense, therefore, to describe Britain and other, similar societies as 'class' societ-ies. What, however, of the explanatory value of the 'class' concept? As we shall see in the chapters that follow, there is no straightforward answer to this question, not least because of the variety of ways in which 'class' has been defined. In terms of 'class' relations, and perceptions of class, however, there is one important change (or rather, set of changes) that it would be best to acknowl-edge from the outset.

This is the fact that, although class divisions are persistent, the *idea* of 'class' has lost its impor-tance as a central discourse, or political organizing principle, in contemporary societies. This is a con-sequence of changes in jobs, in employment and in localities, as well as quite deliberate and con-scious changes in discursive frameworks. In respect of the latter, for example, in Britain, the Labour Party, for most of the twentieth century, defined itself as the party of the 'working class'. However, 'New Labour' has consciously dis-tanced itself from 'class' connotations of any kind. Poverty is seen as a problem of 'social exclusion' rather than as an outcome of class processes. Thus government policies tend to be directed at equip-ping the individual with the capacities for inclu-sion (training, parenting classes, new skills) rather than at systematic structural or contextual changes that might reduce inequalities (increases in taxa-tion, or employment regulation that would gen-erate 'better' jobs, for example). An emphasis on the individual, of course, is one of the defining features of neo-liberalism.

It could be argued – and indeed, many social theorists have done so (Giddens 1991; Beck and Beck-Gernsheim 2002) – that an increasingly individualistic emphasis within society at large is an outcome of the kinds of structural economic and social changes that have been briefly reviewed above, rather than just a shift in ideas and dominant 'ways of thinking'. The decline – indeed disappearance – of traditional working-class communities has removed an important mechanism of socialization within which collectivist ideas and attitudes were once generated. Although, for most people, work as employment remains of central importance, changes in the nature of work itself, the employment relationship and management styles have all contributed to increasing individualism. In Western countries, increasing affluence has resulted in a greater emphasis on consumption and leisure. Moreover, opportunities to consume have been massively widened (cheap holidays overseas, for example), and information on these opportunities is widely available both in the media and in more recent developments such as the Internet.

In Britain, the example of Association Football may be used as a metaphor through which to illustrate some of the many different strands contributing to the growth of individualism and the decline of collectivism. Football was once the 'people's game' (Walvin 2001, although this did not usually include women). The majority of today's leading clubs began as an extension of their local community, linked to a workplace (Arsenal and West Ham), a working men's social club (Manchester United), a church (Everton) or educational institution (Tottenham Hotspur), and both supporters and players tended to be 'locals'. In a similar vein, financial support for these early ventures was drawn from the local community, and the major shareholders were local employers and businessmen. As with boxing, professional football was (and still is) a way in which working-class youths could achieve upward mobility and economic security – to a point.

Until the 1960s, the wages of football players were regulated at a level that certainly provided a good income, but not excessive riches. The major market in football was in the transfer (of players), and promising young players in the lower divi-

sions were almost invariably sold on to the more successful clubs. Nevertheless, Association Football in Britain, even at the higher levels, retained strong local links until well into the second half of the twentieth century. This rootedness in local working-class communities meant that 'football's politics, such as they are, have tended to loiter on the left wing' (Ronay 2007). Even in the 1960s, 1970s and 1980s major figures in football, such as Bill Shankly and Brian Clough, identified themselves as socialists, and traced their beliefs back to childhoods spent in areas dominated by heavy industry and trade union influence.

The regulation of footballers' wages ended in the 1960s. Wages increased, but not dramatically, and were still restricted by the ability of clubs to pay. However, the nature of football in Britain was changing, as the more successful clubs opened up their shareholdings via stock market flotations. The erosion of the 'traditional' working-class fan base and football's growing attraction for the middle classes meant that the successful clubs became increasingly attractive in financial terms, grounds were improved, and ticket prices rose dramatically. The really big change, however, came in 1992 when the sale of television rights, at a stroke, massively increased the money available to the clubs, particularly the more successful clubs. The introduction of the Premiership (an elite 'super league', replacing the old First Division) hugely increased the financial polarization between the top and bottom clubs. The leading teams have become global brands, and local links have to a large extent disappeared. The clubs themselves are now up for grabs, either as the playthings of the international super-rich, or as sound commercial investments. Footballers' wages now average £12,300 a week and the top players have become multimillionaires. The international trade in the top players means that national, as well as local, links have been attenuated. Local heroes have been replaced by international celebrities.

As a recent commentary has argued (Ronay 2007):

in its own way modern British football is a deeply political affair. Just take a look at the Premiership to find out what 15 years of hot-housed free-market capitalism looks like . . . The players have come to represent an acme of consumption, a brutally linear expression of a certain way of living. In our footballers we see a funfair mirror reflection of the same forces working on the people watching them from the stands. We don't admire them, so much as aspire to their lifestyle . . . The top tier of British football stands as an extreme expression of a certain kind of politics, rampant capitalism with the volume turned up to 11.

This brief excursion into the recent history of British football has been made not in order to sentimentalize the past, or as a yearning for the 'good old days', but as a (hopefully) accessible illustration of the many different factors that have fed into the generation of an increasingly individualistic perspective in Britain and other countries. The erosion of local communities, the deregulation of the labour market, the growth of commercialism and the impact of the media have polarized the game and created in Britain a global leisure industry marked by a highly individualistic culture. The example of football may be seen as an extreme case of the processes that fuel increasing individualism in society at large.

However, in this book it will be argued that although it is pointless to attempt to deny, or ignore, this individualistic societal shift, this does not mean, as some have argued, that 'class is dead'. 'Class' still persists as systematically structured social and economic disadvantage, which is reproduced over the generations. With regard to the explanatory value of the concept of 'class', it will be argued that we should not attempt to cling on to old frameworks, but also that it is equally important not to discard approaches and techniques that are still relevant to the analysis of contemporary societies. Indeed, in this book it will be further suggested that at times, the pursuit of the currently fashionable within sociology (in particular, in respect of 'culture' and 'identity') has resulted in a loss of sociological 'cutting edge' as far as discussions of class inequalities are concerned (see Crompton and Scott 2005). A 'return to structures' is required.

[. . .]

In the 1980s and 1990s, feminist thinking made a major contribution to the 'identity politics' which, it has been argued (and as already discussed in chapter 2), has largely replaced 'old' class politics. From the beginning of the 1980s, left-leaning parties suffered successive electoral defeats in both Britain and the United States, and there was a neo-liberal 'return to the market' in government policies ('Reaganomics' in the US, 'Thatcherism' in Britain). Towards the end of the 1980s, government regimes in the self-proclaimed state 'socialist' countries in the Eastern bloc progressively collapsed.[3] They have been replaced by governments which have, with varying degrees of enthusiasm, embraced the doctrine of neo-liberalism and 'market forces'.

A powerful subtext in these debates is that the 'failure of the left' is also a failure of socialist theory; that socialists have remained encumbered for too long by the trappings of outdated ideologies which required revision and updating. The major thesis associated with such arguments, which reflects the changes discussed above, is that the decline of mass production, and with it a mass labour force, has led to the declining significance of the (mass, male) 'working class' and thus of class *politics*. The political parallel of mass production was Keynesian economics in combination with varying degrees of centralized planning and organization; when such political accommodations finally collapsed at the end of the 1970s the vacuum was filled by the neo-liberal 'return to the market', which has further fragmented class politics. Thus 'class', at least in its now obsolete mass, manual, male, working class dimensions, is of declining significance, and must be replaced by a new emphasis on ecological and feminist issues, a concern for internationalism together with a move away from authoritarian centralism, and a recognition of the centrality of consumption, rather than outdated 'productivism' (Hall and Jaques 1989: 11–12).

This apparent decline of 'class politics' seemed also to signify the unravelling of yet another element of the 'industrial society' thesis which, as has been described in previous chapters (pp. 17, 28), was a significant element of the 'orthodox consensus' which prevailed in post-war sociology in Britain and America. This was the Lipset Rokkan thesis concerning the institutionalization of class politics (1967). It argued that as nation states mature, political divisions (parties) come to reflect relatively stable class cleavages in society. Thus political representation allows for the expression of class interests within the framework of democratic politics. This model was extensively criticized, but the British case, in broad outline, did correspond to the bipartisan 'class containment' model; with the middle and upper classes tending to vote Conservative, the lower and working classes for Labour. Nevertheless, as we have noted, both parties gave broad support to 'welfarist' policies such as increased educational provision, the development of public housing, and support for the National Health Service. However, from the 1960s onwards, the link between class and voting has apparently become increasingly tenuous – that is, a process of 'dealignment' (between employment class and voting behaviour) has occurred (Clark et al. 1993).

The significance of 'new social movements' which, according to Offe (1985a), have 'transformed the boundaries of institutional politics' has also been emphasized. Offe describes the 'old politics' – that is, the major political issues in Western Europe from the immediate post-war years until the early 1970s – as being centrally concerned with issues of economic growth, distribution and security. As described by the Lipset–Rokkan thesis, old politics was also marked by a considerable degree of consensus – on the desirability of economic growth, of welfare provision and so on – and distributive conflict organized politics along broadly 'class' lines; parties of the unionized working class competing with bourgeois parties which included both the old and elements of the 'new' (that is, lower-level, white-collar) middle class. However, the accommodative basis of the old politics has been challenged by both the New Right and the growth of new social movements, which include the peace movement, ecological movements and human rights and feminist movements.

The neo-liberal New Right was highly critical of the extent of state involvement characteristic of the 'old politics', which it saw both as acting as a brake upon economic recovery and as eroding the base of individual responsibilities and undermining civil society. New social movements are similarly critical of the state's capacity to resolve the major problems which they identify, but, Offe argues, they seek not to 'roll back' the state or 'reprivatize' civil society but to *transform* political action through the development of a non-institutional politics which will bring about permanent changes. The feminist slogan 'the personal is political' may be used to describe this approach to political action, which is also characterized by relatively non-hierarchical modes of organization, mass protests (for example, against the Iraq war) and, often, direct action.

New social movements, Offe argues, represent a significant break with class politics. The bases of their organization do not correspond to socioeconomic classes, or their corresponding left/right ideologies, but '[are] rather coded in *categories* taken from the movements' issues, such as gender, age, locality etc., or, in the case of environmental and pacifist movements, the human race as a whole' (Offe 1985b: 831; my emphasis). Class, in the sense of socio-economic status, is related to new social movements, however, in that much of their membership is drawn from the 'new' new middle class – that is, the educated, socially aware elements of the middle class who grew up within the economic security of the old politics and found employment within the institutions it created (that is, in administration, health, education, etc.). The 'new' new middle class may be distinguished from the 'old' new middle class of lower-level, white-collar workers. Such groupings have politicized, not on behalf of a class, but around the wider issues addressed by new social movements: 'New middle class politics, in contrast to most working class politics, as well as old middle class politics, is typically the politics *of* a class but not *on behalf of* a class' (Offe 1985b: 833).

These academic debates relating to politics, it must be remembered, were taking place at a time in which (particularly in Britain), left-of-centre political parties endured successive electoral defeats (the Conservative government was in power from 1979 to 1997). A major feature of 'New Labour' has been its conscious attempt to distance itself from 'old politics', in particular the major representatives of 'class politics' such as the trade unions. Indeed the transformation of Labour politics might itself be seen as yet another instance of the increasing lack of relevance of 'class' in contemporary political debates.

[. . .]

It is true that there have been massive social changes. As summarized above, changes in the structure and location of paid employment, together with changes in the management of employees, have eroded the presumed bases of collective, class-based identities and action. Increases in women's employment not only created unmanageable difficulties for employment-aggregate class analysis, but have also underlined the significance of non-class inequalities (which would include race and age as well as sex) in employment. The declining political relevance of class would seem to contribute further to the case for the irrelevance of the concept. However, it has been argued above that it is premature to assert that an 'epochal shift' has taken place, and that the phenomena associated with what may loosely be described as 'globalization' may best be understood as reflecting the resurgence of neo-liberalism and the intensification of capitalism. It is important not to underestimate the significance of the changes that have occurred, but their significance should not be overestimated either.

[. . .]

It is not difficult to demonstrate the persistent inequalities of class as revealed by occupational measures. 'Professional and managerial' class groupings earn more money, live in better housing, are more likely to gain higher-level qualifications and go to university, have a greater life expectancy, and are much less likely to have a long-term limiting illness (Reid 1998). In their defence of 'class analysis', Goldthorpe and Marshall (1992) laid much emphasis on the continuing class differences in opportunity revealed by studies of education and social mobility. The empirical persistence of occupational class inequalities is an important fact that should continue to be repeated and emphasized. The research programmes associated with disputes over measures of class may have ended, but this is no justification for not continuing to use these measures. Alternative measures incorporating consumption indicators are unreliable and unstable. However, this approach to 'class analysis' is relatively narrow. It does not incorporate other major dimensions of occupational inequality such as sex, age and race. More fundamentally, perhaps, the most common analytical tool that is used to demonstrate the persistence of class – occupational measures – do not adequately incorporate 'cultural' dimensions which are also vital in the production and reproduction of class inequalities.

NOTES

1. 'Liberalism' does not describe a single doctrine, and the term may encompass conflicting perspectives. For example, although all liberals would emphasize the importance of the rights and freedoms of the individual – whereas social liberals would argue that forms of support, usually provided by the state (education, welfare supports, etc.), are required in order that the individual may truly exercise these freedoms – economic liberalism argues that the inequality that arises from unequal bargaining positions (in the

absence of coercion) is a natural outcome of free competition. Indeed, economic liberals would argue that the social supports advocated by social liberals interfere with market competition and should therefore be opposed or, at the very least, kept to a minimum.

2. So called after the economist J. M. Keynes. Keynes advocated a 'mixed economy' of public and private ownership, in which the state used its powers to smooth out market fluctuations. State intervention in the economy was also accompanied by the expansion of welfare policies and other market protections. In short (and in sharp contrast to classic economic liberalism or *laissez-faire*), Keynesian economics advocates direct state intervention in markets of all kinds.

3. There were and are, of course, many on the socialist left who had always maintained that the centrally planned regimes of the Soviet Union were not in fact 'socialist', but nevertheless, even such critical socialist analyses have suffered from 'guilt by association' as discredited regimes crumbled apace.

REFERENCES

Beck, U. and Beck-Gernsheim, E. 2002: *Individualization*. Sage: London.

Clark, T. N., Lipset, S. M. and Rempel, M. 1993: The declining political significance of social class. *International Sociology*, 8 (3), 293–316.

Crompton, R. and Scott, J. 2005: Class analysis: beyond the cultural turn. In Devine, F., Savage, M., Scott, J. and Crompton, R. (eds) *Rethinking Class: Culture, Identities and Lifestyles*. Palgrave: Basingstoke, pp. 186–203.

Giddens, A. 1991: *Modernity and Self Identity*. Polity: Cambridge.

Goldthorpe, J. H. and Marshall, G. 1992: The promising future of class analysis: a response to recent critiques. *Sociology*, 26 (3), 381–400.

Gregg, P. and Wadsworth, J. 2001: Everything you ever wanted to know about measuring worklessness and polarization at the household level but were afraid to ask. *Oxford Bulletin of Economics and Statistics*, 63, 777–806.

Hall, S. and Jaques, M. (eds) 1989: *New Times: The Changing Face of Politics in the 1990s*. Lawrence & Wishart: London.

Harvey, D. 2005: *A Brief History of Neoliberalism*. Oxford University Press: Oxford.

Lipset, S. M. and Rokkan, S. (eds) 1967: *Party Systems and Voter Alignments*. Free Press: New York.

Offe, C. 1985a: 'Work' – a central sociological category? In *Disorganized Capitalism*. Polity: Cambridge.

Offe, C. 1985b: New social movements: challenging the boundaries of institutional politics. *Social Research*, 52 (4), 817–68.

Reid, I. 1998: *Class in Britain*. Polity: Cambridge.

Ronay, B. 2007: Anyone want to play on the left? *Guardian*, Wednesday 25 April.

Walvin, J. 2001: *The Only Game*. Pearson Education: London.

28. The Social Model of Disability

Colin Barnes, Geof Mercer & Tom Shakespeare

In this section, we will explore in more detail the dominant, individual, model of disability, and then contrast it with a social model of disability that was originally advanced by a small group of disabled activists, and which, without taking direct inspiration from any sociological perspective, emulates the critical approach endorsed by the sociological imagination thesis.

The individual model of disability

By the beginning of the twentieth century, the individual approach to disability – which sees its diagnosis and solution in medical knowledge – was securely entrenched. The focus is on bodily 'abnormality', disorder or deficiency, and the way in which this in turn 'causes' some degree of 'disability' or functional limitation. For example, people who have quadriplegia cannot use their arms and are therefore unable to wash or dress themselves. However, this functional 'incapacity' is used as the basis for a wider classification of the individual as (an) 'invalid'. Once they have been categorized in this way, the 'disability' becomes their defining characteristic and their incapacity is generalized. This forms the basis for a 'personal tragedy' approach, where the individual is regarded as a victim, and as someone who is in need of 'care and attention', and dependent on others – a perspective which has been at the heart of contemporary social welfare policies designed to help disabled people cope with 'their disability' (Oliver, 1983, 1990; Finkelstein, 1993).

The recommended solution lies in curative and rehabilitative medical intervention, with an increasing involvement of allied health practitioners, psychologists and educationalists. To acquire an impairment is to become the object of professional attention. This 'expert' defines an individual's needs and how these should be met. The aim is to overcome, or at least minimize, the negative consequences of the individual's 'disability'. The rehabilitative focus has underpinned a growing range of policy initiatives designed by various professional 'experts' to address the 'special needs' and 'personal difficulties' of disabled individuals.

The basic medical concern is to diagnose the bodily or intellectual 'abnormality' and advise on appropriate treatment. There is an associated administrative and policy interest in translating the individual's 'disability' into specific needs – for welfare benefits and services (Albrecht, 1976). In Britain, this has stimulated a debate about the most appropriate definition and measure of 'disability'.

Initially, the individual's 'abnormality or loss' was translated into a particular level of incapacity. For example, the British National Insurance Benefit Regulations in the 1960s advised that the loss of fingers and a leg amputated below the knee constituted a 50 per cent disability, while the loss of three fingers and the amputation of a foot or the loss of an eye translated into a 30 per cent rating (Sainsbury, 1973: 26–7). Such a mechanistic approach (though still an element in the assessment process for the Severe Disablement Allowance) came under increasing criticism from policy-makers and social researchers. There was also a widening of the definition of 'disability' to include:

1 'anatomical, physiological or psychological abnormality or loss', such as those without an arm or a leg, or who are 'blind, or deaf or paralysed'; and

2 chronic illness which interferes with physiological or psychological processes, such as arthritis, epilepsy and schizophrenia (Townsend, 1979: 686–7).

In addition, there was a reinterpretation of physical incapacity so that it was now defined in terms of the inability to perform essential activities of daily living.

[. . .]

The most influential intervention in these debates was the World Health Organization's (WHO) decision to complement its *International Classification of Disease* (WHO, 1976) with a scheme that detailed the consequences of disease. These discussions resulted in a threefold distinction in its new *International Classification of Impairments, Disabilities and Handicaps* (ICIDH) which was introduced in 1981. The explanatory document (WHO, 1980) defined the key terms as follows:

- *Impairment* 'Any loss or abnormality of psychological, physiological or anatomical structure or function' (p. 27).
- *Disability* 'Any restriction or lack (resulting from an impairment) of ability to perform an activity in the manner or within the range considered normal for a human being' (p. 28).
- *Handicap* 'A disadvantage for a given individual, resulting from an impairment or disability, that limits or prevents the fulfilment

of a role (depending on age, sex, social and cultural factors) for that individual' (p. 29).

In shorthand terms, 'impairment' includes those parts or systems of the body which do not work 'properly', and 'disability' centres on those things that people cannot do, primarily basic skills of everyday living. Most of the novelty of the WHO schema lies in the interpretation of 'handicap'. This extends the notion of 'consequences' to difficulties in carrying out social roles, while acknowledging that these vary across social groups and cultural contexts. The disablement process is represented in terms of distinctive but linked areas of consequences (WHO, 1980: 30) (see Figure 28.1).

There is a close correspondence between this *ICIDH* approach and that followed in the OPCS national surveys of disability conducted between 1985 and 1988. The latter selected as the main areas of functional limitation:

- Reaching and stretching
- Dexterity
- Seeing
- Hearing
- Personal care
- Continence
- Communication
- Locomotion
- Behaviour
- Intellectual functioning

An overall measure of ten levels of severity of 'disability' was constructed for the OPCS study based on the above activities. This emphasis on the individual's functional limitations has won international favour. As an illustration, the Americans with Disabilities Act of 1990 defines disability as an 'impairment that substantially limits one or more of the major life activities', with 'normal' functioning again the yardstick.

[. . .]

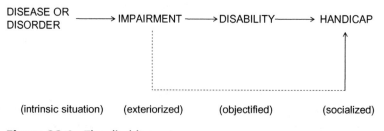

DISEASE OR DISORDER ——→ IMPAIRMENT ——→ DISABILITY ——→ HANDICAP

(intrinsic situation)   (exteriorized)   (objectified)   (socialized)

Figure 28.1 The disablement process

Towards a social model of disability

During the 1970s and 1980s, disabled activists and their organizations voiced increasing criticism of the individual, medical model of disability. In developing what became known as a social approach to disability, disabled people in Britain argued that it is society which disables people with impairments, and therefore any meaningful solution must be directed at societal change rather than individual adjustment and rehabilitation. The social model riposte to the individual, medical approach is that 'disability is not the measles' (Rioux and Bach, 1994).

The Union of the Physically Impaired Against Segregation (UPIAS) was in the vanguard of those calling for an alternative model of disability. In its manifesto document *Fundamental Principles* (1976), UPIAS placed the responsibility for disability squarely on society's failures: 'In our view it is society which disables physically impaired people. Disability is something imposed on top of our impairments by the way we are unnecessarily isolated and excluded from full participation in society. Disabled people are therefore an oppressed group in society' (UPIAS, 1976: 14).

The close connection between impairment, disability and handicap is rejected in the UPIAS model. While it broadly accepted the medical definition of impairment, the meaning of disability was turned on its head:

- *Impairment* Lacking part or all of a limb, or having a defective limb, organ or mechanism of the body.
- *Disability* The disadvantage or restriction of activity caused by a contemporary social organization which takes no or little account of people who have physical impairments and thus excludes them from participation in the mainstream of social activities (UPIAS, 1976: 3–4).

Subsequent discussions among disabled people and their organizations have amended the reference to 'physical impairments' so that any impairment (including sensory and intellectual examples) fall within the potential scope of disability.

Whereas impairment is regarded as an individual attribute, disability is not. Instead it is described as 'the outcome of an oppressive relationship between people with . . . impairments and the rest of society' (Finkelstein, 1980: 47). Once defined as a disabled person, the individual is stigmatized, and social expectations about how, for example, those with a visual or hearing impairment should behave, or what they are capable of doing, exert an influence independent of their impairment. The assumption that the form of disability – that is, social oppression – is universal is rejected by those following a social approach who point to the cultural and historical variation which characterizes disability.

Similarly, from the social model perspective, the measurement of disability adopted by the OPCS disability surveys requires substantial refurbishment. It is about a focus on 'disabling barriers and attitudes'. Hence an alternative approach to measuring disability is required. An indication of how the survey researcher who adopts a social model approach would focus on different issues is illustrated by Mike Oliver's (1990: 7–8) alternative formulation of the questions used to assess 'disability' in the 1980s by OPCS:

1   OPCS: '*Can you tell me what is wrong with you?*'
      Oliver: 'Can you tell me what is wrong with society?'
2   OPCS: '*What complaint causes your difficulty in holding, gripping or turning things?*'
      Oliver: 'What defects in the design of everyday equipment like jars, bottles and tins causes you difficulty in holding, gripping or turning them?'
3   OPCS: '*Are your difficulties in understanding people mainly due to a hearing problem?*'
      Oliver: 'Are your difficulties in understanding people mainly due to their inability to communicate with you?'
4   OPCS: '*Do you have a scar, blemish or deformity which limits your daily activities?*'

Oliver: 'Do other people's reactions to any scar, blemish or deformity you may have limit your daily activities?'

5   OPCS: *'Have you attended a special school because of a long-term health problem or disability?'*

Oliver: 'Have you attended a special school because of your education authority's policy of sending people with your health problem/disability to such places?'

6   OPCS: *'Does your health problem/disability prevent you from going out as often or as far as you would like?'*

Oliver: 'What is it about the local environment that makes it difficult for you to get about in your neighbourhood?'

7   OPCS: *'Does your health problem/disability make it difficult for you to travel by bus?'*

Oliver: 'Are there any transport or financial problems which prevent you from going out as often or as far as you would like?'

8   OPCS: *'Does your health problem/disability affect your work in any way at present?'*

Oliver: 'Do you have problems at work because of the physical environment or the attitudes of others?'

9   OPCS: *'Does your health problem/disability mean that you need to live with relatives or someone else who can help or look after you?'*

Oliver: 'Are community services so poor that you need to rely on relatives or someone else to provide you with the right level of personal assistance?'

10   OPCS: *'Does your present accommodation have any adaptations because of your health problem/disability?'*

Oliver: Did the poor design of your house mean that you had to have it adapted to suit your needs?'

The social model approach concentrates on a set of causes established externally: that is, as obstacles imposed on disabled people which limit their opportunities to participate in society. Hence, measures of disability should provide a way of monitoring the effects of physical, social and economic disabling barriers experienced by disabled people – their social exclusion – and the impact of anti-discrimination policies. In contrast, 'personal tragedy theory has served to individualize the problems of disability and hence leave social and economic structures untouched' (Oliver, 1986: 16).

In advancing a critique of the personal tragedy model, the disabled people's movement has generated a social model of disability which argues for a radical reformulation of our understanding of disability (Table 28.1). It advances very different answers to key questions such as: 'What is the nature of disability? What causes it? How is it experienced?' (Oliver, 1996b: 29–30). This goes beyond a social model standpoint, to the development of a more comprehensive social *theory* of disability: 'the social model of disability is not a substitute for social theory, a materialist history of disability not an explanation of the welfare state' (Oliver, 1996b: 41).

Of course, a 'materialist history' is but one among a range of theoretical explanations used by sociologists. It is here that a 'sociology of disability' must explore in detail the argument that 'society disables' people with impairments. Contributions to the development of a social theory of disability have ranged widely. It is important to consider work in allied areas, such as medical sociology and its analysis of what is termed 'chronic illness and disability' (Bury, 1997). In a similar way, the social model's references to 'disabling barriers' demands a more comprehensive examination of the processes and structures associated with social oppression and discrimination, whether at everyday levels, or in the workings of the state and social policy. Forms of domination also raise complex issues relating to culture and politics: not simply as sites of domination, but as arenas of resistance and challenge by disabled people.

Table 28.1 Two models of disability

Individual model	Social model
personal tragedy theory	social oppression theory
personal problem	social problem
individual treatment	social action
medicalization	self-help
professional dominance	individual and collective responsibility
expertise	experience
individual identity	collective identity
prejudice	discrimination
care	rights
control	choice
policy	politics
individual adjustment	social change

Source: adapted from Oliver, 1996a: table 2.1.

The social model focuses on the experience of disability, but not as something which exists purely at the level of individual psychology, or even interpersonal relations Instead, it considers a wide range of social and material factors and conditions, such as family circumstances, income and financial support, education, employment, housing, transport and the built environment, and more besides. At the same time, the individual and collective conditions of disabled people are not fixed, and the experience of disability therefore also demonstrates an 'emergent' and temporal character. This spans the individual's experience of disability, in the context of their overall biography, social relationships and life history, the wider circumstances of disabling barriers and attitudes in society, and the impact of state policies and welfare support systems.

Yet the claims of the social model should not be exaggerated:

The social model is not about showing that every dysfunction in our bodies can be compensated for by a gadget, or good design, so that everybody can work an 8-hour day and play badminton in the evenings. It's a way of demonstrating that everyone – even someone who has no movement, no sensory function, and who is going to die tomorrow – has the right to a certain standard of living and to be treated with respect (Vasey, 1992: 44).

[. . .]

A theoretically informed sociology will approach disability as a social state rather than as biological difference. Attention is given to the role of choice, meaning and agency in the experience of impairment/disability. This links with analyses of the social construction of disability – across societies and over time – although the complexity of this process should not be underestimated. If disabled people are characterized by their separation from the 'normal' population, specific representations of disability may be both contested and contradictory. The general trend since the nineteenth century, in Western societies, has entailed a medical takeover of disability and the intervention of a multitude of allied health and social welfare practitioners. Disabled people have been effectively marginalized and excluded from the 'mainstream' of social life; and this aspect of disabling society needs to be explored in the context of unequal power and social resources.

Over the last two centuries, disabled people have been kept more 'out of sight', and disability has almost been a 'taboo' subject. The fact that disability is now being subjected to social and political analysis is due, not to the work of sociologists, but to the pioneering studies of disabled people themselves. Recent decades are characterized by disabled people 'fighting back'. This is evident in their promotion of a social model in opposition to the traditional orthodoxy. It has been reinforced by a significant politicization of disabled people and their organizations, on an international scale, that can claim to be a disabled people's movement of social, cultural and political protest.

REFERENCES

Albrecht, G. L. (ed.) 1976: *The Sociology of Physical Disability and Rehabilitation*. Pittsburgh: The University of Pittsburgh Press.

Bury, M. 1997: *Health and Illness in a Changing Society.* London: Routledge.

Finkelstein, V. 1980: *Attitudes and Disabled People: Issues for Discussion.* New York: World Rehabilitation Fund.

Finkelstein, V. 1993: The commonality of disability. In J. Swain, V. Finkelstein, S. French, and M. Oliver (eds), *Disabling Barriers – Enabling Environments,* London: Sage, in association with the Open University, 9–16.

Oliver, M. 1983: *Social Work with Disabled People.* Basingstoke: Macmillan.

Oliver, M. 1986: 'Social Policy and Disability: some theoretical issues'. *Disability, Handicap and Society,* 1(1): 5–17.

Oliver, M. 1990: *The Politics of Disablement.* Basingstoke: Macmillan.

Oliver, M. 1996a: *Understanding Disability: From Theory to Practice.* London: Macmillan.

Oliver, M. 1996b: A sociology of disability or a disablist sociology? In L. Barton (ed.), *Disabil-ity & Society: Emerging Issues and Insights,* London: Longman, 18–42.

Rioux, M. H. and Bach, M. (eds) 1994: *Disability Is Not Measles.* North York, Ontario: L'Institut Roeher Institute.

Sainsbury, S. 1973: *Measuring Disability.* Occasional Papers on Social Administration, no. 54. London: Bell.

Townsend, P. 1979: *Poverty in the United Kingdom.* Harmondsworth: Penguin.

UPIAS. 1976: *Fundamental Principles of Disability.* London: Union of the Physically Impaired Against Segregation.

Vasey, S. 1992: 'A Response to Liz Crow'. *Coalition,* September, 42–4.

WHO. 1976: *International Classification of Disease.* 9th Revision. Geneva: World Health Organization.

WHO. 1980: *International Classification of Impairments, Disabilities and Handicaps.* Geneva: World Health Organization.

Theme 5 – Further Reading

Rosemary Crompton's (2008) *Class and Stratification: An Introduction to Current Debates* (Cambridge: Polity) is an excellent discussion which does exactly what it says. On gender inequality, see Raewyn Connell's (2009) *Gender* (Cambridge: Polity), for disability Colin Barnes and Geof Mercer's (2002) *Disability* (Cambridge: Polity) is very good, and for 'race' and ethnicity a good start is Robert Miles's (2003) *Racism*, second edition (London: Routledge). A more detailed set of readings debating the intersection of inequalities is Peter Kivisto and Elizabeth Hartung's (2007) *Intersecting Inequalities: Class, Race Sex and Sexualities* (Englewood Cliffs, NJ: Prentice Hall), though this goes well beyond introductory level.

Giddens and Sutton *Sociology* 7th *Edition* (2013)

Giddens *Sociology* covers social inequality both within and across societies, hence the block of Chapters 12, 13 and 14 provides a comprehensive coverage. In addition, other inequalities are covered in: Chapter 11 for disability, pages 464–73; Chapter 15 for gender inequality, pages 651–9; Chapter 16 for 'race' and ethnicity, pages 675–700; Chapter 20 for educational inequality, pages 883–99; Chapter 21 for crime and inequality, pages 938–50 and Chapter 23 for national identity and inequality, pages 1024–9.

Part 6

Relationships and the Life-Course

The human life-cycle appears to be universal. Individuals are born, they pass through childhood, youth, adulthood and old age before eventually, they die. This commonsense view is not entirely false, but sociologically speaking it is only a partial description. This becomes evident when we reflect on some of the terms used to describe people who are at particular stages of life. We are used to childhood, but what about adolescents, teenagers, youth, young adults, the 'young old' and the 'old old'? All of these categories are currently in use to describe stages of life in the developed societies, but some of them are very recent indeed. The concept of the teenager, for example, did not emerge until the 1950s when rapid economic growth enabled young people to become consumers, generating new forms of youth culture including pop music and fashion. Similarly, differentiating older people into the young old (65–74) and old old (75–84) only made sense once average life expectancy had risen significantly, creating social groups with common experiences.

What these examples show is that individual life stages are shaped by particular social contexts and cannot be accounted for by a simple biological life-cycle model. For this reason, sociologists now use the more flexible and less fixed concept of the life-course to study human existence. In Reading 29, Stephen Hunt outlines the arguments in favour of a life-course approach and works through some of the consequences of this. In

particular, he illustrates how the social changes associated with globalization are having an effect on people's experiences of the life-course.

While life-course studies have replaced those rooted in the biological life-cycle, the study of human sexuality has moved in a similar direction. Before the 1960s, heterosexuality was assumed to be the 'normal' human condition around which norms of sexual behaviour revolved. Of course, other forms of sexual orientation and behaviour existed, but these were thought to be marginal and limited to a small number of individuals. However, with the emergence of lesbian and gay social movements, this view was shown to be false. Academic interest in sexuality began to explore the history of sexuality and the way that sexual identities changed over time. One of the early pioneers in this field was Jeffrey Weeks who drew attention to the fact that sexuality is not a simple biological matter. On the contrary, it is a complex, constantly changing and highly significant aspect of human life that hitherto had received scant attention from sociologists. In Reading 30, Weeks begins from the standpoint that sexuality is a 'social and historical construct' and goes on the explore the consequences of this understanding.

One element of intimate relations that seems to be ever-present, regardless of sexual orientation is romantic love. If pop songs, novels and film are a guide, love must be *the* most significant part of all our lives. Yet many social historians have already convinced us that romantic love hasn't always been at the centre of personal relationships. Far from it. In previous times, people have formed relationships and married for companionship, financial stability, familial cooperation and other quite rational reasons. By comparison, love appears unstable, random and in the words of Ulrich Beck and Elisabeth Beck-Gernsheim in Reading 31, frankly chaotic. Beck and Beck-Gernsheim argue that the transformation of women's position in modern societies has complicated intimate relations even more. As more women move into better-paid work, achieving higher levels of independence, they become less likely to remain in relationships which they don't find fulfilling or satisfying. At the same time the loss of traditional manufacturing jobs and consequent challenge to the stereotype of men as breadwinners, has seen men questioning their social roles and identities. In short, one consequence of the movement towards greater gender equality has been that intimate relations are ever more dependent on the most unreliable element to keep people together, namely, love. How can individuals plan their lives and careers and societies achieve stability on such a flimsy and fragile basis?

An enormous amount of research effort has been expended studying the changing demographic structure of societies. As people live longer due to better diet, wider access to medicine and less onerous working lives, many governments and policy-makers have become concerned about the dependency ratio – the balance between the growing dependent population (mainly children and retired people) and the shrinking working population. How can we afford reasonable pensions and health care for older people when fewer workers are engaged in creating the wealth? Is it fair to expect younger generations to bear the financial burden of an ageing population? Although this kind of analysis and questioning may seem quite legitimate, many sociologists and gerontolo-

gists see it as essentially ageist in tone, blaming or scapegoating older people. In Reading 32, Bill Bytheway explores some of the contours of contemporary ageism in many of our unstated assumptions, media portrayals and humour. What Bytheway makes clear is the paradoxical situation we find ourselves in. While we don't yet find jokes about older people offensive in the way that we do with jokes about ethnicity (take a look at birthday cards poking fun at the ageing process), unlike ethnicity or, say, gender we will all be old eventually.

The final reading in this section (Reading 33) seems a highly appropriate one to end with, an excerpt from Norbert Elias's *The Loneliness of the Dying*. However, we ought to note that the sociology of death, dying and bereavement is a very recent addition to the discipline's specialist fields. The way that people handle social interaction at the end of life and the effects of death on survivors are issues that were largely ignored in sociology. Today, that has now changed and interest in the study of death and dying is growing; death, as Elias says, really is a problem of the living, not the dead. Elias argues that in modern societies death and dying is a subject that many people do not like to talk about. Perhaps because it is too painful to consider, but perhaps also because the death of others reminds us of our own inevitable demise in a society that prides itself on its ability to prolong life through medical intervention. Elias's concern here is to work through some of the consequences of our inability to talk about and prepare for dying and death. Many people today die in hospitals rather than at home and though it might be said that this is the 'best' place for gravely ill people to be, Elias argues that it often ensures a very lonely death. Even so, more recent studies into the hospice movement show that there are other ways of dealing with the inevitable end of human life which may be more satisfactory than this bleak picture suggests.

29. Life-Cycle or Life-Course?

Stephen Hunt

For many decades the life-cycle approach to human existence dominated sociological and anthropological thinking and grounded research studies. Much appeared to be associated with observations concerning biological and psychological processes. This was perhaps understandable. For human beings there are perhaps few things that are certain in this world. Some events are nonetheless fairly predictable. In this sense, the 'biological cycle' of life would seem to be an inevitable one. Human beings are living organisms with observable biological patterns which are dictated by their physiological constitution. There are inevitable, if uneven, biological processes which take the individual from infanthood into adult maturity and old age: growth and physical decline, and eventually death. All these are universal human experiences, unchanging processes which are shared with other animal species. Variations are, of course, to be discerned since historically speaking high rates of infant mortality have been common and living one's three score years and ten has proved to be by no means a forgone conclusion in many previous societies and for the majority of people in the Third World today. The ageing process can therefore be impacted, for good or for bad, by a range of social and environmental variables that interact with the range of biological factors responsible for differing rates of morbidity and mortality.

In simple terms, the 'life-cycle' can be reduced to a developmental model or models which outline the social and psychological change encountered as a person passes through the major 'stages' of life: childhood, adolescence, mid-life, old age, and eventually death. Much of the early literature on the subject seemed to reflect an underlying commonsense conviction which reduced behaviour and outlooks associated with these stages to the 'biological clock' in that ageing was seen as merely a biological process. Although focusing upon inevitable biological development as the principal bedrock to the life-cycle, these changes were, and frequently still are, associated with psychological repercussions.

In considering biological factors, there is the also the importance of the human reproductive system. In the case of females, there will be the commencement of menstruation, the years when a woman is fertile, and the time when her capacity to reproduce comes to an end. Yet even these biological 'stages' have long been subject to social construction. In Western society this is perhaps most evident through the medicalization of natural processes which has frequently framed them into so-called inevitable 'stages of life'. In many instances, the feminist critique has identified this as a reflection of 'patriarchy' – one which associates the end of the female reproductive capacity with the inevitable onslaught of menopause and all of its perceived accompanying ills.

[. . .]

In sociological terms, there has never been a complete agreement on the precise length and nature of the life-cycle in human society. Although the sociological endeavour has identified patterns and processes common to most societies, different and contrasting models of the life-cycle have been constructed. Among the most well-known (but now often widely criticized) frameworks is the eight-stage model of the life-cycle presented by Erik Erikson (1959). It was one which epitomized much of the thinking about the life-cycle. Erikson's model was typical in that it was a developmental one which attempted to present the maturational relationship between the biological, chronological, psychological and social aspects of human progress through the life-cycle as a fairly universal phenomenon. For Erikson, the basic biological processes are probably more or less similar in all human societies, although crucially the rate and quality of biological change is subject to wide individual variation in terms of both genetic and environmental variables which, in turn, are supplemented by social arrangements.

[. . .]

It was clear that at the end of the twentieth century the notion of a life-cycle became almost impossible to sustain, despite recognition of the complexities and variations involved in historical and cross-cultural analysis. Partly this was due to a greater acceptance that the models produced were biased towards experiences in Western societies and even then were increasingly less easy to conceptually and practically apply. Secondly, life-cycle models appeared to put far too much emphasis on age as a form of social stratification. Other social variables, especially in contemporary society, also had a considerable impact, forging different experiences and variation in the life-cycle. This included structured inequalities such as social class, ethnicity and gender.

Next, in rejecting the life-cycle model sociologists began to display a greater acknowledgement that although each stage of life is linked to the biological process of ageing, the life-course is largely a social construction and that earlier models were often forged by enculturated views of the world. For this reason, people in one society may experience a stage of life quite differently from another, or not at all. This acceptance allowed for a greater cross-cultural approach and an enhanced appreciation of the similarities and differences between societies. Finally, further differentiation was recognized in Western societies by the increasing chance of discontinuities in life and the complex variety of experiences of being an adult. In relationships there might be the possible experience of divorce, remarriage, or cohabitation. Changes in the labour market structure, including redundancy, job retraining and early retirement, similarly complicated the picture. This meant that transitions and status passages were not simply linear but became ever more characterized by synchronicity (the coincidence of events) and even reversibility (Du Bois-Reymond 1998). Given the evidence, then, the notion of life-cycle appeared increasingly redundant. In contrast, that of the 'life-course' had the attraction of being more flexible, more workable. The term 'life-course' does not, unlike that of 'life-cycle', assume a stable social system but one that is constantly changing. It recognized that in Western societies in particular, constant change and variation is to be expected. More widely, however, the term life-course allowed for a greater historical and cross-cultural comparison, and this seemed important given the changing nature of contemporary society and, indeed, a changing global order.

[. . .]

There are various direct or indirect ways by which late- or postmodernist writers have approached the subject of the life-course and some of their speculations have been implicit in the above discussions, not least of all that of globalization. Yet, perhaps most obviously, postmodernist theorists argue that it is arduous to suggest that people go through such clearly demarcated stages of life as in previous decades. For instance, it is now difficult to stipulate where childhood ends and adolescence begins and whether age norms still hold, although it is apparent that to one degree or another some expectations remain. What is clearly lacking is the rigidity. Writers such as Featherstone and Hepworth (1991) and Bauman (1988) see the postmodern life-course as characterized by a number of overlapping, often disparate conditions associated with the blurring of traditional chronological boundaries and the integration of formally segregated periods of life. Fixed definitions of childhood, middle age and old age are eroding under pressure from two cultural directions that have accompanied the profound shifts in the political economy of labour, retirement, and traditionally structured forms of inequality such as social class. This has various repercussions. One is that in late- or postmodern culture, the prospect of an endless life has been revived through images of perpetual youth and a blurring of traditional life-course boundaries. Now life in Western societies is reduced to a series of individual choices and projected plans for the future that have little community significance. It follows that rites of passage in Western societies are mostly optional, not compulsory aspects of social life and are likely to disappear with the rise of individualism and the decline of the community setting where they were once an integral part of life and helped establish social identity.

In Western societies we are now inclined to anticipate risks and future possibilities at least partly by choice. However, the stance taken by late- or postmodernist writers differs in this respect. Giddens argues that choice implies an underlying denial of inevitability which comes with a rational mode of thinking, nothing is inevitable. At the same time, late-modern society is void of communal obligations, and fixed social status and roles. Today, we regard ourselves as highly individualistic. This means that individualism and individual choice are key values (Giddens 1991, 5–6, 147–8). It follows that we may not necessarily pass through stringent and clearly marked out stages of the life-course but make choices and negotiate risks surrounding such matters as whether to marry or have children, or at what age we wish to retire – a more or less previously assumed inevitable life event.

Postmodernist writers are less likely to talk in terms of life-course 'risks' as emphasized by Giddens, and more in terms of the uncertainty and unpredictability in the life-course. One of the key uncertainties comes from the fragmentation of 'self'. There is now a search for 'self', personal identity and meaning. Postmodernity confronts people with pluralism and choice, but also with an absence of tradition which means that there is very little help provided by society in establishing identities and in selecting moral guides to living.

Postmodernity has also brought something different for the life-span. There is increasing demographic evidence that life-expectancy is drawing closer to life-span potential. Hence, Westerners ideally anticipate long, active and healthy lives. However, the features of postmodern ageing also derive from cultural industries that distribute pleasure and leisure across an unrestricted range of objects, identities, styles and expectations. In doing so, claims Katz, 'such industries recast the life-span in "fantastic ways", in particular, "the masking of ageing and the fantasy of timelessness"' (Katz 1995, 69). Whether the contemporary approach to the life-span is quite as radical as Katz suggests is open to debate. What is clear, however, is that its restructuring does have weighty consequences for various aspects of the life-course.

REFERENCES

Bauman, Z. (1988) 'Is There a Postmodern Sociology?', *Theory, Culture and Society*, 5 (2): 217–37.

Du Bois-Reymond, M. (1998) '"I Don't Want to Commit Myself Yet": Young People's Life Concepts', *Journal of Youth Studies*, 1 (1): 63–79.

Erikson, E. (1959) *Identity and the Life-Cycle*, London: Norton.

Featherstone, M. and Hepworth, M. (1991) 'The Mask of Ageing and the Postmodern Life Course', in M. Featherstone, M. Hepworth, and B. Turner (eds) *The Body Process and Cultural Theory*, London: Sage.

Giddens, A. (1991) *Modernity and Self-Identity: Self and Society in the Late Modern Age*, Cambridge: Polity.

Katz, S. (1995) 'Imagining the Life-Span: from Pre-Modern Miracles to Post-Modern Fantasies', in M. Featherstone and A. Wernick (eds) *Images of Ageing: Cultural Representations of Later Life*, New York: Routledge.

30. Social Constructions of Sexuality

Jeffrey Weeks

At the heart of the new sexual history is the assumption that sexuality is a social and historical construct. In the famous words of Foucault, 'Sexuality must not be thought of as a kind of natural given which power tries to hold in check, or as an obscure domain which knowledge tries gradually to uncover. It is the name that can be given to a historical construct' (Foucault, 1979, p. 105).

Leaving aside the ambiguities of and problems with this statement, I want to emphasize the revolution in the approach to sexuality that this symbolized. Of all social phenomena, sex has been most resistant to social and historical explanations. It seems the most basic, the most natural thing about us, the truth at the heart of our being. This has been reflected until very recently in even the most sophisticated studies of sexuality. As pioneering sexual theorists sought to chronicle the varieties of sexual experience throughout different periods and different cultures, they assumed that beating at the centre of all this was a core of natural sexuality, varying in incidence and power, no doubt, as a result of chance historical factors, the weight of moral and physical repression, the patterns of kinship, and so on, but nevertheless basically unchanging in biological and psychological essence.

Such an assumption governed equally the naturalist approaches of the early sexologists and the metatheoretical approaches of such Freudo-marxists as Reich and Marcuse. It dominated the thoughts of functionalist anthropologists with their commitment to cultural relativism as much as the evolutionists they displaced. It lurked as effortlessly behind the sexual writings of cultural

radicals as behind the work of moral conservatives. It was the taken-for-granted of sexual studies (see Weeks, 1985, Part 2).

The new sexual history has changed that. Its origins are disparate, owing, as I have already indicated, something to sociology and anthropology (their emphasis on cultural relativism, social organization and micro-studies: Gagnon and Simon, 1974; Plummer, 1975), something to psychoanalysis (especially the challenge offered by the theory of the unconscious to fixed gender and sexual positions: Coward, 1983), something to the new sexual movements of the early 1970s (their critique of existing social and sexual categories: Weeks, 1977), something to the new social history (in as far as these diverse strands can be disentangled from the new history). Foucault's work made such an impact in the early 1980s because, in part at least, it complemented and helped to systematize work already going on. Unifying the new approach were several common themes.

First, there was a general rejection of sex as an autonomous realm, a natural domain with specific effects, a rebellious energy that the social controls.

Once you begin to see sexuality as a 'construct', as a series of representations, as an 'apparatus' with a history of its own, many of the older certainties dissolve. It is no longer appropriate to state, as Malinowski did, that 'Sex really is dangerous', the source of most human trouble from Adam and Eve on (Malinowski, 1963, p. 127). Instead, we are forced to ask: why is it that sex is regarded as dangerous? We can no longer speculate about the inevitable conflict between the powerful instinct of sex and the demands of culture. Instead, we need to ask why our culture has conceived of sexuality in this way.

Second, it followed that the new sexual history assumed the social variability of sexual forms, beliefs, ideologies and behaviours. Sexuality has not only a history, but many histories, each of which needs to be understood both in its uniqueness and as part of an intricate pattern.

Third, it became necessary to abandon the idea that the history of sexuality can usefully be understood in terms of a dichotomy of pressure and release, repression and liberation. 'Sexuality' as a domain of social interest and concern is produced by society in complex ways. It is a result of diverse social practices that give meaning to human activities, of social definitions and self-definitions, of struggles between those who have the power to define, and those who resist. Sexuality is not a given. It is a product of negotiation, struggle and human agency.

The most important outcome of the resulting historical approach to sexuality is that it opens up the whole field to critical analysis and assessment. It becomes possible to relate sexuality to other social phenomena and to ask new types of question (new at least to the field of sex research). Questions such as the following: how is sexuality shaped, and how is it articulated with economic, social and political structures – in a word, how is it 'socially constructed'? Why and how has the domain of sexuality achieved such a critical organizing and symbolic significance? Why do we think it so important? If sexuality is constructed by human agency, to what extent can it be changed?

Questions such as these have produced an impressive flood of new work – and new questions – across a range of issues from the shaping of reproduction (e.g. Petchesky, 1986) to the social organization of disease (e.g. Mort, 1987), from the pre-Christian origins of the western preoccupation with the association between sex and truth (Foucault, 1987, 1988) to the making of the modern body (Gallagher and Laqueur, 1987).

I'll take a further example from an area which I myself have been particularly interested in – the history of homosexuality. Fifteen years ago there was virtually nothing in the way of serious historical studies of same-sex activity. Such writings as existed assumed an unchanging essence of homosexuality across cultures and over the millennia of human history, as if one could readily identify the experience of the modern gay subcultures with the socially sanctioned male intergenerational sexual patterns of ancient Greece or the institutionalized crossdressing of certain pre-industrial tribal societies.

I became convinced [. . .] that this was an inadequate way of seeing this particular past, and my early researches persuaded me that there had been significant shifts in attitudes to, and the organization of, same-sex erotic activities. In particular, it became clear that the idea that there was such a thing as a homosexual person, and an associated homosexual identity, was of comparatively recent origin, no more, in most western cultures at least, than two or three hundred years old (Weeks, 1977). Other work carried on at the same time was reaching similar conclusions (see Smith-Rosenberg, 1975; Katz, 1976; Foucault, 1979).

Since the 1970s this approach has been much debated, and has occasioned a great deal of controversy. There is by no means unanimous agreement about it (Boswell, 1983). It has at the same time become the major hypothesis for the study of homosexual history. For example, a conference at the Free University of Amsterdam in December 1987 brought together over five hundred people from all over the world to debate the relevance of 'essentialist' versus 'constructionist' perspectives in addressing the question 'Homosexuality, Which Homosexuality?'. The history papers covered a wide range of topics, from Aristotelean philosophy to the sexual and emotional proclivities of Eleanor Roosevelt. But central to the majority of them was a sensitivity to historical context that illumined hitherto obscure issues, and largely confirmed the 'constructionist' hypothesis (Altman et al., 1989; Franklin and Stacey, 1988).

But sensitivity to context is one thing; doing away with a unifying concept of sexuality is quite another. One of the problems with the new sexual history is that it is in danger of becoming a history without a proper subject. The history of sexuality is at the same time a history of a category of thought, which, if we follow Foucault, has a delimited history; and a history of changing erotic practices, subjective meanings, social definitions and patterns of regulation whose only unity lies in their common descriptor. 'Sexuality' is an unstable category, in constant flux (Padgug, 1979).

It is, nevertheless, a vital one. All societies find it necessary to organize the erotic possibilities of the body in one way or another. They all need, as Plummer suggests, to impose 'who restrictions' and 'why restrictions' to provide the permissions, prohibitions, limits and possibilities through which erotic life is organized (Plummer, 1984). But they do so in a wider variety of ways. The study of sexuality therefore provides a critical insight into the wider organization of a culture. The important question then becomes not what traditional disciplines such as history or sociology can contribute to our understanding of sexuality, but rather what the study of the sexual can contribute to our grasp of the historical, the social and the political.

Sex, politics and society

This brings me to the second of the major issues I want to explore: what indeed does the new history of sexuality tell us about the relationship of sexuality to other elements of social life, and especially what insights does it give to the nature of power and politics in the modern world?

'To some', the feminist scholar Gayle Rubin has argued, 'sexuality may seem to be an unimportant topic, a frivolous diversion from the more critical problems of poverty, war, disease, racism, famine, or nuclear annihilation. But it is precisely at times such as these, when we live with the possibility of unthinkable destruction, that people are likely to become dangerously crazy about sexuality' (Rubin, 1984, p. 267).

Why is this so? Why is sexuality so thoroughly bound up with the modern play of power, as Foucault suggested (Foucault, 1979)? What is it about sexuality that makes it so susceptible to anxiety, conflict and moralizing zeal?

The first point to make is that this is not always the case. Although our culture attributes a peculiar significance to the sexual, there is plentiful anthropological and historical evidence to suggest that other cultures interpret the possibilities of the body quite differently (Caplan, 1987). While all societies have to make arrangements for the organization of erotic life, not all do so with the obsessive concern we show in the west. Different cultures have varying responses to childhood sexuality, marriage, homosexuality, even reproduction. Some societies display so little interest in erotic activity that they have been labelled more or less 'asexual'. Islamic cultures, by contrast, have developed a lyrical view of sex with sustained attempts to integrate the religious and the sexual – as long, that is, as it was heterosexual (Bouhdiba, 1985; Weeks, 1986, pp. 25–6).

We in the west are heirs of a Christian tradition which has tended to see in sex a focus for moral anguish and conflict, producing an enduring dualism between the spirit and the flesh, the mind and the body. It has produced a culture which simultaneously disavows the body while being obsessively preoccupied with it.

Michel Foucault was centrally concerned with this issue. He abandoned the original scheme for his *History of Sexuality* and went back to the ancient Greeks and Romans in the two volumes published at the very end of his life (Foucault, 1987, 1988) precisely because of his growing conviction that the western preoccupation with the relationship between sex and truth was of very ancient lineage, and crucial to the understanding of power and subjectivity. For the ancients, he argued, concern with the pleasures of the body was only one, and not necessarily the most important, of the preoccupations of life, to be set alongside dietary regulations and the organization of household relations. We, on the other hand, seek the truth of our natures in our sexual desires. In the course of that shift, with pre-Christian as well as Christian origins, sexuality has emerged as a domain of danger as well as pleasure, emotional anxiety as well as moral certainty.

I do not wish here to assess the merits and defects of this argument. I cite it because it illustrates the major point I want to make. The new social history takes for granted that sexuality as an historical phenomenon is in fact a consequence of an obsessive social preoccupation with the body and its possibilities for erotic pleasure. As a result, far from being stubbornly resistant to social moulding, it is a peculiarly sensitive conductor of cultural influences, and hence of social and political divisions.

There are five broad categories of social relations which both are constructed around and in turn shape and reshape sex and gender relations (Weeks, 1986, 1989). First, there are the kinship and family systems that place individuals in relationship to one another, and constitute them as human subjects with varying needs and desires, conscious and unconscious. Second, there are the economic and social organizations that shape social relations, statuses and class divisions, and provide the basic preconditions and ultimate limits for the organization of sexual life. Third, there are the changing patterns of social regulation and organization, formal and informal, legal and moral, populist and professional, religious and secular, unintended consequences as well as organized and planned responses. Fourth, there are the changing forms of political interest and concern, power and policies. Finally, there are the cultures of resistance which give rise to oppositional subcultures, alternative forms of knowledge and social and sexual movements.

These are quite general categories. They have had different weighting at different historical conjunctures. But their intricate and complex interaction in the West has produced a culture which assigns a critical role to sexuality in the definition of subjectivity and self, morality and sin, normality and abnormality.

Modern sexuality has been shaped and defined at the intersection of two absolutely central concerns: with who and what we are as human subjects and social individuals; and with the nature and direction of the society as a whole. And as the state, as the organizing focus of the social sphere, has become more and more concerned with the lives of its members, for the sake of moral uniformity, economic wellbeing, national security or hygiene and health, so it has become more and more involved with the sex lives of individuals, providing the rationale for techniques of moral and legal management, detailed intervention into private lives and scientific exploration of the subject of sex.

As a result, sexuality has become an increasingly important political as well as moral issue, condensing a number of critical issues: with the norms of family life, the relations between men and women, adults and children, and the nature of normality and abnormality. These are central issues in any culture. The debate about them has become increasingly heated and bitter in recent years because debates about sexuality are debates about the type of society we want to live in. As sex goes, so goes society (Weeks, 1986, p. 36).

[. . .]

This brings me to the final theme I want to pursue: the implications of the new sexual history for our understanding of the historic present. As I suggested earlier, a major stimulus to the study of our sexual pasts has come from preoccupations that were clearly located in the present. Feminist history is, for example, by definition a history that has current political concerns at its heart. Thus a book produced by the London Feminist History Group, called *The Sexual Dynamics of History*, observes that 'Our link with contemporary political struggles gives our work as historians a special edge, because our analysis is constantly being reworked and developed' (London Feminist History Group, 1983, p. 1).

At the very least this implies that the questions that are asked of the past are prompted by the concerns of the present. Sometimes these questions can lead to the exploration of new or neglected themes. A good example here is the interest in the history and politics of male violence against women, whose starting point is very much recent experience (for instance, Cameron and Frazer, 1987; Theweleit, 1987, 1990). Sometimes the result is a re-examination of well-worn but controversial subjects in new ways. For example, Boswell's (1980) work on attitudes to homosexuality in the early Christian church is a work of great (traditional) scholarship, but is clearly also part of a fierce debate within both the Roman Catholic Church and the gay community about the real implications of the Christian tradition's attitudes towards homosexuality.

But there is something more at stake than simply finding new or better ways of addressing the past. Sexuality is a highly contentious issue in contemporary society, and at the centre of some highly influential political programmes. I have mentioned feminism and lesbian and gay politics. Perhaps even more important today are the projects of moral regeneration that lie close to the centre of the politics of the New Right in some at least of its manifestations. In the resulting political struggles around sexuality the past is freely raided for its contemporary relevance – as, for example, in the capture by the Thatcher government in Britain of the idea of Victorian values (Walvin, 1987; Weeks, 1989). The new sexual history is important in so far as it contributes to these debates, and to the extent that it illuminates the present.

I do not mean by this that historians should only study the recent past, or concentrate on issues that are of current concern. But at the very least, if the perspectives I have described on the historical construction of sexuality have any merit, the new sexual history should be able to undermine the certainty with which the past is called in to redress the difficulties of the present. As we have seen, sensitive studies of sexual behaviour in other cultures (e.g. Caplan, 1987), or at other times within our own, serve to problematize the whole idea of a single history. Instead they direct our attention to the variety of forces and practices that shape sexual categories.

The historic present is a product of many histories, some of very ancient lineage, some very recent. What we can use the new sexual history for is to question the taken-for-granted, challenge our own culturally specific preoccupations, and to try to see whether what we assume is natural is not in fact social and historical. At the same time, we can explore the continuities and the discontinuities of our sexual histories.

Let's take as an example the ways in which our culture is responding to a crisis that is both personal and social, medical and moral, and also highly political – that relating to AIDS. This is a new problem in that it is a new, or at least newly discovered, disease or group of diseases. It is also a phenomenon that is very closely connected with sexuality, both because it can be sexually transmitted and because, at least in the West, the people most affected so far have been gay men.

What is most striking is the degree to which, in reacting to AIDS, people call on pre-existing discourses and shape them to the current crisis. As Frank Mort (1987) has shown, for example, there is a substantial medico-moral tradition, going back at least to the early nineteenth century, linking beliefs about health and disease to notions of moral and immoral sex, 'dangerous sexualities'. The linkage of AIDS with homosexual lifestyles evokes a rich tradition that sees homosexuality as itself a disease (Weeks, 1977). Even the question of whether people with AIDS should be segregated and confined refers back to a heated debate in the late nineteenth century about whether the most effective means of controlling the spread of syphilis was by compulsorily testing and confining prostitutes (Walkowitz, 1980).

These are political and moral debates where more is at stake than mere historical accuracy. But it so happens that all the issues I have just referred to have been the object of investigation by the new sexual historians, who have effectively demonstrated the social conditions for the emergence of these discourses. It is too much to hope, perhaps, that their work would dispel illusions and prejudices. But at the very least it should force us to pause and ask about the conditions which are shaping our interventions. What their work underlines above all is the living nature of the past – and the historical nature of the present.

REFERENCES

Altman, D., Vance, C., Vicinus, M. and Weeks, J., (eds) (1989) *Which Homosexuality?* (London: GMP).

Boswell, J. (1980) *Christianity, Social Tolerance and Homosexuality* (Chicago: University of Chicago Press).

Boswell, J. (1983) 'Revolutions, Universals, Categories', *Salmagundi*, No. 58/59.

Bouhdiba, A. (1985) *Sexuality in Islam* (London: Routledge & Kegan Paul).

Cameron, D. and Frazer, E. (1987) *The Lust to Kill* (Cambridge: Polity Press).

Caplan, P. (1987) *The Cultural Construction of Sexuality* (London: Tavistock).

Coward, R. (1983) *Patriarchal Precedents* (London: Routledge & Kegan Paul).

Foucault, M. (1979) *History of Sexuality: Vol. 1, An Introduction* (London: Allen Lane).

Foucault, M. (1987) *History of Sexuality: Vol. 2, The Use of Pleasure* (London: Viking).

Foucault, M. (1988) *History of Sexuality: Vol. 3, Care of the Self* (London: Viking).

Franklin, S. and Stacey, J. (1988) 'Dyketactics in Difficult Times. A Review of the "Homosexuality, Which Homosexuality?" Conference', *Feminist Review*, No. 29, Summer.

Gagnon, J. and Simon, W. (1974) *Sexual Conduct* (London: Hutchinson).

Gallagher, C. and Laqueur, T. (eds) (1987) *The Making of the Modern Body* (Berkeley, CA: University of California Press).

Katz, J. (1976) *Gay American History* (New York: Thomas Croswell).

London Feminist History Group (1983) *The Sexual Dynamics of History* (London: Pluto).

Malinowski, B. (1963) *Sex, Culture and Myth* (London: Hart-Davis).

Mort, F. (1987) *Dangerous Sexualities* (London: Routledge & Kegan Paul).

Padgug, R. A. (1979) 'Sexual Matters', *Radical History Review*, No. 20, Spring/Summer.

Petchesky, R. P. (1986) *Abortion and Women's Choice* (London: Verso).

Plummer, K. (1975) *Sexual Stigma* (London: Routledge & Kegan Paul).

Plummer, K. (1984) 'Sexual Diversity', in K. Howells (ed.) *Sexual Diversity* (Oxford: Basil Blackwell).

Rubin, G. (1984) 'Thinking Sex', in C. Vance (ed.) *Pleasure and Danger* (London: Routledge & Kegan Paul).

Smith-Rosenberg, C. (1975) 'The Female World of Love and Ritual', in C. Smith-Rosenberg *Disorderly Conduct* (Oxford: Oxford University Press).

Theweleit, K. (1987, 1990) *Male Fantasies*, vols 1 and 2 (Cambridge: Polity Press).

Walkowitz, J. (1980) *Prostitution and Victorian Society* (Oxford: Oxford University Press).

Walvin, J. (1987) *Victorian Values* (London: André Deutsch).

Weeks, J. (1977) *Coming Out* (London: Quartet).

Weeks, J. (1985) *Sexuality and Its Discontents* (London: Routledge & Kegan Paul).

Weeks, J. (1986) *Sexuality* (London: Tavistock).

Weeks, J. (1989) *Sex, Politics and Society* (2nd edn) (London: Routledge & Kegan Paul).

31. The Normal Chaos of Love

Ulrich Beck & Elisabeth Beck-Gernsheim

One can love all sorts of things and people: Andalusia, one's grandmother, Goethe, black fishnet stockings against white skin, cheese sandwiches, the warm smile of a bosomy woman, fresh rolls, the movement of clouds *and* legs, Erna, Eva, Paul, Heinz-Dietrich – and one can do all this simultaneously, successively, excessively, silently, with hands, teeth, words, looks and great intensity. But sexual love (whatever form it takes) is so overwhelmingly powerful, so engrossing that we often reduce the vast range of our loving potential to longing for a caress, a word, a kiss – need I go on?

The everyday battle between the sexes, noisy or muted, inside, outside, before, after and alongside marriage is perhaps the most vivid measure of the hunger for love with which we assault each other. 'Paradise now!' is the cry of the worldly whose heaven or hell is here or nowhere. The cry echoes in the rage of the frustrated and those in pursuit of freedom, knowing that freedom plus freedom does not equal love, but more likely means a threat to it or even its end.

People marry for the sake of love and get divorced for the sake of love. Relationships are lived as if they were interchangeable, not because we want to cast off our burden of love but because the law of true love demands it. The latter-day tower of Babel built on divorce decrees is a monument to disappointed, overrated love. Even cynicism sometimes fails to conceal that it is an embittered late variant of love. People raise the drawbridges of their longings because this seems the only, the best way of protecting themselves against unbearable pain.

A lot of people speak of love and family as earlier centuries spoke of God. The longing for salvation and affection, the fuss made over them, the unrealistic pop-song truisms hidden deep in our hearts – all this smacks of religiosity, of a hope of transcendence in everyday life [. . .].

This residual and new secular religion of love leads to bitter religious controversies between two sides determined to defend their individuality, fought out in the privacy of the home or in the offices of divorce lawyers and marriage counsellors. In these modern times our addiction to love is *the* fundamentalist belief to which almost everyone has succumbed, especially those who are against fundamentalist creeds. Love is religion after religion, the ultimate belief after the end of all faith (this analogy is elucidated in chapter 6 below). It fits in with our environment about as well as the Inquisition would with an atomic power station, or a daisy with a rocket to the moon. And still love's icons blossom in us, watered by our deepest wishes.

Love is the god of privacy. 'Real socialism' may have vanished with the Iron Curtain, but we are still living in the age of real pop lyrics (see 'Romanticism now: love as a pop song in chapter 6 below). Romanticism has won and the therapists are raking it in.

The meaning of existence has not been lost; life is not hollow, at least under the lure and pressure of daily life. Some powerful force has pushed its way in and filled up the gap where, according to previous generations, God, country, class, politics or family were supposed to hold sway. I am what matters: I, and You as my assistant; and if not You then some other You.

Love, however, should on no account be equated here with fulfilment. That is its glowing side, the physical thrill. Even Eros's powerful allure, its hidden promises awakening our lust, suggesting delights both novel and familiar, does not mean fulfilment, or even require it. Achieving the goal often turns the sight of the flesh which seemed so delightful a moment ago into an alien white mass shorn of any appeal with the clothes so perfunctorily stripped off it.

How easily having one's hopes fulfilled can turn into a chilly gaze! Where only a moment ago overwhelming urgency made a knotted tangle of two walking taboos, merging me and you, all boundaries gone, now we are staring at one another with critical eyes, rather like meat inspectors, or even butchers who see the sausages where others see cattle and pigs.

Anyway there is little hope for anyone who confuses storming the heights with living on the plains, surrounded by the bogs and pitfalls of love. Love is pleasure, trust, affection and equally their opposites – boredom, anger, habit, treason, loneliness, intimidation, despair and laughter. Love elevates your lover and transforms him/her into the source of possible pleasures where others only detect layers of fat, yesterday's stubble and verbosity.

Love knows no grace, however, nor does it stick to vows or keep contracts. Whatever is said, intended or done is no more inevitably linked than the movements of mouth or hands are with other parts of the body. In what court can a spurned or misunderstood lover sue for his/her rights? Who says what is just or true or right in matters of love?

Previous generations hoped and believed that if both sexes were given a sense of freedom and equality then true love would blossom in all its radiance, heartbreak and passion; love and inequality are after all as mutually exclusive as fire and water. Now that we seem to have caught hold of at least the tip of this ideal, we find ourselves faced with the opposite problem: how can two individuals who want to be or become equals and free

discover the common ground on which their love can grow? Among the ruins of outdated lifestyles freedom seems to mean breaking out and trying something new, following the beat of one's own drum, and falling out of step with the rest.

Perhaps the two parallel lines will eventually meet, in the far distant future. Perhaps not. We shall never know.

[. . .]

Pop songs still sing the praises of eternal love. According to recent surveys, living with someone is still regarded as the ideal, as the place where one finds closeness, warmth and affection, an antithesis to the cold concrete wastes outside.

But at the same time there are deep cracks across the picture of the family. On stage and screen, in novels and tongue-tied autobiographies, wherever one turns there is the sound of battle. The battle between the sexes is the central drama of our times; business is flourishing for marriage counsellors, the family courts are booming, divorce figures are high and even in everyday life among very normal families one can hear someone quietly wondering, 'Why, oh why is living together so difficult?'

The way to find an answer is suggested in a remark by Norbert Elias: 'Often enough one cannot understand what is happening today if one does not know what happened yesterday' (1985: viii). So first of all we shall take a look at the past. It will show us that where people gradually cast off the commitments, dictates and taboos of premodern society they began to put new hopes in love, but equally found themselves in new predicaments. The combination of these two factors produced the explosive mixture we know as contemporary love.

Love becomes more important than ever

Severing traditional ties

Comparisons between premodern and modern society always emphasize that human lives used to be determined by a multitude of traditional ties – from family business and village community, homeland and religion to social status and gender role. Such ties always have a double face [. . .].

On the one hand they rigorously restrict the individual's choices, on the other they offer familiarity and protection, a stable footing and certain identity. Where they exist, a person is never alone but integrated into a larger unit. Take religion, for example:

The fact that our ancestors were bound to Christian beliefs . . . generally meant that their little world, their microcosm, was tied to another, larger world, the macrocosm. . . . The result of this bond between microcosm and macrocosm, sheltering hundreds and thousands of little worlds within the unifying greater world, which in turn, according to Christian belief, rested in God's all-encompassing embrace, was not just that even the lowliest person never fought in vain or was left to fend for himself. . . . It also must have given our ancestors an emotional stability which could not be easily thrown off-balance even by the worst ragings of pestilence, famine and war. (Imhof 1984: 23)

With the transition to modern society, changes took place on many levels and they brought about a far-reaching individualization process, cutting people off from their traditional ties, beliefs and social relationships. This process began, as Weber explained in his *Protestant Ethic* (1985), with the teachings of the Reformation, which cancelled any certainty of salvation and dismissed people into a deep inner isolation. This process has continued on many levels over the succeeding centuries; it can be seen in our complex economic system with its intricate infrastructure, and in increased secularization, urbanization, personal mobility and so on. More and more people have been affected by it, and it has reached unique dimensions in the present. As a result each of us is increasingly both expected and forced to *lead our own life* outside the bounds of any specific community or group.

For the individual this severing of traditional ties means being freed of previous constraints and obligations. At the same time, however, the support and security offered by a close-knit society

begin to disappear. As secularization gains ground, as new living patterns emerge, as value systems and religions compete for people's minds, many landmarks which previously provided orientation, meaning and a personal anchoring place in a larger universe have vanished.

[. . .]

The fundamental theme behind marriage is not just the social structure of our lives; it is also increasingly a matter of *identity*. This is the aspect revealed particularly by psychological studies of marriage: in seeking an exchange on many levels with our partner we are also seeking ourselves. We are searching for the history of our life; we want to reconcile ourselves with hurts and disappointments, plan our goals and share our hopes. We mirror ourselves in the other, and our image of a You is also an idealized image of I: 'You are an image of my secret life' (Schellenbaum 1984: 142ff), 'my better self' (Rückert). Marriage is becoming an institution 'specialized in the development and maintenance of the individual self' (Ryder 1979: 365). Love and identity are becoming closely interwoven.

So in the initial stage, falling in love:

Being in love is the search for one's own destiny a search for one's own self, to the very bottom. This is achieved through the other person, in dialogue with her, in the encounter where each person seeks recognition in the other, in accepting, in understanding, in the confrontation and liberation of what was and of what is. (Alberoni 1983)

And equally in the intimate exchanges of a couple who have been together for years:

The past with its unsolved questions and sorrows is set free. Or rather the past and the present which everyone is made up of are on the lookout for answers to the question 'Who am I and why am I here?' And what one looks for above all is someone else who wants to hear the questions, as if one can only understand oneself if someone else is listening and as if one's history can only become complete in someone else's ear. . . . So the image each partner has of him/herself and the world is born and confirmed, corrected and changed in talking together . . . the question of personal identity is constantly being discussed, 'Who am I and who are you?' (Wachinger 1986: 70–1)

Marriage counsellors, and even more so the divorce figures, can confirm that this dialogue which is sought so passionately at the beginning often falters or dries up, hesitates, is blocked by silent taboos, interrupted or completely cut off. Why does this happen? That is the question to be looked into in the following sections. We shall trace how both phenomena – the growing longing and the frequent failure – have a common root. Simplified into one sentence, the disappointments inherent in our idea of love just as much as the hopes we invest in it are an outcome of our modern concern with being ourselves.

Love is more difficult than ever

The pros and cons of a life of one's own

The old loyalties within premodern society were framed by strict rules and regulations on how to behave. As these have gradually been shed, life has come to seem less confined, with more room to choose and more possibilities to choose from; in many ways it is less restricted and more flexible than before (for an exemplary study of this, see Berger et al. 1973). But this change also implies that each of us is confronted with having to take decisions on numerous levels, from the mundane matters of which resort and which make of car, to long-term matters like how many children and which kind of school. We are expected to be responsible citizens and critical consumers, price-conscious and good to the environment, up-to-date on nuclear energy and the right dosage of the right medicine. As analysts of modern times have noted, 'living with an oversupply of options' (Riesman 1981: 123) often overtaxes the individual.

What has so far been overlooked is the fact that when an individual does not live alone, but with someone else, the stress factors multiply; all the issues which affect the partner directly or indirectly – which television programme, which

excursion, which furniture, which routine – have to be fed into the decision-making process as ideas and wishes, habits and norms of *two different* people. The results are predictable: *the more complex the decisions are, the more likely they are to lead to quarrels.*

The likelihood that the couple will disagree is further increased by the fact that on the reverse side of being free to choose, one comes up against new restrictions. In one sense everyone is free to plan and decide, and in another the logic of individualism gets in the way. As the family as an economic unit is gradually breaking down, new ways of making a living are emerging which depend on the labour market and the individual. How individuals find jobs depends on the laws of the market – flexibility and mobility, for instance, or competition and career – which give very little consideration to private commitments. Those who do not obey these laws risk their jobs, incomes and social standing.

Here we can see a series of structural developments within society, the effect of which is particularly obvious in post-war Germany. Mobility in all its forms – geographical, social, daily moves between job and family, work and leisure, training, work-place and retirement – continues to force people away from their established ties (to neighbours, colleagues, local customs and so on). Similarly, many people find that their education cuts them off from the milieu in which they grew up. Having achieved a professional qualification means one has more chances on the job market; this pattern of achievement, which of course affects whole groups of people, nonetheless forces each one to plan and decide on his/her own behalf and take personal responsibility for success or failure.

This external description covers only some of the changes involved. The logic behind individualization steers basically adaptable biographies in certain predetermined directions, and therefore has inner consequences for those involved. It leads to a battle over 'space of one's own' in the literal and figurative sense, in a search for oneself and for fulfilling one's own potential. The fact that these words crop up all the time in interviews, therapy and literature does not imply we are all suffering from an outbreak of collective egoism. In fact the talk of finding oneself and doing one's own thing precisely reflects the pressures affecting everyone in their normal lives – demands to be mobile, get educated, find a job – and reaching deep into the innermost recesses of their heart and minds. As a result these themes are now appearing *en masse* in individual biographies in the guise of private problems. When life turns into a 'do-it-yourself biography' (Berger et al. 1973: passim), discovering your own potential is 'not just a new shining star at the zenith of our value system but a cultural answer to new challenges in life' (Baden-Württemberg Provincial Government 1983: 32) or, in succinct form, a social must.

The question immediately arises: how much room is there left in a do-it-yourself biography with all its pressures and restrictions for a partner with his/her own plans and problems? How can the other person avoid becoming an additional hindrance, if not a disruptive factor? To what extent is it possible to share one's life if social circumstances compel one to concentrate on one's own interests? Situations are bound to arise in which, despite the very best intentions, two monads who instead of building up a shared universe have to defend their own separate universes end up arguing, sometimes in a civilized tone, and sometimes bitterly, with no holds barred.

From this viewpoint it is intriguing to compare the new ideas about love, marriage and intimate relationships recommended in self-help books. The trend, presented in all kinds of variations, some mild, some crass, is to give self-assertion top priority, not just in the office and the bus but at home too. The magic formula is known as authenticity. The much-quoted postulates of gestalt therapy, reproduced on countless greetings cards, coffee mugs and posters pinned over beds, put the message most clearly:

I do my thing, and you do your thing.
I am not in this world to live up to your expectations

And you are not in this world to live up to mine.
You are you and I am me, and if by chance we find each other it's beautiful
If not it can't be helped.

(Perls and Stevens 1969: 4)

Quite a contrast to love poems like Rückert's! Most self-help books do not go that far, admittedly, but they point in the same direction. Where they used to call for adaptation they now recommend conscious separation. What they teach is constructive disagreement: 'saying no in love' (Schellenbaum 1984). Therapy tries to encourage the view that 'it is not at all desirable for two people who love each other to be *one* heart and *one* soul' (Preuss 1985; emphasis in the original). And they recommend 'laying down as many aspects of daily life together as possible in a marriage contract', from the right to 'personal freedom' all the way to 'arrangements in case of separation' (Partner 1984).

Phrases like these reflect the basic pattern behind individualization applied to living with a partner. It is an attempt to find a way of enabling independent individuals with their own aims and rights to perform the difficult balancing act of living their own lives and yet sharing them with someone else. One cannot help suspecting, however, that this fundamental dilemma is sometimes being treated with remedies which tend to enlarge the problem rather than solve it. If we are told that 'arguing binds people together' (Bach and Wyden 1969), how often is the result the desired creative tension, and how often, to borrow the up-beat title of one such book, 'creative divorce' (Krantzler 1974)?

Should such negotiations break down, according to a different book, there can be a 'successful divorce', – by no means to be thought of as a failure – but one which 'has been pre-considered in terms of personal upward mobility, with stress laid not nearly so much on what is being left, and may therefore be lost, as on what lies ahead that may be incorporated into a new and better image'. After the successful divorce, this behaviour-modification book tells us, 'Little Affairs' may be useful. . . The person with a 'Positive Self Image' need not worry about promiscuity. *All* these affairs will be 'meaningful' because they will all contribute to the 'self's reservoir of experiences'. (Ehrenreich and English 1979: 276)

If love fails again, if this hope is extinguished, then what you must do is find a new one. The motto is 'How To Be Your Own Best Friend' (Ehrenreich and English 1979: 176). Is that the only remaining hope? Does the individualization which induced our romantic longings necessarily and always lead to a post-romantic world?

In the post-romantic world, where the old ties no longer bind, all that matters is *you:* you can be what you *want* to be; you *choose* your life, your environment, even your appearance and your emotions . . . The old hierarchies of protection and dependency no longer exist, there are only free contracts, freely terminated. The marketplace, which long ago expanded to include the relations of production, has now expanded to include *all* relationships. (Ehrenreich and English 1979: 276)

It is not only that everyone's life has become more flexible and adaptable; one can choose to live with someone else in a wide variety of ways. Pre-industrial society laid down strict rules for couples to ensure their economic survival. Marriage was teamwork, with men and women having separate spheres and children being welcomed as helping hands and heirs. And nowadays? We have an endless series of questions to answer. Should the wife work outside the home, yes or no, full- or part-time? Should the husband aim straight up the career ladder, or share in the housework or even stay at home as a househusband? Are children a good idea, and if yes, when and how many? If yes, who is going to look after them, if no, who is responsible for contraception? It is becoming increasingly likely that sooner or later, in some respect or another, the partners are going to differ. And this will not necessarily be for personal reasons, unwillingness to compromise or sheer bloody-mindedness. It will be because their biographies as employees face them with clear limits and prevent them from structuring their lives as they might wish if they are to avoid difficulties in their work-places.

As well as all the substantial decisions to be made, there is the time aspect to consider. Every decision can be revoked in the course of a marriage. In fact decisions have to be revocable so that other outside demands can be met. The individualized biography assumes that everyone can update and optimize his/her decisions, and these in turn are affected by the new psychological approach expecting everyone to be open to new challenges, inquisitive and willing to learn. Such postulates are no doubt a great help in warding off the mute indifference which can befall couples trapped in a dreary marital routine. They do, however, have their dangers. What happens if one spouse is quite content with the way things are, while the other is not, or when both want to change but in different directions?

There are couples who both once agreed that it would be best for her to devote herself completely to the family. After a few years, however, bored by the monotony and isolation of domestic life, she wants to go back to work. Her husband, quite happy with the familiar pattern, feels endangered by the change and insists on his customary rights. Or take the example of couples who got married in the 1960s with conventional ideas of fidelity and a few years later read about 'open marriage' as an ideal. What if one of them now wants to hold on to the security of familiar habits, while the other longs to sample the attractions of novelty? Who is in the right?

Sometimes no one is. Right and wrong turn into vague categories as soon as there is no longer a shared standard but just the standards of *two* biographies affected by different expectations and restraints, and on top of all that a rapid change of stereotypes. There is more and more space available for subjective interpretations into which people's wishes can flow, and often both spouses have them, if of different kinds. And the outcome is a huge number of married people feeling misunderstood, injured and betrayed.

[. . .]

Change has been rapid. What initially was a prerogative of the men – shaking off old patterns of behaviour – has since the late nineteenth century, and especially since the 1960s, also become feasible for women. This is particularly apparent in education; although new openings became available to them at the turn of the century, the real shift took place fifty years later with offers of education to everybody in the 1960s. The disadvantages for girls, which had long been taken for granted, were now deliberately questioned, and the success of these efforts surpassed all expectations. Within only twenty years the marked differences in levels of schooling gave way to almost equal numbers of girls and boys in state education at every level, all the way up to university.

Working away from home is another example. Although the model of housewife and mother was an ideal of the bourgeois family, women in the lower strata had always been forced to earn money because their husband's wage was rarely enough to support the family. And in the late nineteenth century even in the middle classes, where work within the family gradually lost any links with the production process, more women found themselves forced to look for a source of income; the number of women who had no private means and had to make a living rose. In middle-class society, however, such work was restricted in time, defined only to last until marriage; the woman's place was still in the home.

Really far-reaching changes took place in the 1950s. The first move in Germany, as in other industrial countries, was a marked rise in the number of married women working outside the home. This was followed by a tendency for married women to continue to work until their first child was born, and to return to work after the children had grown up, The second stage, again in all industrial societies, is marked by pronounced shifts in the number of women with children working away from home – working mothers. Nowadays work for them is much more than an interim phase; 'Not working is becoming an exceptional situation for women, increasingly limited to the phase of caring for small children' (Willms 1983: 111).

Demographic changes also play a role. Since the beginning of the century life expectancy has been rising and has reached an all-time high in the late twentieth century. By contrast, the number of children has drastically sunk, a tendency which began in Europe in the late nineteenth century and has accelerated since the 1960s. The combined effects of these two developments has decisively altered the standard female biography. The task which had become women's main occupation after the extended family had broken up and been replaced by the bourgeois family – raising children – now occupies in purely temporal terms an ever-smaller portion of her life. Now there is a phase which historically speaking is quite new, the 'empty nest' years, where the woman is no longer tied to or needed in her mother role (Imhof 1981: 180f.).

As a result of these changes in education, professional openings, family life, legislation and the like, working women have fewer family commitments, and are coming to expect less support from their husbands; they have to be in some, often contradictory, form independent and able to support themselves. The subjective aspect is of course that women are finding out, in fact having to find out, what they expect of life and making their own plans which are not necessarily focused on the family but on their own personalities. They must plan how to take care of themselves, first of all financially, and to do without a husband if need be. They can no longer consider themselves appendages of the family, but as individual people with corresponding rights and interests, their own futures and their own options.

Here are the classical lines from the final scene of Ibsen's *A Doll's House* (1878–9):

HELMER: . . . Is this the way you neglect your most sacred duties?

NORA: What do you consider is my most sacred duty?

HELMER: Do I have to tell you that? Isn't it your duty to your husband and children?

NORA: I have another duty, just as sacred.

HELMER: You can't have. What duty do you mean?

NORA: My duty to myself.

HELMER: Before everything else, you're a wife and a mother.

NORA: I don't believe that any longer. I believe that before everything else I'm a human being – just as much as you are . . . or at any rate I shall try to become one.

What is interesting here is how such changes affect relationships between the sexes. Clearly there is potential here for a new kind of bond no longer restricting man and woman to the daily grind of making a living, as in pre-industrial society, or, as in the bourgeois nineteenth-century model, to antithetical gender roles which complemented one another but presupposed the woman's subordination. Instead there is now the chance of a bond of fellow spirits, or putting it more cautiously, a partnership between two people who are close to one another in character and attitude to life. This is the bond so longed for in the writings of the women's movement, that most wonderful thing that shines out as a hope at the end of *A Doll's House*:

HELMER: Nora – can't I ever be anything more than a stranger to you?

NORA: Oh, Torvald – there would have to be the greatest miracle of all . . .

HELMER: What would that be – the greatest miracle of all?

NORA: Both of us would have to be so changed that – Oh, Torvald, I don't believe in miracles any longer.

HELMER: But I'll believe. Tell me: 'so changed that . . .'?

NORA: That our life together could be a real marriage.

The striking thing here is of course not so much the high hopes and the possible miracles but the other side, the disappointments and failures which nowadays dog so many marriages and liaisons. Quite obviously, as standard biographies have changed, living together has become more diffi-cult for both sexes. The ideas discussed above on the curbs we all face in choosing how to lead our lives remained imprecise in one crucial respect: they presupposed that both men and women can behave as true partners, sharing the decision-making – a state of affairs which is by no means given.

Now we can complete the picture. The new factor altering love and marriage is not that some-body – meaning the man – has become more himself, more individual in the course of modern times, as the sociologists have traced. What is new is the individual *female* biography, freeing the woman of family duties, and sending her out into the world with an impetus which has been increas-ing since the 1960s. To put it even more point-edly, as long as it was only the man who developed his potential and the woman was complementarily obliged to look after him and others, family cohe-sion remained more or less intact – at the cost of her own interests or personality. Now, however, this 'division of modernity' [. . .] cannot be main-tained any longer and we are witnessing a new period in the history of women.

REFERENCES

Alberoni, F. (1983) *Verliebt sein und Lieben: Rev-olution zu zweit*. Stuttgart (*Falling in Love*), New York.

Bach, G. R. and Wyden, P. (1969) *The Intimate Enemy: How to Fight Fair in Love and Mar-riage*. New York.

Baden-Württemberg Provincial Government (1983) *Bericht der Kommission 'Zukunftsperspe-ktiven gesellschaftlicher Entwicklungen', erstellt im Auftrag der Landesregierung von Baden-Württemberg*. Stuttgart.

Berger, P. L., Berger, B. and Kellner, H. (1973) *The Homeless Mind: Modernization and Con-sciousness*. New York.

Ehrenreich, B. and English, D. (1979) *For Her Own Good: 150 Years of the Experts' Advice for Women*. London.

Elias, N. (1985) Foreword. In M. Schröter, *'Wo zwei zusammen kommen in rechter Ehe...':*

Sozio- und psychogenetische Studien über Ehe-schliessungsvorgänge vom 12. bis 15. Jahrhundert, Frankfurt: vii-xi.

Ibsen, H. (1986) *A Doll's House and Other Plays*, trans. Peter Watts. Harmondsworth.

Imhof, A. E. (1981) *Die gewonnenen Jahre*. Munich.

Imhof, A. E. (1984) *Die verlorenen Welten*. Munich.

Krantzler, M. (1974) *Creative Divorce: A New Opportunity for Personal Growth*. New York.

Partner, P. (1984) *Das endgültige Ehebuch für Anfänger und Fortgeschrittene*. Munich.

Perls, F. and Stevens, J. O. (1969) *Gestalt Therapy Verbatim*. Lafayette, California.

Preuss, H. G. (1985) *Ehepaartherapie: Beitrag zu einer psychoanalytischen Partnertherapie in der Gruppe*. Frankfurt.

Riesman, D. (1981) Egozentrik in Amerika. *Der Monat*, 3: 111–23.

Ryder, N. B. (1979) The Future of American Fertility. *Social Problems*, 26/3: 359–70.

Schellenbaum, P. (1984) *Das Nein in der Liebe: Abgrenzung und Hingabe in der erotischen Beziehung*. Stuttgart.

Wachinger, L. (1986) *Ehe: Einander lieben-einander lassen*. Munich.

Weber, M. (1985) *The Protestant Ethic and the Spirit of Capitalism*. London (Ger, orig. 1905).

Willms, A. (1983) Segregation auf Dauer?: Zur Entwicklung des Verhältnisses von Frauenarbeit und Männerarbeit in Deutschland. In W. Müller, A. Willms and J. Handl (eds) *Strukturwandel der Frauenarbeit 1880–1980*: 107–81. Frankfurt.

32. Ageing and Ageism

Bill Bytheway

How is age significant in our everyday lives? On the day that this is being written, there is a feature in the daily newspaper about the Dean of a threatened London Medical College. The journalist writes that she (the Dean):

was 50 last year ('Dreadful!' she shrieks) but has the energy and dynamism of someone at least a decade younger.

(*The Guardian 2*, 20 January 1993: 8)

It is worth asking what this statement represents. It includes two elements: the reported response of the Dean to reaching 50 – dreadful – and the journalist's assessment of the Dean's energy and dynamism – equivalent to a younger person's. There is no escaping the double message that the fiftieth birthday was not enjoyed and that energy and dynamism are associated with younger people.

Now listen to this exchange based on an interview by a researcher (*RA*) with two health centre receptionists (*SD* and *RM*):

RA: Can I be indelicate and ask your age?
SD: 41 I am.
RM: 26.
RA: Oh, there we are.
SD: She's showing off.
RA: Isn't she just!
RM: Put 21 for me.
RA: Put 21? No, 26 is young. I can't remember being 26 (laugh).

Note how the 'indelicate question' generates all kinds of comments: SD accuses RM of showing off; RM wants to lie; RA associates herself with SD, unable to remember being as young as RM; and so on until all three end up laughing.

So are we all sensitive to revealing our age? How self-conscious do we feel when asked outright how old we are? Do we shriek? Do we feel our energy ebbing? Do we feel uncomfortable as we stutter over the answer? Do we find ourselves elaborating it with comment about how we feel and what we do? Or do we feel comfortable about our age, willing and able to provide a direct and simple answer, seeing it as part of an ordinary biographical introduction? Or do we feel affronted because we fail to see how our age is relevant? Do we find ourselves wondering why we are being asked our age? Do we avoid answering it?

In addition to these personal responses – shrieking, laughing, bemoaning, denying or whatever – our answer to the question can be used for more formal or bureaucratic purposes. Just like height, weight, IQ tests, number of children, health and income, age is a personal characteristic that can be measured on a standard scale. What then happens is crucial to understanding ageism. It is almost always included in application forms for benefits, jobs and services. In the processing of these forms, age is often set against age-specific norms and expectations as in the case of the steelworker. When we deviate from these norms, we may be applauded for being younger than we are – 'Fifty last year! You're acting like a 40-year-old. Aren't you wonderful!' – and, if needs be, regulations regarding age are overlooked. Or, the norms may be mobilized in order to put pressure, deny us resources, or channel us in particular directions – 'We'll be keeping a very close eye on you!'

Age in newspapers

Age figures in many different contexts. A real newspaper story reads as follows (names have been changed):

Brown, 45, was at the 'centre of the web' in a plot to cheat the City Council by dishonestly using highly confidential information, it was alleged. It was passed to him by Joe Green, 47, a committee chairman . . .

In the dock with Brown are ex-councillors Green and White, 49; and businessman John Grey, 45.

There is nothing particularly unusual about this story – again it appeared in a newspaper that happened to be at hand at the time of writing – and the ages of the defendants are unexceptional. None of the defendants are reported as being appalled by or proud of their age. And their ages seem irrelevant to the issue being reported – so why are they included?

Perhaps it is because the defendants' ages indicate that they are all of the same middle-aged generation. Interesting – but significant? And surely not the reason for their ages being reported. The answer is that including age is standard journalistic practice. And why? Because age conveys precise information in the minimum of space (just two typographical symbols), information that directly contributes to the construction of an image of the person being described.

But why is it not necessary to add the word 'years' after the two-digit numbers: 'Brown, 45 years, was at the centre of the web . . .'? How do we know that Brown was 45 years of age and not 45 stones in weight? Because we all know that age is typically reported in newspapers solely as a number: it has become standard practice. In this sense it is part of the language, something that we have to learn if we are to make sense of newspapers.

We also know that someone involved in such a newspaper story is quite likely to be 45 years of age (and unlikely to be 45 stones in weight). If we had read: 'Brown, 18, was at the centre of the web . . .'? we would have been confused. Surely Brown was more than 18 years of age? Could he be 18 stone? But why would the journalist report his weight? And wouldn't the journalist have written: 'Brown, who weighs 18 stones, was at the centre of the web . . .'?

So it is convention backed up by expectations that ensures that we will understand that the 45 refers to age. This simple argument indicates how important and pervasive age has become in the relationship between the individual and society. It is not you who has decided that age is interesting, so interesting that you are going to ask everyone you meet how old they are. You didn't ask the newspaper how old Brown, Green, White and Grey were. It wasn't you who volunteered your age in a box entitled 'Other Relevant Information' when you applied for a bank loan. Rather it is the dominant values of the society in which we live, values which have emerged over decades if not centuries, that oblige us to be age-conscious and age-alert if we are to understand how to fill in forms and what we read in newspapers, and if we are to sustain meaningful communication with the social institutions around us.

And it is because we have gained such a discerning knowledge of how people behave at various ages that we in turn behave in an age-specific way. At 18 we know we are not expected to attempt to cheat the City Council by using highly confidential information. Most of us don't have such information when were 18 and so we don't even think of cheating the Council – confirming expectations. Just as at 45 we don't even think of lying about our age in order to get into the cinema, because we know that even the most youthful-looking 45-year-old will be let in without a thought being given to age.

To summarize this argument: if we are to fully understand ageism, we have to appreciate the extent to which it is an age-specific society in which we live, and how we have all learned to be age-sensitive while not necessarily being age-conscious.

Ageism: just another 'ism'?

What is an 'ism'? How does ageism relate to sexism and racism? One answer is to assert boldly:

These are three philosophies that we find offensive and which we would expect ordinary, liberal, tolerant, intelligent people to be against.

Gauche though this may sound, it is nevertheless the basis of an understanding. We all know about racism and sexism don't we? And, because we all know we all know about racism and sexism, we have little trouble in talking about and being conscious of racist and sexist issues. The terms acquire meaning through usage and, when misunderstandings or disagreements arise, meanings are clarified by the exchange and analysis of examples, i.e. through further usage.

It is because we all know about racism and sexism, we have no difficulty in knowing what ageism is about. Ageism is prejudice on grounds of age, just as racism and sexism is prejudice on grounds of race and sex. Consider one choice example. An article in *The Independent* (9 January 1993: 39) is headlined: 'Ageism takes off at British Airways', and the first sentence is, 'Do airlines discriminate against older people?' asks Gladys Glascoe of North Thamesmead.' What is significant about this is that the word *ageism* only appears in the headline, and that it is defined implicitly in this first sentence as 'discrimination against older people'. The parallels with gender and race could not be clearer: take out 'older people and put in 'women' or 'the ethnic minorities' and the headline would have had sexism or racism in place of ageism.

Let's suppose Gladys Glascoe is a doctor and had booked in advance. Let's consider the possibilities. There's no problem until she appears. First Dr Glascoe is a woman. 'Oh, I'm sorry. I thought you were a man. I'll just go and change this.' It doesn't matter what 'this' is, Dr Glascoe had been pre-judged to be a man.

Next, Dr Glascoe is black. 'Good afternoon, Dr Glascoe. Now, I'm afraid I have to fill in this form. Nationality?' Whereas had Dr Glascoe been white, the introduction might have been: 'Good afternoon, Dr Glascoe. Now, I'm afraid I have to fill in this form. Nationality, British?' Again Dr Glascoe had been pre-judged to be British.

Next is Age? – there it is on the booking form. Let's guess that Dr Glascoe was born in 1918 (Gladys Glascoe's age is not revealed in the article but she does refer to herself as an 'elderly lady'), and with her answer the booking clerk books her into a seat that is not next to an emergency exit. Why? Because it is British Airways policy not to book 'women of a certain age' into seats adjacent to exits for fear that they will not be able to use the emergency equipment and will block them in an emergency.

This, according to the article, is the ageism that was taking off and again we have a clear example of how people – or perhaps women – are pre-judged on the basis of age. Just as a 58-year-old man is thought incapable of managing concrete blocks, so a woman in her seventies is considered unable to use emergency equipment.

We have to accept then that this is how the word ageism is now being used in the media. As this example clearly indicates, ageism – a term that was first used as recently as 1969 – is becoming part of the vocabulary of the media in the 1990s. As such, the word itself is a phenomenon of growing significance which complicates our attempts to develop a sound understanding of the responses of society to age.

It would be easy to accept this kind of definition – ageism, equivalent to racism and sexism, is discrimination against old people – as the basis of this book and I could set about documenting many examples of such discrimination in considerable detail. There is little doubting that such discrimination does occur and so at the outset, need we quibble about definitions?

Well, as the example of Oldham and Bexley Councils indicates, younger people are discriminated against, too and, as the example of the steelworker indicates, middle-aged people can find their age being used against them. Indeed, one sometimes has the impression in discussing ageism with people involved in employment policies that they perceive ageism to be no more than the unacceptable use of age in the processing of people in the labour market – when you suggest that it also affects very old people living in nursing homes, you are faced with looks of confusion and incomprehension. No matter what our age, there will be times when it is invoked to deny us things that we seek.

With rare exceptions, the way in which we are affected by sexism and racism has a degree of continuity throughout our lives. This does not apply to our experience of ageism. 'No one is born old'; 'We are all growing older from the day we are born'. Such aphorisms confirm the distinctive nature of age as a characteristic of the individual – one which, unlike gender and ethnicity, is constantly changing. It is the only progressive condition with which we all have to live. For these reasons alone, it is essential that we start from scratch; that we set sexism and racism to one side in the development of our understanding of ageism.

Sex and race, along with many other divisions within society such as class and disability, are issues relating to – but not determining – our experience of ageism. The belief that other dimensions are more important than age is a peculiarly clear indication of just how endemic and insidious ageism is. It is the kind of absurd value judgement that we are all inclined to make when we think of age as just another variable.

[. . .]

I first became interested in ageism when Maggie Kuhn visited the UK in 1978. On television she demonstrated that ageism was something that was serious and, in the magazine, *New Age*, she defined ageism simply as 'discrimination against people on the basis of chronological age' (Whitehouse 1978). Shortly afterwards, I commented in the same magazine:

It was the first article I had read which used the term in a serious and unqualified way. The term has often been used by others, but rather coyly as though the speaker feared the audience might think that a joke was being made.

(Bytheway 1980: 29)

Three years later, I was asked to take part in a review symposium on the book *Vitality and Aging* (Fries and Crapo 1981). In working through this my initial concern was with the statistical analyses of the authors. I came to realize, however, that they were forwarding a thesis which implied that we were moving towards a society characterized by a 'long life of vigour and vitality ending suddenly, one day, on schedule' (1981: 135). Without anticipating it, I found myself concluding my review with the comment that Fries and Crapo were articulating 'a markedly ageist thesis'; that they were 'engaged in the construction of a biological basis for social discrimination between living people' (Bytheway 1982: 391). It was clear that their argument was preparing the ground for old-age euthanasia: for easing the rapid passage of those who appear to have reached the 'natural' end of their long lives. It was this that made me first appreciate the biological base and the potentially awesome power of ageism.

I collaborated with Julia Johnson on the organization of the 1988 conference of the British Society of Gerontology in Swansea and, through this, it became apparent to us that there was a continuing neglect of the concept of ageism, and this led to our formulating the following 'working definition':

1   Ageism is a set of beliefs originating in the biological variation between people and relating to the ageing process.
2   It is in the actions of corporate bodies, what is said and done by their representatives, and the resulting views that are held by ordinary ageing people, that ageism is made manifest.
In consequence of this, it follows that:
(a)   Ageism generates and reinforces a fear and denigration of the ageing process, and stereotyping presumptions regarding competence and the need for protection.
(b)   In particular, ageism legitimates the use of chronological age to mark out classes of people who are systematically denied resources and opportunities that others enjoy, and who suffer the consequences of such denigration, ranging from well-meaning patronage to unambiguous vilification.

(Bytheway and Johnson 1990)

[. . .]

Taking on ageism

In our article on defining ageism (Bytheway and Johnson 1990), we put forward four suggestions for anti-ageist action. First, we should abandon ageist language. In particular, we should abandon the word 'elderly' and begin to use a relative rather than an absolute age vocabulary. In March 1993, I spent an hour expounding the argument against 'elderly' and 'old age' to a group of 21 students from eleven different countries who were attending a short course in social gerontology at the International Institute of Ageing in Malta. They quickly agreed that there was no point at which someone became elderly and that this invalidated categorizations of people as elderly. They were reluctant, however, to let go of the word itself. They recognized that the alternative older was relative, was not exclusionary, did not set people apart, but they wanted to retain 'elderly'. 'People get grey hair, they are more frail, they need services, we need a name for it', one said.

'What is this *it*?', I countered. 'I don't deny we all grow older. I don't deny that people in their nineties are of a great age and that most have real needs. I don't deny we need a technical vocabulary, but what is this it that has to be called "elderly"?'

Second, we should recognize age for what it is. Upon reading this, a colleague astutely asked us what age is. In truth our suggestion was a limply worded acknowledgement that certain things are undeniable. No matter now committed one is to the social constructionist approach, there comes a point when one has to face the reality in front of one's eyes and, indeed, the reality of the condition of one's much-used body. The following section addresses this issue.

Third, we should stop using age as an institutional regulator. As I have suggested at various points in this book, age bars are ageist. Fourth, we should abandon the us–them mentality. We should begin to think in inclusionary ways, seeing ourselves in a broader temporal context, in terms of our lives as a whole rather than our lives at present.

[. . .]

If we are to be effective in challenging ageism, we have to recognize the significance of difference. Perhaps the following account (Macdonald and Rich 1983: 7–12) of the personal discovery of ageism will demonstrate the importance of this. It also reveals the potential we all have for being thoroughly ageist in our relations with older people and, in particular, in our ability to conceptualize them as being apart from us.

Through their involvement in the women's movement in the USA, Cynthia Rich had got to know Barbara Macdonald – 21 years her senior – in 1974. Regarding her knowledge of ageism at that time, Rich writes:

'Ageism' is hardly a word in my vocabulary. It has something to do with job discrimination in middle age. And aging itself I see as simply 'failing', a painful series of losses, an inevitable confrontation with the human condition.

(Macdonald and Rich 1983: 10)

Feeling part of the women's movement – 'we are all women together' – and having noticed that other older friends had never talked about ageing, she had assumed that they had 'transcended' it. 'I could have the illusion of the richness of difference without having to confront the reality of difference' (Macdonald and Rich 1983: 9). After living with Rich for three years, Macdonald began to write about ageism in 1977, and it was only then that Rich became aware of her own ageism:

Slowly, I begin to see that the fear of the stigma of age, and total ignorance of its reality in the lives of old women, flow deep in myself, in other women I know, in the women's movement. That our society breeds ignorance and fear of both aging and death. That the old woman carries the burden of that stigma, and with remarkable, unrecognized, unrecorded courage I begin to see that I myself am aging, was always aging, and that only powerful forces could have kept me – from self-interest alone – from working to change the social and economic realities of older women. That ageism is part of the air both Barbara and I have breathed since we were born, and that it is unthinkable that women should continue to be indifferent to the meaning of the whole of our lives, until we are old ourselves.

(Macdonald and Rich 1983: 11–12)

This powerful statement sustains the distinctiveness of old women – as remarkable, unrecognized, unrecorded, courageous people. It could be argued that the use of 'old' not 'older' emphasizes not just difference but also a distinction between us and them. Be that as it may, it also asserts loudly that ageing is a shared experience, that we are all subject to the fear and ignorance of ageism, and that the power of ageism should be challenged in ways that promote a holistic and undivided view of 'the whole of our lives'.

REFERENCES

Bytheway, B. (1980) Is ageism just a joke? *New Age*, 12, 29–30.

Bytheway, B. (1982) Review symposium, *Ageing and Society*, 2 (3), 389–91.

Bytheway, B. and Johnson, J. (1990) On defining ageism, *Critical Social Policy*, 27, 27–39.

Fries, J. F. and Crapo, L. M. (1981) *Vitality and Aging*. San Francisco: W. H. Freeman.

Macdonald, B. and Rich, C. (1983) *Look Me in the Eye: Old Women, Aging and Ageism*. London: The Women's Press.

Whitehouse, A. (1978) The Gray Panther rides again! *New Age*, 5, 7–8.

33. The Loneliness of the Dying

Norbert Elias

Many people die gradually; they grow infirm, they age. The last hours are important, of course. But often the parting begins much earlier. Their frailty is often enough to sever the ageing from the living. Their decline isolates them. They may grow less sociable, their feelings less warm, without their need for people being extinguished. That is the hardest thing – the tacit isolation of the ageing and dying from the community of the living, the gradual cooling of their relationships to people to whom they were attached, the separation from human beings in general, who gave them meaning and security. The declining years are hard not only for those in pain, but for those who are left alone. The fact that, without being specifically intended, the early isolation of the dying occurs with particular frequency in the more advanced societies is one of the weaknesses of these societies. It bears witness to the difficulties that many people have of identifying with the ageing and dying.

[. . .]

Death is a problem of the living. Dead people have no problems. Of the many creatures on this earth that die, it is human beings alone for whom dying is a problem. They share birth, illness, youth, maturity, age and death with the animals. But they alone of all living beings *know* that they shall die; they alone can anticipate their own end, are aware that it can come at any time, and take special precautions – as individuals and as groups – to protect themselves against the danger of annihilation.

[. . .]

By and large, in developed societies the dangers threatening people, particularly that of death, are more predictable, while the need for protective superhuman powers has grown more temperate. One cannot doubt that, with increasing social uncertainty, and with the decreasing ability of people to foresee and – to an extent – control their own fate over long periods, these needs would grow stronger again.

The attitude to dying and the image of death in our societies cannot be completely understood without reference to this relative security and predictability of individual life and the correspondingly increased life expectancy. Life grows longer, death is further postponed. The sight of dying and dead people is no longer commonplace. It is easier in the normal course of life to forget death. Death is sometimes said to be 'repressed'. An American coffin-manufacturer observed recently: 'The present-day attitude to death leaves planning for a funeral, if it happens at all, to late in life.'[1]

[. . .]

An experience I had in my younger days has taken on a certain significance for me, now that I am older. I attended a lecture by a well-known physicist at Cambridge. He came in shuffling, dragging his feet, a very old man. I caught myself wondering, Why does he drag his feet like that? Why can he not walk like a normal human being? I at once corrected myself. He can't help it, I told myself. He is very old.

My spontaneous youthful reaction to the sight of an old man is very typical of the kind of feelings aroused today, and perhaps still more in earlier periods, in healthy people in the normal age groups by the sight of old people. They know that old people, even when they are quite healthy, often have difficulty in moving in the same way as healthy people in all other age groups except small children. They know this, but in a remote way. They cannot imagine a situation where their own legs or trunk do not obey the commands of their will, as is normal.

I use the word 'normal' deliberately here. That people grow different in old age is often involuntarily seen as a deviation from the social norm. The others, the normal age groups, often have difficulty in empathizing with older people in their experience of ageing – understandably. For most younger people have no basis in their experience for imagining how it feels when muscle tissue gradually hardens and perhaps becomes fatty, when connective tissue multiplies and cell renewal slows down. The physiological processes are well known to science and in part well understood. There is extensive literature on the subject. Much less understood, and far less frequently touched on in the literature, is the experience of ageing itself. This is a comparatively little discussed topic. It is certainly not without importance for the treatment of the old by those who are not – or not yet – old, and not merely for their medical treatment, to have a closer understanding of the experiential aspect of the process of ageing, and of dying as well. But, as I have mentioned, there are clearly very special difficulties in the way of empathy here. It is not easy to imagine that one's own body, which is so fresh and often so full of pleasant feelings, could become sluggish, tired and clumsy. One cannot imagine it and, at bottom, one does not want to. To put it differently, identification with the ageing and dying understandably poses special difficulties for people of other age groups. Whether consciously or unconsciously, people resist the idea of their own ageing and dying as best they can.

[. . .]

The technical perfection of the prolongation of life is certainly not the only factor contributing to the isolation of the dying in our day. The greater internal pacification of developed industrial states and the marked advance of the embarrassment threshold in face of violence gives rise in these societies to a usually tacit but noticeable antipathy of the living towards the dying – an antipathy that many members of these societies cannot overcome even if they cannot approve it. Dying, however it is viewed, is an act of violence. Whether people are the perpetrators or whether it is the blind course of nature that brings about the sudden or gradual decay of a human being is ultimately of no great importance to the person concerned. Thus, a higher level of internal pacification also contributes to the aversion towards death, or more precisely towards the dying. So does a higher level of civilizing restraint. There is no shortage of examples. Freud's protracted death from cancer of the larynx is one of the most telling. The growth became more and more ill-smelling. Even Freud's trusted dog refused to go near him. Only Anna Freud, strong and unwavering in her love for the dying father, helped him in these last weeks and saved him from feeling deserted. Simone de Beauvoir described with frightening exactness the last months of her friend Sartre, who was no longer able to control his urinary flow and was forced to go about with plastic bags tied to him, which overflowed. The decay of the human organism, the process that we call dying, is often anything but odourless. But developed societies inculcate in their members a rather high sensitivity to strong smells.

All these are really only examples of how we have failed to come to terms with the problems of the dying in developed societies. What I have said here is merely a small contribution to the diagnosis of problems that still have to be solved. This diagnosis, it seems to me, ought to be developed further. By and large, we are not yet fully aware that dying in more developed societies brings with it special problems which have to be faced as such.

The problems I have raised here are, as you may see, problems of medical sociology. Present-day medical measures relate mainly to individual aspects of the physiological functioning of a person – the heart, the bladder, the arteries and so on – and as far as these are concerned medical technique in preserving and prolonging life is undoubtedly more advanced than ever before. But to concentrate on medically correcting single organs, or areas of organs that are functioning more and more badly, is really worthwhile only for the sake of the person within whom all these part-processes are integrated. And if the problems of the individual part-processes cause us to forget those of the integrating person, we really devalue what we are doing for these part-processes themselves. The decay of persons that we call ageing and dying today poses for their fellow human beings, including doctors, a number of unperformed and largely unrecognized tasks. The tasks I have in mind here remain concealed if the individual person is considered and treated as if he or she existed solely for her- or himself, independently of all other people. I am not quite sure how far doctors are aware that a person's relationships to others have a codetermining influence both on the genesis of pathological symptoms and on the course taken by an illness. I have here raised the problem of the relationship of people to the dying. It takes, as you see, a special form in more developed societies, because in them the process of dying is isolated from normal social life to a greater degree than it was earlier. A result of this isolation is that people's experience of ageing and dying, which in earlier societies was organized by traditional public institutions and phantasies, tends to be dimmed by repression in later societies. Perhaps, in pointing to the loneliness of the dying, one makes it easier to recognize, within developed societies, a nucleus of tasks that remain to be done.

I am aware that doctors have little time. I also know that people and their relationships are given more attention by them now than they were earlier. What does one do if dying people would rather die at home than in hospital, and one knows that they will die more quickly at home? But perhaps that is just what they want. It is perhaps not yet quite superfluous to say that care for people sometimes lags behind the care for their organs.

NOTE

1. B. Deborah Frazier, 'Your Coffin as Furniture – For Now', *International Herald Tribune,* 2 October 1979.

Theme 6 – Further Reading

One of the best introductory texts on the life-course is Stephen Hunt's (2005) *The Life Course: A Sociological Introduction* (Basingstoke: Palgrave Macmillan). Jenny Hockey and Allison James's (2002) *Social Identities Across the Life Course* (Basingstoke: Palgrave Macmillan) is a stimulating account of life-course changes drawing on recent work on emotions, embodiment and postmodernity. A good collection of readings on ageing can then be approached, such as Miriam Bernard and Thomas Scharf's (2007) *Critical Perspectives on Ageing Societies* (Bristol: Policy Press). On sexuality, Véronique Mottier's (2008) *Sexuality: A Very Short Introduction* (Oxford: Oxford University Press) is a brief, but remarkably comprehensive starting point. To find out what sociologists have to say about death and dying, try Glennys Howarth's (2006) excellent, *Death and Dying: A Sociological Introduction* (Cambridge: Polity).

Giddens and Sutton *Sociology 7th Edition* (2013)

Chapters 9 and 10 are the main resources for this theme along with Chapter 15 on gender and sexualities, pages 625–51 and Chapter 20 on education across the life course, pages 903–13.

Part 7

Interaction and Communication

Complex communication is a fundamental feature of everyday life, from face-to-face conversations and interactions in real time to the one-way transmissions of mass media like television programmes and films and, more recently, synchronous or asynchronous multi-user chatrooms and blogs on the worldwide web. Human communication is more than just the use of vocal language but also involves the reading and interpretation of signs, symbols and body language. In this section, the readings aim to give a flavour of this diverse and wide-ranging subject.

The interactionist tradition of sociology originating in the early work of Max Weber and the theoretical ideas of George Herbert Mead has been a continual source of insights into intentional and unintentional communications. In particular, symbolic interactionism has a long history of research into small-scale interactions and social situations. And though functionalists theorized the place of social roles and positions in the wider society, it was interactionists who delved into roles and positions to discover exactly how roles are played by specific individuals as well as the ways in which they are able to maintain a sense of self amid the demands and norms of pre-existing roles. No one has been more successful in this endeavour than Erving Goffman, whose work continues to inspire new generations of sociologists. In Reading 34, Goffman takes us into the often surprising ways in which people present themselves in social situations. Adopting a 'dramaturgical' approach – that is, one that draws parallels

between stage plays and real life – Goffman employs a range of now familiar concepts. For instance, waiters and waitresses may comport themselves very differently when front stage in the restaurant and backstage in the kitchens, sometimes to the extent that their performances appear to be those of two separate characters. What we can learn from such studies is the lengths to which people will go to preserve their sense of self in situations which threaten to submerge it amid the expectations of others.

Of course, like all other social phenomena, structures of class, gender, ethnicity and other inequalities influence our interactions. For example, in patriarchal societies, the quality and character of interactions tend to be shaped by the dominant position of men. Research studies have shown how boys in classroom situations simply talk for longer and more often than girls, interrupting them in order to demonstrate their control over the situation, while the body language of women in interview situations involving men tends to be more submissive and unthreatening than men's. Feminist research has called into question the apparent 'normality' of women adopting feminine norms of behaviour, demonstrating how femininity is a highly constraining frame within which girls are taught to become women. Feminine norms are based on strict codes of acceptable behaviour and tight control of bodily movement. One area in which this can be observed is sports and athletics, which demand something akin to the opposite of femininity to be successful. Reading 35 takes the simple act of throwing a ball, which is so fundamental to many sports, as its focus. The excerpt from Iris Marion Young's influential article sets out to explain why girls appear to have physical difficulties in throwing, exemplified in the criticism boys often level at each other, 'you throw like a girl'. Young argues that there exists a distinct feminine style of bodily comportment and movement which presents severe difficulties for girls when activities demand free movement of limbs and an opening up of the body. Such activities force girls to break with feminine norms and the difficulties encountered are therefore not physical but socially created.

Reading 36 by Jack Shaheen takes us into the area of media representations of social groups. Representations are important in our media saturated societies as they hold up a mirror to society and social relations. A body of feminist work argues that the way many fashion and entertainment outlets present idealized images of impossibly thin women is contributing to young women's increasing concern about their own body image as well as an increasing number of eating disorders. This is a good example of the power of media representations. Shaheen investigates the Hollywood film industry's representation of Arabs over a long time period. He shows that the industry works with a strictly limited set of negative and highly offensive stereotypes about Arabs from Sheikhs as sexual predators, Arabs as terrorists and Arab women as mere sex objects. The consistent and persistent misrepresentation of Arab people in this way, he suggests, is partly the result of the need to find an easy target to play the 'bad guy' and partly a consequence of indifference and lazy research. Shaheen suggests it will continue until Arabs themselves become part of the Hollywood production process.

The last two readings deal with aspects of the latest technology to impact on human communication, the Internet. In Reading 37 James Slevin reflects on how the Internet has already changed our social life. Like all adopted new technologies, the Internet has moved very rapidly from being the preserve of the wealthy to becoming part of the very fabric of societies and a key factor in the speeding up of globalization.

We buy products and services, do our personal banking, communicate with friends and businesses, play games across continents, carry out research, watch television programmes, keep up with current events and even do our dating over the Internet. In sum, the Internet is no longer an interesting diversion from real life, but is a crucial part of real life in the twenty-first century. However, assessments of the impact of the Internet on society tend to be polarized between those who see it as a negative development that is essentially destructive of social relations and others who see enormous potential and promise in its new opportunities for global communications. Slevin provides a sober alternative to such widely divergent viewpoints, focusing on the need for our active engagement in shaping the role of the Internet in our social lives.

A very good illustration of this is contained in Howard Rheingold's discussion of his involvement in attempts to build a virtual community online (in Reading 38). Rheingold tells us about his experiences communicating with people in distant locations and the extant forms of mutual assistance that evolved from this virtual community. Countering the widespread fears of the Internet as promoting the abuse and the corruption of children as well as the dumbing down of society, this piece is a much more optimistic account of the potential of the Internet for fostering genuine human communication via social networks. Accepting that there are legitimate criticisms of virtual communities and that many problems still have to be dealt with, Rheingold argues that the virtual community is potentially as real as any physical one.

34. Presenting the Self in Social Life

Erving Goffman

Interaction (that is, face-to-face interaction) may be roughly defined as the reciprocal influence of individuals upon one another's actions when in one another's immediate physical presence. *An* interaction may be defined as all the interaction which occurs throughout any one occasion when a given set of individuals are in one another's continuous presence; the term 'an encounter' would do as well. A 'performance' may be defined as all the activity of a given participant on a given occasion which serves to influence in any way any of the other participants. Taking a particular participant and his performance as a basic point of reference, we may refer to those who contribute the other performances as the audience, observers, or co-participants. The pre-established pattern of action which is unfolded during a performance and which may be presented or played through on other occasions may be called a 'part' or 'routine'.[1] These situational terms can easily be related to conventional structural ones. When an individual or performer plays the same part to the same audience on different occasions, a social relationship is likely to arise. Defining social role as the enactment of rights and duties attached to a given status, we can say that a social role will involve one or more parts and that each of these different parts may be presented by the performer on a series of occasions to the same kinds of audience or to an audience of the same persons.

[...]

Often a performance will involve only one focus of visual attention on the part of performer and audience, as, for example, when a political speech is presented in a hall or when a patient is talking to a doctor in the latter's consulting-room. However, many performances involve, as constituent parts, separate knots or clusters of verbal interaction. Thus a cocktail party typically involves several conversational subgroups which constantly shift in size and membership. Similarly, the show maintained on the floor of a shop typically involves several foci of verbal interaction, each composed of attendant–customer pairs.

Given a particular performance as a point of reference, it will sometimes be convenient to use the term 'front region' to refer to the place where the performance is given. The fixed sign-equipment in such a place has already been referred to as that part of front called 'setting'. We will have to see that some aspects of a performance seem to be played not to the audience but to the front region.

The performance of an individual in a front region may be seen as an effort to give the appearance that his activity in the region maintains and embodies certain standards. These standards seem to fall into two broad groupings. One grouping has to do with the way in which the performer treats the audience while engaged in talk with them or in gestural interchanges that are a substitute for talk. These standards are sometimes referred to as matters of politeness. The other group of standards has to do with the way in which the performer comports himself while in visual or aural range of the audience but not necessarily engaged in talk with them. I shall use the term 'decorum' to refer to this second group of standards, although some excuses and some qualifications will have to be added to justify the usage.

[. . .]

We are accustomed to assuming that the rules of decorum that prevail in sacred establishments, such as churches, will be much different from the ones that prevail in everyday places of work. We ought not to assume from this that the standards in sacred places are more numerous and more strict than those we find in work establishments. While in church, a woman may be permitted to sit, daydream, and even doze. However, as a saleswoman on the floor of a dress shop, she may be required to stand, keep alert, refrain from chewing gum, keep a fixed smile on her face even when not talking to anyone, and wear clothes she can ill afford.

[. . .]

It was suggested earlier that when one's activity occurs in the presence of other persons, some aspects of the activity are expressively accentuated and other aspects, which might discredit the fostered impression, are suppressed. It is clear that accentuated facts make their appearance in what I have called a front region; it should be just as clear that there may be another region – a 'back region' or 'backstage' – where the suppressed facts make an appearance.

A back region or backstage may be defined as a place, relative to a given performance, where the impression fostered by the performance is knowingly contradicted as a matter of course. There are, of course, many characteristic functions of such places. It is here that the capacity of a performance to express something beyond itself may be painstakingly fabricated; it is here that illusions and impressions are openly constructed. Here stage props and items of personal front can be stored in a kind of compact collapsing of whole repertoires of actions and characters. Here grades of ceremonial equipment, such as different types of liquor or clothes, can be hidden so that the

audience will not be able to see the treatment accorded them in comparison with the treatment that could have been accorded them. Here devices such as the telephone are sequestered so that they can be used 'privately'. Here costumes and other parts of personal front may be adjusted and scrutinized for flaws. Here the team can run through its performance, checking for offending expressions when no audience is present to be affronted by them; here poor members of the team, who are expressively inept, can be schooled or dropped from the performance. Here the performer can relax; he can drop his front, forgo speaking his lines, and step out of character.

[. . .]

Obviously, control of backstage plays a significant role in the process of 'work control' whereby individuals attempt to buffer themselves from the deterministic demands that surround them. If a factory worker is to succeed in giving the appearance of working hard all day, then he must have a safe place to hide the jig that enables him to turn out a day's work with less than a full day's effort.[2] If the bereaved are to be given the illusion that the dead one is really in a deep and tranquil sleep, then the undertaker must be able to keep the bereaved from the workroom where the corpses are drained, stuffed, and painted in preparation for their final performance.[3] If a mental hospital staff is to give a good impression of the hospital to those who come to visit their committed kinfolk, then it will be important to be able to bar visitors from the wards, especially the chronic wards, restricting the outsiders to special visiting-rooms where it will be practicable to have relatively nice furnishings and to ensure that all patients present are well dressed, well washed, well handled and relatively well behaved. So, too, in many service trades, the customer is asked to leave the thing that needs service and to go away so that the tradesman can work in private. When the customer returns for his automobile – or watch, or trousers, or radio – it is presented to him in good working order, an order that incidentally conceals the amount and kind of work that had to be done, the number of mistakes that were first made before getting it fixed, and other details the client would have to know before being able to judge the reasonableness of the fee that is asked of him.

Service personnel so commonly take for granted the right to keep the audience away from the back region that attention is drawn more to cases where this common strategy cannot be applied than to cases where it can. For example, the American filling-station manager has numerous troubles in this regard.[4] If a repair is needed, customers often refuse to leave their automobile overnight or all day, in trust of the establishment, as they would do had they taken their automobile to a garage. Further, when the mechanic makes repairs and adjustments, customers often feel they have the right to watch him as he does his work. If an illusionary service is to be rendered and charged for, it must, therefore, be rendered before the very person who is to be taken in by it. Customers, in fact, not only disregard the right of the station personnel to their own back region but often also define the whole station as a kind of open city for males, a place where an individual runs the risk of getting his clothes dirty and therefore has the right to demand full backstage privileges. Male motorists will saunter in, tip back their hats, spit, swear, and ask for free service or free travel advice. They will barge in to make familiar use of the toilet, the station's tools, the office telephone, or to search in the stockroom for their own supplies.[5] In order to avoid traffic lights, motorists will cut right across the station driveway, oblivious to the manager's proprietary rights.

NOTES

1. For comments on the importance of distinguishing between a routine of interaction and any particular instance when this routine is played through, see John von Neumann and Oskar Morgenstern, *The Theory of Games and Economic Behaviour* (second edition; Princeton University Press, 1947), page 49.

2. See Orvis Collins, Melville Dalton, and Donald Roy, 'Restriction of Output and Social Cleavage in Industry', *Applied Anthropology* (now *Human Organization*), iv, pages 1–14, especially page 9.

3. Mr Habenstein has suggested in seminar that in some states the undertaker has a legal right to prevent relatives of the deceased from entering the workroom where the corpse is in preparation. Presumably the sight of what has to be done to the dead to make them look attractive would be too great a shock for non-professionals and especially for kinfolk of the deceased. Mr Habenstein also suggests that kinfolk may want to be kept from the undertaker's workroom because of their own fear of their own morbid curiosity.

4. The statements which follow are taken from a study by Social Research, Inc., of two hundred small-business managers.

5. At a sports car garage the following scene was reported to me by the manager regarding a customer who went into the storeroom himself to obtain a gasket, presenting it to the manager from behind the storeroom counter:

Customer: 'How much?'
Manager: 'Sir, where did you get in and what would happen if you went behind the counter in a bank and got a roll of nickels and brought them to the teller?'
Customer: 'But this ain't a bank.'
Manager: 'Well, those are my nickels. Now, what did you want, sir?'
Customer: 'If that's the way you feel about it, O.K. That's your privilege. I want a gasket for a '51 Anglia.'
Manager: 'That's for a '54.'

While the manager's anecdote may not be a faithful reproduction of the words and actions that were actually interchanged, it does tell us something faithful about his situation and his feelings in it.

35. Throwing Like a Girl

Iris Marion Young

The basic difference which Straus observes between the way boys and girls throw is that girls do not bring their whole bodies into the motion as much as the boys. They do not reach back, twist, move backward, step, and lean forward. Rather, the girls tend to remain relatively immobile except for their arms, and even the arm is not extended as far as it could be. Throwing is not the only movement in which there is a typical difference in the way men and women use their bodies. Reflection on feminine comportment and body movement in other physical activities reveals that these also are frequently characterized, much as in the throwing case, by a failure to make full use of the body's spatial and lateral potentialities.

Even in the most simple body orientations of men and women as they sit, stand, and walk, one can observe a typical difference in body style and extension. Women generally are not as open with their bodies as men in their gait and stride. Typically, the masculine stride is longer proportional to a man's body than is the feminine stride to a woman's. The man typically swings his arms in a more open and loose fashion than does a woman and typically has more up and down rhythm in his step. Though we now wear pants more than we used to, and consequently do not have to restrict our sitting postures because of dress, women still tend to sit with their legs relatively close together and their arms across their bodies. When simply standing or leaning, men tend to keep their feet further apart than do women, and we also tend more to keep our hands and arms touching or shielding our bodies. A final indicative difference is the way each carries books or parcels; girls and women most often carry books embraced to their chests, while boys and men swing them along their sides.

The approach persons of each sex take to the performance of physical tasks that require force, strength, and muscular coordination is frequently different. There are indeed real physical differences between men and women in the kind and limit of their physical strength. Many of the observed differences between men and women in the performance of tasks requiring coordinated strength, however, are due not so much to brute muscular strength, but to the way each sex *uses* the body in approaching tasks. Women often do not perceive themselves as capable of lifting and carrying heavy things, pushing and shoving with significant force, pulling, squeezing, grasping, or twisting with force. When we attempt such tasks, we frequently fail to summon the full possibilities of our muscular coordination, position, poise, and bearing. Women tend not to put their whole bodies into engagement in a physical task with the same ease and naturalness as men. For example, in attempting to lift something, women more often than men fail to plant themselves firmly and make their thighs bear the greatest proportion of the weight. Instead, we tend to concentrate our effort on those parts of the body most immediately connected to the task—the arms and shoulders—rarely bringing the power of the legs to the task at all. When turning or twisting something, to take another example, we frequently concentrate effort in the hand and wrist, not bringing to the task the power of the shoulder, which is necessary for its efficient performance.[1]

The previously cited throwing example can be extended to a great deal of athletic activity. Now most men are by no means superior athletes, and their sporting efforts more often display bravado than genuine skill and coordination. The relatively untrained man nevertheless engages in sport generally with more free motion and open reach than does his female counterpart. Not only is there a typical style of throwing like a girl, but there is a more or less typical style of running like a girl, climbing like a girl, swinging like a girl, hitting like a girl. They have in common, first, that the whole body is not put into fluid and directed motion, but rather, in swinging and hitting, for example, the motion is concentrated in one body part; and second, that the woman's motion tends not to reach, extend, lean, stretch, and follow through in the direction of her intention.

For many women as they move in sport, a space surrounds them in imagination which we are not free to move beyond; the space available to our movement is a constricted space. Thus, for example, in softball or volleyball women tend to remain in one place more often than men, neither jumping to reach nor running to approach the ball. Men more often move out toward a ball in flight and confront it with their own countermotion. Women tend to wait for and then *react* to its approach rather than going forth to meet it. We frequently respond to the motion of a ball coming toward us as though it were coming *at* us, and our immediate bodily impulse is to flee, duck, or otherwise protect ourselves from its flight. Less often than men, moreover, do women give self-conscious direction and placement to their motion in sport. Rather than aiming at a certain place where we wish to hit a ball, for example, we tend to hit it in a 'general' direction.

Women often approach a physical engagement with things with timidity, uncertainty, and hesitancy. Typically, we lack an entire trust in our bodies to carry us to our aims. There is, I suggest, a double hesitation here. On the one hand, we often lack confidence that we have the capacity to

do what must be done. Many times I have slowed a hiking party in which the men bounded across a harmless stream while I stood on the other side warily testing out my footing on various stones, holding on to overhanging branches. Though the others crossed with ease, I do not believe it is easy for *me*, even though once I take a committed step I am across in a flash. The other side of this tentativeness is, I suggest, a fear of getting hurt, which is greater in women than in men. Our attention is often divided between the aim to be realized in motion and the body that must accomplish it, while at the same time saving itself from harm. We often experience our bodies as a fragile encumberance, rather than the media for the enactment of our aims. We feel as though we must have our attention directed upon our body to make sure it is doing what we wish it to do, rather than paying attention to what we want to do *through* our bodies.

All the above factors operate to produce in many women a greater or lesser feeling of incapacity, frustration, and self-consciousness. We have more of a tendency than men to greatly underestimate our bodily capacity.[2] We decide beforehand – usually mistakenly – that the task is beyond us, and thus give it less than our full effort. At such a half-hearted level, of course, we cannot perform the tasks, become frustrated, and fulfill our own prophecy. In entering a task we frequently are self-conscious about appearing awkward, and at the same time do not wish to appear too strong. Both worries contribute to our awkwardness and frustration. If we should finally release ourselves from this spiral and really give a physical task our best effort, we are greatly surprised indeed at what our bodies can accomplish. It has been found than women more often than men underestimate the level of achievement they have reached.[3]

None of the observations which have been made thus far about the way women typically move and comport their bodies applies to all women all of the time. Nor do those women who manifest some aspect of this typicality do so in the same degree. There is no inherent mysterious connection between these sorts of typical comportments and being a female person. Many of them result, as will be developed later, from lack of practice in using the body and performing tasks. Even given these qualifications, one can nevertheless sensibly speak of a general feminine style of body comportment and movement.

[. . .]

The modalities of feminine bodily comportment, motility, and spatiality which I have described here are, I claim, common to the existence of women in contemporary society to one degree or another. They have their source, however, in neither anatomy nor physiology, and certainly not in a mysterious feminine 'essence'. Rather, they have their source in the particular *situation* of women as conditioned by their sexist oppression in contemporary society.

Women in sexist society are physically handicapped. Insofar as we learn to live out our existence in accordance with the definition that patriarchal culture assigns to us, we are physically inhibited, confined, positioned, and objectified. As lived bodies we are not open and unambiguous transcendences which move out to master a world that belongs to us, a world constituted by our own intentions and projections. To be sure, there are actual women in contemporary society to whom all or part of the above description does not apply. Where these modalities are not manifest in or determinative of the existence of a particular woman, however, they are definitive in a negative mode – as that which she has escaped, through accident or good fortune, or more often, as that which she has had to overcome.

One of the sources of the modalities of feminine bodily existence is too obvious to dwell upon at length. For the most part, girls and women are not give the opportunity to use their full bodily capacities in free and open engagement with the world, nor are they encouraged as much as boys to develop specific bodily skills.[4] Girl play is often more sedentary and enclosing than the play of boys. In school and after school activities girls are not encouraged to engage in sport, in the controlled use of their bodies in achieving well-defined goals. Girls, moreover, get little practice at 'tinkering' with things, and thus at developing spatial skill. Finally, girls are not asked often to perform tasks demanding physical effort and strength, while as the boys grow older they are asked to do so more and more.[5]

The modalities of feminine bodily existence are not merely privative, however, and thus their source is not merely in lack of practice, though this is certainly an important element. There is a specific positive style of feminine body comportment and movement, which is learned as the girl comes to understand that she is a girl. The young girl acquires many subtle habits of feminine body comportment – walking like a girl, tilting her head like a girl, standing and sitting like a girl, gesturing like a girl, and so on. The girl learns actively to hamper her movements. She is told that she must be careful not to get hurt, not to get dirty, not to tear her clothes, that the things she desires to do are dangerous for her. Thus she develops a bodily timidity which increases with age. In assuming herself as a girl, she takes herself up as fragile. Studies have found that young children of both sexes categorically assert that girls are more likely to get hurt than boys,[6] and that girls ought to remain close to home while boys can roam and explore.[7] The more a girl assumes her status as feminine, the more she takes herself to be fragile and immobile, and the more she actively enacts her own body inhibition. When I was about thirteen, I spent hours practicing a 'feminine' walk which was stiff, closed, and rotated from side to side.

Studies which record observations of sex differences in spatial perception, spatial problem solving, and motor skills have also found that these differences tend to increase with age. While very young children show virtually no differences in motor skills, movement, spatial perception, etc., differences seem to appear in elementary school and increase with adolescence. If these findings are accurate, they would seem to support the conclusion that it is in the process of growing up as a girl that the modalities of feminine bodily comportment, motility, and spatiality make their appearance.[8]

There is, however, a further source of the modalities of feminine bodily existence which is perhaps even more profound than these. At the root of those modalities, I have stated in the previous section, is the fact that the woman lives her body as *object* as well as subject. The source of this is that patriarchal society defines woman as object, as mere body, and that in sexist society women are in fact frequently regarded by others as objects and mere bodies. An essential part of the situation of being a woman is that of living the ever present possibility that one will be gazed upon as a mere body, as shape and flesh that presents itself as the potential object of another subject's intentions and manipulations, rather than as a living manifestation of action and intention.[9] The source of this objectified bodily existence is in the attitude of others regarding her, but the woman herself often actively takes up her body as a mere thing. She gazes at it in the mirror, worries about how it looks to others, prunes it, shapes it, molds and decorates it.

This objectified bodily existence accounts for the self-consciousness of the feminine relation to her body and resulting distance she takes from her body. As human, she is a transcendence and subjectivity, and cannot live herself as mere bodily object. Thus, to the degree she does live herself as mere body, she cannot be in unity with herself, but must take a distance from and exist in discontinuity with her body. The objectifying regard which 'keeps her in her place' can also account for the spatial modality of being positioned and for why women frequently tend not to move openly, keeping their limbs enclosed around themselves. To open her body in free active and open extension and bold outward directedness is for a woman to invite objectification.

The threat of being seen is, however, not the only threat of objectification which the woman lives. She also lives the threat of invasion of her body space. The most extreme form of such spatial and bodily invasion is the threat of rape.

But we are daily subject to the possibility of bodily invasion in many far more subtle ways as well. It is acceptable, for example, for women to be touched in ways and under circumstances that it is not acceptable for men to be touched, and by persons – i.e., men – whom it is not acceptable for them to touch.[10] I would suggest that the enclosed space which has been described as a modality of feminine spatiality is in part a defense against such invasion. Women tend to project an existential barrier enclosed around them and discontinuous with the 'over there' in order to keep the other at distance. The woman lives her space as confined and enclosed around her at least in part as projecting some small area in which she can exist as a free subject.

NOTES

1. It should be noted that this is probably typical only of women in advanced industrial societies, where the model of the Bourgeois woman has been extended to most women. It would not apply to those societies, for example, where most people, including women, do heavy physical work. Nor does this particular observation, of course, hold true of those women in our own society who do heavy physical work.

2. See A. M. Gross, 'Estimated versus actual physical strength in three ethnic groups,' *Child Development*, 39 (1968), pp. 283–90. In a test of children at several different ages, at all but the youngest age level, girls rated themselves lower than boys rated themselves on self-estimates of strength, and as the girls grow older, their self-estimates of strength become even lower.

3. See Marguerite A. Cifton and Hope M. Smith, 'Comparison of Expressed Self-Concept of Highly Skilled Males and Females Concerning Motor Performance,' *Perceptual and Motor Skills* 16 (1963): 199–201. Women consistently underestimated their level of achievement in skills such as running and jumping far more often than men did.

4. Nor are girls provided with examples of girls and women being physically active. See Mary E. Duquin, 'Differential Sex Role Socialization Toward Amplitude Appropriation,' *Research Quarterly* (American Alliance for Health, Physical Education, and Recreation) 48 (1977): 288–92. Survey of textbooks for young children revealed that children are thirteen times more likely to see a vigorously active man than a vigorously active woman, and three times more likely to see a relatively active man than a relatively active woman.

5. Sherman (Julia A. Sherman, 'Problems of Sex Differences in Space Perception and Aspects of Intellectual Functioning,' *Psychological Review* 74 (1967): 290–9) argues that it is the differential socialization of boys and girls in being encouraged to 'tinker,' explore, etc., that accounts for the difference between the two in spatial ability.

6. See L. Kolberg, 'A Cognitive-Developmental Analysis of Children's Sex-Role Concepts and Attitudes,' in E. E. Maccoby, ed., *The Development of Sex Differences* (Palo Alto: Stanford University Press, 1966), 101.

7. Lenore J. Weitzman, 'Sex Role Socialization,' in Jo Freeman, ed., *Woman: A Feminist Perspective* (Palo Alto: Mayfield Publishing Co., 1975), 111–12.

8. E. E. Maccoby and C. N. Jacklin, *The Psychology of Sex Differences* (Stanford, CA: Stanford University Press, 1974), 93–94.

9. The manner in which women are objectified by the gaze of the Other is not the same phenomenon as the objectification by the Other that is a condition of self-consciousness in Sartre's account. See *Being and Nothingness*, trans. Hazel E. Barnes (New York: Philosophical Library, 1956), part III. While the basic ontological category of being-for-others is an objectified for itself, the objectification that women are subject to is being regarded as a mere in-itself. On the particular dynamic of sexual objectification, see Sandra Bartky, 'Psychological Oppression,' in Sharon Bishop and Margorie Weinzweig, ed., *Philosophy and Women* (Belmont, CA: Wadsworth Publishing Co., 1979), 33–41.

10. See Nancy Henley and Jo Freeman, 'The sexual politics of interpersonal behavior,' in Freeman ed., *Woman: A Feminist Perspective*, pp. 391–401.

36. Hollywood's Misrepresentation of Arabs

Jack G. Shaheen

In this first comprehensive review of Arab screen images ever published, I document and discuss virtually every feature that Hollywood has ever made – more than 900 films, the vast majority of which portray Arabs by distorting at every turn what most Arab men, women, and children are really like. In gathering the evidence for this book, I was driven by the need to expose an injustice: cinema's systematic, pervasive, and unapologetic degradation and dehumanization of a people.

When colleagues ask whether today's reel Arabs are more stereotypical than yesteryear's, I can't say the celluloid Arab has changed. That is the problem. He is what he has always been – the cultural 'other.' Seen through Hollywood's distorted lenses, Arabs look different and threatening. Projected along racial and religious lines, the stereotypes are deeply ingrained in American cinema. From 1896 until today, filmmakers have collectively indicted all Arabs as Public Enemy #1 – brutal, heartless, uncivilized religious fanatics and money-mad cultural 'others' bent on terrorizing civilized Westerners, especially Christians and Jews. Much has happened since 1896 – women's suffrage, the Great Depression, the civil rights movement, two world wars, the Korean, Vietnam, and Gulf wars, and the collapse of the Soviet Union. Throughout it all, Hollywood's caricature of the Arab has prowled the silver screen. He is there to this day – repulsive and unrepresentative as ever.

What is an Arab? In countless films, Hollywood alleges the answer: Arabs are brute murderers, sleazy rapists, religious fanatics, oil-rich dimwits, and abusers of women. 'They [the Arabs] all look alike to me,' quips the American heroine in the movie *The Sheik Steps Out* (1937). 'All Arabs look alike to me,' admits the protagonist in *Commando* (1968). Decades later, nothing had changed. Quips the US Ambassador in *Hostage* (1986), 'I can't tell one [Arab] from another. Wrapped in those bed sheets they all look the same to me.' In Hollywood's films, they certainly do.

Pause and visualize the reel Arab. What do you see? Black beard, headdress, dark sunglasses. In the background – a limousine, harem maidens, oil wells, camels. Or perhaps he is brandishing an automatic weapon, crazy hate in his eyes and Allah on his lips. Can you see him?

Think about it. When was the last time you saw a movie depicting an Arab or an American of Arab heritage as a regular guy? Perhaps a man who works ten hours a day, comes home to a loving wife and family, plays soccer with his kids, and prays with family members at his respective mosque or church. He's the kind of guy you'd like to have as your next door neighbor, because – well, maybe because he's a bit like you.

But would you want to share your country, much less your street, with any of Hollywood's Arabs? Would you want your kids playing with him and his family, your teenagers dating them? Would you enjoy sharing your neighborhood with fabulously wealthy and vile oil sheikhs with an eye for Western blondes and arms deals and intent on world domination, or with crazed terrorists, airplane hijackers, or camel-riding bedouins?

Real Arabs

Who exactly are the Arabs of the Middle East? When I use the term 'Arab,' I refer to the 265 million people who reside in, and the many more millions around the world who are from, the 22 Arab states. The Arabs have made many contributions to our civilization. To name a few, Arab and Persian physicians and scientists inspired European thinkers like Leonardo da Vinci. The Arabs invented algebra and the concept of zero. Numerous English words – algebra, chemistry, coffee, and others – have Arab roots. Arab intellectuals made it feasible for Western scholars to develop and practice advanced educational systems.

In astronomy Arabs used astrolabes for navigation, star maps, celestial globes, and the concept of the center of gravity. In geography, they pioneered the use of latitude and longitude. They invented the water clock; their architecture inspired the Gothic style in Europe. In agriculture, they introduced oranges, dates, sugar, and cotton, and pioneered water works and irrigation. And, they developed a tradition of legal learning, of secular literature and scientific and philosophical thought, in which the Jews also played an important part.

There exists a mixed ethnicity in the Arab world – from 5000 BC to the present. The Scots, Greeks, British, French, Romans, English, and others have occupied the area. Not surprisingly, some Arabs have dark hair, dark eyes, and olive complexions. Others boast freckles, red hair, and blue eyes.

Geographically, the Arab world is one-and-a-half times as large as the United States, stretching from the Strait of Hormuz to the Rock of Gibraltar. It's the point where Asia, Europe, and Africa come together. The region gave the world three major religions, a language, and an alphabet.

In most Arab countries today, 70 percent of the population is under age 30. Most share a common language, cultural heritage, history, and religion (Islam). Though the vast majority of them are Muslims, about 15 million Arab Christians (including Chaldean, Coptic, Eastern Orthodox, Episcopalian, Roman Catholic, Melkite, Maronite, and Protestant), reside there as well.

Two Fulbright-Hayes lectureship grants and numerous lecture tours sponsored by the United States Information Service (USIS) enabled me to travel extensively throughout the region. While lecturing and living in fifteen Arab countries, I came to discover that like the United States, the Arab world accommodated diverse, talented, and hospitable citizens: lawyers, bankers, doctors, engineers, bricklayers, farmers, computer programmers, homemakers, mechanics, businesspeople, store managers, waiters, construction workers, writers, musicians, chefs, architects, hairdressers, psychologists, plastic surgeons, pilots, and environmentalists.

Their dress is traditional and Western, The majority are peaceful, not violent; poor, not rich; most do not dwell in desert tents; none are surrounded by harem maidens; most have never seen an oil well or mounted a camel. Not one travels via 'magic carpets.' Their lifestyles defy stereotyping.

As for Americans of Arab heritage, prior to World War I, nearly all the Arabs immigrating to America were Christians: Lebanese, Palestinians, and Syrians. Today, the majority of the United States' Arab-American population is also Christian; about 40 percent are Muslim.

Through immigration, conversion, and birth, however, Muslims are America's fastest growing religious group; about 500,000 reside in the greater Los Angeles area. America's six to eight million Muslims frequent more than 2,000 mosques, Islamic centers, and schools. They include immigrants from more than 60 nations, as well as African-Americans. In fact, most of the world's 1.1 billion Muslims are Indonesian, Indian, or Malaysian. Only 12 percent of the world's Muslims are Arab. Yet, moviemakers ignore this reality, depicting Arabs and Muslims as one and the same people. Repeatedly, they falsely project all Arabs as Muslims and all Muslims as Arabs. As a result, viewers, too, tend to link the same attributes to both peoples.

[. . .]

Why is it important for the average American to know and care about the Arab stereotype? It is critical because dislike of 'the stranger,' which the Greeks knew as xenophobia, forewarns that when one ethnic, racial, or religious group is vilified, innocent people suffer. History reminds us that the cinema's hateful Arab stereotypes are reminiscent of abuses in earlier times. Not so long ago – and sometimes still – Asians, American Indians, blacks, and Jews were vilified.

Ponder the consequences. In February 1942, more than 100,000 Americans of Japanese descent were displaced from their homes and interred in camps; for decades blacks were denied basic civil rights, robbed of their property, and lynched; American Indians, too, were displaced and slaughtered; and in Europe, six million Jews perished in the Holocaust.

This is what happens when people are dehumanized.

Mythology in any society is significant. And, Hollywood's celluloid mythology dominates the culture. No doubt about it, Hollywood's renditions of Arabs frame stereotypes in viewer's minds. The problem is peculiarly American. Because of the vast American cultural reach via television and film – we are the world's leading exporter of screen images – the all-pervasive Arab stereotype has much more of a negative impact on viewers today than it did thirty or forty years ago.

Nowadays, Hollywood's motion pictures reach nearly everyone. Cinematic illusions are created, nurtured, and distributed world-wide, reaching viewers in more than 100 countries, from Iceland to Thailand. Arab images have an effect not only on international audiences, but on international moviemakers as well. No sooner do contemporary features leave the movie theaters than they are available in video stores and transmitted onto TV screens. Thanks to technological advances, old silent and sound movies impugning Arabs, some of which were produced before I was born, are repeatedly broadcast on cable television and beamed directly into the home.

Check your local guides and you will see that since the mid-1980s, appearing each week on TV screens, are fifteen to twenty recycled movies projecting Arabs as dehumanized caricatures: *The Sheik* (1921), *The Mummy* (1932), *Cairo* (1942), *The Steel Lady* (1953), *Exodus* (1960), *The Black Stallion* (1979), *Protocol* (1984), *The Delta Force* (1986), *Ernest In the Army* (1997), and *Rules of Engagement* (2000). Watching yesteryear's stereotypical Arabs on TV screens is an unnerving experience, especially when pondering the influence celluloid images have on adults and our youth.

[. . .]

In this book, I list and discuss, in alphabetical order, more than 900 feature films displaying Arab characters. Regrettably, in all these I uncovered only a handful of heroic Arabs; they surface in a few 1980s and 1990s scenarios. In *Lion of the Desert* (1981), righteous Arabs bring down invading fascists. Humane Palestinians surface in *Hanna K* (1983) and *The Seventh Coin* (1992). In *Robin Hood, Prince of Thieves* (1991), a devout Muslim who 'fights better than twenty English knights,' helps Robin Hood get the better of the evil Sheriff of Nottingham. In *The 13th Warrior* (1999), an Arab Muslim scholar befriends Nordic warriors, helping them defeat primitive cavemen. And in *Three Kings* (1999), a movie celebrating our commonalities and differences, we view Arabs as regular folks, with affections and aspirations. This anti-war movie humanizes the Iraqis, a people who for too long have been projected as evil caricatures.

Most of the time I found moviemakers saturating the marketplace with all sorts of Arab villains. Producers collectively impugned Arabs in every type of movie you can imagine, targeting adults in well-known and high-budgeted movies such as *Exodus* (1960), *Black Sunday* (1977), *Ishtar* (1987), and *The Siege* (1998); and reaching out to teenagers with financially successful schlock movies such as *Five Weeks in a Balloon* (1962), *Things Are Tough All Over* (1982), *Sahara*

(1983), and *Operation Condor* (1997). One constant factor dominates all the films: Derogatory stereotypes are omnipresent, reaching youngsters, baby boomers, and older folk.

I am not saying an Arab should never be portrayed as the villain. What I am saying is that almost *all* Hollywood depictions of Arabs are *bad* ones. This is a grave injustice. Repetitious and negative images of the reel Arab literally sustain adverse portraits across generations. The fact is that for more than a century producers have tarred an entire group of people with the same sinister brush.

Hundreds of movies reveal Western protagonists spewing out unrelenting barrages of uncontested slurs, calling Arabs: 'assholes,' 'bastards,' 'camel-dicks,' 'pigs,' 'devil-worshipers,' 'jackals,' 'rats,' 'rag-heads,' 'towel-heads,' 'scum-buckets,' 'sons-of-dogs,' 'buzzards of the jungle,' 'sons-of-whores,' 'sons-of-unnamed goats,' and 'sons-of-she-camels.'

Producers fail to recognize that 'Allah' is Arabic for God, that when they pray, Arab Christians and Muslims, use the word 'Allah.' When producers show Jewish and Christian protagonists contesting Arab Muslims, the Western hero will say to his Arab enemy in a scornful and jeering manner, 'Allah.' The character's disrespectful 'Allah's' mislead viewers, wrongly implying that devout Arab Muslims do not worship the 'true God' of the Christians and Jews, but some tribal deity.

Still other movies contain the word 'Ayrab,' a vulgar Hollywood epithet for Arab that is comparable to dago, greaser, kike, nigger, and gook.

[. . .]

Arabs are almost always easy targets in war movies. From as early as 1912, decades prior to the 1991 Gulf War, dozens of films presented allied agents and military forces – American, British, French, and more recently Israeli – obliterating Arabs. In the World War I drama *The Lost Patrol* (1934), a brave British sergeant (Victor McLaughlin) guns down 'sneaky Arabs, those dirty, filthy swine.' An American newsreel cameraman (John Wayne) helps wipe out a 'horde of [Arab] tribesmen' in *I Cover the War* (1937).

In *Sirocco* (1951), the first Hollywood feature film projecting Arabs as terrorists, Syrian 'fanatics' assail French soldiers and American arms dealer Harry Smith (Humphrey Bogart). *The Lost Command* (1966) shows French Colonel Raspeguy's (Anthony Quinn) soldiers killing Algerians. And, Israelis gun down sneaky bedouins in two made-in-Israel films, *Sinai Guerrillas* (1960) and *Sinai Commandos* (1968).

Arabs trying to rape, kill, or abduct fair-complexioned Western heroines is a common theme, dominating scenarios from *Captured by Bedouins* (1912), to *The Pelican Brief* (1993). In *Brief*, an Arab hitman tries to assassinate the protagonist, played by Julia Roberts. In *Captured*, desert bandits kidnap a fair American maiden, but she is eventually rescued by a British officer. As for her bedouin abductors, they are gunned down by rescuing US Cavalry troops.

Arabs enslave and abuse Africans in about ten films, including *A Daughter of the Congo* (1930), *Drums of Africa* (1963), and *Ashanti* (1979). Noted African-American filmmaker Oscar Micheaux, who made 'race movies' from 1919 to 1948, also advanced the Arab-as-abductor theme in his *Daughter of the Congo*. Though Micheaux's movies contested Hollywood's Jim Crow stereotypes of blacks, *A Daughter of the Congo* depicts lecherous Arab slavers abducting and holding hostage a lovely Mulatto woman and her maid. The maiden is eventually rescued by the heroic African-American officers of the 10th US Cavalry.

Anti-Christian Arabs appear in dozens of films. When the US military officer in *Another Dawn* (1937) is asked why Arabs despise Westerners, he barks: 'It's a good Moslem hatred of Christians.' Islam is also portrayed as a violent faith in *Legion of the Doomed* (1959). Here, an Arab is told, 'Kill him before he kills you.' Affirms the Arab as he plunges a knife into his foe's gut, 'You speak the words of Allah.' And, in *The Castilian* (1963), Spanish Christians triumph over Arab Muslim zealots. How? By releasing scores of squealing pigs! Terrified of the pigs, the reel Arabs retreat.

Arabs invade the United States and terrorize innocents in *Golden Hands of Kurigal* (1949), *Terror Squad* (1988), *True Lies* (1994), and *The Siege* (1998). *The Siege* is especially alarming. In it, Arab immigrants methodically lay waste to Manhattan. Assisted by Arab-American auto mechanics, university students, and a college teacher, they blow up the city's FBI building, kill scores of government agents, blast theatergoers, and detonate a bomb in a crowded bus.

I discussed the movie's violent images with director Edward Zwick in New York on April 2, 1998. Zwick told me that because some scenes show innocent Arab-Americans being tossed indiscriminately into detention centers, the film would 'provoke thought.' Provoke violence, more likely, I thought.

[. . .]

Sheikhs

The word 'sheikh' means, literally, a wise elderly person, the head of the family, but you would not know that from watching any of Hollywood's 'sheikh' features, more than 160 scenarios, including the Kinetoscope short *Sheik Hadj Tahar Hadj Cherif* (1894) and the Selig Company's *The Power of the Sultan* (1907) – the first movie to be filmed in Los Angeles. Throughout the Arab world, to show respect, people address Muslim religious leaders as sheikhs.

Moviemakers, however, attach a completely different meaning to the word. As Matthew Sweet points out, 'The cinematic Arab has never been an attractive figure . . . in the 1920s he was a swarthy Sheik, wiggling his eyebrows and chasing the [Western] heroine around a tiled courtyard. After the 1973 oil crisis . . .' producers revitalized the image of the fabulously wealthy and slothful sheikh, only this time he was getting rich at the expense of red-blooded Americans; 'he became an inscrutable bully – a Ray-Ban-ed variation of the stereotypes of the Jewish money lender.'[1]

Instead of presenting sheikhs as elderly men of wisdom, screenwriters offer romantic melodramas portraying them as stooges-in-sheets, slovenly, hook-nosed potentates intent on capturing pale-faced blondes for their harems. Imitating the stereotypical behavior of their lecherous predecessors – the 'bestial' Asian, the black 'buck,' and the 'lascivious' Latino – slovenly Arabs move to swiftly and violently deflower Western maidens. Explains Edward Said, 'The perverted sheikh can often be seen snarling at the captured Western hero and blonde girl . . . [and saying] "My men are going to kill you, but they like to amuse themselves before."'[2]

Early silent films, such as *The Unfaithful Odalisque* (1903), *The Arab* (1915), and *The Sheik* (1921), all present bearded, robed Arab rulers as one collective stereotypical lecherous cur. In *The Unfaithful Odalisque*, the sheikh not only admonishes his harem maiden, he directs a Nubian slave to lash her with a cat-o'-nine-tails. In *The Sheik* (1921), Sheikh Ahmed (Valentino) glares at Diana, the kidnapped British lovely and boasts: 'When an Arab sees a woman he wants, he takes her!'

Flash forward 33 years. Affirms the sheikh in *The Adventures of Hajji Baba* (1954): 'Give her to me or I'll take her!'

Moving to kidnap and/or seduce the Western heroine, clumsy moneyed sheikhs fall all over themselves in more than 60 silent and sound movies, ranging from *The Fire and the Sword* (1914) to *Protocol* (1984). Sheikhs disregard Arab women, preferring instead to ravish just one Western woman.

[. . .]

The movies of the 1980s are especially offensive. They display insolent desert sheikhs with thick accents threatening to rape and/or enslave starlets: Brooke Shields in *Sahara* (1983), Goldie Hawn in *Protocol* (1984), Bo Derek in *Bolero* (1984), and Kim Basinger in *Never Say Never Again* (1986).

[. . .]

The time is long overdue for Hollywood to end its undeclared war on Arabs, and to cease misrepresenting and maligning them.

All I ask of filmmakers is to be even-handed, to project Arabs as they do other people – no better, no worse. They should enjoy at the very least relative immunity from prejudicial portrayal.

Established professionals and young, energetic moviemakers should step forward and create movies that change the way viewers perceive reel Arabs. They should incorporate this axiom: The denigration of one people, one religion, is the denigration of all people, all religions. As Holocaust survivor and Nobel Prize winner Elie Wiesel reminds us, no human race is superior, no religious faith is inferior; every nation has its share of bad people and good people.

I challenge Hollywood's producers to acknowledge unjust portraits of the past century and embrace Wiesel's wisdom, taking the high ground and projecting Arabs as ordinary and decent world citizens.

NOTES

1. Sweet, M. (2000) 'Movie Targets,' *The Independent* 30ᵗʰ July 2000. Available online at http://www.independent.co.uk/arts-entertainment/films/features/movie-targets-710042.html
2. Said, E. (1997) *Covering Islam: How the Media and the Experts Determine How We See The Rest Of the World*. U.S.: Random House Inc., pp. 19–20.

37. The Internet Galaxy

James Slevin

Although the internet is being actively adopted into the day-to-day lives of many millions of people, there is a growing unease that this is happening without full cognizance of the consequences of its use. The opportunities created by the internet mean many different things to different people. It is useful first to consider some ideas that Zuboff discusses in her work *In the Age of the Smart Machine*.[1] Zuboff argues that many of the choices we face regarding new intelligent technologies concern different ways of conceptualizing and distributing knowledge, and this has led her to recognize a number of alternative futures arising from the 'smart machine'. Second, I shall carry Zuboff's arguments through to the internet, where we also see two alternative perspectives developing. I shall argue, however, that overly positive or dismal accounts of the impact of the internet on modern life are not conducive to the development of an active engagement with the unpredictable environment in which we live today.

Alternative futures in the age of the smart machine

Zuboff's study analyses the introduction of new intelligent technologies such as the computer into the workplace during the 1980s. It provides us with an excellent starting point for relating the rise of the internet to the conditions of reflexive modernization. She describes how people fear 'that today's working assumptions could not be relied upon to carry them through, that the future would not resemble the past or the present' (pp. 4–5). She goes on to ask:

Should the advent of the smart machine be taken as an invitation to relax the demands upon human comprehension and critical judgement? Does the massive diffusion of computer technology throughout our workplaces necessarily entail an equally dramatic loss of meaningful employment opportunities? Must the new electronic milieu engender a world in which individuals have lost control over their daily work lives? (p. 5)

These are all questions which we might ask about the internet today.

In examining these questions Zuboff refers to the two faces of intelligent technology. On the one hand, such technology can be used to *automate* organizational processes and procedures such that it provides 'substitutes for the human body that reach an even greater degree of certainty and precision' (p. 8). On the other, such technology can be used to '*informate*' organizational processes and procedures such that it introduces

an additional dimension of reflexivity: it makes its contribution to the product, but it also reflects back on its activities and on the system of activities to which it is related. Information technology not only produces action but also produces a voice that symbolically renders events, objects, and processes so that they become visible, knowable, and shareable in a new way. (p. 9)

Zuboff claims that a succession of dilemmas results from the introduction of intelligent technologies into the workplace. These slot directly into the conditions that describe reflexive modernization. First, there are the dilemmas associated with the changing grounds of knowledge.

These involve the emergence of intellective skills that often supplant the body as a primary source of knowledge. Individuals have to develop skills, for example, that allow them to confidently monitor other people or processes relevant to their tasks without necessarily being physically present themselves. Second, there are the dilemmas associated with the blurring of the traditional opposition between those in authority and those in positions of subordination. As the demand for new intellective skills increases, the dismantling of traditional hierarchies progresses. Third, there are the dilemmas related to attempts to bolster threatened authority hierarchies with new techniques of control that draw on the intelligent technology's tendency to extend the visibility of organizational processes. However, as Zuboff explains, such efforts 'engage a series of organizational responses that, ironically, weaken managerial authority even more profoundly' (p. 16).

She argues that we are in danger of failing to meet the challenges of 'informating' technology by polarizing two approaches. If intelligent technology is used

only to intensify the automaticity of work, it can reduce skill levels and dampen the urge toward more participatory and decentralized forms of management . . . In contrast, an approach to technology deployment that emphasizes its informating capacity uses technology to do far more than routinize, fragment, or eliminate jobs. It uses the new technology to increase the intellectual content of work at every organizational level, as the ability to decipher explicit information and make decisions informed by that understanding becomes broadly distributed among organizational members. (p. 243)

She warns that 'a redistribution of authority is both the basis upon which intellective skill development can proceed and the necessary implication of its success. Unless informating is taken up as a conscious strategy, rather than simply being allowed to unfold without any anticipation of its consequences, it is unlikely to yield up its full value' (pp. 309–10).

The internet: towards a positive or a negative pole?

As the contours of intensified globalization, decentred authority and intensified reflexivity continue to interlace with both modern institutions and with individual life, it is possible to recognize Zuboff's dilemmas within the development and deployment of the internet. While aware of the complexities this conceals, I would suggest that the perspectives on the impact of the internet on society tend towards two poles of optimism and pessimism. I shall deal with each of these in turn.

An unclouded celebration of the internet's opportunities

In circumstances of late modernity it is not difficult to be somewhat naively optimistic about the opportunities the internet offers. Those tending toward this positive pole are by no means confined to groups seeking to sell new computers or internet accounts. They can also be found among a wide range of technological crusaders convinced that the internet is about to change the world. Indeed, most internet users would admit to having been somewhat inspired by awe when they first launched a homepage or heard the distant voice of a stranger coming from their computer. In a world in which interaction has become increasingly stretched across time and space, the internet is acting as a catalyst, releasing a pent-up demand for more reciprocal and sophisticated control over the exchange and use of information.

Clearly, the internet seems to go some way in fulfilling this demand for positive forms of control and is helping nation-states, economic organizations and individuals to cope with the consequences of intensifying globalization, the emergence of post-traditional forms of organization and the expansion and intensification of social reflexivity. On an unprecedented level, the internet is presenting individuals and organizations with new opportunities for responsive action by allowing them to display their integrity and maintain and build up the trust of others in their actions. It also offers new ways of accessing such information anywhere and at any time. As such, the internet is radically altering the degree to which individuals and organizations can enter freely into discourses across extended time-space. It opens up new opportunities for dialogue and deliberation, empowers people to make things happen rather than have things happen to them, and facilitates new forms of solidarity and cooperation.

Let me describe some features of internet use which have contributed to certain accounts of the internet tending toward this positive pole. First, confronted by accelerated risk and uncertainty, with citizens critically questioning many of their actions and policies, governments have been making clear their intent to use the internet in order to be more open and responsive towards their citizenry. In November 1996 the Conservative government in Great Britain published 'Government Direct', a green paper in which it set out its ideas for using information technology to empower people in their dealings with government; and this vision was taken further by the Labour government which came into power in 1997. The green paper was published on the government information service website.[2] Here, visitors were invited to participate in the debate on how government should use IT to serve people better and were able to submit their contributions via e-mail. Additional webpages provided access to a virtual library of responses which had already been submitted by various officials, citizens and organizations.

A similar initiative was unveiled by the Dutch Ministry of Transport in the Netherlands in 1996. The ministry set up an interactive forum called the 'Digital Roundabout',[3] a website where ministry officials, citizens and interested organizations could meet and discuss various policy issues. Discussions focused on projects which were posted on the website, which also enabled participants to enter into real-time debate via a chat system and to contribute to newsgroup discussions. What all these public sector initiatives have in common is that they are not aimed merely at providing one-way channels for funnelling official information about national, regional and local government projects, but rather at two-way interfaces for facilitating dialogue, sharing knowledge and giving participants an opportunity to make a difference.

A second feature of internet use which has given cause for optimism for some is that, like governments, commercial organizations are also displaying their intention to use internet technology to revitalize their external and internal communications. The Boeing Company,[4] for example, has designed and implemented an intranet to facilitate and support the dissemination of information within the organization. Like many modern organizations, the company is assessing and rethinking its managerial information flows and decentralizing its operations. Intranets have become key tools in many such projects. Like the examples discussed earlier, this intranet offers its users a wide range of webpages and interactive forums. Employees can access information without having to wait for it to filter down through traditional lines of communication. The interactive forums create a sphere in which employees can discuss their ideas, share knowledge and engage in collaborative work across organizational boundaries.[5]

A similar initiative has been undertaken by the Ford Motor Company,[6] connecting up some 120,000 computers at offices and production units around the world. Webpages provide users with marketing information, analyses of competitors' components and information on suppliers. A product development system houses information on the assembling and testing of vehicles, and lets designers, engineers and suppliers collaborate using the same data. Teams working on one kind of vehicle have their own website where they can publish progress reports, ask questions, warn about problems and actively build quality into their work processes. Knowledge sharing is helping the organization to reduce the time it takes to get new vehicles to market from thirty-six to twenty-four months. The company is also considering linking its 15,000 dealers to its intranet as this will open up possibilities for custom ordering and cars 'made on demand'.[7] As such, intranets and extranets are radically changing the nature of supply chains of commercial organizations, offering new opportunities for partnering and alliances, cutting out some 'infomediaries' and introducing new ones.

A third feature of internet use which contributes to the feeling of optimism is the way individuals using the internet are experiencing matching transformations in their day-to-day lives. Let us focus a while on the internet relay chat channel '#Gay.nl'.[8] It first took shape as a permanent channel with a small group of regular users in 1993, although it existed intermittently well before that. Today, it frequently has over a hundred users online at a time, sometimes reaching over 130 at weekends. Channel users vary in age and social background, and come from all over the Netherlands, and also from other countries. By no means all users are gay; some are just interested or genuinely curious. Although much of the discourse includes having a bit of fun and a laugh, #Gay.nl is indicative of how the internet is helping individuals cope with modern everyday life. The channel creates a forum in which they can negotiate the standardized influences of sexual values, acquire knowledge and skills, and forge new commitments and mutuality. The channel operators, consisting of a group of regular users, run a #Gay.nl webpage[9] which provides information about the channel, invitations to meetings and hyperlinks to various other webpages, including those belonging to channel users. Users frequently meet up face to face, and a number of organized channel meetings are held every year where on some occasions over fifty people have been known to turn up.

The #Gay.nl webpage also lists channel rules which prohibit harassment and abusive language. However, transgressors typing gay abuse are rarely 'kicked off' the channel immediately. Experienced channel users often first ignore them and then enter into discussion with them, challenging their views, and after a good deal of amusement and banter the incident is soon over. Despite various security systems, more aggressive attacks sometimes result in the channel being taken over completely. While they attempt to sort the problem out, the operators simply create a temporary channel with a different name. Sometimes the discourse in the main channel is logged by the operators so that they can later analyse incidents in order to deal with them more effectively in the future.

The internet and the fear that chaos might overwhelm the world

Balanced against these positive images of the consequences of internet use is, however, an opposite set of complex attitudes which, taken together, tend towards a rather more cynical and sometimes even pessimistic pole. Here the centrifugal tendencies and the dislocating character of internet use are brought to the forefront. The internet, more than any other medium, is seen by some as eroding 'community' and 'emptying' day-to-day life by allowing individuals and organizations to enter into a virtual time-space which is seen as competing with reality and which clouds whatever they do with a sense of inauthenticity. Accompanying this are worries that individuals and organizations using the internet are in danger of becoming dispersed and rendered powerless by the fragmenting of experience, resulting in conditions which preclude, rather than facilitate, collaborative action.

One of the most dismal and disturbing visions of the future of social interaction is suggested by Castells in the general conclusion to his three-volume work *The Information Age: Economy, Society and Culture*. In *End of Millennium*, the final volume,[10] Castells concludes that a 'network logic', which he describes as 'a dynamic, self-expanding form of organization of human activity', is transforming all domains of social and economic life (pp. 336–7). He believes that a new world is beginning to emerge, a network society, consisting of network enterprises, network states and networks of people, a world 'dominated by a network geometry' and connected by way of global financial networks which he sees as 'the nerve center of informational capitalism' (p. 343).

Castells observes that this new system of production is sharply differentiated according to people's characteristics. On the one hand, there are those whom he defines as 'self-programmable labor'. He explains, 'whoever is educated, in the proper organizational environment, can reprogram him/herself toward the endlessly changing task of the production process.' On the other hand, there are those whom he defines as 'generic labor' or as 'human terminals'. Generic labor, according to Castells, is 'assigned a given task, with no reprogramming capability, and it does not presuppose the embodiment of information and knowledge beyond the ability to receive and execute signals' (p. 341). He explains that the network geometry is 'incarnated by different subjects, even though these subjects often work with historical materials provided by the values and organizations inherited from industrial capitalism and statism' (pp. 350–1).

Under this new system, Castells warns, 'a considerable number of humans . . . are irrelevant, both as producers and consumers, from the perspective of the system's logic' (p. 344). The 'social exclusion and economic irrelevance of segments of societies, of areas of cities, of regions, and of entire countries' constitute what he calls the 'Fourth World' (p. 337). Under the informational paradigm, he writes,

the space of flows dominates the space of places of people's cultures . . . dominant functions and values in society are organized in simultaneity without contiguity; that is, in flows of information that escape from experience embodied in any locale . . . dominant values and interests are constructed without reference to either past or future, in the timeless landscape of computer networks and electronic media, where all expressions are either instantaneous, or without predictable sequencing. All expressions, from all times and from all spaces, are mixed in the same hypertext, constantly rearranged, and communicated at any time, anywhere, depending on the interests of senders and the moods of receivers. (pp. 349–50)

Yet despite his warning, Castells also claims that 'societies of the Information Age cannot be reduced to the structure and dynamics of the network society' (p. 352). However, desperate attempts by some groups and areas to link up with the global networks and to escape marginality have led to what Castells calls the 'perverse connection', a concept he uses to analyse criminal activity (p. 337). He is rather sceptical and not very hopeful regarding new avenues of social change. On the one hand, he observes the 'retrenchment of dominant global elites in immaterial palaces made out of communication networks and information flows'. On the other, he describes proactive identity-based social movements where people's experience remains 'confined to multiple, segregated locales, subdued in their existence and fragmented in their consciousness. With no Winter Palace to be seized, outbursts of revolt may implode, transformed into everyday senseless violence.' This is truly a frightening prospect. In the Information Age, Castells claims, instead of social classes, we are witnessing the rise of 'tribes' and 'cultural communes' (p. 352). And, as a reaction against social exclusion, marginalization and economic irrelevance, he sees the beginnings of 'the exclusion of the excluders by the excluded' (p. 354).

A way ahead

In his thoughtful and wide-ranging argument, I think Castells like Zuboff is right to point out that while new communication networks are opening up new opportunities for human intervention, they also create new uncertainties. Moreover, these new technologies are spreading the consciousness that the world we live in today is a highly risky and unpredictable environment. However, while being on our guard against euphoric interpretations and the excesses of futurology, we must be careful not to present an overly dismal account of the transformations taking place. I want to argue in this vein that Castells's conclusions are, in many respects, one-sided and too negative. I shall elaborate this argument by briefly considering six important aspects of his work: (1) his notion of 'network logic'; (2) his distinction between 'self-programmable labor' and 'generic labor'; (3) his conception of people as 'human terminals'; (4) his notion of the 'Fourth World'; (5) his conception of senders with 'interests' and receivers with 'moods'; and (6) his account of the 'rise of tribes'.

The notion of 'network logic' Castells uses the notion of 'network logic' to explain why particular social processes are as they are. He even portrays 'network logic' as some kind of self-expanding form of organization, which is somehow similar to a nerve centre. This portrayal invites a view that network enterprises, network states and networks of people are all governed by the teleology of a system which supplants that of actors themselves. I take the view, however, that not even the most worrying features of modern societies come about, persist or disappear because a network's geometry forces them to do so. All networks of social interaction consist of 'social practices, situated in time-space, and organized in a skilled and knowledgeable fashion by human agents'.[11] Of course, human knowledgeability, as Giddens argues, is always bounded by unacknowledged conditions and by unintended consequences of human activity.[12] But even this is a very complex process and it cannot so easily be referred to as involving the characteristics of network society being simply 'incarnated by different subjects'. Moreover, our world today is connected by a dazzling variety of networks, as Castells himself admits, so it would seem all too simplistic to suggest that networks create unitary conditions. Consequently, I do not believe that the notion of 'network logic' explains very much at all.

The distinction between 'self-programmable labor' and 'generic labor' Castells's distinction between

'self-programmable labor' and 'generic labor' suggests that there are those who are bestowed with a good deal of fortune and those who are bestowed with a good deal of bad luck. Yet many questions cloud such a distinction, not least that of how to go about establishing to which group one might belong. While all networks promote horizontal relationships, they by no means do away with hierarchical authority altogether. Participants in networks may thus have at their disposal varying degrees of authority: their options are not restricted to being either connected or unconnected. We might also wonder how we became 'self-programmable labor' or 'generic labor'. Is this feature pre-set by the system too? And is there any chance, or danger, that we might at some point in time change positions?

The designation of people as 'human terminals' According to Castells, the designation of people as 'human terminals' describes a considerable proportion of humans, probably growing in number. However, I think it conjures up a quite inadequate vision of people as cultural dopes. Moreover, Castells seems also to suggest something far worse: the idea that if people do not perform according to the 'network logic', they will simply be switched off. While there may indeed exist significant differentials of power in network society, I do not think that any individual can be satisfactorily interpreted in this way. It renounces once again the idea that all individuals are skilled and knowledgeable human agents, as Giddens so rightly emphasizes, and fails to recognize that 'all forms of dependence offer some resources whereby those who are subordinate can influence the activities of their superiors.'[13] Moreover, capitalist ventures would not make much profit if they switched nearly everybody off.

The notion of the 'Fourth World' Castells's notion of the 'Fourth World', I think, fails to recognize the extent to which in many ways we now all live in *one* world, a world in which there are no others. Our world today may have become increasingly decentred, but it has also become all-enveloping.

As Giddens writes, the day-to-day actions of an individual today are globally consequential. The notion of the 'Fourth World' distracts us from this accelerating connectedness, and from the fact that it is more and more unlikely that those retrenched in 'immaterial palaces' will find a world from which the mass of the population is excluded even remotely an acceptable place to live in.

The conception of senders with 'interests' and receivers with 'moods' Castells's conception of senders with 'interests' and receivers with 'moods' does not do justice to a new agenda for mediated communication, one in which individuals are potentially both senders and receivers. Even when individuals are excluded from one channel of communication, they can find others to make themselves heard.

The 'rise of tribes' Castells's account of the rise of modern-day tribes is superficial and not at all useful. Premodern tribal culture was very confined in terms of its time-space span. Equipped with access to modern communication networks, social groups in the late modern age have access to unprecedented opportunities for cultivating images and controlling their diffusion. This, I think, precludes any serious comparison with tribalism of the past.

In the light of Castells's warnings we need urgently to follow Zuboff's advice that it is necessary to take up a conscious strategy, rather than to simply allow new forms of human interaction to unfold without any anticipation of their consequences. The unpredictable environment we live in today demands our active engagement. Yet while Castells elaborates on some trends that may configure society in the early twenty-first century, he makes no attempt to sketch a way out of the problems they may create. And, as I already stated in the introduction, isn't an alternative path of development the surest way to avert some of the perverse and unintended consequences of networked social interaction?

If we are to develop positive ways of using the internet, we need to develop a more informed understanding and a firmer grasp of what it amounts to and what its consequences are for modern culture, and use such knowledge to cope more effectively with the current crisis in the management of risk. Contributing to the further polarization of the different perspectives tending towards either the pole of optimism or the pole of pessimism would serve only to continue a rather fruitless debate; instead I want to take both of these perspectives seriously. Taken together, they reveal that it is no accident that the internet has originated in an environment bequeathed to us by the developments that have transformed modern societies. These are developments for which the internet is also an essential tool. As a consequence, there is much to be said in support of arguments which sensitize us to the dual potentialities of information technology, referring as they do to the capability of the same technology to produce one set of effects or their opposite.[14]

Any benefit from such an insight cannot, however, be satisfactorily pursued from the premises of the internet understood simply as a *new medium*. Instead we must first attempt to develop a framework which may help us to properly understand how the internet is resulting in new ways of relating to others and to ourselves. It must be a framework which does not treat the 'uncertainization' of modern life merely as a backdrop, but one in which the internet is treated comprehensively as a contextualized social phenomenon. Such a framework must enable us to break away from lists of arbitrary strengths which are offered in praise or in defence of this new medium: moreover, its weaknesses may become challenges which we might be able to do something about.

NOTES

1. S. Zuboff, *In the Age of the Smart Machine*. (Basic Books, New York, 1989).
2. Government Direct: A Prospectus for the Electronic Delivery of Government Services, http://www.open.gov.uk/citu/gdirect/greenpaper/index.htm.

3. Ministry of Transport, Public Works and Water Management, http://www.dgv.minvenw.nl/home/categorie.asp?categorie+dvp.

4. Boeing Company, http://www.boeing.com/.

5. J. E. Fook, 'Boeing's intranet flies high', *Internet Week*, 24 Jan. 1997.

6. Ford Motor Company, http://www.ford.com/global/index-d.html.

7. M. J. Cronin, 'Ford's intranet success', *Fortune*, 30 Mar. 1998.

8. Internet relay chat channel #Gay.nl can be found on EF-net using the following servers: irc2.sci.kun.nl, or irc.sci.kun.nl, irc.xs4all.nl or stealth.net.

9. #Gay.nl home page, http://www.gaynl.demon.nl/.

10. M. Castells, *End of Millennium*, vol. 3 of *The Information Age: Economy, Society and Culture* (Blackwell, Oxford, 1998).

11. A. Giddens, *A Contemporary Critique of Historical Materialism*, vol. 1: *Power, Property and the State* (Macmillan, London, 1981), p. 19.

12. Ibid.

13. A. Giddens, *The Constitution of Society: Outline of the Theory of Structuration* (Polity Press, Cambridge, 1984), p. 16.

14. R. E. Walton, *Up and Running: Integration, Information Technology and the Organization* (Harvard Business School Press, Boston, 1989), pp. 26–8.

38. Building Virtual Communities

Howard Rheingold

'Daddy is saying "Holy moly!" to his computer again!'

Those words have become a family code for the way my virtual community has infiltrated our real world. My seven-year-old daughter knows that her father congregates with a family of invisible friends who seem to gather in his computer. Sometimes he talks to them, even if nobody else can see them. And she knows that these invisible friends sometimes show up in the flesh, materializing from the next block or the other side of the planet.

Since the summer of 1985, for an average of two hours a day, seven days a week, I've been plugging my personal computer into my telephone and making contact with the WELL (Whole Earth 'Lectronic Link) – a computer conferencing system that enables people around the world to carry on public conversations and exchange private electronic mail (e-mail). The idea of a community accessible only via my computer screen sounded cold to me at first, but I learned quickly that people can feel passionately about e-mail and computer conferences. I've become one of them, I care about these people I met through my computer, and I care deeply about the future of the medium that enables us to assemble.

I'm not alone in this emotional attachment to an apparently bloodless technological ritual. Millions of people on every continent also participate in the computer-mediated social groups known as virtual communities, and this population is growing fast. Finding the WELL was like discovering a cozy little world that had been flourishing without me, hidden within the walls of my house; an entire cast of characters welcomed me to the troupe with great merriment as soon as I found the secret door. Like others who fell into the WELL, I soon discovered that I was audience, performer, and scriptwriter, along with my companions, in an ongoing improvisation. A full-scale subculture was growing on the other side of my telephone jack, and they invited me to help create something new.

The virtual village of a few hundred people I stumbled upon in 1985 grew to eight thousand by 1993. It became clear to me during the first months of that history that I was participating in the self-design of a new kind of culture. I watched the community's social contracts stretch and change as the people who discovered and started building the WELL in its first year or two were joined by so many others. Norms were established, challenged, changed, reestablished, rechallenged, in a kind of speeded-up social evolution.

The WELL felt like an authentic community to me from the start because it was grounded in my everyday physical world. WELLites who don't live within driving distance of the San Francisco Bay area are constrained in their ability to participate in the local networks of face-to-face acquaintances. By now, I've attended real-life WELL marriages, WELL births, and even a WELL funeral. (The phrase 'in real life' pops up so often in virtual communities that regulars abbreviate it to IRL.) I can't count the parties and outings where the invisible personae who first acted out their parts in the debates and melodramas on my computer screen later manifested in front of me in the physical world in the form of real people, with faces, bodies, and voices.

I remember the first time I walked into a room full of people IRL who knew many intimate details of my history and whose own stories I knew very well. Three months after I joined, I went to my first WELL party at the home of one of the WELL's online moderators. I looked around at the room full of strangers when I walked in. It was one of the oddest sensations of my life. I had contended with these people, shot the invisible breeze around the electronic watercooler, shared alliances and formed bonds, fallen off my chair laughing with them, become livid with anger at some of them. But there wasn't a recognizable face in the house. I had never seen them before.

My flesh-and-blood family long ago grew accustomed to the way I sit in my home office early in the morning and late at night, chuckling and cursing, sometimes crying, about words I read on the computer screen. It might have looked to my daughter as if I were alone at my desk the night she caught me chortling online, but from my point of view I was in living contact with old and new friends, strangers and colleagues:

I was in the Parenting conference on the WELL, participating in an informational and emotional support group for a friend who just learned his son was diagnosed with leukemia.

I was in MicroMUSE, a role-playing fantasy game of the twenty-fourth century (and science education medium in disguise), interacting with students and professors who know me only as "Pollenator."

I was in TWICS, a bicultural community in Tokyo; CIX, a community in London; CalvaCom, a community in Paris; and Usenet, a collection of hundreds of different discussions that travel around the world via electronic mail to millions of participants in dozens of countries.

I was browsing through Supreme Court decisions, in search of information that could help me debunk an opponent's claims in a political debate elsewhere on the Net, or I was retrieving this morning's satellite images of weather over the Pacific.

I was following an eyewitness report from Moscow during the coup attempt, or China during the Tiananmen Square incident, or Israel and Kuwait during the Gulf War, passed directly from citizen to citizen through an ad hoc network patched together from cheap computers and ordinary telephone lines, cutting across normal geographic and political boundaries by piggybacking on the global communications infrastructure.

I was monitoring a rambling real-time dialogue among people whose bodies were scattered across three continents, a global bull session that seems to blend wit and sophomore locker-room talk via Internet Relay Chat (IRC), a medium that combines the features of conversation and writing. IRC has accumulated an obsessive subculture of its own among undergraduates by the thousands from Adelaide to Arabia.

People in virtual communities use words on screens to exchange pleasantries and argue, engage in intellectual discourse, conduct commerce, exchange knowledge, share emotional support, make plans, brainstorm, gossip, feud, fall in love, find friends and lose them, play games, flirt, create a little high art and a lot of idle talk. People in virtual communities do just about everything people do in real life, but we leave our bodies behind. You can't kiss anybody and nobody can punch you in the nose, but a lot can happen within those boundaries. To the millions who have been drawn into it, the richness and vitality of computer-linked cultures is attractive, even addictive.

There is no such thing as a single, monolithic, online subculture; it's more like an ecosystem of subcultures, some frivolous, others serious. The cutting edge of scientific discourse is migrating to virtual communities, where you can read the electronic pre-preprinted reports of molecular biologists and cognitive scientists. At the same time, activists and educational reformers are using the same medium as a political tool. You can use virtual communities to find a date, sell a lawnmower, publish a novel, conduct a meeting.

Some people use virtual communities as a form of psychotherapy. Others, such as the most addicted players of Minitel in France or Multi-

User Dungeons (MUDs) on the international networks, spend eighty hours a week or more pretending they are someone else, living a life that does not exist outside a computer. Because MUDs not only are susceptible to pathologically obsessive use by some people but also create a strain on computer and communication resources, MUDding has been banned at universities such as Amherst and on the entire continent of Australia.

Scientists, students, librarians, artists, organizers, and escapists aren't the only people who have taken to the new medium. The U.S. senator who campaigned for years for the construction of a National Research and Education Network that could host the virtual communities of the future is now vice president of the United States. As of June 1993, the White House and Congress have e-mail addresses.

Most people who get their news from conventional media have been unaware of the wildly varied assortment of new cultures that have evolved in the world's computer networks over the past ten years. Most people who have not yet used these new media remain unaware of how profoundly the social, political, and scientific experiments under way today via computer networks could change all our lives in the near future.

[. . .]

The distributed nature of the telecommunications network, coupled with the availability of affordable computers, makes it possible to piggyback alternate networks on the mainstream infrastructure.

We temporarily have access to a tool that could bring conviviality and understanding into our lives and might help revitalize the public sphere. The same tool, improperly controlled and wielded, could become an instrument of tyranny. The vision of a citizen-designed, citizen-controlled worldwide communications network is a version of technological utopianism that could be called the vision of 'the electronic agora.' In the original democracy, Athens, the agora was the market-

place, and more – it was where citizens met to talk, gossip, argue, size each other up, find the weak spots in political ideas by debating about them. But another kind of vision could apply to the use of the Net in the wrong ways, a shadow vision of a less utopian kind of place – the Panopticon.

Panopticon was the name for an ultimately effective prison, seriously proposed in eighteenth-century Britain by Jeremy Bentham (1843). A combination of architecture and optics makes it possible in Bentham's scheme for a single guard to see every prisoner, and for no prisoner to see anything else; the effect is that all prisoners act as if they were under surveillance at all times. Contemporary social critic Michel Foucault, in *Discipline and Punish* (1977), claimed that the machinery of the worldwide communications network constitutes a kind of camouflaged Panopticon; citizens of the world brought into their homes, along with each other, the prying ears of the state. The cables that bring information into our homes today are technically capable of bringing information out of our homes, instantly transmitted to interested others. Tomorrow's version of Panoptic machinery could make very effective use of the same communications infrastructure that enables one-room schoolhouses in Montana to communicate with MIT professors, and enables citizens to disseminate news and organize resistance to totalitarian rule. With so much of our intimate data and more and more of our private behavior moving into cyberspace, the potential for totalitarian abuse of that information web is significant and the cautions of the critics are worth a careful hearing.

The wise revolutionary keeps an eye on the dark side of the changes he or she would initiate. Enthusiasts who believe in the humanitarian potential of virtual communities, especially those of us who speak of electronic democracy as a potential application of the medium, are well advised to consider the shadow potential of the same media. We should not forget that intellectuals and journalists of the 1950s hailed the advent of the greatest educational medium in history – television.

Because of its potential to change us as humans, as communities, as democracies, we need to try to understand the nature of CMC, cyberspace, and virtual communities in every important context – politically, economically, socially, cognitively. Each different perspective reveals something that the other perspectives do not reveal. Each different discipline fails to see something that another discipline sees very well. We need to think together here, across boundaries of academic discipline, industrial affiliation, nation, if we hope to understand and thus perhaps regain control of the way human communities are being transformed by communications technologies.

We can't do this solely as dispassionate observers, although there is certainly a strong need for the detached assessment of social science. Community is a matter of emotions as well as a thing of reason and data. Some of the most important learning will always have to be done by jumping into one corner or another of cyberspace, living there, and getting up to your elbows in the problems that virtual communities face.

I care about what happens in cyberspace, and to our freedoms in cyberspace, because I dwell there part of the time. The author's voice as a citizen and veteran of virtual community-building is one of the points of view presented in this book: I'm part of the story I'm describing, speaking as both native informant and as uncredentialed social scientist. Because of the paucity of first-person source material describing the way it feels to live in cyberspace, I believe it is valuable to include my perspective as participant as well as observer. In some places, like the WELL, I speak from extensive experience; in many of the places we need to examine in order to understand the Net, I am almost as new to the territory as those who never heard about cyberspace before. Ultimately, if you want to form your own opinions, you need to pick up a good beginner's guidebook and plunge into the Net for yourself. It is possible, however, to paint a kind of word-picture, necessarily somewhat sketchy, of the varieties of life to be found on the Net.

[. . .]

Important critical questions have been asked about the idea of virtual community and the influence of virtual communications on human relationships. We must all address these questions if we aspire to steer the course of the technology rather than passively experiencing the changes the technology triggers. If there is something disturbing about finding community through a computer screen (and who can deny that the image of disembodied geeks who move only our fingers while staring at a tube is disturbing?), we should also consider whether it is disturbing for hundreds of millions of people to drive for hours every day in our single-passenger automobiles to cities of inhuman scale, where we spend our days in front of screens inside cubicles within skyscrapers full of people who don't know each other. Yes, we should focus on the pitfalls of spending our days in front of screens, but we should not lose sight of those cubicles, skyscrapers, cities, and automobiles when we seek the sources of our alienation.

The rubber tire and the elevator both played their part in the construction of a technology-centric community. And they are both second-generation fruits of industrialized capitalism. Virtual community sits atop a hierarchy of abstractions – language, technology, computing, networking many-to-many discussion. Virtual community is also built upon a succession of technologies and ways of life we chose to use and live in and be shaped by, because they gave many people freedom and power. Now, the biggest challenge to our freedom is our need to know how to wield the powers of new communication media. New tools exist. Who will use them, and how will they use them? Those who already have power and wealth to defend also have the knowledge of how to use media to influence and persuade others.

Technologies and literacies that help individuals and groups to dictate the conditions under which other people live are profoundly political instruments, although this seems to go against the grain of the common wisdom. Certain tools themselves are political by their nature. In order to frame critiques of the notion of virtual community, it helps to examine the ways in which the rapidly evolving communication media constitute a political environment – and look especially closely at the ways we choose not to examine that environment.

[. . .]

Social networks emerge when people interact with each other continually, and they have to be useful or they wouldn't exist. Your social network can find you a job or a husband, information you need, recommendations for restaurants and investments, babysitters and bargains, a new religion, emotional support. Before writing letters became commonplace, social networks were confined to those people who saw each other face to face. Writing, public postal systems, telegraph, telephone, and the Internet each brought new means of extending one's social network to include people who are not in the immediate geographical vicinity, who share an interest rather than a location.

It has been argued that these increasingly mediated relationships are, for the most part, increasingly superficial. As I look at the way more and more of our social communication is migrating to email and cell phone, instant message and online greeting card, I tend to agree. At the same time, it certainly is possible to maintain deep relationships through letters, telephone calls, or online chats. Like all technologies, communication tools come with a price: Alienation might be the cost of the power of abstraction. We might do better by ourselves by paying more attention to how we're using the powers of abstraction.

Social network analysis provides a useful framework for discussing the impact of online socializing. It counters the critique of virtual communities as alienating, dehumanizing substitutes for more direct, less mediated human contact. The notion of 'strong ties and weak ties' is a useful part of that conceptual framework. The classic document explicating this idea is 'The Strength of Weak Ties' (Granovetter, 1973). A weak tie is an alumnus of your alma mater, a stronger tie would be members of your college sorority or fraternity you actually lived with, an even stronger tie would be your roommate. A social network with a mixture of strong ties, familial ties, lifelong friend ties, marital ties, business partner ties, is important for people to obtain the fundamentals of identity, affection, emotional and material support. But without a network of more superficial relationships, life would be harder and less fun in many ways. Weaker ties multiply people's social capital, useful knowledge, ability to get things done.

When asking questions about the impact of any technology on community, I have learned to avoid romanticizing the notion of community, of assuming a state of pastoral existence that once existed in pretechnology small towns. There is an indisputable merit to living your life in the same place, loving or hating or putting up with the same people day after day, making decisions together with people you don't necessarily like, reducing the number of your social relationships and perhaps increasing their depth. But there is a cost to this long lost *Gemeinschaft* of the village, the hamlet, the small town, as well. If the shadows of urban and mediated experience are alienation and superficiality, the shadows of the traditional community are narrow-mindedness and bigotry.

REFERENCES

Bentham, Jeremy. *Works*, vol. 4. Edited by J. Bowring. Edinburgh: William Tait, 1843.

Foucault, Michel. *Discipline and Punish: The Birth of the Prison*. Translated from the French by Alan Sheridan. New York: Pantheon, 1977.

Granovetter, Mark. 'The Strength of Weak Ties.' *American Journal of Sociology* 78 (1973): 1360–80.

Theme 7 – Further Reading

All students should read something by Erving Goffman as no one writes on social and symbolic interactions with quite such an enthusiasm. To this end, we suggest his 1990 [1969] book, *The Presentation of Self in Everyday Life* (Harmondsworth: Penguin) or the more analytical (2003) *Interaction Ritual: Essays on Face to Face Behaviour* (New York: Pantheon Books). On the social impact of the Internet and how it might be managed, James Slevin's (2000) *The Internet and Society* (Cambridge: Polity) is worth the effort. On the mass media of communications, there are lots of possibilities, but Graeme Burton's (2010) *Media and Society: Critical Perspectives*, 2nd edition (Buckingham: Open University Press) is among the best guides to this field.

Giddens and Sutton *Sociology 7th Edition* (2013)

Chapter 8 is the starting point for interaction studies, while Chapter 18 covers the field of the media and communications. Issues of social interaction and communications also occur in Chapter 10 on gender relations, pages 395–414 and 416–20; Chapter 20 on socialization processes, pages 871–83 and Chapter 21 on deviance, pages 927–9.

Part 8 Health and the Body

Good health is widely perceived as a prerequisite for a good life and governments spend enormous amounts on preventing and treating illness. Traditionally, research studies of health and illness were dominated by medical and health service professionals and epidemiologists seeking to better understand diseases in order to produce more effective prevention and treatments. What role could there possibly be for sociologists in the study of health and illness? The American sociologist Talcott Parsons, who opened up the whole field to sociological enquiry, provided the definitive answer to this question.

Parsons argued that there are important social aspects to health and illness. Individuals do not simply become physically ill. Illness is a condition that has to be confirmed and validated by a doctor before people are allowed to relinquish some of their duties and responsibilities. Should they decide not to seek this confirmation, their employer will probably not accept that they are ill and if they remain ill and unavailable for longer than the doctor believes necessary, even friends and relatives may start to question their condition. Illness then, is clearly a social state as well as a physical or mental condition. Similarly, to be ill is to play a social role which carries expectations that have to be fulfilled for the performance to be taken seriously. Parsons deserves credit for recognizing the sociological significance of health and illness and for creating a general framework to aid our understanding.

However, as Bryan Turner explains in Reading 39, Parsons's ideas were subject to merciless critique from later sociologists and the concept of the sick role has fallen from favour. How can the sick role model cope with chronic illness, which is not amenable to cure and a return to 'normality'? Where do disability and the experience of disabled people fit into the thesis? Is the sick role limited to the experience of acute illness in the developed societies? Turner provides a welcome defence of Parsons's basic thesis. Of course not all societies around the world treat illness in the same way and the specific sick role discussed by Parsons cannot be extended to the rest of the world. Nevertheless, Turner argues that all societies have to deal with illness and the general concept of a sick role carrying social expectations can be deployed in a comparative way to analyse similarities and differences.

The experience of health and illness differs not only across societies but across social groups too. Women live, on average, longer than men in most societies. Working-class men tend to have poorer health than middle- and upper-class men. A starker contrast is that between the developed world and developing societies. People in the latter suffer from illness and diseases that have been brought under control or eliminated in the rich countries long ago. Medicines available to relatively wealthy populations are still unavailable in large parts of the developing world, a situation made highly visible in relation to the skewed distribution of anti-viral drugs used in the treatment of HIV/AIDS in recent years. Health inequalities have been the subject of much research in the sociology of health and illness.

Women's experience of health and illness in the developed societies is particularly complex. On the one hand, women's average life expectancy is longer than men's, but on the other, women make more visits to doctors and report more illness and distress than men. In Reading 40, Lesley Doyal tries to make sense of the picture of women's health experience that emerges from health statistics and sociological research. In contrast to one commonsense viewpoint that women's biology predisposes them to more illness – child bearing, gynaecological problems and mental-health issues, for example – she argues that we cannot understand women's experience without locating it within their social and psychological circumstances. What makes women sick is not their weak physiological constitution but a complex combination of biological factors, social expectations, roles and duties and the organization of health care services.

When we talk about health and illness, many people have in their mind a typical picture of contracting a disease, having treatment for it and then being 'cured' before being returned to good health. This picture is becoming less and less accurate as chronic illness has become the normal experience for many more people. The broad movement from acute to chronic conditions such as arthritis, diabetes, osteoporosis and high blood pressure, brings with it changes in the doctor–patient relationship and a new focus on health management rather than curing illness. Patients who live with chronic conditions and have to find ways of coping with them on a daily basis, very often have expert levels of knowledge about their conditions. Indeed, in many cases they may have a more extensive knowledge of particular conditions

and management regimes than the doctors who advise them. In this situation, the deferential relationship portrayed in Parsons's discussion of the sick role, may be eroded. We can see some evidence of this in patients' increasing willingness to seek out alternative and complementary therapies even without the sanctioning or approval of their doctor.

Reading 41 discusses the patient's experience of illness, the body and health care in the context of a society that is becoming more used to managing chronic illness and where patients have to try to maintain and manage their personal identities during illness and recovery. Drawing on ideas of 'illness narratives' and, in particular, the work of Arthur Frank, Mike Bury explores competing arguments suggesting that chronic illness: (a) creates 'biographical disruption', which can be problematic in the maintenance of personal identity, and (b) that, as many more people now live with chronic conditions or are in long-term remission, such conditions have become normalized as 'part of life's journey' rather than being simply disruptive. Frank found the early stages of his own diagnoses of heart disease and testicular cancer to be highly disruptive to the point of marking a break between past and present and the future. But later, he also saw new opportunities for reflection and learning in the 'remission society' as he began (along with many others) to rethink and re-evaluate his life, and in that sense his work can be read as a positive account of how lay people may be able to move beyond the medicalization of health and illness. However, Bury points out that such personal narratives, though instructive, do not take social structures and inequalities into account and therefore fall short of a thoroughly sociological approach.

Although modern medicine is still widely seen as a positive development, enabling people to prevent and combat illnesses and live longer, healthier lives, some scholars take a radically different view. Some argue that medicine has been wrongly credited with health improvements that are the result of improved diet and less physically demanding working environments, while others argue that modern medicine is itself the cause of illness. Ivan Illich used the concept of iatrogenesis – physician-created illness – to illustrate some of the ways in which the medical profession has become too powerful, leading to the general acceptance of potentially dangerous treatments and toxic medicines. In Reading 42, Illich reminds us that a proportion of healthy people who go into hospital contract potentially deadly infections such as MRSA and C.diff, while others are damaged or die during surgery as a result of medical incompetence. In a wider sense, the whole of society has become medicalized as health services place more and more demands on economic resources as new, technology-driven techniques spread. Instead of reducing over time as public health improves, health costs continue to spiral upwards. Illich also argues that the reliance on a burgeoning health service deskills people in relation to their own health and prevents them from taking full control of their own lives. This is a damning picture of medicine, though any properly rounded perspective would also acknowledge that many people also owe their lives to the skill and expertise of medical professionals.

Our final reading outlines a relatively recent field, the sociology of the body, which arose, partly, from research studies of health and illness. In Reading 43, Chris Shilling – whose early interest in the body helped to shape the field – explains some of the factors leading to a wider sociological interest in the human body and embodiment. The body is at the centre of many contemporary concerns such as the development of genetic treatments, cosmetic surgery and body modification, eating disorders and bodily imagery and new reproductive technologies. The body has become much more a project to be worked on rather than a natural and fixed entity to be accepted. The sociology of the body has developed in this context and research studies have tended to raise new questions about the body rather than leading us to any consensus on what 'the body' actually is.

39. Defending Parsons's Sick Role

Bryan S. Turner

The basic position in the sociological approach to illness and disease is that being sick is fundamentally a social state of affairs rather than being a narrowly defined biochemical malfunction of the organism. Sociology is concerned to explain the social causes of sickness, the character of sickness as a social role and the human response to sickness in terms of feeling, language and social action. The notion of sickness as a social role is very closely associated with the sociology of Parsons (1951) who first conceptualized the notion of the sick role. Parsons's contribution to medical sociology has been extensive, although unfortunately the evaluation of his contribution is often confined to commentaries on the sick role. Although there has been extensive evaluation of Parsons's formulation of the sick role (Frank, 1991; Gerhardt, 1989; Levine and Kozloff, 1978), the general character of Parsonian medical sociology has been somewhat neglected (Holton and Turner, 1986).

There were four areas to Parsons's contribution to medical sociology broadly conceived. First, Parsons was interested in the ethical character of the professions in relation to the profit motive of capitalist society. He sought to argue that there was a distinctive feature to the learned and caring professions, namely that they were organized in terms of service to the community which did not reflect the dominant values of capitalist society. Secondly, he was concerned to analyse the effect of the social structure and culture on the general features of health; Parsons's work on the family in relation to stress would be one illustration of this component of his sociology Thirdly, Parsons analysed the relationship between death, religion and the gift of life which he saw as part of a more general problem of meaning. Fourthly, Parsons developed the concept of the sick role as implicitly a critique of biologism in the conceptualization of illness. In this latter respect Parsons's concept of the sick role provided a major alternative to the medical model. The Parsonian approach to medical sociology may be regarded as an action system theoretical orientation. The approach is functionalist (functionalism analyses social activities in terms of their contribution to the maintenance of a social system or institution) in that Parsons argued that if the definition of sickness and disability were too lenient or general, then severe social strains would be exerted on the social system bringing about considerable dysfunction in the achievement of general goals (Mechanic, 1968). The social control and regulation of sickness is brought about by what may be termed the sick-role mechanism. The consequence is that in western societies general practitioners are concerned with clinical situations where they are professionally obliged to certify illness in order to explain the patient's failure to comply with social expectations.

The sick role can be defined in terms of four components. The first aspect is that the sick role legitimates social withdrawal from a number of obligations, such as those relating to work and family duties. The idea is that a sick person ought to stay at home and take rest in order to facilitate recovery. The second feature of the role is that a sick person is exempted from responsibility for their medical condition; the assumption is that they cannot get better without professional help and support. The third component is that the person has a social obligation to improve and get better: the legitimation of sickness as a basis for social withdrawal from roles is conditional on the patient's full acceptance of an obligation to get better by cooperating with the professional recommendations of a competent doctor. The fourth element within the sick role is therefore an expectation that the person will seek out competent health care from a trained physician. As a consequence, the sick role describes the role-set or social system of the doctor–patient relationship which is structured in terms of the pattern variables, which Parsons had outlined in a discussion of professionalism.

The concept of the sick role was elaborated by Parsons against a background in which the American medical profession was beginning to take some notice of the idea of psychosomatic illness and to realize that the emotional connection between the doctor and patient was an important aspect of both the diagnostic and therapeutic processes. Parsons had also become aware of the relevance of Freudian psychoanalysis for the study of sickness, especially Freud's notion of transference. These intellectual influences brought Parsons to a realization that there was a significant issue of motivation in the process of becoming sick and getting better. Given the concept of the action frame of reference with its voluntaristic premises in Parsonian sociology, there was an important sense in which the social agent decides to be sick. Voluntarism was important because sickness could not be considered merely as an objective condition of the organism without some discussion of the motivation of the individual in relation to the social system. To be sick required certain exemptions from social obligation and a motivation to accept a therapeutic regimen. It was for this reason that Parsons classified sickness as a form of deviant behaviour which required legitimation and social control. While the sick role legitimizes social deviance, it also requires an acceptance of a medical regimen. The sick role was therefore an important vehicle for social control, since the aim of the medical regimen was

to return the sick person to conventional social roles. In some respects, Parsons's analysis of the sick role anticipated a variety of deviancy models of mental illness which subsequently became influential in sociology in the work of Lemert (1967) and Scheff (1966).

In terms of Parsons's pattern variables, the doctor–patient relationship is characterized by its affective neutrality, universalism, functional specificity and orientation to collective norms. The point of this description is to show how the doctor and patient are committed to breaking their relationship rather than forming a social connection as a stable and permanent system of interaction. The sick role is to be a temporary role and it is important that the patient does not become emotionally dependent on the doctor or the doctor become involved in a particularistic relation with the patient. The whole aim of the exercise is to get the patient out of a sick role and back into a social environment involving activism and obligation. A typical sickness episode would be an attack of gastroenteritis where the patient is forced to stay away from work for a limited period of time in order to undertake appropriate medication. The sickness has a limited duration and, where the sick role is successfully occupied, the patient returns to normal expectations after a brief respite from major social duties.

[. . .]

The first major criticism of the Parsonian model is that going to see the doctor may be the end process of a complex system of help-seeking behaviour (Mechanic, 1968: 268ff.). Freidson (1961, 1970) has discussed the importance of the so-called 'lay referral system' in the social process by which lay people consult the physician. Freidson has argued that the lay person only consults the doctor after a series of consultations with significant lay groups. It is the lay culture, not the professional values of the physician, which defines the meaning of illness in a social context. If a person perceives himself to be sick and in need of specialized help, he is likely to find support within his own cultural context only if 'he shows evidence of symptoms the others perceive to be illness and if he interprets them the way the others find plausible' (Freidson, 1970: 289). Once the requirement for specialized health care is acknowledged by the lay culture, then help-seeking behaviour is organized in terms of the lay referral system. The lay referral system has two components: the lay culture and a network of personal influence which is the lay referral structure. A variety of sociological studies (McKinlay, 1973; Scambler et al., 1981; Suchman, 1964) have found that the majority of patients reporting to a doctor had already consulted extensively with lay colleagues and discussed the various symptoms which were subsequently presented to the doctor.

The concept of the lay referral system and lay interventions has produced a significant body of research into the role of social networks in the presentation of illness to a professional physician. One consequence of this research is that we should distinguish between the sick role and the patient role. In particular, Parsons's conception of sickness should be analysed as a contribution to the sociology of the patient role. Not all sick people are patients and not all patients are sick people. This distinction draws attention once more to a set of potential conflicts between the lay cultural analysis of sickness and the professional conceptualization of the patient role.

The distinction also points to the presence of a reservoir of undiagnosed illness in the community. Social surveys of the general population have persistently shown a number of serious conditions which are characteristically undiagnosed; these include high blood pressure, anaemia, bronchitis, obesity and diabetes (Tuckett, 1976: 23ff.). Whether or not these complaints reach the doctor's clinic will depend a great deal on the strength of the network of lay consultations and significant lay groups. Parsons's analysis of the patient role therefore tends to be a rather narrow slice of the total character of illness behaviour and help-seeking behaviour.

The second area of significant criticism of Parsons has been concerned with the character of conflict and disagreement in the doctor–patient relationship. It has been argued that Parsons's model assumes an ideal patient who brings real illness to the doctor, accepts the medical diagnosis without question and complies entirely with the doctor's recommendations; the model also assumes an ideal doctor who has a concern for the total patient, provides an effective diagnosis of the patient's problem with reference to the medical and social context of the patient, and finally is professionally committed to the rapid and effective healing of his client. A large body of sociological research has suggested that Parsons's ideal typical analysis of the doctor–patient relationship is not appropriate as an orientation to actual empirical doctor–patient interaction. For example, much research has been concerned to analyse the typification of patients as 'bad patients' who diverge from this ideal model (Murcott, 1981).

The sick-role model suggests that the doctor–patient relationship is complementary and functional, whereas much medical sociology research has suggested that the relationship is very variable (Bloor and Horobin, 1975). There is a certain contradiction between the expectation that the ideal patient will be well informed and strongly motivated to seek medical help, and the expectation that the patient will submit to the expert knowledge and guidance of the doctor. That is, the patient is expected to be sufficiently informed to bring real rather than trivial symptoms to the doctor but sufficiently compliant to follow the doctor's advice without question or interference. The patient's expert character in deciding to consult the doctor terminates once the patient enters the clinic.

Because the patient is expected to be literally naive, there is considerable conflict, or at least potential conflict, in terms of power, knowledge and status between doctor and patient. Social differences in power and knowledge create a set of conflicting discourses between patient and doctor which in turn produce situations of low trust and minimal confidence. The potential range of conflict appears to be infinite, but one might suggest a continuum between a situation where the patient attempts to get 'better' before the doctor is adequately convinced that health has been restored (Roth, 1963) and a situation where the patient stays 'sick' where the doctor thinks a new drug or therapy may be desirable and appropriate (Sacks, 1976).

The third area of major criticism of the sick-role concept concerns the type of disease which may have an important bearing on the character of the patient/sick role. In general, Parsons's analysis of the sick role refers to acute rather than chronic illness, since Parsons's analysis of the role assumes that the patient will get better. Some diseases may be long term and the sick person is not necessarily excused from commitments and may be expected to cope with a long-term disability. For example, in the case of diabetes mellitus, there is no known cure. With early onset the patient will have to manage a sick role for life in an isolated social context, with increasing forms of disability including blindness. Another example of such long-term management where social responsibilities are not absolved would be epilepsy. Similarly, diseases like Parkinsonism render the patient incapable of maintaining long-term social commitments and, while the disease might enable legitimate withdrawal from social engagement, there is often little opportunity for release from the disease so that the patient could occupy normal social roles.

Parsons's conception of the sick role is also limited in the area of somewhat ambiguous forms of medical illness and deviance from normal patterns of behaviour. For example, pregnancy might eventually cause a woman to withdraw from full-time employment, but it is not entirely clear that Parsons's notion of the sick role would include pregnancy as a legitimate reason for withdrawal from the full range of expectations relating to social roles. Another example would be aging which produces disability and withdrawal from social roles, but it might be somewhat problematic to regard aging as a genuine sick role. If aging is regarded as a form of sickness, then retirement would be a form of transference of the individual to a permanent sick role. In short, there are a wide range of long-term illnesses from diabetes to dementia which force the individual to withdraw from social roles, but may not have the full legitimacy which patients usually expect from the sick role.

A fourth type of criticism of Parsons relates to the problem of the universalistic character of treatment of patients regardless of class, gender or status. Parsons's sick-role formulation assumed that doctors would orientate to the patient on the basis of a universalistic norm irrespective of the particular characteristics of the patient. This assumption about universalism does not appear to be borne out in empirical research. One significant variation in the treatment of patients is explained by social class. Research on medical consultations in the UK, for example, shows that the length of consultations varies with social class so that patients in social class I had an average consultation of 6.1 minutes where members of social class V had a consultation length of 4.4 minutes (Buchan and Richardson, 1973). In a study of elderly patients, Cartwright and O'Brien (1976) found that middle-class patients' consultations lasted for 6.2 minutes whereas consultations for working-class patients lasted for 4.7 minutes.

The content of the consultations also varied according to social class so that middle-class patients would be more likely to receive an explanation of their condition than working-class patients. There are also important variations in terms of gender. For instance, Macintyre and Oldman (1984) have described very different responses from the medical profession to the common complaint of migraine where these differences in response appear to be at least partly related to patients' gender, age and status. They suggest that female sufferers from migraine are more likely to be treated as neurotic females whereas middle-class migraine sufferers who are male are more likely to be regarded as persons exposed to extreme stress and tension from demanding occupational routines. Sociological studies in the USA have shown that there are also extreme variations in the treatment of persons defined as mentally ill according to class, status, gender and ethnicity (Hollingshead and Redlich, 1958). Variations in the treatment of patients by social status are not confined to the interview within the clinical situation. Sudnow (1967) has explored through an ethnographic study variations in medical responses to persons arriving at an emergency unit who are suspected of being dead on arrival. Sudnow was able to show how the medical response varied in terms of the presumed moral character of the patient. For example, patients who were deemed to be alcoholic did not receive the same treatment as those who were deemed to be sober. In short, there are wide variations in the treatment of patients by doctors according to the particularistic status of the patients, and therefore it is difficult to argue that in practice universalistic criteria apply.

[. . .]

Parsons had argued that the specific character of the sick role in American society was the product of a culture that gave special emphasis to individualism, achievement and activism. To be sick in American society was to be inactive and withdrawn from the competitive race of a society which gave an emphasis to moral individualism. Parsons had suggested that different social structures would produce different sick roles and he was particularly concerned to provide a contrast between sickness in state socialist societies and sickness in competitive capitalist society. As a defence of Parsons's legacy, it is interesting therefore to compare different social systems in terms of the presence or absence of this syndrome of individualism-activism-achievement values.

   If the sick role is regarded as an exit from social relations for a temporary respite from social obligations, then we can argue that sickness and health are criteria of social membership and engagement. It is for this reason that Parsons argued that permanent incumbency of the sick role should be regarded as a form of social deviance. In fact the sick role as a form of social withdrawal is widespread in human cultures and clearly not peculiar to modern industrial societies.

For example, in the Islamic Middle East illness behaviour can be a method for legitimating behaviour which deviates from conventional social expectations. In the Nile delta, the possessed male or female may display a variety of symptoms but the social manifestations have a single theme, namely the breaking of social customs (Morsy, 1978). A woman who is sick by possession may reject the offer of a marriage selected by her father, oppose her husband's sexual desires and decline to nurse another's child without social criticism since her deviance is explained by her illness. Medical labels in this context provide an acceptable label for deviant activity and also institutionalize this form of deviance. Thus it is interesting to note that:

> the very term 'uzr' (excuse) provides the illness with a social definition. It offers the 'ma'zur' (excused) a temporary dispensation from the requirements of social canons. (Morsy, 1978: 603)

Those afflicted with illness ('uzr') are able to maintain a marginal position in society while avoiding the ultimate punishments of social exclusion traditionally connected with serious forms of deviance. The illness of the excused is normally terminated by re-engagement in a variety of collective rituals which have a medical-social character.

   Anthropological research points to the fact that all known societies have what we might call culturally patterned disorders which are social roles in which deviance is legitimated and indeed institutionalized as an available social pattern. Research from a variety of pre-modern societies indicates the widespread prevalence of these culturally patterned forms of disorder which we may simply regard as sick roles. Anthropological investigation of North American tribes shows that behaviour which we might want to call 'psychotic' is in fact institutionalized by ritual and custom (Barnouw, 1979; Bishop, 1975; Hay, 1971). In western society a common expression for deviant behaviour is the concept of the 'berserk' by which we attempt to describe abnormal deviant behaviour of a frenetic character. The word berserk is itself a corruption of a Norse word meaning 'bear's shirt'; in fact the word berserk therefore refers to institutionalized deviant behaviour. The berserk was somebody who occupied a special role in the tribe and was expected to put fear into tribal enemies. The behaviour of the berserk, far from being random and peculiar, was in fact culturally patterned and structured.

These illustrations from pre-modern conditions have two common features. First, sickness is related to marginality and exclusion from mundane activity, despite the fact that these exclusions are themselves ritualized and institutional. Secondly, the cure for such behaviour involves social rituals designed to reintegrate the individual in the social group and reaffirm conventional membership by the expurgation of offending sickness. We can argue that all human societies are organized in terms of rituals of exclusion and inclusion. In traditional Christianity, the primary rituals of inclusion were such sacraments as baptism, confirmation and marriage, while the rituals of exclusion included excommunication, ritual death and various forms of social exclusion. In this respect illness is a form of marginality and the primary mechanisms of therapy are social integration. From this perspective, the important feature of Parsons's analysis of the sick role in the American context is the emphasis on the individual and the individualization of deviance. While in this sick role the incumbent deviates from the values of achievement and engagement, the sick person does not deviate from the values of individualism. In part this is because western medicine itself emphasizes through modern theories of disease the individuality of sickness.

In secular western societies, there are few public rituals by which sickness and health can be demarcated through collective processes. We have lost most of the major ritualized expressions of social membership and social engagement; our rituals are fragmented and secularized. The definition of social membership in contemporary industrial societies is signified by political conceptions of citizenship which in turn typically depend upon the possession of language and therefore a par-

ticular form of education (Gellner, 1983). The rituals of modern society are concerned with definitions of nationalism rather than with medicosocial definitions of deviance and normality. It is characteristic of western societies that when we fall ill, we are isolated from our public activities and we may well be isolated from kin and relatives. Because we are sick, we are removed from public surveillance and inspection, retreating to the privacy of our beds and our private spaces. Alternatively, within the hospital setting we will again be institutionalized, isolated and often prevented from the enjoyments of regular interaction with our kin folk or friends. Illness under these circumstances is alienating and degrading; sickness involves removal and departure rather than reintegration and incorporation within social groups. In this respect, we can support Parsons's contention that in western societies the sick role is a form of social control which regulates the amount of sickness in society, making return to health and work personally and socially desirable.

This pattern of sickness and health presents a sharp contrast with the form of illness behaviour and therapy in contemporary Japan. While Japan and the USA are clearly industrial capitalist societies, they have significantly different cultural systems. Specifically, Japan does not have the individualistic culture which is typical of industrial western societies and therefore the patterns of illness behaviour in Japan do not exhibit individualistic values (Abercrombie et al., 1986).

In Japanese culture there is a more positive approach towards sickness, not simply as the absence of work but as positive vacation and recreation. The Japanese pamper their sick in a way which would be unusual in western societies. The Japanese approach is to emphasize 'ansai' (peace and quietness) as the principal form of therapy for all illness. Hospitalization is a form of vacation which is positively required for the restoration of health. This attitude towards illness and rest may in part explain why the average length of hospital stay for a patient in Japan is far longer than in any other industrial society. Whereas the average length of stay in the USA in the 1970s was 8.1 days and in England and Wales 13.1 days, the average length of stay in Japanese hospitals was 42.9 days. Furthermore, entry into hospital in Japan does not signal the end of close kinship relationships. In Japan, regular contact is maintained with the relatives through a ritualized system of visitation where sharing of food is particularly important. The Japanese hospitalization resembles the treatment of the socially deviant in pre-modern society where illness often brings about an intensification rather than a diminution of social relations:

through the crisis situation of hospitalization, the patient's entire social network becomes activated and reaches a new height of intensity, both positively and negatively. All the participants in the 'drama' are forced to re-examine their human relationships. During the hospitalization, every fibre of the patient's social network is tested. (Ohnuki-Tierney, 1984: 210)

The integration of the kinship system, the patient and the hospital is symbolized by the fact that patients continue to wear their own clothing while in hospital and are not subject to the usual forms of bureaucracy so common in the western system. Entry into hospital in a western system is often accompanied by what have been called 'degradation ceremonies' (Garfinkel, 1956). The degradation has the effect of reinforcing the desirability of health, engagement with the social system and a return to individualistic autonomy and self-reliance.

Conclusion

Although Parsons's concept of the sick role has been the subject of appropriate criticism, the empirical implications of Parsons's theory of sickness have yet to be fully explored. Especially in the framework of comparative sociology, the sick-role concept is a powerful instrument for the analysis of culture and social deviance. Parsons's notion that sickness is subject to social control provides a useful way into the analysis of culture in relation to illness behaviour. His discussion of

sickness brought to the foreground the whole question of responsibility for sickness and the social response to illness behaviour. The notion of the sick role is a critical alternative to the medical model with its emphasis on objective causation of disease within a framework which denies the involvement of the individual and precludes a voluntaristic framework for the analysis of sickness as a form of social action. However, the medical model, by ruling out responsibility absolves the patient from routine tasks and social employments. Because they are no longer responsible, they are no longer subject to moral criticism and legal punishment. In return for this denial of responsibility, the patient may well be subject to various forms of social degradation, however implicit such rituals may be. This question of responsibility and individual autonomy becomes paramount in the analysis of mental illness.

REFERENCES

N. Abercrombie, S. Hill and B. S. Turner (1986), *Sovereign Individuals of Capitalism*, London, Allen and Unwin.

V. Barnouw (1979), *Culture and Personality*, Homewood Ill., The Dawsey Press.

C. A. Bishop (1975), 'Northern Algonkian Cannibalism and Windigo Psychosis', in T. R. Williams (ed.) *Psychological Anthropology*, The Hague, Mouton.

M. Bloor and G. Horobin (1975), 'Conflict and Conflict Resolution in Doctor-Patient Interactions', in C. Cox and A. Mead (eds) *A Sociology of Medical Practice*, London, Macmillan.

I. C. Buchan and I.M. Richardson (1973), 'Time Study of Consultations in General Practice', *Scottish Health Service Studies*, No. 27, Scottish Home and Health Department.

A. Cartwright and M. O'Brien (1976), 'Social Class Variations in Health Care and in the Nature of General Practitioner Consultations', in M. Stacy (ed.), *The Sociology of the NHS*, *Sociological Review*, monograph No. 22.

A. Frank (1991), 'From Sick Role to Health Role: Deconstructing Parsons', in R. Robertson and

B. Turner (eds), *Talcott Parsons: Theorist of Modernity*, London, Sage.

E. Freidson (1961), *Patients' Views of Medical Practice*, New York, Russell Sage Foundation.

E. Freidson (1970), *Profession of Medicine, a Study of the Sociology of Applied Knowledge*, New York, Harper and Row.

H. Garfinkel (1956), 'Conditions of Successful Degradation Ceremonies', *The American Journal of Sociology*, 61: 420–4.

E. Gellner (1983), *Nations and Nationalism*, Oxford, Basil Blackwell.

U. Gerhardt (1989), *Ideas about Illness: An Intellectual and Political History of Medical Sociology*. London, Macmillan.

T. H. Hay (1971), 'The Windigo Psychosis: Psychodynamic, Cultural and Social Factors in Aberrant Behaviour', *American Anthropologist*, 73: 1–19.

A. B. Hollingshead and F. C. Redlich (1958), *Social Class and Mental Illness, a Community Study*, New York, Wiley.

R. J. Holton and B. S. Turner (1986), *Talcott Parsons on Economy and Society*, London, Routledge & Kegan Paul.

E. M. Lemert (1967), *Human Deviance, Social Problems and Social Control*, Englewood Cliffs, New Jersey, Prentice-Hall.

S. Levine and M. A. Kozloff (1978), 'The Sick Role: Assessment and Overview', *The Annual Review of Sociology*, 4: 317–43.

S. Macintyre and D. Oldman (1984), 'Coping with Migraine', in N. Black et al. (eds) *Health and Disease, A Reader*, Milton Keynes, The Open University Press.

J. McKinlay (1973), 'Social Networks, Lay Consultation and Help-seeking Behaviour', *Social Forces*, 53: 275–92.

D. Mechanic (1968) *Medical Sociology*, New York, The Free Press.

S. A. Morsy (1978), 'Sex Differences and Folk Illness in an Egyptian Village', in L. Beck and N. Keddie (eds), *Women in the Muslim World*, Cambridge, Cambridge University Press.

A. Murcott (1981), 'On the Typification of Bad Patients', in P. Atkinson and C. Heath (eds) *Medical Work, Realities and Routines*, London, Gower.

E. Ohnuki-Tierney (1984), *Illness and Culture in Contemporary Japan, An Anthropological View*, Cambridge, Cambridge University Press.

T. Parsons (1951), *The Social System*, London, Routledge & Kegan Paul.

J. A. Roth (1963), *Timetables, Structuring the Passage of Time in Hospital Treatment and Other Careers*, Indianapolis, Bobbs-Merrill.

O. Sacks (1976), *Awakenings*, Harmondsworth, Penguin Books.

A. Scambler, G. Scambler and D. Craig (1981), 'Kinship and Friendship Networks and Women's Demand for Primary Care', *Journal of the Royal College of General Practitioners*, 26: 746–50.

T. J. Scheff (1966), *Being Mentally Ill, A Sociological Theory*, London, Weidenfeld and Nicolson.

E. A. Suchman (1964), 'Sociomedical Variations Among Ethnic Groups', *The American Journal of Sociology*, 70: 319–31.

D. Sudnow (1967), *Passing On, The Social Organisation of Dying*, Englewood Cliffs, New Jersey, Prentice-Hall.

D. Tuckett (ed.) (1976), *An Introduction to Medical Sociology*, London, Tavistock.

40. What Makes Women Sick?

Lesley Doyal

Physical and mental health are basic human needs yet they remain unmet for millions of women. As we shall see, the reasons for this are rarely 'natural' in the sense that they are unavoidable; too often they are, quite literally, 'man-made', requiring feminist imagination(s) for their understanding and ultimately their transformation. But to declare one's feminism in the 1990s requires further elaboration. In particular it necessitates a clear statement on the thorny question of 'difference', which has been at the heart of recent feminist debates.

In this analysis of women's health we will reject both crude universalism and crude difference theories. Instead we will attempt to identify the commonalities in women's situations while at the same time remaining sensitive to the complex social, economic and cultural variety of their lives In other words, we will focus on their 'common difference' (Joseph and Lewis, 1981). Only in this way can we construct a theory that makes both moral and political sense.

[...]

Cultural variations in concepts of sickness and health are now well documented and their significance will be obvious in future chapters (Baer, 1987; Kleinman, 1988; Lock and Gordon, 1988; Lupton, 1994; Whelehan, 1988; Wright and Treacher, 1982). However, they do not mean that we cannot compare the health status of women in different societies. This can still be achieved if we distinguish as clearly as possible between the objective manifestations of 'disease' and the subjective experience of 'illness' (Eisenberg, 1977). These two elements will certainly be inextricably intertwined in the minds and bodies of particular individuals. Yet we can still measure the social distribution of disease and death while also understanding and respecting the cultural relativity of illness.

Women in different cultures who contract tuberculosis or pelvic infection for instance may well experience these diseases in very different ways. However, they will also have a great deal in common. Some will die, most will 'feel ill' (in some sense or other), all will show similar physiological signs (albeit in varying degrees) and all will respond in broadly similar ways to scientifically tested treatments such as antibiotics. It is these commonalities that we can measure, and use to compare the health status of different social groups (Doyal and Gough, 1991, pp. 56–9).

What western medicine defines as mental illness poses more difficult problems of interpretation and measurement since usually there are no objective 'signs' independent of the subjective symptoms. But again, similarities in its effects can be identified across cultures. Whatever the form of their distress, or the words and concepts used to describe it, women with poor mental health will all experience a significant reduction in their capacity for successful participation in their culture. Though each will have their own contribution to make, all will be disabled to a greater or lesser extent in the exercise of their cognitive and emotional capabilities. It is this disability that can be compared between societies (Doyal and Gough, 1991, pp. 62–3).

A picture of health?

All women whose physical or mental health is damaged will therefore be harmed in broadly similar ways, and morbidity and mortality rates can give us a preliminary indication of the global distribution of this harm. Of course, such statistics can provide only a partial picture since they are not measuring the subjective or experiential aspects of illness. Moreover, they offer a negative view of sickness and death rather than a positive picture of well-being. However, they do represent important points of reference between societies and social groups as well as offering clues to structural factors underlying any perceived inequalities.

Inequalities in mortality

In most of the developed countries women can now expect to survive for about 75 years (United Nations, 1991, p. 55). However, this average conceals significant variations in life expectancy between women in different social groups. In Britain women married to men in semiskilled or unskilled jobs are about 70 per cent more likely to die prematurely than those whose husbands are professionals (OPCS, 1986). Similar social divisions are apparent in the United States, where black women now have a life expectancy of 73.5 years compared with 79.2 for white women while their risk of dying in pregnancy or childbirth is three and a half times greater (US National Institutes of 1992, pp. 8, 13). In most underdeveloped countries the social inequalities in health are even more dramatic.

There are also major differences in mortality rates between rich and poor nations. In Latin America and the Caribbean average life expectancy is lower than in developed countries but still relatively high at around 70. In Asia and the Pacific it is 64 and in Africa as low as 54 (UN, 1991 p. 55). The lowest rates recorded for individual countries are in Afghanistan, East Timor, Ethiopia and Sierra Leone, where women can expect to live for only about 43 years (ibid.).

These inequalities are at their most extreme in deaths related to childbearing. In developed countries mortality of this kind is rare, with less than five deaths for every 100,000 live births. In South Asian countries, on the other hand, the rate is more than 650 deaths per 100,000 with the African average a close second at around 600 deaths (UN, 1991, p. 56).

Though these figures are extremely dramatic, they do not show the true extent of the inequalities in reproductive hazards facing women in different parts of the world. The maternal mortality rate reflects the risk a woman runs in each pregnancy. However we also need to examine fertility rates to assess the lifetime risk to an individual woman of dying of pregnancy-related causes. Recent estimates suggest that for a woman in Africa this risk is 1 in 23 compared with only 1 in 10,000 in developed countries (Rooney, 1992). Pregnancy causes almost no deaths among women of reproductive age in developed countries but between a quarter and a third of deaths elsewhere (Fortney et al., 1986). Reproductive deaths are therefore an important indicator both of the different health hazards facing men and women and also of the heterogeneity of women's own experiences.

Turning from mortality to morbidity statistics – from death to disease – we are immediately faced with what appears to be a paradox. Around the world, women usually live longer than men in the same socio-economic circumstances. In most of the developed countries the gap between male and female life expectancy is about 6.5 years (UN, 1991, p. 55). In Latin America and the Caribbean it is 5.0 years, in Africa 3.5 years and in Asia and the Pacific, 3.0 years (ibid.). Only in a few countries in Asia do women have a lower life expectancy than men. Yet despite their generally greater longevity, women in most communities report more illness and distress.

[. . .]

Why do women in most countries have a longer life expectancy than men? Why do women in some countries live nearly twice as long as those in others? Why do rates of morbidity and mortality vary between social classes and ethnic groups? Why do so many women still die in childbirth? Why *do* women report more sickness than men? How does their race or their culture affect women's experiences of health and health care? As we shall see, medical science can offer only limited resources either for answering these questions or for changing the reality that they represent.

The 'biomedical model'

Western medicine offers a powerful framework for describing and classifying much of the sickness afflicting individuals. Using this 'biomedical model' doctors have developed the means to prevent or cure many diseases and to alleviate the symptoms of others. However, many other health problems have remained resistant to their ministrations. This has drawn increasing attention to the limitations of the conceptual schema employed by doctors and other health care providers to understand complex human phenomena. Two aspects of medical practice have come under particular scrutiny: its narrowly biological orientation and its separation of individuals from their wider social environment (Busfield, 1986, p. 28).

It is no longer appropriate (if it ever was) to categorize western medicine as a monolithic unified institution devoted only to hard science and high technology. Recent years have been marked by a revival of interest in public health and a 'humanization' of some areas of research and clinical practice. Yet the natural sciences continue to be seen as the only 'real' basis of medicine, with attention focused predominantly on the internal workings of the human body.

Health and disease are still explained primarily through an engineering metaphor in which the body is seen as a series of separate but interdependent systems (Doyal and Doyal, 1984). Ill health is treated as the mechanical failure of some part of one or more of these systems and the medical task is to repair the damage. Within this model, the complex relationship between mind and body is rarely explored and individuals are separated from both the social and cultural contexts of their lives:

The notion of disease itself refers to a process that unfolds and develops within the individual and what occurs within the individual and what the individual does is the prime subject of medical interest and endeavour, rather than the individual's relationship to others or to the environment or vice versa (Busfield, 1986, p. 25).

This biological and individualistic orientation of modern medicine has led to enormous successes in our understanding of different types of disease and their treatment. Indeed, it was precisely the concentration of effort made possible by this explanatory model that led to major achievements such as anaesthesia, antisepsis, antibiotics, analgesia and a wide range of other therapies that most people in developed countries now take for granted. The 'magic bullet' that works is a powerful weapon indeed. However, its obvious success has led to a neglect of prevention and an over-reliance on this curative model, both in explaining the causes of disease and in exploring the different ways in which illness is experienced.

[. . .]

Gendered research

However, it is not just its narrowly biological orientation that limits the capacity of medicine to deal with women's health problems. Even within its own terms there is growing evidence that both the priorities and the techniques of biomedical research reflect the white male domination of the profession (Kirchstein, 1991). Bias has been identified in the choice and the definition of problems to be studied, the methods employed to carry out the research, and the interpretation and application of results (Cotton, 1990; Rosser, 1992, pp. 129–30). While women are in the majority as health care providers, they continue to be in the minority as practising doctors (Doyal, 1994;

Lorber, 1984). They hold few positions of power and therefore have little influence on how funds are allocated or research carried out (Rosser, 1992; US National Institutes of Health, 1992; Witz, 1992).

There has been relatively little basic research into non-reproductive conditions that mainly affect women – incontinence and osteoporosis for instance. In the United States, Congressional Hearings in 1990 showed that only 13 per cent of government research funds were spent on health issues specific to women (US National Institutes of Health, 1992). Even the menstrual cycle itself has not been extensively researched. Hence we have little detailed knowledge about an extremely important aspect of women's bodily functioning that generates a large amount of distress and many medical consultations (Koblinsky et al., 1993). Where health problems affect both men and women, few studies have explored possible differences between the sexes in their development, symptoms and treatment (American Medical Association, 1991).

Researchers working on coronary heart disease, for example, have continued to act as though it were only a 'male' problem, despite the fact that it is the single most important cause of death in postmenopausal women, killing half a million a year in the United States. The Physician Health Study, which demonstrated the effectiveness of daily aspirin consumption in preventing cardiovascular disease, had a sample of 20,000 men but no women, while the sample in the 'Mr. Fit' study of the relationship between heart disease, cholesterol and lifestyle consisted of 15,000 men (Freedman and Maine, 1993, p. 165). AIDS, too, has been treated for research purposes as a predominantly male disease. Though it is now growing faster among women than among men, we still know very little about the differential effects it may have on them (Bell, 1992; Denenberg, 1990; Kurth, 1993).

As long as most biomedical research continues to be based on male samples there will be significant gaps in our knowledge about women. Even more importantly, treatments tested only on men

will continue to be given to women, when they may not be appropriate to their needs (Hamilton, 1985). There have recently been indications, for example, that anti-depressant drugs can have very different effects on men and women and may affect women differently during the various phases of the menstrual cycle. However, preliminary testing excluded women, despite the fact that they are the major users of the drugs (ibid.).

It is clear that biomedicine has generated valuable knowledge that has been used to improve the health of individual women. But, as we have seen, this understanding is often partial and sometimes erroneous. This is because research has selectively ignored many of the biological differences between the sexes while paying little or no attention to the particularity of women's psychological and social circumstances.

REFERENCES

American Medical Association, Council on Ethical and Judicial Affairs (1991) 'Gender disparities in clinical decision making', *Journal of American Medical Association*, vol. 266, no. 4, pp. 559–62.

Baer, H. (ed.) (1987) *Encounters with Biomedicine: case studies in medical anthropology* (New York: Gordon and Breach).

Bell, N. (1992) 'Women and AIDS: too little, too late?', in H. Bequaert Holmes and L. Purdy (eds) *Feminist Perspectives in Medical Ethics* (Bloomington: Indiana University Press).

Busfield, J. (1986) *Managing Madness: changing ideas and practices* (London: Hutchinson).

Cotton, P. (1990) 'Is there still too much extrapolation from data on middle aged white men?', *Journal of the American Medical Association*, vol. 263, no. 8, pp. 1049–50.

Denenberg, R. (1990) 'Unique aspects of HIV infection in women', in The ACT UP/NY Women and AIDS Book Group, *Women, AIDS and Activism* (Boston, Mass.: South End Press).

Doyal, L. (1994) 'Changing medicine: the politics of women's health', in J. Gabe, D. Kellehar and G. Williams (eds) *Challenging Medicine* (London: Tavistock).

Doyal, L. and Doyal, L. (1984) 'Western Scientific Medicine: a philosophical and political prognosis', in L. Birke and J. Silvertown (eds) *More than the Parts: biology and politics* (London: Pluto Press).

Doyal, L. and Gough, I. (1991) *Theory of Human Need* (London: Macmillan).

Eisenberg, L. (1977) 'Disease and illness: distinctions between professional and popular ideas of sickness', *Culture, Medicine and Psychiatry*, vol. 1, pp. 9–23.

Fortney, J., Susanti, I., Gadalla, S., Saleh, S., Rogers, S. and Potts, M. (1986) 'Reproductive mortality in two developing countries', *American Journal of Public Health*, vol. 76, no. 2, pp. 134–8.

Freedman, L. and Maine, D. (1993) 'Women's mortality: a legacy of neglect', in M. Koblinsky, J. Timyan and J. Gay (eds) *The Health of Women: a global perspective* (Boulder, Co: Westview Press).

Hamilton, J. (1985) 'Avoiding methodological and policy making biases in gender-related research', in US Department of Health and Human Services, *Women's Health: report of the Public Health Service Task Force on women's health issues*, vol. II, pp. 54–64 (Washington, DC: US Government Printing Office).

Joseph, G. and Lewis, J. (1981) *Common Differences: conflicts in black and white feminist perspectives* (Boston, Mass.: South End Press).

Kirchstein, R. (1991) 'Research on women's health', *American Journal of Public Health*, vol. 81, no. 3, pp. 291–3.

Kleinman, A. (1988) *The Illness Narratives: suffering, healing and the human condition* (New York: Basic Books).

Koblinsky, M., Campbell, O. and Harlow, S. (1993) 'Mother and more: a broader perspective on women's health', in M. Koblinsky, J. Timyan and J. Gay (eds) *The Health of Women:*

a global perspective (Boulder, Co: Westview Press).

Kurth, A. (1993) 'Introduction: an overview of women and HIV disease', in A. Kurth (ed.) *Until the Cure: caring for women with HIV* (London and New Haven: Yale University Press).

Lock, M. and Gordon, D. (eds) (1988) *Biomedicine Examined* (Dordrecht: Kluwer).

Lorber, J. (1984) *Women Physicians: careers, status and power* (London: Tavistock).

Lupton, D. (1994) *Medicine as Culture: illness, disease and the body in western societies* (Newbury Park, Calif.: Sage).

Office of Population Censuses and Surveys (OCPS) (1986) *Occupational Mortality: Decennial Supplement, England and Wales 1979–80* (London: HMSO).

Rooney, C. (1992) *Antenatal Care and Maternal Health: how effective is it?, A review of the evidence* (Geneva: WHO).

Rosser, S. (1992) 'Re-visioning clinical research: gender and the ethics of experimental design', in H. Holmes and L. Purdy (eds) *Feminist Perspectives in Medical Ethics* (Bloomington and Indianapolis: Indiana University Press).

United Nations (1991) 'The world's women 1970–1990: trends and statistics', *Social Statistics and Indicators*, Series, K, no. 8 (New York: UN).

United States National Institutes of Health (1992) *Opportunities for Research on Women's Health* (NIH Publication no. 92–3457) (Washington, DC: US Department of Health and Human Services).

Whelehan, M. (1988) *Women and Health: cross cultural perspectives* (Granby, Mass.: Bergin and Garvey).

Witz, A. (1992) *Professions and Patriarchy* (London: Routledge).

Wright, P. and Treacher, A. (eds) (1982) *The Problem of Medical Knowledge: examining the social construction of medicine* (Edinburgh: Edinburgh University Press).

41. The Experience of Illness and Recovery

Mike Bury

In this part of the discussion, however, the emphasis shifts to arguments that call for sociological attention to the experience of bodies and health. An emphasis on subjective experience leads Nettleton and Watson (1998) to call, for example, for a sociology of 'embodiment' rather than a sociology of the body. These authors argue that the idea of 'embodiment' reminds us that 'the self and the body are not separate and that experience is invariably, whether conscious or not, embodied' (Nettleton and Watson 1998: 11). In the experience of illness, the 'life-world' of the individual, comprising his or her biography and values, is confronted with bodily change and disruption. 'Biographical work' is needed to attempt to repair and restore a sense of secure self-identity (p. 12). Nettleton and Watson cite the late Irving Zola to the effect that the taken-for-granted character of embodiment, and especially the cultural barriers to speaking about the body, have hitherto created a ring of silence around the subject (p. 20). This private world of bodily experience, or 'embodiment', has been left largely unexamined by sociology, in comparison with many other areas of enquiry.

However, there are now such large literatures on both the sociology of the body and the experience of illness, in the UK and the USA at least, as to make calls for a more explicit focus on the topic somewhat redundant. Mention has already been made of Freund et al.'s summary of research on work and the body in the USA, and this is set within a wider consideration of health experience (Freund et al. 2003). Whilst it is true, as Nettleton and Watson (1998) note, that much socio-

logical writing on the body has been overly theoretical in tone, an increasing number of empirical studies on experiential issues are emerging (their own collection being a case in point). In the rest of this section the discussion will focus on some of the key arguments in Arthur Frank's writings (1991, 1995), which have documented in detail his own personal experience of illness and, through contact with a variety of patient groups, that of others. Whilst falling short, perhaps, of a systematic research programme with a clear methodology, Frank's influential work illustrates many of the themes currently being explored in sociological studies of the body and illness, and can therefore stand as an exemplar.

In his earlier book, *At the Will of the Body* (1991), Frank describes his experience in early middle age of developing heart disease and then, as he was getting over this, discovering that he had testicular cancer. The first part of the book is a poignant account of the disruption and discontinuity that this sequence of events created for him. Frank had to come to terms with an altered body and simultaneously an altered life. The loss involved was not only that of physical functioning, but also of his younger self. Until the onset of his illness, Frank had been able to see his present as a continuous link with his past, but now he had to recognize that his past was over – 'like saying goodbye to a place I had lived in and loved' (Frank 1991: 39). He and his wife had to face the possibility of disruption to the future as well, with the normal expectations about life and survival being compromised. But Frank emphasizes that the sequence of events was not as orderly as his writing about them suggests. This 'disorderliness' he relates partly to the nature of specific illnesses as, in contrast to most cancers, where the fear of sudden death is absent, in heart disease it may be ever present, at least in the acute phase.

The 'differences and particularities' of illnesses and their expression in the body of individuals, Frank argues, are difficult for people dealing with the ill to manage. The employment by health professionals of categories, protocols and guidelines may help the practitioner, but may strike the patient as insensitive. It is the particularities of experience that give meaning to illness for the individual, but these are almost impossible for others to take on board. How each person in the care-receiving/care-giving relationship handles these tensions can play a large part in determining the experience. Care-givers in particular, Frank argues, are 'confronted not with an ordered sequence of illness experiences, but with a stew of panic, uncertainty, fear, denial and disorientation' (Frank 1991: 49), though he adds that even for the sufferer such words have little reality 'until filled with an ill person's own experience'. Current attempts to create 'managed care' and 'evidence-based' practice can easily clash with patient experiences, however much such initiatives are designed to do the opposite. The heterogeneity of illness experience, including the anxiety and dependency it can create, sits uneasily alongside such rational procedures.

In such a situation, the individual patient is vulnerable to the reactions of others, especially those professionals giving immediate care. Frank states that when he was ill, 'I needed others more than I ever have, and I was also most vulnerable to them' (p. 70). The ethos of appearing to be positive before professionals carried its own costs, where recognition and acceptance of fear and pain would have been more reassuring. This was even more acute, as, when treatment for his cancer left Frank with additional problems such as the loss of his hair, the stigma of cancer was 'embodied' in the effects of chemotherapy. Though some of the professionals whom Frank encountered recognized these dimensions of his experience, many

did not. He argues in the book that for medical staff, 'continuing suffering threatens them, so they deny it exists' (p. 101). Echoing the earlier work of the anthropologist Kleinman (1988), Frank argues that 'simply recognizing suffering for what it is, regardless of whether it can be treated, is care' (p. 101).

Despite this call for professionals to 'witness' patients' suffering, there is within *At the Will of the Body*, a more optimistic theme, which emerges at least when recovery or improvement occurs. This is taken up and developed in a further volume, *The Wounded Storyteller* (1995). Frank argues that a number of important changes have occurred in 'late modern' or 'post-modern' societies, which assign illness experience and the body increased relevance. One of the most critical of these is the transition from the predominance of acute life-threatening illnesses (especially the result of infections) to a situation where chronic illnesses and long life expectancy are more typical. Frank argues that, as a result, we now live in a 'Remission Society', where very large numbers of people, possibly the majority, are either suffering from illness or living with its aftermath. Many disorders and diseases which would have once killed the patient can now be managed through technical intervention and treatment, and this produces circumstances in which individuals and their families 'share the worries and daily triumphs of staying well' (Frank 1995: 8).

For Frank, such changes create a social context in which illness is experienced not so much as disruption but as part of 'life's map' or 'life's journey' (Frank 1995: 7). Hence the title of the book. Patients and lay people, Frank argues, are now reclaiming their bodies and their illnesses from 'modernist medicine'. If, in modern societies, medicine colonized the body and illness, and effectively silenced the patient's experience, by subjecting it to the categories and control of medical thought, now lay people can adopt a 'post-colonial' or 'post-modern stance', such that they can articulate their views without necessarily referring to medicine and physicians at all (Frank 1995: 13). Whereas in Frank's earlier discussion the emphasis was partly on the shortcomings of health care staff in reacting to illness, the later work focuses on the lay person's efforts to refashion life with illness as an integral component, rather than with illness denied. This helps explain the recent attention to patient narratives, in sociology and outside it, where the heterogeneity of experience is given full expression, and where it is contrasted with the more technical and scientific view of illness in 'evidence-based' medicine (Bury 2001).

Developing his argument in *At the Will of the Body*, and taking on board Kleinman's approach to illness narratives, Frank suggests that sociology, like medicine, needs to adopt a stance of being a witness to suffering by listening to such narratives (Frank 1995: 24). In this way, social science and medicine can both be situated, he argues, in a new 'ethics of the body' (p. 24). A number of considerations follow from this stance. One of these concerns the question of loss which illness often involves. Illness, Frank contends, is invariably accompanied by a loss of desire, for the mundane (buying clothes, having one's teeth taken care of) as well as for the more important things in life. But, in the new culture described by Frank, illness can also be the opportunity to reflect on the nature of desire and, under some circumstances, find alternative pleasures and sources of positive feelings toward others (p. 40). Illness narratives that give expression to such efforts are the means of repairing damage to the body and the self, and facing the future; 'of re-drawing maps and finding new destinations' (p. 53).

Frank presents a compelling case for rethinking the relationship between the body and the experience of illness in contemporary 'post-modern' cultures. It is also clear from his writings, and from their reception, that they resonate with the experience of many patients and their families. For some sociologists, too, the prospect of exploring how lay-people 'transcend' the loss involved in illness, and reintegrate the body and self on a different level, hold particular attractions (Charmaz 2000: 287). At the very least, such an approach helps to overcome the tendency to rely only on documenting the negative experiences of patients. However, for others, the emphasis in Frank's work on 'restitution', 'chaos' and 'quest' narratives (the latter involving a 'journey' through illness to a new way of living), when linked with the 'ethic' of witness, carries with it strong religious overtones (Williams 1998; Bury 2001). It suggests a form of 'redemption through suffering', and as such may have more problematic connotations. In particular, it implies that health is a matter of 'ongoing moral self-transformation' in which both 'public and private performances are constantly required' (Clarke et al. 2003: 172).

In the viewpoint developed by Frank, health and illness, mind and body, and the natural and the social are couched in 'holistic' terms rather than as interactive. Indeed, towards the end of *The Wounded Storyteller*, Frank speaks of the 'communicative body' pursuing an incomplete project (Frank 1995: 164), which, echoing those who profess a faith, involves a situation where 'recursive processes continuously loop, never conclude'. Whilst for some lay people such a 'project' may be life-enhancing and positive, for others it may prove less appealing, especially in the face of the attraction of a secularized way of approaching pain and suffering, such as 'bracketing it off' and minimizing its impact on self-identity, or in relying more on 'modernist' medical treatment. An emphasis on 'narration' and 'constructed' selfhood needs to be explored carefully, if only to examine the variations in experience which may be found in relation to these different responses to illness and the body. An emphasis on 'narratives' and 'journeys' may also leave the sociological imagination wondering where social structures and social divisions have gone, as subjectivity becomes the focus of attention, at the expense of situating illness in everyday material circumstances and in the social actions of those involved. The insights that Frank brings to the experience of illness and the body express some of the possible weaknesses of a sociology of 'embodiment', as well as its humanitarian strengths.

[...]

Perhaps one of the most definable features of health in contemporary society is its subjective character. Today, in sharp contrast with even a few years ago, official thinking in medical and policy circles is stressing the lay or patient viewpoint. This shift in official discourse results from, and adds to, general changes in social relations. As a result of consumerism and changes in market economies, together with a growing 'populism' and 'informalism' in the surrounding culture, areas of experience that were once hidden from view, or managed by 'objectifying' experts such as doctors, have taken on greater social salience. A focus on the subjective involves playing down the 'grand narratives' of science and technology, or at least putting their authority in recurrent doubt. In turn, these processes raise the profile of lay or patient narratives (Bury 2001). Developments such as life-course research also serve to reinforce 'biographical' processes in health, and thus the importance of personal experience as much as objective 'health status'. Indeed, at times, health in its subjective dimensions seems to be the *leitmotif* of contemporary culture.

These developments in health and illness seem to be here to stay, and many organizations are trying to face up to their implications. The health care professions are particularly in the firing line. As Coulter and Fitzpatrick (2000) argue, health care professionals are now being educated and trained to communicate more effectively with patients and to take their level of satisfaction with the process and outcome of care more seriously. Initiatives to promote shared decision making and 'patient partnership' are now firmly on the agenda of health services in countries such as the UK. Until recently it was widely held that lay people and patients could (and should) know very little about the content of their care; today all manner of information can be accessed about disease and its treatment, as well the management of symptoms in everyday life. Coulter and Fitzpatrick make the point that whilst in the past the patient's viewpoint was seen as a threat to professional

autonomy, today there is a 'substantial momentum' behind making health services more responsive in this regard (p. 462). Professionals will need, in the future, to incorporate the patient's view into their practice in a number of different ways, ranging from informed consent to greater participation in health care planning. This pressure is likely to continue and increase in the future.

Having said this, it is also clear that arguments that we live in an increasingly 'contestable' as well as 'reflexive' culture are particularly relevant to the future for health and health care. For, while the patient or lay view is being emphasized in policy or research circles, the potential for *conflict* between subjective experience and medical authority has received less attention. Yet many examples exist where lay and medical views of health and health care diverge, and where 'partnership' is less evident. This is especially true, perhaps, where views about health and illness go beyond personal experience in the clinic, and begin to engage with wider public health matters. Such disputes are likely to increase in the future. A recent example from the UK can illustrate the point being made here.

In February 1998 an 'early report' by a team of 13 authors from a North London Hospital (Wakefield et al. 1998) appeared in the medical journal *The Lancet* which suggested (on the basis of a study of a small number of patients) that autism might be linked to gastrointestinal disease, and possibly to the combined vaccine for measles, mumps and rubella (MMR). Although the report clearly stated that the link with the MMR vaccine was not proven, it listed all of the 12 cases under review, showing that the children's doctors and/or parents had linked the onset of autism in time to MMR vaccination – with onset often being seen within 24 or 48 hours. Despite its caution about causal influences, the report clearly expressed concern about the triple vaccine. Although one of the leading authors went on to support the continued use of the MMR vaccine (writing to *The Lancet* in May 1998 to say so), the original report, and a press conference on the subject, led to considerable public reaction. This showed little sign of waning with the passage of time. Parents began to campaign around the demand that their children be offered separate vaccinations for the three diseases, pending further enquiry into the side effects of the triple jab, especially its links with autism, and with child-hood bowel disease. These strongly expressed lay views began to appear regularly in the press and in other media.

However, far from accepting the lay viewpoint and agreeing to separate vaccinations, the British government and Department of Health mounted a counter campaign to stem the flow of parental and media-led demand. As Richard Smith, editor of the *British Medical Journal*, noted in a later editorial on 'The discomfort of patient power' (Smith 2002), the government marshalled a considerable body of evidence to show that the MMR vaccine was safe, and that it would be 'folly to offer parents the choice of having their children vaccinated separately against each disease' (p. 497). The government's Chief Medical Officer, Sir Liam Donaldson, appeared frequently on British television and radio in an attempt to reassure parents that medical opinion and research overwhelmingly supported the use of the triple MMR vaccine. In the end, the government had its way, and while some doctors provided separate vaccines privately, the official position held firm, and parental choice in the NHS was denied. As Smith points out in his editorial, although the government had been stressing the patient view, patient partnership and choice in recent policy initiatives, this clearly could not encompass the prospect of patients making 'wrong' or 'foolish' decisions – even though telling individual parents this in the clinic setting would be difficult indeed.

Whatever the rights and wrongs of this particular case (in November 2003 two of the leading authors of the initial report themselves added a further twist to the story by entering into public conflict about the vaccine, and in February 2004 allegations of a conflict of interest were made against the lead author of the original paper), it expressed clearly many of the contours of the 'contestable culture' noted above. The publica-tion of a single report of possible negative effects of immunization, backed up by a dramatic press conference, led to widespread public concern if not panic. The ensuing conflict between parents and medical opinion revealed that the rhetoric about subjective experience and the patient view could only go so far before it clashed with the authority of leading members of the medical pro-fession and more 'objective' (though contested) scientific evidence about the working of the body and medical treatment. The case has not been without its legal dimensions either, with families involved in a complex lawsuit against three drug companies. This shows little sign of resolution (*The Guardian*, 12 May 2004). Behind this example, then, a number of important processes influencing the shape of health and health care in late modern society have been evident.

[. . .]

If there is one idea that runs through each of the arguments summarized briefly above, it is the problematic character of individual beliefs and subjectivity. The desire to stress the rationality of lay thought in everyday life has to be balanced with a consideration of those elements which are more problematic. This poses particular difficul-ties for medical sociology, especially in its efforts to give voice to the lay person or patient. What is involved here is the recognition of the limits of subjectivity, yet without losing the readiness to listen and represent clearly the form and content of lay thought. Much of the contribution of soci-ological research in the health field, discussed at various points in this book, has been to demon-strate the value of lay thought, or patient experi-ence. There is no reason for this to be discontinued or downplayed. But the discussion above does point to the limits of lay thought, as well as to the cultural context of 'post-modern society' in which it is fashioned. There are two points that can be made here. The first is that the tendency to move from an emphasis on lay *beliefs* to one on lay *knowledge* is to court difficulties in tackling health in the future. Prior (2003), for example, has shown that lay knowledge about specific health disorders is often quite limited. His examination of lay thinking about conditions such as Alzheimer's disease or brain injury revealed considerable misunderstanding and ignorance of the facts. What lay people (or carers) know a great deal about, of course, is their own experience, and this can be invaluable in attempting to fashion a more responsive health care system. But this is not the same as saying that lay people are experts about disease – in fact, knowledge is often 'partial or restricted' (Prior 2003: 49). Prior also considers the example of immunization, which, as we have seen, has been of continuing concern. In a study of the reasons for older people refusing an annual 'flu jab', Prior found that some 'refusers' gave no reason of any kind, whereas others showed a lack of knowledge of 'risk assessment, the nature and effects of influenza or of the nature and effects of vaccination against the flu' (p. 51). The second point is that lay beliefs about health and illness need to be set in their context, and not simply accepted as forms of subjective 'truth' – a difficult concept at the best of times. Personal narratives need interpreting and contextualizing, in order to understand what role they perform in everyday life, and what effects they have on others (Bury 2001). Sociological research on health, at the level of lay ideas and everyday experience, needs, therefore, to be based on good empirical evidence and sound theoretical reasoning. In this way the critiques of social and cultural trends surrounding and shaping health, of the kind provided by Shorter, Sontag and Showalter, can be evaluated against sound first-hand research. Again, this is likely to paint a somewhat more complex picture of health in the future than the cultural critics allow, but one which is more accurate perhaps, and more relevant to health in everyday settings.

REFERENCES

Bury, M. 2001: Illness narratives: fact or fiction? *Sociology of Health and Illness*, 23 (3): 263–85.

Charmaz, K. 2000: Experiencing chronic illness. In G. L. Albrecht, R. Fitzpatrick and S. C. Scrimshaw (eds), *The Handbook of Social Studies in Health and Medicine*, London and New York: Sage, 277–92.

Clarke, A. E., Mamo, L., Fishman, J. R., Shim, J. K. and Fosket, J. R. 2003: Biomedicalization: technoscientific transformations of health, illness and U.S. biomedicine. *American Sociological Review*, 68: 161–94.

Coulter, A. and Fitzpatrick, R. 2000: The patient's perspective regarding appropriate health care. In G. L. Albrecht, R. Fitzpatrick, and S. C. Scrimshaw (eds), *The Handbook of Social Studies in Health and Medicine*, London and New York: Sage, 454–64.

Frank, A. W. 1991: *At the Will of the Body: Reflections on Illness*. Boston and New York: Houghton Mifflin.

Frank, A. W. 1995: *The Wounded Storyteller: Body, Illness and Ethics*. Chicago: University of Chicago Press.

Freund, P. E. S., McGuire, M. B. and Podhurst, L. S. 2003: *Health, Illness and the Social Body: A Critical Sociology*, 4th edn. Upper Saddle River, NJ: Prentice-Hall.

Kleinman, A. 1988: *The Illness Narratives: Suffering, Healing and the Human Condition*. New York: Basic Books.

Nettleton, S. and Watson, J. (eds) 1998: *The Body in Everyday Life*. London: Routledge.

Prior, L. 2003: Belief, knowledge and expertise: the emergence of the lay expert in medical sociology. *Sociology of Health and Illness*, 25 (Silver Anniversary Issue): 41–57.

Smith, R. 2002: The discomfort of patient power. *British Medical Journal*, 324: 497–8.

Wakefield, A. J., Murch, S. H., Anthony, A., Linnell, J., Casson, D. M., Malik, M., Berelowitz, M., Dhillon, A. P., Thomson, M. A., Harvey, P., Valentine, A., Davies, S. E. and Walker-Smith, J. A. 1998: Ileal-lymphoidnodular hyperplasia, non-specific colitis, and pervasive developmental disorder in children. *The Lancet*, 351: 637–41.

Williams, G. 1998: The sociology of disability: towards a materialist phenomenology. In T. Shakespeare (ed.), *The Disability Reader: Social Science Perspectives*, London: Cassell, 234–44.

42. The Problem with Medicine

Ivan Illich

During the past three generations the diseases afflicting Western societies have undergone dramatic changes.[1] Polio, diphtheria, and tuberculosis are vanishing; one shot of an antibiotic often cures pneumonia or syphilis; and so many mass killers have come under control that two-thirds of all deaths are now associated with the diseases of old age. Those who die young are more often than not victims of accidents, violence, or suicide.[2]

These changes in health status are generally equated with a decrease in suffering and attributed to more or to better medical care. Although almost everyone believes that at least one of his friends would not be alive and well except for the skill of a doctor, there is in fact no evidence of any direct relationship between this mutation of sickness and the so-called progress of medicine.[3] The changes are dependent variables of political and technological transformations, which in turn are reflected in what doctors do and say; they are not significantly related to the activities that require the preparation, status, and costly equipment in which the health professions take pride.[4] In addition, an expanding proportion of the new burden of disease of the last fifteen years is itself the result of medical intervention in favor of people who are or might become sick. It is doctor-made, or *iatrogenic*.[5]

After a century of pursuit of medical utopia,[6] and contrary to current conventional wisdom,[7] medical services have not been important in producing the changes in life expectancy that have occurred. A vast amount of contemporary clinical care is incidental to the curing of disease, but the damage done by medicine to the health of individuals and populations is very significant. These facts are obvious, well documented, and well repressed.

Doctors' effectiveness – an illusion

The study of the evolution of disease patterns provides evidence that during the last century doctors have affected epidemics no more profoundly than did priests during earlier times. Epidemics came and went, imprecated by both but touched by neither. They are not modified any more decisively by the rituals performed in medical clinics than by those customary at religious shrines.[8] Discussion of the future of health care might usefully begin with the recognition of this fact.

The infections that prevailed at the outset of the industrial age illustrate how medicine came by its reputation.[9] Tuberculosis, for instance, reached a peak over two generations. In New York in 1812, the death rate was estimated to be higher than 700 per 10,000; by 1882, when Koch first isolated and cultured the bacillus, it had already declined to 370 per 10,000. The rate was down to 180 when the first sanatorium was opened in 1910, even though 'consumption' still held second place in the mortality tables.[10] After World War II, but before antibiotics became routine, it had slipped into eleventh place with a rate of 48. Cholera,[11] dysentery,[12] and typhoid similarly peaked and dwindled outside the physician's control. By the time their etiology was understood and their therapy had become specific, these diseases had lost much of their virulence and hence their social importance. The combined death rate from scarlet fever, diphtheria, whooping cough, and measles among children up to fifteen shows that nearly 90 percent of the total decline in mortality between 1860 and 1965 had occurred before the introduction of antibiotics and widespread immunization.[13] In part this recession may be attributed to improved housing and to a decrease in the virulence of micro-organisms, but by far the most important factor was a higher host-resistance due to better nutrition. In poor countries today, diarrhea and upper-respiratory-tract infections occur more frequently, last longer, and lead to higher mortality where nutrition is poor, no matter how much or how little medical care is available.[14] In England, by the middle of the nineteenth century, infectious epidemics had been replaced by major malnutrition syndromes, such as rickets and pellagra. These in turn peaked and vanished, to be replaced by the diseases of early childhood and, somewhat later, by an increase in duodenal ulcers in young men. When these declined, the modern epidemics took over: coronary heart disease, emphysema, bronchitis, obesity, hypertension, cancer (especially of the lungs), arthritis, diabetes, and so-called mental disorders. Despite intensive research, we have no complete explanation for the genesis of these changes.[15] But two things are certain: the professional practice of physicians cannot be credited with the elimination of old forms of mortality or morbidity, nor should it be blamed for the increased expectancy of life spent in suffering from the new diseases. For more than a century, analysis of disease trends has shown that the environment is the primary determinant of the state of general health of any population.[16]

[. . .]

Medicines have always been potentially poisonous, but their unwanted side-effects have increased with their power[17] and widespread use.[18] Every twenty-four to thirty-six hours, from 50 to 80 percent of adults in the United States and the United Kingdom swallow a medically prescribed chemical. Some take the wrong drug; others get an old or a contaminated batch, and others a counterfeit;[19] others take several drugs in dangerous combinations;[20] and still others receive injections with improperly sterilized syringes.[21] Some drugs are addictive, others mutilating, and others mutagenic, although perhaps only in combination with food coloring or insecticides. In some patients, antibiotics alter the normal bacterial flora and induce a superinfection, permitting more resistant organisms to proliferate and invade the host. Other drugs contribute to the breeding of drug-resistant strains of bacteria.[22] Subtle kinds of poisoning thus have spread even faster than the bewildering variety and ubiquity of nostrums.[23] Unnecessary surgery is a standard procedure.[24] *Disabling nondiseases* result from the medical treatment of nonexistent diseases and are on the increase:[25] the number of children disabled in Massachusetts through the treatment of cardiac nondisease exceeds the number of children under effective treatment for real cardiac disease.[26]

Doctor-inflicted pain and infirmity have always been a part of medical practice.[27] Professional callousness, negligence, and sheer incompetence are age-old forms of malpractice.[28] With the transformation of the doctor from an artisan exercising a skill on personally known individuals into a technician applying scientific rules to classes of patients, malpractice acquired an anonymous, almost respectable status.[29] What had formerly been considered an abuse of confidence and a moral fault can now be rationalized into the occasional breakdown of equipment and operators. In a complex technological hospital, negligence becomes 'random human error' or 'system breakdown,' callousness becomes 'scientific detachment,' and incompetence becomes 'a lack of specialized equipment.' The depersonalization of diagnosis and therapy has changed malpractice from an ethical into a technical problem.[30]

[. . .]

The undesirable side-effects of approved, mistaken, callous, or contraindicated technical contacts with the medical system represent just the first level of pathogenic medicine. *Such clinical iatrogenesis* includes not only the damage that doctors inflict with the intent of curing or of exploiting the patient, but also those other torts that result from the doctor's attempt to protect himself against the possibility of a suit for malpractice. Such attempts to avoid litigation and prosecution may now do more damage than any other iatrogenic stimulus.

On a second level,[31] medical practice sponsors sickness by reinforcing a morbid society that encourages people to become consumers of curative, preventive, industrial, and environmental medicine. On the one hand defectives survive in increasing numbers and are fit only for life under institutional care, while on the other hand, medically certified symptoms exempt people from industrial work and thereby remove them from the scene of political struggle to reshape the society that has made them sick. Second-level iatrogenesis finds its expression in various symptoms of social overmedicalization that amount to what I shall call the expropriation of health. This second-level impact of medicine I designate as *social iatrogenesis* [. . .].

On a third level, the so-called health professions have an even deeper, culturally health-denying effect insofar as they destroy the potential of people to deal with their human weakness, vulnerability, and uniqueness in a personal and autonomous way. The patient in the grip of contemporary medicine is but one instance of mankind in the grip of its pernicious techniques.[32] This *cultural iatrogenesis* is the ultimate backlash of hygienic progress and consists in the paralysis of healthy responses to suffering, impairment, and death. It occurs when people accept health management designed on the engineering model, when they conspire in an attempt to produce, as if it were a commodity, something called 'better health.' This inevitably results in the managed maintenance of life on high levels of sublethal illness. This ultimate evil of medical 'progress' must be clearly distinguished from both clinical and social iatrogenesis.

I hope to show that on each of its three levels iatrogenesis has become medically irreversible: a feature built right into the medical endeavor. The unwanted physiological, social, and psychological by-products of diagnostic and therapeutic progress have become resistant to medical remedies. New devices, approaches, and organizational arrangements, which are conceived as remedies for clinical and social iatrogenesis, themselves tend to become pathogens contributing to the new epidemic. Technical and managerial measures taken on any level to avoid damaging the patient by his treatment tend to engender a self-reinforcing iatrogenic loop analogous to the escalating destruction generated by the polluting procedures used as antipollution devices.[33]

I will designate this self-reinforcing loop of negative institutional feedback by its classical Greek equivalent and call it *medical nemesis.* The Greeks saw gods in the forces of nature. For them, nemesis represented divine vengeance visited upon mortals who infringe on those prerogatives the gods enviously guard for themselves. Nemesis was the inevitable punishment for attempts to be a hero rather than a human being. Like most abstract Greek nouns, Nemesis took the shape of a divinity. She represented nature's response to *hubris:* to the individual's presumption in seeking to acquire the attributes of a god. Our contemporary hygienic hubris has led to the new syndrome of medical nemesis.[34]

NOTES

1. Erwin H. Ackerknecht, *History and Geography of the Most Important Diseases* (New York: Hafner, 1965).
2. Odin W. Anderson and Monroe Lerner, *Measuring Health Levels in the United States, 1900–1958*, Health Information Foundation Research Series no. 11 (New York: Foundation, 1960). Marc Lalonde, *A New Perspective on the Health of Canadians: A Working Document* (Ottawa: Government of Canada, April 1974). This courageous

French-English report by the Canadian Federal Secretary for Health contains a multicolored centerfold documenting the change in mortality for Canada in a series of graphs.

3. René Dubos, *The Mirage of Health; Utopian Progress and Biological Change* (New York: Anchor Books, 1959), was the first to effectively expose the delusion of producing 'better health' as a dangerous and infectious medically sponsored disease. Thomas McKeown and Gordon McLachlan, eds., *Medical History and Medical Care; A Symposium of Perspectives* (New York: Oxford Univ. Press, 1971), introduce the sociology of medical pseudo-progress. John Powies, 'On the Limitations of Modern Medicine,' in *Science, Medicine and Man* (London: Pergamon, 1973), i: i-30, gives a critical selection of recent English-language literature on this subject. For the U.S. situation consult Rick Carlson, *The End of Medicine* (New York: Wiley Interscience, 1975). His essay is 'an empirically based brief, theoretical in nature.' For his indictment of American medicine he has chosen those dimensions for which he had complete evidence of a nature he could handle. Jean-Claude Polack, *La Médicine du capital* (Paris: Maspero, 1970). A critique of the political trends that seek to endow medical technology with an effective impact on health levels by a 'democratization of medical consumer products.' The author discovers that these products themselves are shaped by a repressive and alienating bourgeois class structure. To use medicine for political liberation it will be necessary to 'find in sickness, even when it is distorted by medical intervention, a protest against the existing social order.'

4. Daniel Greenberg, 'The "War on Cancer": Official Fiction and Harsh Facts,' *Science and Government Report*, vol. 4 (December 1, 1974). This well-researched report to the layman substantiates the view that American Cancer Society proclamations that cancer is curable and progress has been made are 'reminiscent of Vietnam optimism prior to the deluge.'

5. *Dorland's Illustrated Medical Dictionary*, 25th ed. (Philadelphia: Saunders, 1974): 'Iatrogenic (*iatro* – Gr. physician, *gennan* – Gr. to produce). Resulting from the activity of physicians. Originally applied to disorders induced in the patient by autosuggestion based on the physician's examination, manner, or discussion, the term is now applied to any adverse condition in a patient occurring as the result of treatment by a physician or surgeon.'

6. Heinrich Schipperges, *Utopien der Medizin: Geschichte und Kritik der ärtztlichen Ideologie des 19. Jh.* (Salzburg: Müller, 1966). A useful guide to the historical literature is Richard M. Burke, *An Historical Chronology of Tuberculosis*, 2nd ed. (Springfield, Ill.: Thomas, 1955).

7. For an analysis of the agents and patterns that determine the epidemic spread of modern misinformation throughout a scientific community, see Derek J. de Sofia Price, *Little Science, Big Science* (New York: Columbia Univ. Press, 1963).

8. On the clerical nature of medical practice, see 'Cléricalisme de la fonction médicale? Médecine et politique. Le "Sacerdoce" médical. La Relation thérapeutique. Psychanalyse et christianisme,' *Le Semeur*, suppl. 2 (1966–67).

9. J N. Weisfert, 'Das Problem des Schwindsuchtskranken in Drama und Roman,' *Deutscher Journalistenspiegel* 3 (1927): 579–82. A guide to tuberculosis as a literary motive in 19th-century drama and novel. E. Ebstein, 'Die Lungen-schwindsucht in der Weltliteratur,' *Zeitschrift für Bücherfreunde* 5 (1913).

10. René and Jean Dubos, *The White Plague: Tuberculosis, Man and Society* (Boston: Little, Brown, 1953). On the social, literary, and scientific aspects of 19th-century tuberculosis; an analysis of its incidence.

11. Charles E. Rosenberg, *The Cholera Years: The United States in 1832, 1849, and 1866* (Chicago: Univ. of Chicago Press, 1962). The New York epidemic of 1832 was a moral dilemma from which deliverance was sought in fasting and prayer. By the time of the epidemics of 1866, the culture that had produced New York slums had as well produced chloride of lime.

12. W. J. van Zijl, 'Studies on Diarrheal Disease in Seven Countries,' *Bulletin of the World Health Organization* 35 (1966): 249–61. Reduction in diarrheal diseases is brought about by a better water supply and sanitation, never by curative intervention.

13. R. R. Porter, *The Contribution of the Biological and Medical Sciences to Human Welfare*, Presidential Address to the British Association for the Advancement of Science, Swansea Meeting, 1971 (London: the Association, 1972), p. 95.

14. N. S. Scrimshaw, C. E. Taylor, and John E. Gordon, *Interactions of Nutrition and Infection* (Geneva: World Health Organization, 1968).

15. John Cassel, 'Physical Illness in Response to Stress,' Antología A7, mimeographed (Cuernavaca: CIDOC (Centro Intercultural de Documentación), 1971).

16. One of the clearest early statements on the paramount importance of the environment is J. P. Frank, *Akademische Rede vom Volkselend als der Mutter der Krankheiten* (Pavia, 1790; reprint ed., Leipzig: Barth, 1960). Thomas McKeown and R. G. Record, 'Reasons for the Decline in Mortality in England and Wales During the Nineteenth Century,' *Population Studies* 16 (1962): 94–122. Edwin Chadwick, *Report on the Sanitary Condition of the Labouring Population of Great Britain, 1842*, ed. M. W. Flinn (Chicago: Aldine, 1965), concluded a century and a half ago that 'the primary and most important measures and at the same time the most practical, and within the rec-ognized providence of public administration, are drainage, the removal of all refuse from habitations, streets, and roads, and the improvement of the supplies of water.' Max von Petterkofer, *The Value of Health to a City: Two Lectures Delivered in 1873*, trans. Henry E. Sigerist (Baltimore: Johns Hopkins, 1941), calculated a century ago the cost of health to the city of Munich in terms of average wages lost and medical costs created. Public services, especially better water and sewage disposal, he argued, would lower the death rate, morbidity, and absenteeism and this would pay for itself. Epidemiological research has entirely confirmed these humanistic convictions, Delpit-Morando, Radenac, and Vilain, *Disparités régionales en matière de santé*, Bulletin de Statistique du Ministère de la Santé et de la Sécurité Sociale No. 3, 1973; Warren Winkelstein, Jr., 'Epidemiological Considerations Underlying the Allocation of Health and Disease Care Resources,' *International Journal of Epidemiology* 1, no. 1 (1972): 69–74; F. Fagnani, *Santé, consommation médicale et environnement: Problèmes et méthodes* (Paris: Mouton, 1973).

17. L. Meyler, *Side Effects of Drugs* (Baltimore: Williams & Wilkins, 1972). *Adverse Reactions Titles*, a monthly bibliography of titles from approximately 3,400 biomedical journals published throughout the world; published in Amsterdam since 1966 *Allergy Information Bulletin*, Allergy Information Association, Weston, Ontario.

18. P. E. Sartwell, 'Iatrogenic Disease: An Epidemiological Perspective,' *International Journal of Health Services* 4 (winter 1974): 89–93.

19. Pharmaceutical Society of Great Britain, *Indentification of Drugs and Poisons* (London: the Society, 1965). Reports on drug adulteration and analysis. Margaret Kreig, *Black Market Medicine* (Englewood Cliffs, NJ: Prentice-Hall, 1967), reports

that an increasing percentage of articles sold by legitimate professional pharmacies are inert counterfeit drugs indistinguishable in packaging and presentation from the trademarked product.

20. Morton Mintz, *By Prescription only*, 2nd ed. (Boston: Beacon Press, 1967). Solomon Garb, *Undesirable Drug Interactions, 1974–75*, rev. ed. (New York: Springer, 1975). Includes information on inactivation, incompatibility, potentiation, and plasma binding, as well as on interference with elimination, digestion, and test procedures.

21. B. Opitz and H. Horn, 'Verhütung iatrogener Infektionen bei Schutzimpfungen,' *Deutsches Gesundheitswesen* 27/24 (1972): 1131–6. On infections associated with immunization procedures.

22. Harry N. Beaty and Robert G. Petersdorf, 'Iatrogenic Factors in Infectious Disease,' *Annals of Internal Medicine* 65 (October 1966): 641–56.

23. Every year a million people – that is, 3 to 5 percent of all hospital admissions – are admitted primarily because of a negative reaction to drugs. Nicholas Wade, 'Drug Regulation: FDA Replies to Charges by Economists and Industry,' *Science* 179 (1973): 775–7.

24. Eugene Vayda, 'A Comparison of Surgical Rates in Canada and in England and Wales,' *New England Journal of Medicine* 289 (1973): 1224–9, shows that surgical rates in Canada in 1968 were 1.8 times greater for men and 1.6 times greater for women than in England. Discretionary operations such as tonsillectomy and adenoidectomy, hemorrhoidectomy, and inguinal herniorrhaphy were two or more times higher. Cholecystectomy rates were more than five times greater. The main determinants may be differences in payment of health services and available hospital beds and surgeons. Charles B. Lewis, 'Variations in the Incidence of Surgery,' *New England Journal of Medicine* 281 (1969): 880–4, finds three- to fourfold variations in regional rates for six common surgical procedures in the U.S.A. The number of surgeons available was found to be the significant predictor in the incidence of surgery. See also James C. Doyle, 'Unnecessary Hysterectomies: Study of 6,248 Operations in Thirty-five Hospitals During 1948,' *Journal of the American Medical Association* 151 (1953): 360–5. James C. Doyle, 'Unnecessary Ovariectomies: Study Based on the Removal of 704 Normal Ovaries from 546 Patients,' *Journal of the American Medical Association* 148 (1952): 1105–11. Thomas H. Weller, 'Pediatric Perceptions: The Pediatrician and Iatric Infectious Disease,' *Pediatrics* 51 (April 1973): 595–602.

25. Clifton Meador, 'The Art and Science of Nondisease,' *New England Journal of Medicine* 272 (1965): 92–5. For the physician accustomed to dealing only with pathologic entities, terms such as 'nondisease entity' or 'nondisease' are foreign and difficult to comprehend. This paper presents, with tongue in check, a classification of nondisease and the important therapeutic principles based on this concept. Iatrogenic disease probably arises as often from treatment of nondisease as from treatment of disease.

26. Abraham B. Bergman and Stanley J. Stamm, 'The Morbidity of Cardiac Nondisease in School Children,' *New England Journal of Medicine* 276 (1967): 1008–13. Gives one particular example from the 'limbo where people either perceive themselves or are perceived by others to have a nonexistent disease. The ill effects accompanying some nondiseases are as extreme as those accompanying their counterpart diseases ... the amount of disability from cardiac nondisease in children is estimated to be greater than that due to actual heart disease.' See also J. Andrioia, 'A Note on Possible Iatrogenesis of Suicide,' *Psychiatry* 36 (1973): 213–18.

27. Clinical iatrogenesis has a long history. Plinius Secundus, *Naturalis Historta* 29.19: 'To protect us against doctors there is no law against ignorance, no example of capital punishment. Doctors learn at our risk, they experiment and kill with sovereign impunity, in fact the doctor is the only one who may kill. They go further and make the patient responsible: they blame him who has succumbed.' In fact, Roman law already contained some provisions against medically inflicted torts, 'damnum injuria datum per medicum.' Jurisprudence in Rome made the doctor legally accountable not only for ignorance and recklessness but for bumbling. A doctor who operated on a slave but did not properly follow up his convalescence had to pay the price of the slave and the loss of the master's income during his protracted sickness. Citizens were not covered by these statutes, but could avenge malpractice on their own initiative.

28. Montesquieu, *De l'esprit des lois*, bk. 29, chap. 14, b (Paris: Pléiade, 1951). The Roman laws ordained that physicians should be punished for neglect or lack of skill (the Cornelian laws, *De Sicariis*, inst. iv. tit. 3, de lege Aquila 7). If the physician was a person of any fortune or rank, he was only condemned to deportation, but if he was of low condition he was put to death. In our institutions it is otherwise. The Roman laws were not made under the same circumstances as ours: in Rome every ignorant pretender meddled with physic, but our physicians are obliged to go through a regular course of study and to take degrees, for which reason they are supposed to understand their profession. In this passage the 17th-century philosopher demonstrates an entirely modern optimism about medical education.

29. For German internists, the time the patient can spend face-to-face with his doctor has now been reduced to 1.7 minutes per visit. Heinrich Erdmann, Heinz-Günther Over-rath, and Wolfgang and Thure Uxkull, 'Organisationsprobleme der ärztlichen Krankenversorgung: Dargestellt am Beispiel einer medizinischen Universitätsklinik,' *Deutsches Arzteblatt-Ärztliche Mitteilungen* 71 (1974): 3421–6. In general practice, this time was (in 1963) about 3 minutes. See T. Geyer, *Verschwörung* (Hilchenbach: Medizinpolitischer Verlag, 1971), p. 30.

30. For the broader issue of genetic rather than individual damage, see John W. Goffman and Arthur R. Tamplin, 'Epidemiological Studies of Carcinogenesis by Ionizing Radiation,' in *Proceedings of the Sixth Berkeley Symposium on Mathematical Statistics and Probability*, Univ. of California, July 1970, pp. 235–77. The presumption is all too common that where uncertainty exists about the magnitude of carcinogenic effects, it is appropriate to continue the exposure of humans to the risk. The authors show that it is neither appropriate nor good public-health practice to demand human epidemiological evidence before stopping exposure. The argument against ionizing radiation from nuclear generation of electrical energy can be applied to all medical treatment in which there is uncertainty about genetic impact. The competence of physicians to establish levels of tolerance for entire populations must be questioned on theoretical grounds.

31. The distinction of several levels of iatrogenesis was made by Ralph Audy, 'Man-made Maladies and Medicine,' *California Medicine*, November 1970, pp. 48–53. He recognizes that iatrogenic 'diseases' are only one type of man-made malady. According to their etiology, they fall into several categories: those resulting from diagnosis and treatment, those relating to social and psychological attitudes and situations, and those resulting from man-made programs for the control and eradication of disease. Besides iatrogenic clinical entities, he recognizes other maladies that have a medical etiology.

32. 'Das Schicksal des Kranken verkörpert als Symbol das Schicksal der Menschheit im Stadium einer technischen Weltentwicklung': Wolfgang Jacob, *Der kranke Mensch in der technischen Welt*, IX. Internationaler Fortbildungskurs für praktische und wissenschaftliche Pharmazie der Bundesapothekerkammer in Meran (Frankfurt am Main: Werbe- und Vertriebsgesellschaft Deutscher Apotheker, 1971).

33. James B. Quinn, 'Next Big Industry: Environmental Improvement,' *Harvard Business Review* 49 (September–October 1971): 120–30. He believes that environmental improvement is becoming a dynamic and profitable series of markets for industry that pay for themselves and in the end will represent an important addition to income and GNP. Implicitly the same argument is being made for the health-care field by the proponents of no-fault malpractice insurance.

34. The term was used by Honoré Daumier (1810–79). See reproduction of his drawing 'Némésis médicale' in Werner Block, *Der Artzt und der Tod in Bildern aus sechs Jahrhunderten* (Stuttgart: Enke, 1966).

43. Sociology and the Body

Chris Shilling

Sociology has rarely focused on the embodied human as an object of importance in its own right. As bodies were commonly regarded as both natural and individual possessions which lay outside of the legitimate social concerns of the discipline this should come as no 'great surprise.' It was only when sociology began to question the divide between nature and society that theorists conceptualized the body as central both to the human actor and to the sociological enterprise. However, it is also possible to argue that the body has been present at the very heart of the sociological imagination.

Like the human heart, the body in sociology tended to remain hidden from view, yet at the same time it served ultimately to keep alive and nourish that which surrounded it. In being concerned with human societies sociology was inevitably concerned, if only implicitly, with the ways in which embodied subjects externalized, objectified and internalized social institutions (Berger, 1990 [1967]). Although the physical, fleshy body was rarely an object of explicit sociological concern, facets of human embodiment, such as language and consciousness, became central to the development of the discipline. Furthermore, the efforts of contemporary sociologists to address and overcome the dual status of the body in social theory, have now led to a growing collection of work concerned with putting the body back into sociology.

None of this is to argue that classical sociology accomplished anything like an adequate conceptualization of the body, or that sociology has reached that stage in the late twentieth century.

Rather, the relative neglect of the body has continued to prove limiting for a discipline seldom able to acknowledge explicitly the fact that humans have bodies which allow them not only to see, listen and think, but to feel (physically and emotionally), smell and act. In this chapter I want to describe in more detail the dual status of the body in sociology, and trace the rise of the body as an object of study.

The dual status of the body in sociology is illustrated by the briefest of glances at some of the core areas of the discipline. The study of social mobility, of racism, the formation of the 'underclass', social inequalities in health and schooling, and globalization, are all concerned implicitly with the movement, location, care and education of bodies. In different ways, all these areas of study are interested in how and why the social opportunities and life expectancies of people are shaped by the classification and treatment of their bodies as belonging to a particular 'race', sex, class or nationality. In the study of health and illness, for example, inequalities in morbidity and mortality rates have prompted sociologists to ask what it is about the social existence of people that affects their bodies in such dramatic ways. Clearly bodies matter, and they matter enough to form the 'hidden' base of many sociological studies.

[. . .]

Our experience of life is inevitably mediated through our bodies. As Goffman has clearly demonstrated, our very ability to intervene in social life – to make a difference to the flow of daily affairs – is dependent on the management of our bodies through time and space. To put it another way, we have bodies and we act with our bodies. Our daily experiences of living – be they derived from learning in schools, travelling to a place of employment, working in an office, buying and preparing food for a meal, or making love with a partner – are inextricably bound up with experiencing and managing our own and other people's bodies. The birth and death of bodies represent start and end points in human existence, and from the cradle to the crematorium individuals depend upon the multiple caring and interdependent relationships which exist between bodies. The embodiment of humans is central to the intricate techniques involved in the formation and maintenance of families and friendships (Allan, 1989), and societies depend for their very existence on the reproduction of existing and new bodies.

Bodies, then, have occupied a place in the sociological imagination as our experience and management of them form part of the general material out of which social life and social theory is forged. Our experiences of embodiment provide a basis for theorizing social commonality, social inequalities and the construction of difference. We all have bodies and this constitutes part of what makes us human beings possessed of the ability to communicate with each other, and experience common needs, desires, satisfactions and frustrations (Doyal and Gough, 1991).

While human embodiment provides at least the potential for communication and shared experiences, however, bodies are inhabited and treated differently both within and between social systems. As Marcel Mauss pointed out in 1934, cultures have specific 'techniques of the body' which provide their members with identities, govern infancy and adolescence and old age, and inform such activities as resting, talking and walking (1973 [1934]). Furthermore, as the work of Norbert Elias demonstrates, bodily differences vary historically as well as cross-culturally. For example, in the Western world our sensitivity to bodily waste has increased enormously in recent centuries, as has the tendency to perceive the surface of our bodies as an immovable barrier between ourselves and the outside world (Corbin, 1986; Elias, 1978). Bodies also vary on an individual basis. We all have bodies but we are not all able to see, hear, feel, speak and move about independently. Having a body is constraining as well as enabling, and people who are old or disabled often feel more constrained by their bodies than do those who are young and able bodied (Campling, 1981). This point about individual bodies is linked to the more general condition that in addition to the possibilities of agency that exist by virtue of us *having* bodies, we are also constrained by the brute fact of *being* bodies. They constitute a condition which both provides us with life and ensures our ultimate death (Berger and Luckmann, 1967).

The body, then, is present in, as well as absent from, sociology. It is present in that the very subject matter of sociology is embodied and shaped by the opportunities and constraints that follow from having and being a body. While sociology may rarely focus explicitly on the body, it does examine aspects of embodiment and the consequences of embodiment. The sociology of health and illness, for example, is concerned with evaluations which are ultimately related to the consequences of human embodiment (Turner, 1987, 1992a). This is also the case with those studies that have at their centre an interest in consciousness, knowledge and ideology (e.g. Mannheim, 1991). The location of consciousness in the body, and the relationship between ideology, knowledge and the body, is rarely explored (Lakoff, 1987). However, this does not negate the fact that sociological studies are inevitably related, if only implicitly, to certain dimensions of human embodiment.

[. . .]

Why was it that the body emerged as a phenomenon considered worthy of detailed study in its own right in the late twentieth century? The answer to this question involves examining some of the social and academic changes which have had the effect of highlighting the importance of the body in society during this time.

[...]

More specifically, the social and academic changes which have formed the context for the current concern with the body involve the rise of 'second wave' feminism; demographic changes which have focused attention on the needs of the elderly in Western societies; the rise of consumer culture linked to the changing structure of modern capitalism; and the previously mentioned 'crisis' in our certainty about what bodies are.

First, the rise of 'second wave' feminism in the 1960s and its subsequent development placed on the political agenda issues related to the control of fertility and abortion rights. They also formed the context for a more general project among women to 'reclaim' their bodies from male control and abuse. As Gill Kirkup and Laurie Smith Keller (1992) note, self-help groups were important parts of the women's movement in this respect, and they incorporated attempts to further women's knowledge and control over their bodies (e.g. Boston Women's Health Collective, 1971). This is linked to a strong tradition in which women have placed their bodies at risk during political struggles, for example, in the suffragette and nuclear peace movements. Such methods of protest, though not entirely novel, have also been drawn on by new social movements; members of Greenpeace, for example, have put themselves at considerable physical risk in order to increase public awareness of the bodily dangers of pollution.

As well as using the body as a vehicle of political action and protest, feminist analyses of women's oppression brought the body into academic conceptualizations of patriarchy. [...]

In addition to the appearance of the body in general discussions of patriarchy, feminists also undertook more specific studies of the commodification of women's bodies in pornography, prostitution and surrogate motherhood (Singer, 1989). They have also done much to highlight both the differential socialization to which girls'

and boys' bodies are subject (Lees, 1984), and the male-orientated knowledge which has informed the development of the medical services and the treatment of women's bodies during pregnancy and childbirth (Greer, 1971; Martin (1989 [1987]); Miles, 1991; Oakley, 1984). Debates about the role of reproduction and housework in the economy also highlighted the position of women as the prime servicers of men's and children's bodies (Oakley, 1974). For example, Nickie Charles and Marion Kerr (1988) suggested that wives are materially and symbolically responsible for the family's main meal of the day, and explored how these women sacrificed their own bodily needs for rest, recreation and nutrition to ensure their children and husbands were adequately fed and cared for during illness (see also David, 1980; Murcott, 1983).

In sum, feminist work highlighted the fact that women frequently have to learn to live with what can be termed 'over burdened bodies'.

[...]

If the rise of feminism was the first factor to highlight the importance of the body, the second factor concerns the growth in the number of aged in Western societies. This has become a matter of international concern largely because of the economic implications of this demographic trend. Increasing elderly populations have serious implications for social policy and state expenditure in the areas of pensions, medical provision, caring services and accommodation (Turner, 1991). An increased focus on human bodies has come about both as a cause and a consequence of these changes. Medical advances have helped create much greater life expectancy rates in comparison with the last century. At the same time, the medical services have been faced with more problems concerning the health and well-being of the elderly. In a very real sense, they have become victims of their own success. This situation has been made more visible with the rise to power of governments in both the United States and the UK during the 1970s and 1980s that were influenced by the ideas of the 'new right' and were concerned not to increase but to reduce public expenditure commitments.

A related, if less important, reason for the rising academic concern with the body can be seen in the ageing of the sociology profession. While in the early 1980s the life experiences and reflexivity of sociologists fed into a growing interest in the sociology of ageing, this developed into a more general concern with the sociology of the body and how social definitions of bodies have entered into general conceptions of 'youth' and 'aged' which have attached to them different symbolic values. The young, slim and sexual body is highly prized in contemporary consumer culture, whereas ageing bodies tend to be sequestrated from public attention (we rarely, for example, see them engaged in sexual activities in movies).

The third factor which has increased the focus on the body in contemporary society concerns a shift in the structure of advanced capitalist societies in the second half of the twentieth century. Broadly speaking, there has been a shift in emphasis from a focus on hard work in the sphere of production coupled with frugality and denial in the sphere of consumption. Instead, the decline of competitive capitalism based on a labour force inclined to save and invest, the historical shortening of the working week, and the proliferation of production orientated towards leisure, encourages the modern individual to work hard at *consuming* as well as producing goods and services. Related to this, the body in consumer culture has become increasingly central and has helped promote the 'performing self' which treats the body as a machine to be finely tuned, cared for, reconstructed and carefully presented through such measures as regular physical exercise, personal health programmes, high-fibre diets and colour-coded dressing. As Featherstone (1982: 22) argues, within consumer culture the body ceases to be a vessel of sin and presents itself instead as an object for display both inside and outside of the bedroom.

[. . .]

The fourth factor behind the rise of interest in the body is concerned with the tendency mentioned in the introduction for an increase in the potential to control our bodies to be accompanied by a crisis in their meaning. In discussing the increased control that modernity exerted over the body, Turner (1992b) has pointed out that diet was central to the early rationalization of the body. Whereas early dietary schemes were connected to religious values, the nineteenth century saw an increasing scientific literature of diet emerge with the establishment of nutritional sciences. These knowledges were first applied in the realm of social policy to measure the food required by various populations such as prisoners and army recruits, and were applied by the social reformers Charles Booth and Seebohm Rowntree as measurements of poverty levels in the larger British cities. Furthermore, the rationalization of the body was intimately connected to the 'sciences of man' which sought in such places as prisons, armies and workplaces to 're-educate the mind via the discipline and organization of bodies in a regime that sought to maximize efficiency and surveillance' (Turner, 1992b: 123, 126).

Our ability to control the body has continued apace as a result of advances in transplant surgery, artificial insemination, in vitro fertilization and plastic surgery. As John O'Neill (1985) demonstrates, there are now few parts of our body which technology cannot restructure in some way or other. Hair implants can rid the appearance of baldness, false teeth are common and there are a growing number of organs that can be transplanted into the human body. Heart transplant surgery is no longer newsworthy (unless carried out on very young children and even here much of the newsworthiness concerns the ability of science to intervene in the infant body) and eye transplants can restore the ability to see. Pacemakers allow people with defective hearts to function normally, various parts of the body can be restructured using artificial materials, and increasingly sophisticated artificial limbs have become available in recent years.

[. . .]

Horror films provide another example of instabilities in the meaning and boundaries of the body. Here, the threat to the body used to come from an exterior source, whereas it now frequently comes from the interior of the body as a result of its inherent instability. The dominant trend in the 1950s and 1960s was to portray victims as vulnerable to attack from external foes such as aliens from outer space. In the 1970s, though, the body was under threat from demonic *possession*, as in the case of *The Exorcist*. The *Alien* trilogy had both John Hurt and Sigourney Weaver 'giving birth' to monsters, and the threat to the body's interior stability continued to grow in the 1980s with the *Nightmare on Elm Street* series. The ghastly 'Freddy' would emerge from deep within the recesses of the mind, while his victims were dreaming, to mutilate and destroy the powerless body. The *Terminator* films have continued to reflect the instability of what bodies are, with machines becoming increasingly human and humans becoming increasingly machine-like.

An additional manifestation of this crisis in our knowledge of bodies can be found in the difficulties sociologists have had in pinning down precisely what is meant by the body. As Bryan Turner says in his 1984 text, 'In writing this study of the body, I have become increasingly less sure of what the body is' (Turner, 1984: 7).

REFERENCES

Allan, G. (1989) *Friendship, Developing a Sociological Perspective*. New York: Harvester Wheatsheaf.

Berger, P. (1990 [1967]) *The Sacred Canopy. Elements of a Sociological Theory of Religion*. New York: Anchor Books.

Berger, P. and Luckmann, T. (1967) *The Social Construction of Reality*. London: Penguin.

Boston Women's Health Collective (1971) *Our Bodies, Our Selves*. New York: Simon and Schuster.

Campling, J. (ed.) (1981) *Images of Ourselves. Women with Disabilities Talking*. London: RKP.

Charles, N. and Kerr, M. (1988) *Women, Food and Families*. Manchester: Manchester University Press.

Corbin, A. (1986) *The Foul and the Fragrant, Odor and the French Social Imagination*. Cambridge, Mass: Harvard University Press.

David, M. (1980) *The State, the Family and Education*. London: RKP.

Doyal, L. and Gough, I. (1991) *A Theory of Human Need*. Houndmills: Macmillan.

Elias, N. (1978) 'The civilizing process revisited', *Theory and Society*, 5: 243–53.

Featherstone, M. (1982) 'The body in consumer culture', *Theory, Culture and Society*, 1: 18–33.

Greer, G. (1971) *The Female Eunuch*. London: Paladin.

Kirkup, G. and Keller, L. S. (1992) *Inventing Women: Science, Technology and Gender*. Cambridge: Polity Press.

Lakoff, G. (1987) *Women, Fire and Dangerous Things*. Chicago: University of Chicago Press.

Lees, S. (1984) *Losing Out. Sexuality and Adolescent Girls*. London: Hutchinson.

Mannheim, K. (1991) *Ideology and Utopia*. London: Routledge.

Martin, E. (1989 [1987]) *The Woman in the Body*. Milton Keynes: Open University Press.

Mauss, M. (1973 [1934]) 'Techniques of the body', *Economy and Society*, 2: 70–88.

Miles, A. (1991) *Women, Health and Medicine*. Milton Keynes: Open University Press.

Murcott, A. (1983) ' "It's a pleasure to cook for him": Food, mealtimes and gender in some South Wales households', in E. Gamarnikow et al. (eds), *The Public and the Private*. London: Heinemann.

Oakley, A. (1974) *The Sociology of Housework*. London: Martin Robertson.

Oakley, A. (1984) *The Captured Womb: A History of the Medical Care of Pregnant Women*. Oxford: Basil Blackwell.

O'Neill. J. (1985) *Five Bodies: The Human Shape of Modern Society*. Ithaca, NY: Cornell University Press.

Singer, L. (1989) 'Bodies, pleasures, powers', *Differences*, 1: 45–65.

Turner, B. S. (1984) *The Body and Society*. Oxford: Basil Blackwell.

Turner, B. S. (1987) *Medical Power and Social Knowledge*. London: Sage.

Turner, B. S. (1991) 'Recent developments in the theory of the body', in M. Featherstone, M. Hepworth and B. Turner (eds), *The Body: Social Process and Cultural Theory*. London: Sage.

Turner, B. S. (1992a) *Regulating Bodies: Essays in Medical Sociology*. London: Routledge.

Turner, B. S. (1992b) *Max Weber: From History to Modernity*. London: Routledge.

Theme 8 – Further Reading

There are many books covering health and illness, so these selections are the tip of an iceberg. Mildred Blaxter's (2010) *Health* (Cambridge: Polity) is an extremely well-written introduction to the field. Sarah Nettleton's (2013) *The Sociology of Health and Illness*, 3rd edition (Cambridge: Polity) is comprehensive and up to date. And Graham Scambler's (2008) *Sociology as Applied to Medicine* (London: Saunders Elsevier) is written ostensibly for medical students and the health professions, which gives it a somewhat different feel, but it is none the worse for it and is very accessible to sociology students. Then, for a reliable introduction to studies of the body, Alexandra Howson's (2012) *The Body in Society: An Introduction*, 2nd edition (Cambridge: Polity) does a very good job.

Giddens and Sutton *Sociology 7th Edition* (2013)

This section's readings take us back to Chapter 11. However, there is a fair amount of material on health and/or the body in Chapter 8 on body language, pages 303–17; Chapter 9 on the ageing body, pages 356–64 and 370–4; Chapter 14 on unequal life and health chances, pages 581–4 and Chapter 15 on gender and biology, pages 633–43.

Part 9 Crime and Deviance

The study of crime is currently one of the fastest growing subjects with many new university level courses and departments being created. A look at the sheer extent of crime and crime-related media output (both fictional and documentary), particularly in television and film, demonstrates how much interest there is in crime and criminality in society. However, in contrast to the individualization of criminality that makes up the bulk of media representations and crime reporting, sociologists are also interested in broad patterns of crime and victimization. For sociologists, crime is just a smaller subset of the more general category of deviance. While deviance may be defined as non-conformity to generally accepted rules and norms, crime only refers to behaviour that breaks society's laws. Hence, there is something of a difference between criminology, which focuses on crime and the sociology of crime and deviance.

In our first reading in this section (Reading 44), taken from Emile Durkheim's *Rules of Sociological Method* (originally 1895), the basic argument remains strikingly different from contemporary commonsense ideas and political debates. Durkheim argues that in every known society there is deviance and crime and in that sense, these are 'normal' social phenomena. But acknowledging this fact does not mean we should simply accept existing levels. Functionalist analysis suggests that crime performs useful functions for society as a whole. In dealing with it, 'crime

brings together honest men and concentrates them', thus paradoxically, crime acts as a reminder to all of society's moral and legal rules, which have been broken. In this way, crime is functional for society as it strengthens rather than weakens social solidarity. However, for Durkheim, the *level of crime* is a crucial factor. If crime levels are too high, then its negative consequences may outweigh the positive benefits and measures will have to be taken to bring crime down. The problem of course is how to measure accurately phenomena as complex and difficult to pin down as crime and deviance.

Initially working in the Durkheimian functionalist tradition, later sociologists modified and adapted his ideas to bring much-needed empirical research to bear on the crime problem. Making use of criminal statistics, which hold out the promise of providing an accurate picture of crime levels across whole societies, Robert Merton tackled a longstanding question – why are the majority of crimes apparently committed by working-class people, especially men? In Reading 45, Merton connects the cultural goals promoted by America's materialistic economy to the distribution of life chances in society and the adaptive responses of individuals to their situation. The ideology of the 'American Dream' promotes education and hard work as the keys to material success in a meritocratic society. However, Merton argues that America is an unequal society where some social groups and classes have more opportunities than others to succeed by legitimate means. When sections of the manual or 'lower' working classes (as Merton put it) realize that they cannot achieve material success by legitimate means, some turn to acquisitive crime as an adaptation to the structural position they find themselves in. Merton's work is an early example of relative deprivation theory and it provides an effective way into the study of crime patterns. It also helps to explain why the working classes make up the majority in prison populations.

Today the widespread use of prison sentences for a very diverse array of offences is generally accepted. Indeed, in opinion surveys many people say they would like to see prison used even more widely. But the modern prison can only be traced back to the early nineteenth century. In the period preceding this, offenders faced, by modern standards, extremely harsh and cruel punishments. Beatings, floggings, torture and gruesome death penalties were demanded by judicial order. Such physical punishments have been largely abandoned in the developed countries in favour of imposing periods of loss of liberty and more recently a range of community penalties. Why did this change occur? Have we just become more civilized and less likely to approve of torture, even for the most serious of crimes?

In Reading 46 we introduce the influential ideas of French social philosopher and historian Michel Foucault. The reading is from the introduction to his 1975 book, *Discipline and Punish*, in which Foucault traces the shift from one penal regime to the other. Using a graphic eyewitness account of the torture and killing of a man found guilty of attempting to murder the monarch in 1757, Foucault contrasts this with the strict timetable of an early prison regime in which every minute of the prisoner's day is laid out. The striking thing about this comparison is that the two punishments are just a few decades apart. In that time the old regime all but died away

and the new one was installed. Foucault looks at how this happened. The controversial aspect of Foucault's account is that he does not accept that the new prison regime was definitively 'better' or 'more civilized' than the old one. Instead, he suggests that, for a variety of reasons, the old regime of public punishments had become ineffective and a more efficient form was necessary. In this way, Foucault's provocative interpretation makes us think much harder about what 'civilization' and 'civilized conduct' actually means.

In recent years, the routine use of prison as the main method of punishment has been called into question. Recidivism rates remain consistently high, prison suicides have been a cause for concern and many have come to see prison regimes as an obstacle to the rehabilitation of offenders in advance of their reintroduction into society. But if not prison, then what? In Reading 47, John Braithwaite argues the case for restorative justice as an alternative, a model that has been used among Maori communities in New Zealand for some time. Restorative justice, as the name suggests, aims to restore the community to the situation which existed before the crime was committed by forcing offenders to appreciate the harmful consequences of their actions. To do this, offenders are brought into contact with victims in community settings rather than impersonal courtrooms that are distanced from the site of their offences. Rather than removing offenders from their communities, restorative justice demands that they become more involved in them in order to rebuild social relations. Advocates of restorative justice claim that it is not a 'soft' alternative to prison, but is a more challenging and difficult approach that avoids creating 'schools of crime' in prison settings. Thinking back to Foucault's historical work, could it be argued that the prison regime itself has now become quite ineffective, as did physical punishments at the end of the eighteenth century, and another alternative is now needed?

The final reading is a bold attempt to map the most recent types of crime, namely those that make use of information technologies. The generic name for such crime is cybercrime, though this is a rather vague and probably overly broad definition. For example, many older crimes such as financial fraud, make use of new technology to achieve their aim, but are they really cybercrimes? In Reading 48, David Wall constructs a typology of cybercrimes using examples to illustrate each type, in order to differentiate those new crimes that could not have been committed without networked information technology. First-generation cybercrimes are those involving computers in some way, second-generation cybercrime consists of hackers who are able to find ways into computer networks. However, third-generation or 'true' cybercrimes involve 'botnets' which are used to remotely administer a computer user's machine in order to commit crimes. One notable aspect of cybercrime is its global reach. Because they are based within computer networks, cybercrimes can be committed over vast distances and extremely quickly. Wall argues that cyber crimewaves are 'now measured in hours and minutes rather than months and years', and one aim of his analysis is to understand them better so that their regulation and prevention can be made more effective.

44. The Normality of Deviance

Emile Durkheim

If there is any fact whose pathological character appears incontestable, that fact is crime. All criminologists are agreed on this point. Although they explain this pathology differently, they are unanimous in recognizing it. But let us see if this problem does not demand a more extended consideration.

We shall apply the foregoing rules. Crime is present not only in the majority of societies of one particular species but in all societies of all types. There is no society that is not confronted with the problem of criminality. Its form changes; the acts thus characterized are not the same everywhere; but, everywhere and always, there have been men who have behaved in such a way as to draw upon themselves penal repression. If, in proportion as societies pass from the lower to the higher types, the rate of criminality, i.e., the relation between the yearly number of crimes and the population, tended to decline, it might be believed that crime, while still normal, is tending to lose this character of normality. But we have no reason to believe that such a regression is substantiated. Many facts would seem rather to indicate a movement in the opposite direction. From the beginning of the [nineteenth] century, statistics enable us to follow the course of criminality. It has everywhere increased. In France the increase is nearly 300 per cent. There is, then, no phenomenon that presents more indisputably all the symptoms of normality, since it appears closely connected with the conditions of all collective life. To make crime a social illness would be to concede that sickness is not something accidental, but on the contrary derives in certain cases from the fundamental constitution of the living creature. This would be to erase any distinction between the physiological and the pathological. No doubt it is possible that crime itself will have abnormal forms, as, for example, when its rate is unusually high. This excess is, indeed, undoubtedly morbid in nature. What is normal, simply, is the existence of criminality, provided that it attains and does not exceed, for each social type, a certain level, which it is perhaps not impossible to fix in conformity with the preceding rules.

Here we are, then, in the presence of a conclusion in appearance quite pathological. Let us make no mistake. To classify crime among the phenomena of normal sociology is not to say merely that it is an inevitable, although regrettable phenomenon due to the incorrigible wickedness of men; it is to affirm that it is a factor in public health, an integral part of all healthy societies. This result is, at first glance, surprising enough to have puzzled even ourselves for a long time. Once this first surprise has been overcome, however, it is not difficult to find reasons explaining this normality and at the same time confirming it.

In the first place crime is normal because a society exempt from it is utterly impossible. Crime, we have shown elsewhere, consists of an act that offends certain very strong collective sentiments. In a society in which criminal acts are no longer committed, the sentiments they offend would have to be found without exception in all individual consciousness, and they must be found to exist with the same degree as sentiments contrary to them. Assuming that this condition could actually be realized, crime would not thereby disappear; it would only change its form, for the very cause which would thus dry up the sources of criminality would immediately open up new ones.

Imagine a society of saints, a perfect cloister of exemplary individuals. Crimes, properly so called, will there be unknown, but faults which appear venial to the layman will create there the same scandal that the ordinary offense does in ordinary consciousness. If, then, this society has the power to judge and punish, it will define these acts as criminal and will treat them as such. For the same reason, the perfect and upright man judges his smaller failings with a severity that the majority reserve for acts more truly in the nature of an offense. Formerly, acts of violence against persons were more frequent than they are today, because respect for individual dignity was less strong. As this has increased, these crimes have become more rare; and also, many acts violating this sentiment have been introduced into the penal law which were not included there in primitive times.

In order to exhaust all the hypotheses logically possible, it will perhaps be asked why this unanimity does not extend to all collective sentiments without exception. Why should not even the most feeble sentiment gather enough energy to prevent all dissent? The moral consciousness of the society would be present in its entirety in all the individuals, with a vitality sufficient to prevent all acts offending it – the purely conventional faults as well as the crimes. But a uniformity so universal and absolute is utterly impossible; for the immediate physical milieu in which each one of us is placed, the hereditary antecedents, and the social influences vary from one individual to the next, and consequently diversify consciousness. It is impossible for all to be alike, if only because each one has his own organism and that these organisms occupy different areas in space. That is why even among the lower peoples, where individual originality is very little developed, it nevertheless does exist.

Thus, since there cannot be a society in which the individuals do not differ more or less from the collective type, it is also inevitable that, among these divergences, there are some with a criminal character. What confers this character upon them is not the intrinsic quality of a given act but that definition which the collective conscience lends them. If the collective conscience is stronger, if it has enough authority practically to suppress these divergences, it will also be more sensitive, more exacting, and, reacting against the slightest deviations with the energy it otherwise displays only against more considerable infractions, it will attribute to them the same gravity as formerly to crimes. In other words, it will designate them as criminal.

Crime is, then, necessary; it is bound up with the fundamental conditions of all social life and by that very fact it is useful, because these conditions of which it is a part are themselves indispensable to the normal evolution of morality and law.

45. Crime as Deviant Adaptation

Robert Merton

Contemporary American culture appears to approximate the polar type in which great emphasis upon certain success-goals occurs without equivalent emphasis upon institutional means. It would of course be fanciful to assert that accumulated wealth stands alone as a symbol of success just as it would be fanciful to deny that Americans assign it a place high in their scale of values. In some large measure, money has been consecrated as a value in itself, over and above its expenditure for articles of consumption or its use for the enhancement of power. 'Money' is peculiarly well adapted to become a symbol of prestige. As Simmel emphasized, money is highly abstract and impersonal. However acquired, fraudulently or institutionally, it can be used to purchase the same goods and services. The anonymity of an urban society, in conjunction with these peculiarities of money, permits wealth, the sources of which may be unknown to the community in which the plutocrat lives or, if known, to become purified in the course of time, to serve as a symbol of high status. Moreover, in the American Dream there is no final stopping point. The measure of 'monetary success' is conveniently indefinite and relative. At each income level, as H. F. Clark found, Americans want just about twenty-five per cent more (but of course this 'just a bit more' continues to operate once it is obtained). In this flux of shifting standards, there is no stable resting point, or rather, it is the point which manages always to be 'just ahead.' An observer of a community in which annual salaries in six figures are not uncommon reports the anguished words of one victim of the American Dream: 'In this town, I'm snubbed socially because I only get a thousand a week. That hurts.'[1]

To say that the goal of monetary success is entrenched in American culture is only to say that Americans are bombarded on every side by precepts which affirm the right or, often, the duty of retaining the goal even in the face of repeated frustration. Prestigeful representatives of the society reinforce the cultural emphasis. The family, the school and the workplace – the major agencies shaping the personality structure and goal formation of Americans – join to provide the intensive disciplining required if an individual is to retain intact a goal that remains elusively beyond reach, if he is to be motivated by the promise of a gratification which is not redeemed. As we shall presently see, parents serve as a transmission belt for the values and goals of the groups of which they are a part – above all, of their social class or of the class with which they identify themselves. And the schools are of course the official agency for the passing on of the prevailing values, with a large proportion of the textbooks used in city schools implying or stating explicitly 'that education leads to intelligence and consequently to job and money success.'[2]

[. . .]

Coupled with this positive emphasis upon the obligation to maintain lofty goals is a correlative emphasis upon the penalizing of those who draw in their ambitions. Americans are admonished 'not to be a quitter' for in the dictionary of American culture, as in the lexicon of youth, 'there is no such word as "fail".' The cultural manifesto is clear: one must not quit, must not cease striving, must not lessen his goals, for 'not failure, but low aim, is crime'.

Thus the culture enjoins the acceptance of three cultural axioms: first, all should strive for the same lofty goals since these are open to all; second, present seeming failure is but a way-station to ultimate success; and third, genuine failure consists only in the lessening or withdrawal of ambition.

[...]

It is in these terms and through these processes that contemporary American culture continues to be characterized by a heavy emphasis on wealth as a basic symbol of success, without a corresponding emphasis upon the legitimate avenues on which to march toward this goal. How do individuals living in this cultural context respond? And how do our observations bear upon the doctrine that deviant behavior typically derives from biological impulses breaking through the restraints imposed by culture? What, in short, are the consequences for the behavior of people variously situated in a social structure of a culture in which the emphasis on dominant success-goals has become increasingly separated from an equivalent emphasis on institutionalized procedures for seeking these goals?

[...]

We here consider five types of adaptation, as these are schematically set out in the following table, where (+) signifies 'acceptance,' (−) signifies 'rejection,' and (±) signifies 'rejection of prevailing values and substitution of new values'.

A typology of modes of individual adaptation[3]

Modes of Adaptation	Culture Goals	Institutionalized Means
I. Conformity	+	+
II. Innovation	+	−
III. Ritualism	−	+
IV. Retreatism	−	−
V. Rebellion[4]	±	±

Examination of how the social structure operates to exert pressure upon individuals for one or another of these alternative modes of behavior must be prefaced by the observation that people may shift from one alternative to another as they engage in different spheres of social activities. These categories refer to role behavior in specific types of situations, not to personality. They are types of more or less enduring response, not types of personality organization.

[...]

Innovation

Great cultural emphasis upon the success-goal invites this mode of adaptation through the use of institutionally proscribed but often effective means of attaining at least the simulacrum of success – wealth and power. This response occurs when the individual has assimilated the cultural emphasis upon the goal without equally internalizing the institutional norms governing ways and means for its attainment.

[...]

Whatever the differential rates of deviant behavior in the several social strata, and we know from many sources that the official crime statistics uniformly showing higher rates in the lower strata are far from complete or reliable, it appears from our analysis that the greatest pressures toward deviation are exerted upon the lower strata. Cases in point permit us to detect the sociological mechanisms involved in producing these pressures. Several researchers have shown that specialized areas of vice and crime constitute a 'normal' response to a situation where the cultural emphasis upon pecuniary success has been absorbed, but where there is little access to conventional and legitimate means for becoming successful. The occupational opportunities of people in these areas are largely confined to manual labor and the lesser white-collar jobs. Given the American stigmatization of manual labor *which has been found to hold rather uniformly in all social classes,*[5] and the absence of realistic opportunities for advancement beyond this level, the result is a marked tendency toward deviant behavior. The status of unskilled labor and the consequent low income cannot readily compete *in terms of established standards of worth* with the promises of power and high income from organized vice, rackets and crime.[6]

For our purposes, these situations exhibit two salient features. First, incentives for success are provided by the established values of the culture *and* second, the avenues available for moving toward this goal are largely limited by the class structure to those of deviant behavior. It is the *combination* of the cultural emphasis and the social structure which produces intense pressure for deviation. Recourse to legitimate channels for 'getting in the money' is limited by a class structure which is not fully open at each level to men of good capacity.[7] Despite our persisting open-class ideology,[8] advance toward the success-goal is relatively rare and notably difficult for those armed with little formal education and few economic resources. The dominant pressure leads toward the gradual attenuation of legitimate, but by and large ineffectual, strivings and the increasing use of illegitimate, but more or less effective, expedients.

Of those located in the lower reaches of the social structure, the culture makes incompatible demands. On the one hand, they are asked to orient their conduct toward the prospect of large wealth – 'Every man a king,' said Malden and Carnegie and Long – and on the other, they are largely denied effective opportunities to do so institutionally. The consequence of this structural inconsistency is a high rate of deviant behavior. The equilibrium between culturally designated ends and means becomes highly unstable with progressive emphasis on attaining the prestige-laden ends by any means whatsoever. Within this context, Al Capone represents the triumph of amoral intelligence over morally prescribed 'failure,' when the channels of vertical mobility are closed or narrowed *in a society which places a high premium on economic affluence and social ascent for all its members.*[9]

This last qualification is of central importance. It implies that other aspects of the social structure, besides the extreme emphasis on pecuniary success, must be considered if we are to understand the social sources of deviant behavior. A high frequency of deviant behavior is not generated merely by lack of opportunity or by this exaggerated pecuniary emphasis. A comparatively rigidified class structure, a caste order, may limit opportunities far beyond the point which obtains in American society today. It is only when a system of cultural values extols, virtually above all else, certain *common* success-goals *for the population at large* while the social structure rigorously restricts or completely closes access to approved modes of reaching these goals *for a considerable part of the same population*, that deviant behavior ensues on a large scale. Otherwise said, our egalitarian ideology denies by implication the existence of non-competing individuals and groups in the pursuit of pecuniary success. Instead, the same body of success-symbols is held to apply for all. Goals are held to transcend class lines, not to be bounded by them, yet the actual social organization is such that there exist class differentials in accessibility of the goals. In this setting, a cardinal American virtue, 'ambition,' promotes a cardinal American vice, 'deviant behavior.'

NOTES

1. Leo C. Rosten, *Hollywood* (New York, 1940), 40.
2. Malcolm S. MacLean, *Scholars, Workers and Gentlemen* (Harvard University Press, 1938), 29.
3. There is no lack of typologies of alternative modes of response to frustrating conditions. Freud, in his *Civilization and Its Discontents*

(p. 30 ff) supplies one; derivative typologies, often differing in basic details, will be found in Karen Horney, *Neurotic Personality of Our Time* (New York, 1937); S. Rosenzweig, 'The experimental measurement of types of reaction to frustration,' in H. A. Murray et al., *Explorations in Personality* (New York, 1938), 585–99; and in the work of John Dollard, Harold Lasswell, Abram Kardiner, Erich Fromm. But particularly in the strictly Freudian typology, the perspective is that of types of individual responses, quite apart from the place of the individual within the social structure. Despite her consistent concern with 'culture,' for example, Horney does not explore differences in the impact of this culture upon farmer, worker and businessman, upon lower-, middle-, and upper-class individuals, upon members of various ethnic and racial groups, etc. As a result, the role of 'inconsistencies' in culture is *not* located in its differential impact upon diversely situated groups. Culture becomes a kind of blanket covering all members of the society equally, apart from their idiosyncratic differences of life-history. It is a primary assumption of our typology that these responses occur with different frequency within various sub-groups in our society precisely because members of these groups or strata are differentially subject to cultural stimulation and social restraints. This sociological orientation will be found in the writings of Dollard and, less systematically, in the work of Fromm, Kardiner and Lasswell.

4.   This fifth alternative is on a plane clearly different from that of the others. It represents a transitional response seeking to *institutionalize* new goals and new procedures to be shared by other members of the society. It thus refers to efforts to *change* the existing cultural and social structure rather than to accommodate efforts *within* this structure.

5.   National Opinion Research Center, *National Opinion on Occupations*, April, 1947. This research on the ranking and evaluation of ninety occupations by a nationwide sample presents a series of important empirical data. Of great significance is their finding that, despite a slight tendency for people to rank their own and related occupations higher than do other groups, there is a substantial agreement in ranking of occupations among all occupational strata. More research of this kind is needed to map the cultural topography of contemporary societies. (See the comparative study of prestige accorded major occupations in six industrialized countries: Alex Inkeles and Peter H. Rossi, 'National comparisons of occupational prestige,' *American Journal of Sociology*, 1956, 61, 329–39.)

6.   See Joseph D. Lohman, 'The participant observer in community studies,' *American Sociological Review*, 1937, 2, 890–8 and William F. Whyte, *Street Corner Society* (Chicago, 1943). Note Whyte's conclusions: 'It is difficult for the Cornerville man to get onto the ladder [of success], even on the bottom rung. . . . He is an Italian, and the Italians are looked upon by upper-class people as among the least desirable of the immigrant peoples . . . the society holds out attractive rewards in terms of money and material possessions to the 'successful' man. For most Cornerville people these rewards are available only through advancement in the world of rackets and politics' (273–4).

7.   Numerous studies have found that the educational pyramid operates to keep a large proportion of unquestionably able but economically disadvantaged youth from obtaining higher formal education. This fact about our class structure has been noted with dismay, for example, by Vannevar Bush in his governmental report, *Science: The Endless Frontier*. Also, see W. L. Warner, R. J. Havighurst and M. B. Loeb, *Who Shall Be Educated?* (New York, 1944).

8.   The shifting historical role of this ideology is a profitable subject for exploration.

9.   The role of the Negro in this connection raises almost as many theoretical as practical

questions. It has been reported that large segments of the Negro population have assimilated the dominant caste's values of pecuniary success and social advancement, but have 'realistically adjusted' themselves to the 'fact' that social ascent is presently confined almost entirely to movement within the

caste. See Dollard, *Caste and Class in a Southern Town* (New Haven, 1937), 66 ff; Donald Young, *American Minority Peoples* (New York, 1932), 581; Robert A. Warner, *New Haven Negroes* (New Haven, 1940), 234. See also the subsequent discussion in this chapter.

46. The Birth of Prison

Michel Foucault

On 2 March 1757 Damiens the regicide was condemned 'to make the *amends honorable* before the main door of the Church of Paris', where he was to be 'taken and conveyed in a cart, wearing nothing but a shirt, holding a torch of burning wax weighing two pounds'; then, 'in the said cart, to the Place de Grève, where, on a scaffold that will be erected there, the flesh will be torn from his breasts, arms, thighs and calves with red-hot pincers, his right hand, holding the knife with which he committed the said parricide, burnt with sulphur, and, on those places where the flesh will be torn away, poured molten lead, boiling oil, burning resin, wax and sulphur melted together and then his body drawn and quartered by four horses and his limbs and body consumed by fire, reduced to ashes and his ashes thrown to the winds' (*Pièces originales . . .*, 372–4).

'Finally, he was quartered,' recounts the *Gazette d'Amsterdam* of 1 April 1757. 'This last operation was very long, because the horses used were not accustomed to drawing; consequently, instead of four, six were needed; and when that did not suffice, they were forced, in order to cut off the wretch's thighs, to sever the sinews and hack at the joints . . .

'It is said that, though he was always a great swearer, no blasphemy escaped his lips; but the excessive pain made him utter horrible cries, and he often repeated: 'My God, have pity on me! Jesus, help me!' The spectators were all edified by the solicitude of the parish priest of St Paul's who despite his great age did not spare himself in offering consolation to the patient.'

Bouton, an officer of the watch, left us his account: 'The sulphur was lit, but the flame was so poor that only the top skin of the hand was burnt, and that only slightly. Then the executioner, his sleeves rolled up, took the steel pincers, which had been especially made for the occasion, and which were about a foot and a half long, and pulled first at the calf of the right leg, then at the thigh, and from there at the two fleshy parts of the right arm; then at the breasts. Though a strong, sturdy fellow, this executioner found it so difficult to tear away the pieces of flesh that he set about the same spot two or three times, twisting the pincers as he did so, and what he took away formed at each part a wound about the size of a six-pound crown piece.

'After these tearings with the pincers, Damiens, who cried out profusely, though without swearing, raised his head and looked at himself, the same executioner dipped an iron spoon to the pot containing the boiling potion, which he poured liberally over each wound. Then the ropes that were to be harnessed to the horses were attached with cords to the patient's body; the horses were then harnessed and placed alongside the arms and legs, one at each limb.

'Monsieur Le Breton, the clerk of the court, went up to the patient several times and asked him if he had anything to say. He said he had not; at each torment, he cried out, as the damned in hell are supposed to cry out 'Pardon, my God! Pardon, Lord.' Despite all this pain, he raised his head from time to time and looked at himself boldly. The cords had been tied so tightly by the men who pulled the ends that they caused him indescribable pain. Monsieur Le Breton went up to him again and asked him if he had anything to say; he said no. Several confessors went up to him and spoke to him at length; he willingly kissed the crucifix that was held out to him; he opened his lips and repeated: 'Pardon, Lord.'

'The horses tugged hard, each pulling straight on a limb, each horse held by an executioner. After a quarter of an hour, the same ceremony was repeated and finally, after several attempts, the direction of the horses had to be changed, thus: those at the arms were made to pull towards the head, those at the thighs towards the arm, which broke the arms at the joints. This was repeated several times without success. He raised his head and looked at himself. Two more horses had to be added to those harnessed to the thighs, which made six horses in all. Without success.

'Finally, the executioner, Samson, said to Monsieur Le Breton that there was no way or hope of succeeding, and told him to ask their Lordships if they wished him to have the prisoner cut into pieces. Monsieur Le Breton, who had come down from the town, ordered that renewed efforts be made, and this was done; but the horses gave up and one of those harnessed to the thighs fell to the ground. The confessors returned and spoke to him again. He said to them (I heard him): 'Kiss me, gentlemen.' The parish priest of St Paul's did not dare to, so Monsieur de Marsilly slipped under the rope holding the left arm and kissed him on the forehead. The executioners gathered round and Damiens told them not to swear, to carry out their task and that he did not think ill of them; he begged them to pray to God for him, and asked the parish priest of St Paul's to pray for him at the first mass.

'After two or three attempts, the executioner Samson and he who had used the pincers each drew out a knife from his pocket and cut the body at the thighs instead of severing the legs at the joints; the four horses gave a tug and carried off the two thighs after them, namely, that of the right side first, the other following; then the same was done to the arms, the shoulders, the arm-pits and the four limbs; the flesh had to be cut almost to the bone, the horses pulling hard carried off the right arm first and the other afterwards.

'When the four limbs had been pulled away, the confessors came to speak to him; but his executioner told them that he was dead, though the truth was that I saw the man move, his lower jaw moving from side to side as if he were talking. One of the executioners even said shortly afterwards that when they had lifted the trunk to throw it on the stake, he was still alive. The four limbs were untied from the ropes and thrown on the stake set up in the enclosure in line with the scaffold, then the trunk and the rest were covered with logs and faggots, and fire was put to the straw mixed with this wood.

'. . . In accordance with the decree, the whole was reduced to ashes. The last piece to be found in the embers was still burning at half-past ten in the evening. The pieces of flesh and the trunk had taken about four hours to burn. The officers of whom I was one, as also was my son, and a detachment of archers remained in the square until nearly eleven o'clock.

'There were those who made something of the fact that a dog, which had lain the day before on the grass where the fire had been, had been chased away several times, and had always returned. But it is not difficult to understand that an animal found this place warmer than elsewhere' (quoted in Zevaes, 201–14).

Eighty years later, Léon Faucher drew up his rules 'for the House of young prisoners in Paris':

'Art. 17. The prisoners' day will begin at six in the morning in winter and at five in summer. They will work for nine hours a day throughout the year. Two hours a day will be devoted to instruction. Work and the day will end at nine o'clock in winter and at eight in summer,

Art. 18. *Rising*. At the first drum-roll, the prisoners must rise and dress in silence, as the supervisor opens the cell doors. At the second drum-roll, they must be dressed and make their beds. At the third, they must line up and proceed to the chapel for morning prayer.

There is a five-minute interval between each drum-roll.

Art. 19. The prayers are conducted by the chaplain and followed by a moral or religious reading. This exercise must not last more than half an hour.

Art. 20. *Work*. At a quarter to six in the summer, a quarter to seven in winter, the prisoners go down into the courtyard where they must wash their hands and faces, and receive their first ration of bread. Immediately afterwards, they form into work-teams and go off to work, which must begin at six in summer and seven in winter.

Art. 21. *Meal*. At ten o'clock the prisoners leave their work and go to the refectory; they wash their hands in their courtyards and assemble in divisions. After the dinner, there is recreation until twenty minutes to eleven.

Art. 22. *School*. At twenty minutes to eleven, at the drum-roll, the prisoners form into ranks, and proceed in divisions to the school. The class lasts two hours and consists alternately of reading, writing, drawing and arithmetic.

Art. 23. At twenty minutes to one, the prisoners leave the school, in divisions, and return to their courtyards for recreation. At five minutes to one, at the drum-roll, they form into work-teams.

Art. 24. At one o'clock they must be back in the workshops: they work until four o'clock.

Art. 25. At four o'clock the prisoners leave their workshops and go into the courtyards where they wash their hands and form into divisions for the refectory.

Art. 26. Supper and the recreation that follows it last until five o'clock: the prisoners then return to the workshops.

Art. 27. At seven o'clock in the summer, at eight in winter, work stops; bread is distributed for the last time in the workshops. For a quarter of an hour one of the prisoners or supervisors reads a passage from some instructive or uplifting work. This is followed by evening prayer.

Art: 28. At half-past seven in summer, half-past eight in winter, the prisoners must be back in their cells after the washing of hands and the inspection of clothes in the courtyard; at the first drum-roll, they must undress, and at the second get into bed. The cell doors are closed and the supervisors go the rounds in the corridors, to ensure order and silence' (Faucher, 274–82).

We have, then, a public execution and a time-table. They do not punish the same crimes or the same type of delinquent. But they each define a certain penal style. Less than a century separates them. It was a time when, in Europe and in the United States, the entire economy of punishment was redistributed. It was a time of great 'scandals' for traditional justice, a time of innumerable projects for reform. It saw a new theory of law and crime, a new moral or political justification of the right to punish; old laws were abolished, old customs died out. 'Modern' codes were planned or drawn up: Russia, 1769; Prussia, 1780; Pennsylvania and Tuscany, 1786; Austria, 1788; France, 1791, Year IV, 1808 and 1810. It was a new age for penal justice.

Among so many changes, I shall consider one: the disappearance of torture as a public spectacle. Today we are rather inclined to ignore it; perhaps, in its time, it gave rise to too much inflated rhetoric; perhaps it has been attributed too readily and too emphatically to a process of 'humanization', thus dispensing with the need for further analysis. And, in any case, how important is such a change, when compared with the great institutional transformations, the formulation of explicit, general codes and unified rules of procedure; with the almost universal adoption of the jury system, the definition of the essentially corrective character of the penalty and the tendency, which has become increasingly marked since the nineteenth century, to adapt punishment to the individual offender? Punishment of a less immediately physical kind, a certain discretion in the art of inflicting pain, a combination of more subtle, more subdued sufferings, deprived of their visible display, should not all this be treated as a special case, an incidental effect of deeper changes? And yet the fact remains that a few decades saw the disappearance of the tortured, dismembered, amputated body, symbolically branded on face or shoulder, exposed alive or dead to public view. The body as the major target of penal repression disappeared.

[. . .]

At the beginning of the nineteenth century, then, the great spectacle of physical punishment disappeared; the tortured body was avoided; the theatrical representation of pain was excluded from punishment. The age of sobriety in punishment had begun. By 1830–48, public executions, preceded by torture, had almost entirely disappeared. Of course, this generalization requires some qualification. To begin with, the changes did not come about at once or as part of a single process. There were delays. Paradoxically, England was one of the countries most loath to see the disappearance of the public execution: perhaps because of the role of model that the institution of the jury, public hearings and respect of habeas corpus had given to her criminal law; above all, no doubt, because she did not wish to diminish the rigour of her penal laws during the great social disturbances of the years 1780–1820. For a long time Romilly, Mackintosh and Fowell Buxton failed in their attempts to attenuate the multiplicity and severity of the penalties laid down by English law – that 'horrible butchery', as Rossi described it. Its severity (in fact, the juries regarded the penalties laid down as excessive and were consequently more lenient in their application) had even increased: in 1760, Blackstone had listed 160 capital crimes in English legislation, while by 1819 there were 223. One should also take into account the advances and retreats that the process as a whole underwent between 1760 and 1840; the rapidity of reform in certain countries such as Austria, Russia, the United States, France under the Constituent Assembly, then the retreat at the time of the counter-revolutions in Europe and the great social fear of the years 1820–48; more or less temporary changes introduced by emergency courts or laws; the gap between the laws and the real practice of the courts (which was by no means a faithful reflection of the state of legislation). All these factors account for the irregularity of the transformation that occurred at the turn of the century.

It should be added that, although most of the changes had been achieved by 1840, although the mechanisms of punishment had by then assumed their new way of functioning, the process was far from complete. The reduction in the use of torture was a tendency that was rooted in the great transformation of the years 1760–1840, but it did not end there; it can be said that the practice of the public execution haunted our penal system for a long time and still haunts it today. In France, the guillotine, that machine for the production of rapid and discreet deaths, represented a new ethic of legal death. But the Revolution had immediately endowed it with a great theatrical ritual. For years it provided a spectacle. It had to be removed to the Barrière Saint-Jacques; the open cart was replaced by a closed carriage; the condemned man was hustled from the vehicle straight to the scaffold; hasty executions were organized at unexpected times. In the end, the guillotine had to be placed inside prison walls and made inaccessible to the public (after the execution of Weidmann in 1939), by blocking the streets leading to the prison in which the scaffold was hidden, and in which the execution would take place in secret (the execution of Buffet and Bontemps at the Santé in 1972). Witnesses who described the scene could even be prosecuted, thereby ensuring that the execution should cease to be a spectacle and remain a strange secret between the law and those it condemns. One has only to point out so many precautions to realize that capital punishment remains fundamentally, even today, a spectacle that must actually be forbidden.

Similarly, the hold on the body did not entirely disappear in the mid-nineteenth century. Punishment had no doubt ceased to be centred on torture as a technique of pain; it assumed as its principal object loss of wealth or rights. But a punishment like forced labour or even imprisonment – mere loss of liberty – has never functioned without a certain additional element of punishment that certainly concerns the body itself: rationing of food, sexual deprivation, corporal punishment, solitary confinement. Are these the unintentional, but inevitable, consequence of imprisonment? In fact, in its most explicit practices, imprisonment has always involved a certain degree of physical pain. The criticism that was often levelled at the penitentiary system in the early nineteenth century (imprisonment is not a sufficient punishment: prisoners are less hungry, less cold, less deprived in general than many poor people or even workers) suggests a postulate that was never explicitly denied: it is just that a condemned man should suffer physically more than other men. It is difficult to dissociate punishment from additional physical pain. What would a non-corporal punishment be?

There remains, therefore, a trace of 'torture' in the modern mechanisms of criminal justice – a trace that has not been entirely overcome, but which is enveloped, increasingly, by the non-corporal nature of the penal system.

The reduction in penal severity in the last 200 years is a phenomenon with which legal historians are well acquainted. But, for a long time, it has been regarded in an overall way as a quantitative phenomenon: less cruelty, less pain, more kindness, more respect, more 'humanity'. In fact, these changes are accompanied by a displacement in the very object of the punitive operation. Is there a diminution of intensity? Perhaps. There is certainly a change of objective.

If the penality in its most severe forms no longer addresses itself to the body, on what does it lay hold? The answer of the theoreticians – those who, about 1760, opened up a new period that is not yet at an end – is simple, almost obvious. It seems to be contained in the question itself: since it is no longer the body, it must be the soul. The expiation that once rained down upon the body must be replaced by a punishment that acts in depth on the heart, the thoughts, the will, the inclinations. Mably formulated the principle once and for all: 'Punishment, if I may so put it, should strike the soul rather than the body' (Mably, 326).

It was an important moment. The old partners of the spectacle of punishment, the body and the blood, gave way. A new character came on the scene, masked. It was the end of a certain kind of tragedy; comedy began, with shadow play, faceless voices, impalpable entities. The apparatus of punitive justice must now bite into this bodiless reality.

Is this any more than a mere theoretical assertion, contradicted by penal practice? Such a conclusion would be over-hasty. It is true that, today, to punish is not simply a matter of converting a soul; but Mably's principle has not remained a pious wish. Its effects can be felt throughout modern penality.

REFERENCES

Blackstone, W., *Commentaries on the Laws of England*, vol. 4, 1766–9.
Faucher, L, *De la réforme des prisons*, 1838.
Gazette d'Amsterdam, 1 April, 1757.
Mably, G. de, *De la législation, Oeuvres complètes*, IX, 1789.
Pièces originals et procédures du procès fait à Robert-François Damiens, III, 1757.
Rossi, P. *Traité de droit pénal*, III, 1829.
Zevaes, A. L., *Damiens le régicide*, 1937.

47. Principles of Restorative Justice

John Braithwaite

A teenager is arrested in Halifax for a robbery. The police send him to court where he is sentenced to six months' incarceration. As a victim of child abuse, he is both angry with the world and alienated from it. During his period of confinement he acquires a heroin habit and suffers more violence. He comes out more desperate and alienated than when he went in, sustains his drug habit for the next 20 years by stealing cars, burgles dozens of houses and pushes drugs to others until he dies in a gutter, a death no one mourns. Probably someone rather like that was arrested in Halifax today, perhaps more than one.

Tomorrow another teenager, Sam, is arrested in Halifax for a robbery. He is a composite of several Sams I have seen. The police officer refers Sam to a facilitator who convenes a restorative justice conference. When the facilitator asks about his parents, Sam says he is homeless. His parents abused him and he hates them Sam refuses to cooperate with a conference if they attend. After talking with his parents, the facilitator agrees that perhaps it is best not to involve the parents. What about grandparents? No, they are dead. Brothers and sisters? No, he hates his brothers too. Sam's older sister, who was always kind to him, has long since left home. He has no contact with her. Aunts and uncles? Not keen on them either, because they would always put him down as the black sheep of the family and stand by his parents. Uncle George was the only one he ever had any time for, but he has not seen him for years. Teachers from school? Hates them all. Sam has dropped out. They always treated him like dirt. The facilitator does not give up: 'No one ever treated you

okay at school?' Well, the hockey coach is the only one Sam can ever think of being fair to him. So the hockey coach, Uncle George and older sister are tracked down by the facilitator and invited to the conference along with the robbery victim and her daughter, who comes along to support the victim through the ordeal.

These six participants sit on chairs in a circle. The facilitator starts by introducing everyone and reminding Sam that while he has admitted to the robbery, he can change his plea at any time during the conference and have the matter heard by a court. Sam is asked to explain what happened in his own words. He mumbles that he needed money to survive, saw the lady, knocked her over and ran off with her purse. Uncle George is asked what he thinks of this. He says that Sam used to be a good kid. But Sam had gone off the rails. He had let his parents down so badly that they would not even come today. 'And now you have done this to this poor lady I never thought you would stoop to violence,' continues Uncle George, building into an angry tirade against the boy. The hockey coach also says he is surprised that Sam could do something as terrible as this. Sam was always a troublemaker at school. But he could see a kindly side in Sam that left him shocked about the violence. The sister is invited to speak, but the facilitator moves on to the victim when Sam's sister seems too emotional to speak.

The victim explains how much trouble she had to cancel the credit cards in the purse, how she had no money for the shopping she needed to do that day. Her daughter explains that the most important consequence of the crime was that her mother was now afraid to go out on her own. In particular, she is afraid that Sam is stalking her, waiting to rob her again. Sam sneers at this and seems callous throughout. His sister starts to sob. Concerned about how distressed she is, the facilitator calls a brief adjournment so she can comfort her, with help from Uncle George. During the break, the sister reveals that she understands what Sam has been through. She says she was abused by their parents as well. Uncle George has never heard of this, is shocked, and not sure that he believes it.

When the conference reconvenes, Sam's sister speaks to him with love and strength. Looking straight into his eyes, the first gaze he could not avoid in the conference, she says that she knows exactly what he has been through with their parents. No details are spoken. But the victim seems to understand what is spoken of by the knowing communication between sister and brother. Tears rush down the old woman's cheeks and over a trembling mouth.

It is his sister's love that penetrates Sam's callous exterior. From then on he is emotionally engaged with the conference. He says he is sorry about what the victim has lost. He would like to pay it back, but has no money or job. He assures the victim he is not stalking her. She readily accepts this now and when questioned by the facilitator says now she thinks she will feel safe walking out alone. She wants her money back but says it will help her if they can talk about what to do to help Sam find a home and a job. Sam's sister says he can come and live in her house for a while. The hockey coach says he has some casual work that needs to be done, enough to pay Sam's debt to the victim and a bit more. If Sam does a good job, he will write him a reference for applications for permanent jobs. When the conference breaks up, the victim hugs Sam and tearfully wishes him good luck. He apologises again. Uncle George quietly slips a hundred dollars to Sam's sister to defray the extra cost of having Sam in the house, says he will be there for both of them if they need him.

Sam has a rocky life punctuated by several periods of unemployment. A year later he has to go through another conference after he steals a bicycle. But he finds work when he can, mostly stays out of trouble and lives to mourn at the funerals of Uncle George and his sister. The victim gets her money back and enjoys taking long walks alone. Both she and her daughter say that they feel enriched as a result of the conference, have a little more grace in their lives.

I will return to the meanings of this story.

Institutional collapse

Few sets of institutional arrangements created in the West since the industrial revolution have been as large a failure as the criminal justice system. In theory it administers just, proportionate corrections that deter. In practice, it fails to correct or deter, just as often making things worse as better. It is a criminal *injustice* system that systematically turns a blind eye to crimes of the powerful, while imprisonment remains the best-funded labour market programme for the unemployed and indigenous peoples. It pretends to be equitable, yet one offender may be sentenced to a year in a prison where he will be beaten on reception and then systematically bashed thereafter, raped, even infected with AIDS, while others serve 12 months in comparatively decent premises, especially if they are white-collar criminals.

While I do believe that Canada's criminal justice system is more decent than ours in Australia, all Western criminal justice systems are brutal, institutionally vengeful, and dishonest to their stated intentions. The interesting question is why are they such failures. Given that prisons are vicious and degrading places, you would expect fear of ending up in them would deter crime.

There are many reasons for the failures of the criminal justice system to prevent crime. I will give you just one, articulated in the terms of my theory in *Crime, Shame and Reintegration*.[1] The claim of this theory is that the societies that have the lowest crime rates are the societies that shame criminal conduct most effectively. There is an important difference between reintegrative shaming and stigmatization. While reintegrative shaming prevents crime, stigmatization is a kind of shaming that makes crime problems worse. Stigmatization is the kind of shaming that creates outcasts; it is disrespectful, humiliating. Stigmatization means treating criminals as evil people who have done evil acts. Reintegrative shaming means disapproving of the evil of the deed while treating the person as essentially good. Reintegrative shaming means strong disapproval of the act but doing so in a way that is respecting of the person. Once we understand this distinction, we can see why putting more police on the street can actually increase crime. More police can increase crime if they are systematically stigmatizing in the way they deal with citizens. More police can reduce crime if they are systematically reintegrative in the way they deal with citizens.

We can also understand why building more prisons could make the crime problem worse. Having more people in prison does deter some and incapacitates others from committing certain crimes, like bank robberies, because there are no banks inside the prison for them to rob, though there certainly are plenty of vulnerable people to rape and pillage. But because prisons stigmatize, they also make things worse for those who have criminal identities affirmed by imprisonment, those whose stigmatization leads them to find solace in the society of the similarly outcast, those who are attracted into criminal subcultures, those who treat the prison as an educational institution for learning new skills for the illegitimate labour market. On this account, whether building more prisons reduces or increases the crime rate depends on whether the stigmatizing nature of a particular prison system does more to increase crime than its deterrent and incapacitative effects reduce it.

[. . .]

What is restorative justice?

Restorative justice means restoring victims, a more victim-centred criminal justice system, as well as restoring offenders and restoring community. First, what does restoring victims mean? It means restoring the *property loss* or the *personal injury*, repairing the broken window or the broken teeth (see Table 47.1). It means restoring a *sense of security*. Even victims of property crimes such as burglary often suffer a loss of security when the private space of their home is violated. When the criminal justice system fails to leave women secure about walking alone at night, half the population is left unfree in a rather fundamental sense.

Victims suffer loss of dignity when someone violates their bodies or shows them the disrespect of taking things which are precious to them. Sometimes this disrespectful treatment engenders victim shame: 'He abused me rather than some other woman because I am trash', 'She stole my dad's car because I was irresponsible to park it in such a risky place'. Victim shame often triggers a shame–rage spiral wherein victims reciprocate indignity with indignity through vengeance or by their own criminal acts.

Disempowerment is part of the indignity of being a victim of crime. According to Pettit and Braithwaite's republican theory of criminal justice,[2] a wrong should not be defined as a crime unless it involves some domination of us that reduces our freedom to enjoy life as we choose. It follows that it is important to *restore any lost sense of empowerment* as a result of crime. [. . .]

The way that Western legal systems handle crime compounds the disempowerment that victims feel, first at the hands of offenders and then at the hands of a professional, remote justice

Table 47.1   What does restoring victims mean?

Restoring victims
- Restore property loss
- Restore injury
- Restore sense of security
- Restore dignity
- Restore sense of empowerment
- Restore deliberative democracy
- Restore harmony based on a feeling that justice has been done
- Restore social support

system that eschews their participation. The lawyers, in the words of Nils Christie 'steal our conflict'.[3] The western criminal justice system has, on balance, been corrosive of deliberative democracy, though the jury is one institution that has preserved a modicum of it. Restorative justice is deliberative justice; it is about people deliberating over the consequences of a crime, how to deal with them and prevent their recurrence. This contrasts with the professional justice of lawyers deciding which rules apply to a case and then constraining their deliberation within a technical discourse about that rule application. So restorative justice restores the *deliberative control of justice by citizens*.

[. . .]

Restoring community is advanced by a proliferation of restorative justice rituals in which social support around specific victims and offenders is restored. At this micro level, restorative justice is an utterly bottom-up approach to restoring community. At a meso level, important elements of a restorative justice package are initiatives to foster community organization in schools, neighbourhoods, ethnic communities, churches, [and] through professions who can deploy restorative justice in their self-regulatory practices. At a macro level, we must better design institutions of deliberative democracy so that concern about issues like unemployment and the effectiveness of labour market programmes have a channel through which they can flow from discussions about local injustices up into national economic policy-making debate.

[. . .]

In the alienated urban context where community is not spontaneously emergent in a satisfactory way, a criminal justice system aimed at restoration can construct a community of care around a specific offender or a specific victim who is in trouble. That is what the story of Sam is about. With the restorative justice conferences

being convened in multicultural metropolises like Auckland, Adelaide, Sydney and Singapore, the selection principle as to who is invited to the conference is the opposite to that with a criminal trial. We invite to a criminal trial those who can inflict most damage on the other side. With a conference we invite those who might offer most support to their own side – Sam's sister, uncle and hockey coach, the victim's daughter.

In terms of the theory of reintegrative shaming, the rationale for who is invited to the conference is that the presence of those on the victim side structures shame into the conference, the presence of supporters on the offender's side structures reintegration into the ritual. Conferences can be run in many different ways from the story of Sam's conference. Maori people in New Zealand tend to want to open and close their conferences with a prayer. The institutions of restorative justice we build in the city must be culturally plural, quite different from one community to another depending on the culture of the people involved. It is the empowerment principle of restorative justice that makes this possible – empowerment with process control.

From a restorative perspective, the important thing is that we have institutions in civil society which confront serious problems like violence rather than sweep them under the carpet, yet do so in a way that is neither retributive nor stigmatizing. Violence will not be effectively controlled by communities unless the shamefulness of violence is communicated. This does not mean that we need criminal justice institutions that set out to maximize shame. On the contrary, if we set out to do that we risk the creation of stigmatizing institutions.[4] All we need do is nurture micro-institutions of deliberative democracy that allow citizens to discuss the consequences of criminal acts, who is responsible, who should put them right and how.

[. . .]

Some criminologists in the West are critical of countries like Singapore, Indonesia and Japan where crime in the streets is not a major problem because they think individualism in these societies is crushed by communitarianism or collective obligation. Their prescription is that Asian societies need to shift the balance away from communitarianism and allow greater individualism. I don't find that a very attractive analysis.

Some Asian criminologists are critical of countries like the US and Australia because they think these societies are excessively individualistic, suffering much crime and incivility as a result. According to this analysis, the West needs to shift the balance away from individualism in favour of communitarianism, shift the balance away from rights and toward collective responsibilities. I don't find that a very attractive analysis either.

Both sides of this debate can do a better job of learning from each other. We can aspire to a society that is strong on rights and strong on responsibilities, that nurtures strong communities and strong individuals. Indeed, in the good society strong communities constitute strong individuals and vice versa. Our objective can be to keep the benefits of the statist revolution at the same time as we rediscover community-based justice. Community justice is often oppressive of rights, often subjects the vulnerable to the domination of local elites, subordinates women, can be procedurally unfair and tends to neglect structural solutions. Mindful of this, we might reframe the two challenges posed earlier [. . .]:

1   *Helping indigenous community justice to learn from the virtues of liberal statism – procedural fairness, rights, protecting the vulnerable from domination.*
2   *Helping liberal state justice to learn from indigenous community justice – learning the restorative community alternatives to individualism.*

This reframed agenda resonates with the writings of Canadians such as Donald Clairmont[5] and Marianne Nielsen, who writes that native communities 'will have the opportunity of taking the best of the old, the best of the new and learning from others' mistakes so that they can design a system that may well turn into a flagship of social change'.[6] Together these two questions ask how we save and revive traditional restorative justice practices in a way that helps them become procedurally fairer, in a way that respects fundamental human rights, that secures protection against domination? The liberal state can be a check on oppressive collectivism, just as bottom-up communitarianism can be a check on oppressive individualism. A healing circle can be a corrective to a justice system that can leave offenders and victims suicidally alone; a Charter of Rights and Freedoms a check on a tribal elder who imposes a violent tyranny on young people. The bringing together of these ideals is an old prescription – not just liberty, not just community, but liberté, egalité, fraternité. Competitive individualism has badly fractured this republican amalgam. The social movement for restorative justice does practical work to weld an amalgam that is relevant to the creation of contemporary urban multicultural republics. Day to day it is not sustained by romantic ideals in which I happen to believe like deliberative democracy. They want to do it for Sam and for an old woman who Sam pushed over one day. That is what enlists them to the social movement for restorative justice; in the process they are, I submit, enlisted into something of wider political significance.

NOTES

1. Braithwaite, J. (1989) *Crime, Shame and Reintegration* (Cambridge: Cambridge University Press).
2. Pettit, P. and Braithwaite, J. (1993) *Not Just Deserts: A Republican Theory of Criminal Justice* (Oxford: Oxford University Press).
3. Christie, N. (1977) 'Conflicts as Property', *British Journal of Criminology*, 17:1, pp. 1–15.
4. Retzinger, S. and Scheff, T. (1966) 'Strategy for Community Conferences: Emotions and Social Bonds', in B. Galaway and J. Hudson, (eds.), *Restorative Justice: International Perspectives* (Monsey, NY: Criminal Justice Press).

5. Clairmont, D. (1994) 'Alternative Justice Issues for Aboriginal Justice', Unpublished Manuscript, Atlantic Institute of Criminology.

6. Nielsen, M. (1992) 'Criminal Justice and Native Self-Government', in R. Silverman and M. Nielsen (eds) *Aboriginal Peoples and Canadian Criminal Justice* (Toronto: Butterworths), p. 255.

48. How Serious are Cybercrimes?

David S. Wall

How easy it is to jump to conclusions. A young woman sits alone with her laptop in the corner of her favourite internet café. She has just pressed the send button and is looking over her shoulder. But why? Who is she, what is she doing, what has she done? She looks vulnerable, nervous, possibly a little worried. Perhaps she has just become the victim of a cyber-stalker, or is she replying to a blackmailer? Perhaps, she has unwittingly just given her personal information to an identity thief? On the other hand, she could be a major fraudster, a cyber-terrorist, a notorious hacker or a mass spammer. With that one click she may have just caused a cybercrime wave that will simultaneously victimize tens of thousands of people all over the planet and cause untold misery.

Actually, it is not clear at all who she is or what she is doing because the internet distorts conventional reference points and forces us to challenge our previously held assumptions, particularly about crime and the internet. This book is an exploration of a new era of criminal activity – cybercrime – so-called because it is being rapidly transformed by networked technologies that expand the reach of individuals who have access to networked computers. This technological transformation of crime is an ongoing process – indeed, while this book was being written a step-change occurred that takes us towards an entirely new generation of automated cybercrime, which, although still in its early stages, I have tried to capture here.

A simple reading of history shows that the relationship between crime and technology is by no means new and that the potential for creating harm never seems to be far away from any apparently beneficial technological development. Although the hardware used to implement technological ideas may change across the span of time, many of the basic crime ideas remain familiar, particularly those which exploit chains of trust supported by technology. Some of the nineteenth-century wire frauds perpetrated by tapping into the early electric telegraph systems, for example, bear an uncanny resemblance to modern day hacks. This long standing, though 'uneasy', relationship between crime and technology also extends to ideas about crime prevention and security – the architects of the pyramids, for example, employed sophisticated security technologies to thwart tomb raiders – a few wrong or unexpected moves and . . . slam! . . . the tomb entrance was sealed forever – not so different in principle to the automated surveillant technologies installed at airports to detect potential terrorist actions by identifying abnormal patterns of movement. And on the subject of the electric telegraph, no sooner had it been invented than it was being used to catch criminals, as murderer John Tawell reflected upon in the moments before his execution in 1845. After murdering his mistress and fleeing to London by train, Tawell's description was telegraphed forward by the police and he was arrested upon his arrival (Standage, 1998: 51).

Today the technological cat-and-mouse game between offender and investigator remains much the same as in the past. Offenders still exploit new technologies while the investigators catch up quickly and then use those same technologies for investigation, apprehension and prevention. What has changed significantly in late modern times, however, has been the increase in personal computing power within a globalized communications network. The time frame during which harmful behaviour occurs and changes substantively is now much shorter in this era of networking. It is also particularly worrying that the length of time for a cybercrime opportunity to turn into a cybercrime wave is now measured in hours and minutes rather than months and years. As a consequence, networked technology has become more than simply a 'force multiplier' – not only are ideas about committing crime, its investigation and prevention being shared on a global scale, but high levels of computing power also enable these ideas to be put into practice across the global networks. So fast has been the rate of change that this book has already been revised considerably during the course of writing, living proof of Moore's calculation that one internet year is approximately equal to three months or less in real-time (based upon Moore, 1965: 114) [. . .] not only have networked technologies changed the criminal process to create a new generation of hackers and crackers, fraudsters and pornographers and the like, but these have themselves now been superseded. A third generation of cybercrimes (the first being computer crimes and the second being hacking) is emerging which is almost completely caused by networked technologies that are themselves converging with others. It can now be argued, for example, that earlier concerns about 'hacking' have become sidelined because 'botnets' of many thousands of 'zombie' computers infected by remote administration trojans can now automate the hacking process and also the process by which offenders engage with their victims. [. . .]

Individually, cybercrimes may not be particularly serious and surveys of individual victimizations, police actions and prosecutions show the figures to be quite low, despite expectations to the contrary. However, these local statistics tend not to grasp the global picture as their true seriousness lies in their aggregate impact. We have now entered the world of low-impact, multiple victim crimes where bank robbers no longer have to plan meticulously thefts of millions of dollars; new technological capabilities mean that one person can now commit millions of robberies of $1 each. This 'de-minimism' creates a number of important challenges for law enforcement and the policing of offenders. On the one hand, criminal justice systems are not geared up to deal with such offences. On the other hand, the realism, indeed digital realism, of cybercrime is such that the more a behaviour is mediated by new technology, the more it can be governed by that same technology. So, in addition to the prospect of being faced with 'ubiquitous' and automated victimization, we also – simultaneously – face the prospect of being exposed to ubiquitous law enforcement and prevention and the potential problems it creates, such as a potential 'pre-crime' agenda.

[. . .]

Why call it 'cybercrime'?

First coined by William Gibson (1982) and then popularized in his 1984 novel *Neuromancer*, the term 'cyberspace' became a popular descriptor of the mentally constructed virtual environment within which networked computer activity takes place. 'Cybercrime' broadly describes the crimes that take place within that space and the term has come to symbolize insecurity and risk online. By itself, cybercrime is fairly meaningless because it tends to be used metaphorically and emotively rather than scientifically or legally, usually to signify the occurrence of harmful behaviour that is somehow related to the misuse of a networked computer system (Wall, 1997; NCIS, 1999). Largely an invention of the media, 'cybercrime' originally had no specific reference point in law in the UK or US and the offending that did become associated with the term was a rather narrow legal construction based upon concerns about hacking. In fact, many of the so-called cybercrimes that have caused concern over the past decade are not necessarily crimes in criminal law. If we could turn the clock back in time then perhaps the term 'cyberspace crime' would have been a more precise and accurate descriptor. However, regardless of its merits and demerits, the term 'cybercrime' has entered the public parlance and we are stuck with it (Wall, 2005). It is argued here and elsewhere in this book that the term has a greater meaning if we construct it in terms of the transformation of criminal or harmful behaviour by networked technology, rather than simply the behaviour itself. As stated earlier, cybercrimes are understood here to be criminal or harmful activities that involve the acquisition or manipulation of information for gain.

Not only has the term 'cybercrime' acquired considerable linguistic agency, but over the past decade 'cybercrimes' have become firmly embedded in public crime agendas as something that must be governed.

[. . .]

The most conventionally accepted 'reliable' data are metrics expressed as statistics; however, the distributed environment in which cybercrime thrives undermines conventional methodologies for collecting data. This is because information about reported victimization does not flow through a single portal such as the police in the same way as does the reporting of street and related crime. In this, cybercrime is little different to other invisible or hidden crimes such as white-collar or organized crime (see Davies et al., 1999). There exist many reports and surveys that purport to estimate the extent of cybercrime, typically covering network abuse and commercial crime (see Ryan and Jefferson, 2003), but very few 'official' sources. This point was raised by the UK All Party Internet Group in May 2004 when it reviewed the Computer Misuse Act 1990: 'One problem is that, officially, the government is not aware of exactly how big a problem cybercrime is, since figures are not audited by the National Audit Office – and this means there is no political pressure to deal with the issue. "The first thing we have to do is find out the extent of the problem. We won't win the battle of resourcing the police

if we don't get the crimes recorded"' (APIG chairman Derek Wyatt, cited by Broersma, 2004).

But, even if there did exist the possibility to collate 'official' statistics, there remains the additional problem of applying standardized conceptualizations of 'crime' to systematic reporting or recording methodologies, with the consequence that they are hard, if not impossible, to replicate. Frequently cited for many years as a source of information about cybercrimes were the intrusion statistics published online by the Computer Emergency Response Team (CERT) at Carnegie Mellon University. Reports rose from six in 1988 to 137,529 in 2003, and these statistics were initially accepted as a barometer of cybercrime activity. However, because confusion arose from these being mainly low-level and often automated reports of intrusions with few representing actual crimes, CERT discontinued the 'Incidents reported' data stream in 2003 with the following statement: '[g]iven the widespread use of automated attack tools, attacks against Internet-connected systems have become so commonplace that counts of the number of incidents reported provide little information with regard to assessing the scope and impact of attacks. Therefore, as of 2004, we will no longer publish the number of incidents reported' (CERT/CC Statistics 1988–2005, at www.cert.org/stats/cert_stats.html).

An indication of the inexact science of cybercrime estimation was given in October 2005 when John Leyden, a journalist from *The Register*, deconstructed claims by an anti-spyware firm about the level of infections caused by spyware (Leyden, 2005). The data upon which the statistics were based were collected by Webroot's *Phileas* automatic web crawler, which proactively sought out data about active spyware (Webroot, 2005: 13). The findings were dramatic and revealed high levels of spurious infections. However, Leyden subsequently found that the methods used to calculate the statistics clumped together benign 'cookies' with much more malicious spyware such as trojans and keylogger programs. Once the cookies were removed from the calculation the average number of spyware infections on each PC fell from 18 to 4.5

(Leyden, 2005). While still relatively high, the revised calculations radically change the meaning of the statistics and any conclusions that can be drawn from them. This example highlights graphically the need to understand first the methodological assumptions underlying the compilation of statistics.

In addition to the 'incidents reported' lists are a number of self-reporting victimization surveys run by organizations such as the US National White-Collar Crime Center and the National Fraud Information Center. Most focus specifically upon the business and financial sector. Currently one of the most frequently cited sources of data is the Computer Studies Institute/Federal Bureau of Investigation (CSI/FBI, 2005, 2006) annual computer security survey which questions US businesses about their experience of victimization. Similarly, companies such as Experian, KPMG and others produce occasional (rigorous) surveys. In the UK, similar surveys have been conducted by the Department of Trade and Industry (DTI, 2004), also the National Hi-Tech Crime Unit (NHTCU, 2002) and the National Criminal Intelligence Service (NCIS, 2003). The survey results tend to find high rates of victimization, but it is important to note that most businesses are more likely to become victims of crime simply because of the risks they are exposed to in the course of their day-to-day operations, both online and off. So problems of data interpretation arise when survey data collected for quite specific purposes or specific corporate or client bodies are used to support general observations about the impact of the internet, or its impact on individuals. Such generalizations can fuel sensational news stories which subsequently depict the internet as ungovernable and criminogenic, when in fact, information such as that related to online frauds suggests that the internet is very secure for personal online transactions and that the main risk lies in the vulnerability of input and output procedures (APACS, 2005; Wall, 2002).

The most effective way that statistics about patterns of individual victimization can be reliably captured is through surveys of individuals. To this end there are some encouraging signs, because the main victimization surveys in the UK and US have either recently incorporated, or are currently in the process of incorporating, questions about online victimization. In the UK in 2002–3, the British Crime Survey (BCS) incorporated a small number of questions about individual internet victimizations. The BCS canvasses a sample of about 37,000 people (75 per cent response rate) about their experience of victimization (Allen et al., 2005: 3; Wilson et al., 2006). Complementing the BCS is the Offending, Crime and Justice Survey (OCJS), which asks a smaller sample of 12,000 about their experience of offending. The results of the BCS of 2002–3 and the first OCJS survey in 2003 were made available in mid-2005 and did not show the high levels of prevalence previously anticipated by the reported incident data (Allen et al., 2005). Only 2 per cent of respondents reported that they had been the victim of a hack during the previous year; 21 per cent reported receiving an offensive email. Interestingly, levels of internet card fraud were found to be lower than other forms of card fraud (Allen et al., 2005: vi). These early findings, replicated by the BCS 2003–4 findings (Wilson et al., 2006: 7) lend weight to the argument established in this book that cybercrimes may not be individually as serious as many of the statistics claim, but their seriousness lies in their globalized aggregate volume. This observation brings into question whether cybercrimes can be quantified by traditional local and national recording methods, or whether they should be considered within a much larger global context.

REFERENCES

Allen, J., Forrest, S., Levi, M., Roy, H. and Sutton, M. (2005) 'Fraud and technology crimes: findings from the 2002/03 British Crime Survey and 2003 Offending, Crime and Justice Survey', Home Office Online Report 34/05, at www.homeoffice.gov.uk/rds/pdfs05/rdsolr3405.pdf.

APACS (2005) 'UK card fraud losses reach £504.8m: criminals increase their efforts as chip and PIN starts to make its mark', APACS press release, 8 March, London: APACS, at www.apacs.org.uk/downloads/ cardfraudfigures%20national&regional%20-%208mar05.pdf.

Broersma, M. (2004) 'Boost UK govt cybercrime resources', *Computer Weekly*, 17 May, at www.computerweekly.com/articles/article.asp?liArticleID_130607&liArticleTypeI_1&liCategoryID_6&liChannelID_22&liFlavourID_1&sSearch_&nPage_1.

CSI/FBI (2005) *CSI/FBI Computer Crime and Security Survey 2005*, San Francisco: Computer Security Institute.

CSI/FBI (2006) *CSI/FBI Computer Crime and Security Survey 2006*, San Francisco: Computer Security Institute.

Davies, P., Francis, P. and Jupp, V. (eds) (1999) *Invisible Crimes: Their Victims and their Regulation*, London: Macmillan.

DTI (2004) *Information Security Breaches Survey 2004*, London: Department of Trade and Industry.

Gibson, W. (1982) 'Burning chrome', *Omni Magazine*, July.

Leyden, J. (2005) 'Webroot guesstimates inflate UK spyware problem', *The Register*, 20 October, at www.theregister.co.uk/2005/10/20/webroot_uk_spyware_guesstimates/.

Moore, G. E. (1965) 'Cramming more components onto integrated circuits', *Electronics*, 38 (8): 114–17.

NCIS (1999) *Project Trawler: Crime On The Information Highways*, London: National Criminal Intelligence Service.

NCIS (2003) *United Kingdom Threat Assessment of Serious and Organised Crime 2003*, London: National Criminal Intelligence Service.

NHTCU (2002) *Hi-Tech Crime: The impact on UK Business*, London, National Hi-Tech Crime Unit.

Ryan, J. and Jefferson, T. (2003) 'The use, misuse and abuse of statistics in information security research', Proceedings of the 2003 ASEM National Conference, St. Louis, MO, at www.attrition.org/archive/misc/use_misuse_abuse_stats_infosec_research.pdf.

Standage, T. (1998) *The Victorian Internet: The Remarkable Story of the Telegraph and the Nineteenth Century's Online Pioneers*, London: Phoenix.

Wall, D. S. (1997) 'Policing the virtual community: the internet, cybercrimes and the policing of cyberspace', in P. Francis, P. Davies and V. Jupp (eds), *Policing Futures*, London: Macmillan, 208–36.

Wall, D. S. (2002) *DOT.CONS: Internet Related Frauds and Deceptions upon Individuals within the UK*, Final Report to the Home Office, March (unpublished).

Wall, D. S. (2005) 'The Internet as a conduit for criminals', in A. Pattavina (ed.), *Information Technology and The Criminal Justice System*, Thousand Oaks, CA: Sage, 77–98.

Webroot (2005) *The State of Spyware, Q2*, Webroot Software Inc., October, at www.webroot.com/pdf/2005-q2-sos.pdf.

Wilson, D., Patterson, A., Powell, G. and Hembury, R. (2006) 'Fraud and technology crimes: findings from the 2003/04 British Crime Survey, the 2004 Offending, Crime and Justice Survey and administrative sources', *Home Office Online Report 09/06*, at www.homeoffice.gov.uk/rds/pdfs06/rdsolr0906.pdf.

Theme 9 – Further Reading

A good place to begin is with Tony Lawson and Tim Heaton's (2009) *Crime and Deviance* (Basingstoke: Palgrave Macmillan), which is an introductory text that is still right up to date with the latest issues and theories. Martin Innes's (2003) *Understanding Social Control: Crime and Social Order in Late Modernity* (Buckingham: Open University Press) is well written and casts a broader net to take in general issues of social control as well as crime and deviance. Issues of restorative justice are confidently handled and effectively presented in James Dignan's (2004) *Understanding Victims and Restorative Justice* (Buckingham: Open University Press). Finally, a more advanced level text that is worth considering, as it handles theories especially well, is David Downes and Paul Rock's (2011) *Understanding Deviance: A Guide to the Sociology of Crime and Rule-Breaking*, 6th edition (Buckingham: Open University Press).

Giddens and Sutton *Sociology 7th Edition* (2013)

Chapter 21 reviews the field of the sociology of crime and deviance. Other issues of deviance and crime can be found in Chapter 8 on interaction rules and their breaking, pages 317–22; Chapter 13 on crime and social exclusion, pages 548–53; Chapter 15 on changing attitudes to sexuality, pages 634–5 and 643–51 and crime and deviance in sex work, pages 659–64; Chapter 16 on ethnicity and crime, pages 696–700 and Chapter 23 on war crimes and genocide, pages 1028–40 and terrorism, pages 1041–6.

Part 10

Political Sociology

The study of politics in sociology has conventionally dealt with the relationship between social structures, such as social class, and political power. In practice this has meant investigating political systems such as democracy and authoritarianism, electoral voting patterns, party political allegiances and the role of political ideologies as well as the expression of dissent through non-established channels including the activities of social movements. However, as the world of politics itself has changed, so too has political sociology. As a result of recent events, the field now takes in wars, genocide and terrorism, while social movement studies has expanded considerably in a period when many people express deep dissatisfaction with formal party politics and mistrust their politicians. This section reflects some of these changes.

In Reading 49, Steven Lukes discusses his theory of power, a basic concept in political sociology. Although his original book was published in 1975, this extract is from the 2008 second edition in which Lukes is able to reflect on his earlier work. The originality of Lukes's thesis is his delineation of three perspectives on power. One-dimensional views of power see it as the ability to get one's own way even in the face of opposition. This is very much the kind of definition adopted by Max Weber and one that is influenced by a state-centred politics. The main problem though is that this is very much an intentional view of power which sees it as deliberate attempts to exert power over others. For Lukes, this is a very narrow view. Two-dimensional views include the main tenets of position one, but add that power is often exercised not deliberately, but simply by virtue of existing social arrangements. An example here would be the power afforded to men simply because they are able to take advantage of the opportunities to exercise it over women in patriarchally organized societies. Lukes argues for a three-dimensional view, that adds internal constraints and beliefs through which people willingly acquiesce to structures of domination, which are acquired through the internalization of ideological beliefs.

With a few notable exceptions, sociologists have not paid enough attention to war. This is surprising given that there is a well-established conflict tradition dealing with class and other intra-society conflicts. Perhaps the relatively short event timeframe in which wars take place has led to sociologists deferring their study to historians. This is unfortunate, as the consequences of war have now been shown to be far-reaching in the shaping of future social and international relations, and there is now a growing interest in understanding war and its aftermath.

While the twentieth century was the age of international wars which cost millions of lives and mobilized entire national populations, since the late twentieth century there have been numerous conflicts which do not fit this pattern. In Reading 50, Mary Kaldor outlines her thesis that we are in a period of 'new wars', which differ significantly from previous ones. The crucial difference between old and new wars is, in a word, globalization. New wars involve multinational peacekeeping forces, international aid agencies, coalitions of governments (the 'international community') and draw in combatants from across the world to fight in particular theatres. But new wars differ in other ways too. They involve identity politics, that is they are fought *for* particular identities rather than those identities being incidental to other economic or military goals. Finally, they tend to be fought using guerrilla tactics due to the combatants' relative lack of resources, and thus involve diverse actors including paramilitaries, criminal gangs and warlords as well as armed forces. Kaldor argues that ways will have to be found to prevent such conflicts becoming chronic in the future.

In Reading 51 we turn to the phenomenon of the social movement, which arose and became more common with the onset of modernity. Social movements used to be considered quite marginal to the mainstream of political sociology, but since the emergence of a wave of 'new social movements' in the 1960s and 1970s based on non-violence and direct action, that has changed. Environmental or green movements, student movements, lesbian and gay movements, disabled people's movements as well as anti-nuclear and peace movements and more have all scored successes in bringing new issues to public attention. Here, David Meyer and Sidney Tarrow outline the thesis that movements are becoming permanent features of modern societies as they become more numerous, more diverse and involve new social constituencies. The movement form also appears to be gradually becoming institutionalized or established, which may change people's perception of them. We may therefore be heading towards a social movement society where new forms of politics and political representation are emerging.

Not all social movements adopt non-violent methods. Some of the terrorist activity across the world in recent years bears a striking resemblance to key aspects of new social movements. For example, much of it is organized in relatively loose forms and there is a global dimension that brings terror to geographically disparate locations. Recent terrorism also differs from previous forms as it is not based on nationalism or the pursuit of independence, but involves small groups or cells seeking vengeance and destruction. In Reading 52, Walter Laqueur calls this type of political violence the 'new terrorism' and provides examples to illustrate the argument. His chief concern is the emergence of new terrorism at a time when weapons of mass destruction are becoming more readily available than ever before, holding out the prospect of a very uncertain future. Unlike the old terrorism that had clearly defined political aims, it is more difficult to see how the new terrorism could compromise or be brought into negotiations.

A growing number of academics seeking ways of dealing with the threats posed by the global challenge of new wars and terrorism have turned away from state-centred international political solutions. Instead, many have turned towards the concept of 'cosmopolitan democracy' for solutions. In Reading 53, Daniele Archibugi makes the case for this project, which, she argues, is the best hope for us all in the twenty-first century. At its roots, cosmopolitan democracy is a project aiming to achieve a worldwide social order based on global democracy and the rule of law. This desire is not new and can be traced back to at least the eighteenth century. However, contemporary scholars sense a real opportunity to begin the process of making such an ambitious project a reality. This is because democracy seems to have won the battle of ideas following the collapse of the Soviet Union and communism and a new wave of democratization across the world.

However, processes of globalization may make the concept of global citizenship more tangible and the desire for a global democracy more widespread. Of course cosmopolitan democracy remains something of a utopian project, as the problems of generating even regional unity in the European Union show. Nonetheless, Archibugi argues that the conditions for pursuing such a project have never been more favourable or necessary.

49. Defining Power

Steven Lukes

Thirty years ago I published a small book entitled *Power: A Radical View* (hereafter *PRV*). It was a contribution to an ongoing debate, mainly among American political scientists and sociologists, about an interesting question: how to think about power theoretically and how to study it empirically. But underlying that debate another question was at issue: how to characterize American politics – as dominated by a ruling elite or as exhibiting pluralist democracy – and it was clear that answering the second question required an answer to the first. My view was, and is, that we need to think about power broadly rather than narrowly – in three dimensions rather than one or two – and that we need to attend to those aspects of power that are least accessible to observation: that, indeed, power is at its most effective when least observable.

[. . .]

Introduction

This chapter presents a conceptual analysis of power. In it I shall argue for a view of power (that is, a way of identifying it) which is radical in both the theoretical and political senses (and I take these senses in this context to be intimately related). The view I shall defend is, I shall suggest, ineradicably evaluative and 'essentially contested' (Gallie 1955–6)[1] on the one hand; and empirically applicable on the other. I shall try to show why this view is superior to alternative views. I shall further defend its evaluative and contested character as no defect, and I shall argue that it is 'operational', that

is, empirically useful in that hypotheses can be framed in terms of it that are in principle verifiable and falsifiable (despite currently canvassed arguments to the contrary). And I shall even give examples of such hypotheses – some of which I shall go so far as to claim to be true.

[. . .]

The one-dimensional view

This is often called the 'pluralist' view of power, but that label is already misleading, since it is the aim of Dahl, Polsby, Wolfinger and others to demonstrate that power (as they identify it) is, in fact, distributed pluralistically in, for instance, New Haven and, more generally, in the United States' political system as a whole. To speak, as these writers do, of a 'pluralist view' of, or 'pluralist approach' to, power, or of a 'pluralist methodology', is to imply that the pluralists' conclusions are already built into their concepts, approach and method. I do not, in fact, think that this is so. I think that these are capable of generating non-pluralist conclusions in certain cases. Their view yields elitist conclusions when applied to elitist decision-making structures, and pluralist conclusions when applied to pluralist decision-making structures (and also, as I shall argue, pluralist conclusions when applied to structures which it identifies as pluralist, but other views of power do not). So, in attempting to characterize it, I shall identify its distinguishing features independently of the pluralist conclusions it has been used to reach.

In his early article 'The Concept of Power', Dahl describes his 'intuitive idea of power' as 'something like this: *A* has power over *B* to the extent that he can get *B* to do something that *B* would not otherwise do' (Dahl 1957, in Bell et al. (eds) 1969: 80). A little later in the same article he describes his 'intuitive view of the power relation' slightly differently: it seemed, he writes, 'to involve a successful attempt by *A* to get *a* to do something he would not otherwise do' (ibid., p. 82). Note that the first statement refers to *A*'s capacity ('. . . to the extent that he can get *B* to do something . . .'), while the second specifies a successful attempt – this, of course, being the difference between potential and actual power, between its possession and its exercise. It is the latter – the exercise of power – which is central to this view of power (in reaction to the so-called 'elitists'' focus on power reputations). Dahl's central method in *Who Governs?* is to 'determine for each decision which participants had initiated alternatives that were finally adopted, had vetoed alternatives initiated by others, or had proposed alternatives that were turned down. These actions were then tabulated as individual "successes" or "defeats": The participants with the greatest proportion of successes out of the total number of successes were then considered to be the most influential' (Dahl 1961: 336).[2] In short, as Polsby writes, 'In the pluralist approach . . . an attempt is made to study specific outcomes in order to determine who actually prevails in community decision-making' (Polsby 1963: 113). The stress here is on the study of concrete, observable *behaviour*. The researcher, according to Polsby, 'should study actual behavior, either at first hand or by reconstructing behavior from documents, informants, newspapers, and other appropriate sources' (ibid., p. 121). Thus the pluralist methodology, in Merelman's words, 'studied actual behavior, stressed operational definitions, and turned up evidence. Most important, it seemed to produce reliable conclusions which met the canons of science' (Merelman 1968: 451).

(It should be noted that among pluralists, 'power', 'influence', etc., tend to be used interchangeably, on the assumption that there is a 'primitive notion that seems to lie behind *all* of these concepts' (Dahl 1957, in Bell et al. (eds) 1969: 80). *Who Governs?* speaks mainly of 'influence', while Polsby speaks mainly of 'power'.)

The focus on observable behaviour in identifying power involves the pluralists in studying *decision-making* as their central task. Thus for Dahl power can be analysed only after 'careful examination of a series of concrete decisions' (1958: 466); and Polsby writes

one can conceive of 'power' – 'influence' and 'control' are serviceable synonyms – as the capacity of one actor to do something affecting another actor, which changes the probable pattern of specified future events. This can be envisaged most easily in a decision-making situation. (1963: 3–4)

and he argues that identifying 'who prevails in decision-making' seems 'the best way to determine which individuals and groups have "more" power in social life, because direct conflict between actors presents a situation most closely approximating an experimental test of their capacities to affect outcomes' (p. 4). As this last quotation shows, it is assumed that the 'decisions' involve 'direct', i.e. actual and observable, *conflict*. Thus Dahl maintains that one can only strictly test the hypothesis of a ruling class if there are '. . . cases involving key political decisions in which the preferences of the hypothetical ruling elite run counter to those of any other likely group that might be suggested', and '. . . in such cases, the preferences of the elite regularly prevail' (Dahl 1958: 466). The pluralists speak of the decisions being about *issues* in selected [key] 'issue-areas' – the assumption again being that such issues are controversial and involve actual conflict. As Dahl writes, it is 'a necessary though possibly not a sufficient condition that the key issue should involve actual disagreement in preferences among two or more groups' (p. 467).

So we have seen that the pluralists see their focus on behaviour in the making of decisions over key or important issues as involving actual, observable conflict. Note that this implication is not required by either Dahl's or Polsby's definition of power, which merely require that *A* can or does succeed in affecting what *B* does. And indeed in *Who Governs?* Dahl is quite sensitive to the operation of power or influence in the absence of conflict: indeed he even writes that a 'rough test of a person's overt or covert influence is the frequency with which he successfully initiates an important policy over the opposition of others, or vetoes polices initiated by others, or *initiates a policy where no opposition appears* [*sic*]' (Dahl 1961: 66).[3] This, however, is just one among a number of examples of how the test of *Who Governs?* is more subtle and profound than the general conceptual and methodological pronouncements of its author and his colleagues;[4] it is in contradiction with their conceptual framework and their methodology. In other words, it represents an insight which this one-dimensional view of power is unable to exploit.

Conflict, according to that view, is assumed to be crucial in providing an experimental test of power attributions: without it the exercise of power will, it seems to be thought, fail to show up. What is the conflict between? The answer is: between preferences, that are assumed to be consciously made, exhibited in actions, and thus to be discovered by observing people's behaviour. Furthermore, the pluralists assume that *interests* are to be understood as policy preferences – so that a conflict of interests is equivalent to a conflict of preferences. They are opposed to any suggestion that interests might be unarticulated or unobservable, and above all, to the idea that people might actually be mistaken about, or unaware of, their own interests. As Polsby writes

Rejecting this presumption of 'objectivity of interests', we may view instances of intraclass disagreement as intraclass conflict of interests, and interclass agreement as interclass harmony of interests. To maintain the opposite seems perverse. If information about the actual behavior of groups in the community is not considered relevant when it is different from the researcher's expectations, then it is impossible ever to disprove the empirical propositions of the stratification theory [which postulate class interests], and they will then have to be regarded as metaphysical rather than empirical statements. The presumption that the 'real' interests of a class can be assigned to them by an analyst allows the analyst to charge 'false class consciousness' when the class in question disagrees with the analyst. (Polsby 1963: 22–3)[5]

Thus I conclude that this first, one-dimensional, view of power involves a focus on *behaviour* in the making of *decisions* on *issues* over which there is an observable *conflict* of (subjective) *interests*, seen as express policy preferences, revealed by political participation.

The two-dimensional view

In their critique of this view, Bachrach and Baratz argue that it is restrictive and, in virtue of that fact, gives a misleadingly sanguine pluralist picture of American politics. Power, they claim, has two faces. The first face is that already considered, according to which 'power is totally embodied and fully reflected in "concrete decisions" or in activity bearing directly upon their making' (1970: 7). As they write

Of course power is exercised when *A* participates in the making of decisions that affect *B*. Power is also exercised when *A* devotes his energies to creating or reinforcing social and political values and institutional practices that limit the scope of the political process to public consideration of only those issues which are comparatively innocuous to *A*. To the extent that *A* succeeds in doing this, *B* is prevented, for all practical purposes, from bringing to the fore any issues that might in their resolution be seriously detrimental to *A*'s set of preferences. (p. 7)

Their 'central' point' is this: 'to the extent that a person or group – consciously or unconsciously – creates or reinforces barriers to the public airing of policy conflicts, that person or group has power' (p. 8), and they cite Schattschneider's famous and often-quoted words:

All forms of political organization have a bias in favour of the exploitation of some kinds of conflict and the suppression of others, because *organization is the mobilization of bias*. Some issues are organized into politics while others are organized out. (Schattschneider 1960: 71)

The importance of Bachrach and Baratz's work is that they bring this crucially important idea of the 'mobilization of bias' into the discussion of power. It is, in their words, a set of predominant values, beliefs, rituals, and institutional procedures ('rules of the game') that operate systematically and consistently to the benefit of certain persons and groups at the expense of others. Those who benefit are placed in a preferred position to defend and promote their vested interests. More often than not, the 'status quo defenders' are a minority or elite group within the population in question. Elitism, however, is neither foreordained nor omnipresent: as opponents of the war in Vietnam can readily attest, the mobilization of bias can and frequently does benefit a clear majority (1970: 43–4).

What, then, does this second, two-dimensional view of power amount to? What does its conceptual map look like? Answering this question poses a difficulty because Bachrach and Baratz use the term 'power' in two distinct senses. On the one hand, they use it in a general way to refer to all forms of successful control by *A* over *B* – that is, of *A*'s securing *B*'s compliance. Indeed, they develop a whole typology (which is of great interest) of forms of such control – forms that they see as types of power in either of its two faces. On the other hand, they label one of these types 'power' – namely, the securing of compliance through the threat of sanctions. In expounding their position, we can, however, easily eliminate this confusion by continuing to speak of the first sense as 'power', and by speaking of the second as 'coercion'.

Their typology of 'power', then, embraces coercion, influence, authority, force and manipulation. *Coercion*, as we have seen, exists where *A* secures *B*'s compliance by the threat of deprivation where there is 'a conflict over values or course of action between *A* and *B*' (p. 24).[6] *Influence* exists where *A*, 'without resorting to either a tacit or an overt threat of severe deprivation, causes [*B*] to change his course of action' (p. 30). In a situation involving *authority*, '*B* complies because he recognizes that [*A*'s] command is reasonable in terms of his own values' – either because its content is legitimate and reasonable or because it has been arrived at through a legitimate and reasonable procedure (pp. 34, 37). In the case of *force*, *A* achieves his objectives in the face of *B*'s noncompliance by stripping him of the choice between compliance and noncompliance. And *manipulation* is, thus, an 'aspect' or sub-concept of force (and distinct from coercion, influence and authority), since here 'compliance is forthcoming in the absence of recognition on the complier's part either of the source or the exact nature of the demand upon him' (p. 28).

The central thrust of Bachrach and Baratz's critique of the pluralists' one-dimensional view of power is, up to a point, *anti-behavioural:* that is, they claim that it 'unduly emphasises the importance of initiating, deciding, and vetoing' and, as a result, takes 'no account of the fact that power may be, and often is, exercised by confining the scope of decision-making to relatively "safe" issues' (p. 6). On the other hand, they do insist (at least in their book – in response to critics who maintained that if *B* fails to act because he anticipates *A*'s reaction, nothing has occurred and one has a 'non-event', incapable of empirical verification) that their so-called nondecisions which confine the scope of decision-making are themselves (observable) *decisions*. These, however, may not be overt or specific to a given issue or even consciously taken to exclude potential challengers, of whom the status quo defenders may well be unaware. Such unawareness 'does not mean, however, that the dominant group will refrain from making nondecisions that protect or promote their dominance. Simply supporting the established political process tends to have this effect' (p. 50).

A satisfactory analysis, then, of two-dimensional power involves examining both *decision-making* and *nondecision-making*.

[...]

The three-dimensional view

There is no doubt that the two-dimensional view of power represents a major advance over the one-dimensional view: it incorporates into the analysis of power relations the question of the control over the agenda of politics and of the ways in which potential issues are kept out of the political process. Nonetheless, it is, in my view, inadequate on three counts.

In the first place, its critique of behaviourism is too qualified, or, to put it another way, it is still too committed to behaviourism – that is, to the study of overt, 'actual behaviour', of which 'concrete decisions' in situations of conflict are seen as paradigmatic. In trying to assimilate all cases of exclusion of potential issues from the political agenda to the paradigm of a decision, it gives a misleading picture of the ways in which individuals and, above all, groups and institutions succeed in excluding potential issues from the political process. Decisions are choices consciously and intentionally made by individuals between alternatives, whereas the bias of the system can be mobilized, recreated and reinforced in ways that are neither consciously chosen not the intended result of particular individuals' choices. As Bachrach and Baratz themselves maintain, the domination of defenders of the status quo may be so secure and pervasive that they are unaware of any potential challengers to their position and thus of any alternatives to the existing political process, whose bias they work to maintain. As 'students of power and its consequences', they write, 'our main concern is not whether the defenders of the status quo use their power consciously, but rather if and how they exercise it and what effects it has on the political process and other actors within the system' (Bachrach and Baratz 1970: 50).

Moreover, the bias of the system is not sustained simply by a series of individually chosen acts, but also, most importantly, by the socially structured and culturally patterned behaviour of groups, and practices of institutions, which may indeed be manifested by individuals' inaction. Bachrach and Baratz follow the pluralists in adopting too methodologically individualist a view of power. In this both parties follow in the steps of Max Weber, for whom power was the probability of *individuals realizing their wills* despite the resistance of others, whereas the power to control the agenda of politics and exclude potential issues cannot be adequately analysed unless it is seen as a function of collective forces and social arrangements.[7]

[...]

In summary, the three-dimensional view of power involves a *thoroughgoing critique of the behavioural focus*[8] of the first two views as too individualistic and allows for consideration of the many ways in which *potential issues* are kept out of politics, whether through the operation of social forces and institutional practices or through individuals' decisions. This, moreover, can occur in the absence of actual, observable conflict, which may have been successfully averted – though there remains here an implicit reference to potential conflict. This potential, however, may never in fact be actualized. What one may have here is a *latent conflict*, which consists in a contradiction between the interests of those exercising power and the *real interests* of those they exclude.[9] These latter may not express or even be conscious of their interests, but, as I shall argue, the identification of those interests ultimately always rests on empirically supportable and refutable hypotheses.

The distinctive features of the three views of power presented above are summarized below.

One-Dimensional View of Power
Focus on (a) behaviour
　　　　(b) decision-making
　　　　(c) (key) issues

(d) observable (overt) conflict
(e) (subjective) interests, seen as policy preferences revealed by political participation

Two-Dimensional View of Power
(Qualified) critique of behavioural focus
Focus on (a) decision-making and nondecision-making
(b) issues and potential issues
(c) observable (overt or covert) conflict
(d) (subjective) interests, seen as policy preferences or grievances

Three-Dimensional View of Power
Critique of behavioural focus
Focus on (a) decision-making and control over political agenda (not necessarily through decisions)
(b) issues and potential issues
(c) observable (overt or covert), and latent conflict
(d) subjective and real interests

[. . .]

The one-dimensional view of power offers a clear-cut paradigm for the behavioural study of decision-making power by political actors, but it inevitably takes over the bias of the political system under observation and is blind to the ways in which its political agenda is controlled. The two-dimensional view points the way to examining that bias and control, but conceives of them too narrowly: in a word, it lacks a sociological perspective within which to examine, not only decision-making and nondecision-making power, but also the various ways of suppressing latent conflicts within society. Such an examination poses a number of serious difficulties.

These difficulties are serious but not overwhelming. They certainly do not require us to consign the three-dimensional view of power to the realm of the merely metaphysical or the merely ideological. My conclusion, in short, is that a deeper analysis of power relations is possible – an analysis that is at once value-laden, theoretical and empirical.[10] A pessimistic attitude towards the

possibility of such an analysis is unjustified. As Frey as written (1971: 1095), such pessimism amounts to saying: 'Why let things be difficult when, with just a little more effort, we can make them seem impossible?'

NOTES

1. Contrast Parsons's lament that 'Unfortunately, the concept of power is not a settled one in the social sciences, either in political science or in sociology' (Parsons 1957: 139).
2. For a critical discussion of Dahl's use of his own concept of power, see Morriss (1972).
3. Emphasis mine (S.L.) This passage is acutely criticized in Morriss 1972.
4. Another example occurs on pp. 161–2 and p. 321, when Dahl points implicitly towards the process of nondecision-making, by writing of the power of members of the political stratum to determine whether a matter becomes a 'salient public issue' or not.
5. Compare Theodor Geiger's critique of Marx's imputation of 'true interests' to the proletariat which are independent of the wishes and goals of its members: here, writes Geiger, 'the proper analysis of the interest structure of social classes ends – religious mania alone speaks here' (*Die Klassengesellschaft im Schmelzliegel*, Cologne and Hagen, 1949, p. 133 cited and translated in Dahrendorf 1959: 175).
6. On coercion see Nozick 1972; Pennock and Chapman (eds) 1972. See also Wertheimer 1987.
7. See Lukes 1973, chapter 17. Contrast Dahrendorf's decision to 'follow . . . the useful and well-considered definitions of Max Weber', according to which 'the important difference between power and authority consists in the fact that whereas power is essentially tied to the personality of individuals, authority is always associated with social positions or roles' (Dahrendorf 1959: 166).

8. I use the term 'behavioural' [...] to refer to the study of overt and actual behaviour – and specifically concrete decisions. Of course, in the widest sense, the three-dimensional view of power is 'behavioural' in that it is committed to the view that behaviour (action and inaction, conscious and unconscious, actual and potential) provides evidence (direct and indirect) for an attribution of the exercise of power.

9. This conflict is latent in the sense that it is assumed that there *would be* a conflict of wants or preferences between those exercising power and those subject to it, were the latter to become aware of their interests. (My account of latent conflict and real interests is to be distinguished from Dahrendorf's account of 'objective' and 'latent' interests as 'antagonistic interests conditioned by, even inherent in, social positions', in imperatively co-ordinated associations, which are 'independent of [the individual's] conscious orientations' (Dahrendorf 1959: 174, 178). Dahrendorf assumes as sociologically given what I claim to be empirically ascertainable.)

10. For a fine example of such an analysis, see Gaventa 1980.

REFERENCES

Peter Bachrach and Morton S. Baratz, *Power and Poverty. Theory and Practice* (New York: Oxford University Press, 1970).

Roderick Bell, David V. Edwards and R. Harrison Wagner (eds), *Political Power: A Reader in Theory and Research* (New York: The Free Press; London: Collier-Macmillan, 1969).

Robert A. Dahl, 'The Concept of Power', *Behavioral Science*, 2 (1957) pp. 201–5.

Robert A. Dahl, 'A Critique of the Ruling Elite Model', *American Political Science Review*, 52 (1958) pp. 463–9.

Robert A. Dahl, *Who Governs? Democracy and Power in an American City* (New Haven and London: Yale University Press, 1961).

Ralf Dahrendorf, *Class and Class Conflict in Industrial Society* (London: Routledge & Kegan Paul, 1959).

Frederick W. Frey, 'Comment: On Issues and Nonissues in the Study of Power', *American Political Science Review*, 65 (1971) pp. 1081–101.

W. B. Gallie, 'Essentially Contested Concepts', *Proceedings of the Aristotelian Society*, 56 (1955–6) pp. 167–98.

J. Gaventa, *Power and Powerlessness: Quiescence and Rebellion in an Appalachian Valley* (Champaign, IL: University of Illinois Press, 1980).

Steven Lukes, *Emile Durkheim: His Life and Work* (New York: Harper & Row, 1973).

Richard M. Merelman, 'On the Neo-Elitist Critique of Community Power', *American Political Science Review*, 62 (1968) pp. 451–50.

Peter Morriss, 'Power in New Haven: A Reassessment of "Who Governs?"', *British Journal of Political Science*, 2 (1972) pp. 457–65.

Robert Nozick, 'Coercion', in P. Laslett, W. G. Runciman and Q. Skinner (eds), *Philosophy, Politics and Society*, Fourth Series (Oxford: Basil Blackwell, 1972).

Talcott Parsons, 'The Distribution of Power in American Society', *World Politics*, 10 (Oct 1957) pp. 123–43.

J. Roland Pennock and John W. Chapman (eds), *Coercion* (Chicago: Aldine Atherton, 1972).

Nelson W. Polsby, *Community Power and Political Theory* (New Haven and London: Yale University Press, 1963).

E. E. Schattschneider, *The Semi-Sovereign People: A Realist's View of Democracy in America* (New York: Holt, Rinehart & Winston, 1960).

Alan Wertheimer, *Coercion* (Princeton, NJ: Princeton University Press, 1987).

50. New Wars in a Global Age

Mary Kaldor

My central argument is that, during the last decades of the twentieth century, a new type of organized violence developed, especially in Africa and Eastern Europe, which is one aspect of the current globalized era. I describe this type of violence as 'new war'. I use the term 'new' to distinguish such wars from prevailing perceptions of war drawn from an earlier era. [. . .]

I use the term 'war' to emphasize the political nature of this new type of violence, even though, as will become clear in the following pages, the new wars involve a blurring of the distinctions between war (usually defined as violence between states or organized political groups for political motives), organized crime (violence undertaken by privately organized groups for private purposes, usually financial gain) and large-scale violations of human rights (violence undertaken by states or politically organized groups against individuals).

In most of the literature, the new wars are described as internal or civil wars or else as 'low-intensity conflicts'. Yet although most of these wars are localized, they involve a myriad of transnational connections so that the distinction between internal and external, between aggression (attacks from abroad) and repression (attacks from inside the country), or even between local and global, are difficult to sustain. The term 'low-intensity conflict' was coined during the Cold War period by the US military to describe guerrilla warfare or terrorism. Although it is possible to trace the evolution of the new wars from the so-called low-intensity conflicts of the Cold War period, they have distinctive characteristics which

are masked by what is in effect a catch-all term. Some authors describe the new wars as privatized or informal wars[1]; yet, while the privatization of violence is an important element of these wars, in practice, the distinction between what is private and what is public, state and non-state, informal and formal, what is done for economic and what for political motives, cannot easily be applied. A more appropriate term is perhaps 'post-modern', which is used by several authors.[2]

Like 'new wars', it offers a way of distinguishing these wars from the wars which could be said to be characteristic of classical modernity. However, the term is also used to refer to virtual wars and wars in cyberspace[3]; moreover, the new wars involve elements of premodernity and modernity as well. Finally, Martin Shaw uses the term 'degenerate warfare'. For him there is a continuity with the total wars of the twentieth century and their genocidal aspects; the term draws attention to the decay of the national frameworks, especially military forces.

Critics of the 'new war' argument have suggested that many features of the new wars can be found in earlier wars and that the dominance of the Cold War overshadowed the significance of 'small wars' or 'low intensity' conflicts.[4] There is some truth in this proposition. The main point of the distinction between new and old wars was to change the prevailing perceptions of war, especially among policy-makers. In particular, I wanted to emphasize the growing illegitimacy of these wars and the need for a cosmopolitan political response – one that put individual rights and the rule of law as the centrepiece of any international intervention (political, military, civil or economic). Nevertheless, I do think that the 'new war' argument does reflect a new reality – a reality that was emerging before the end of the Cold War. Globalization is a convenient catch-all to describe the various changes that characterize the contemporary period and have influenced the character of war.[5]

Among American strategic writers, there is a discussion about what is known as the Revolution in Military Affairs, or Defence Transformation.[6] The argument is that the advent of information technology is as significant as was the advent of the tank and the aeroplane, or even as significant as the shift from horsepower to mechanical power, with profound implications for the future of warfare. In particular, it is argued that these changes have made modern war much more precise and discriminate. However, the Revolution in Military Affairs is conceived by these writers within the inherited institutional structures of war and the military. They envisage wars on a traditional model in which the new techniques develop in a more or less linear extension from the past. Moreover, they are designed to sustain the imagined character of war which was typical of the Cold War era and utilized in such a way as to minimize own casualties. The preferred technique is spectacular aerial bombing or rapid and dramatic ground manoeuvres which reproduces the appearance of classical war for public consumption but which is rather clumsy as an instrument for influencing the reality on the ground. Hence Baudrillard's famous remark that the Gulf War did not take place.[7] These complex sophisticated techniques were used in the Gulf War of 1991, in the last phases of the war in Bosnia–Herzegovina, in Kosovo, in Afghanistan and, most recently, in Iraq. In most of these cases, they did achieve limited clearly defined goals, but they failed to control the situation on the ground and they caused many civilian casualties.

I share the view that there has been a revolution in military affairs, but it is a revolution in the social relations of warfare, not in technology, even though the changes in social relations are influenced by and make use of new technology. Beneath the spectacular displays are real wars, which, even in the case of the 1991 Iraq war in which hundreds and thousands of Kurds and Shi'ites died, are better explained in terms of my conception of new wars.

[. . .]

'In the images of falling statues', said President Bush on 1 May 2003, as he announced the end of hostilities in Iraq, dressed in fatigues on the deck of USS *Abraham Lincoln*, 'we have witnessed the arrival of a new era.'[8] Like his Defense Secretary, Donald Rumsfeld, President Bush claimed to have discovered a new form of warfare, making use of information technology so that war can be rapid, precise, and low in casualties. In the immediate aftermath of the invasion, military commentators were jubilant. Bush himself described the invasion as 'one of the swiftest advances in history'.[9] Max Boot, writing in *Foreign Affairs*, described the war as 'dazzling'. 'That the United States and its allies won anyway – and won so quickly – must rank as one of the signal achievements of military history.'[10] The ongoing war in Iraq is, indeed, a new type of war but of the kind described in this book. It is true that all kinds of new technologies, ranging from sophisticated satellite-based systems to mobile phones and the Internet, have been used. But if we are to understand the war in ways that are useful to policymakers, then its novel character should not be defined in terms of technology. What is new about the war needs to be analysed in terms of the disintegration of states and the changes in social relations under the impact of globalization rather than in terms of technology.

[. . .]

Effectively, what is happening in Iraq is that the United States is being drawn into a genuinely new type of war. The Americans' belief that they are fighting an old war, adapted and improved by the advent of new technology, actually prevents any strategy towards Iraq that might lead to stability. As in other new wars, the warring parties are both caught up in their own narratives about what they are trying to achieve, and their respective narratives feed on each other. The Americans believe that they are leading a struggle for democracy, and the more they confront resistance, especially of the more spectacular type, the more those who support the war are convinced of the rightness of what they are doing and the more the polarized atmosphere within the United States contributes to the strength of war party. As long as they and others believe in the narrative, it does not matter that the insurgency grows. On the contrary, it perpetuates and substantiates the idea of a long war. At the same time, the more that American behaviour exacerbates the sense of insecurity and humiliation, the more the insurgency grows and the more those that promulgate an idea of a war of the West against Islam, or who identify the Iraqi government, Shi'ites and Kurds with the West in order to promote a sectarian war, gain the upper hand.

As in other new wars, the victims are the civilians, who suffer the vast bulk of the casualties, who are detained by the Americans or taken hostage by the insurgents, and who are displaced from their homes as a consequence of the fighting or the efforts by both sides to establish secure areas. Despite the American attacks on the insurgents and the insurgents' attacks on the Americans, the warring parties rarely directly engage each other; instead the victims are Iraqi civilians or those associated with the nascent Iraqi security forces. This is perhaps the distinguishing characteristic of new wars. Unlike in Bosnia, deliberate attacks on civilians are rare, although they are increasing as the war acquires a sectarian character. But, as in Chechnya, it becomes increasingly difficult to distinguish between ethnic cleansing and counter-insurgency. Civilians are killed, detained, tortured, or displaced from their homes because it is so difficult to distinguish combatants from non-combatants. Civilians are also caught in the crossfire because, unlike Coalition troops, they have no protection.

Each stage of the conflict accelerates the process of unravelling state institutions and shared norms and rules, both inside Iraq and, indeed, within an increasingly polarized United States. In particular, it is the prospect of Iraqi democracy that is being defeated in this war. Those who hope for peaceful ways of managing disagreements through elections and debates have to choose between association with the insurgents, dominated both by repressive Ba'athism and conservative Islam or, worse, al-Qaeda, or associating with the Coalition, which discredits them in the eyes of many of their fellow citizens.

[. . .]

The optimistic view of current developments is the obsolescence of modern war. War, as we have known it for the last two centuries, may, like slavery, have become an anachronism. National armies, navies and airforces may be no more than ritual vestiges of the passing nation-state. 'Perpetual peace', as envisaged by Immanuel Kant, the globalization of civility, and the development of cosmopolitan forms of governance are real possibilities. The pessimistic view is that war, like slavery, can always be reinvented. The capacity of formal political institutions, primarily nation-states, to regulate violence has been eroded and we have entered an era of long-term low-level informal violence, of post-modern warfare. In this book, I have argued that both views are correct. We cannot assume that either barbarism or civility is embedded in human nature. Whether we can learn to cope with the new wars and veer towards a more optimistic future depends ultimately on our own behaviour.

NOTES

1. David Keen, 'When war itself is privatized', *Times Literary Supplement* (December 1995).
2. Mark Duffield, 'Post-modern conflict: warlords, post-adjustment states and private protection', *Journal of Civil Wars* (April

1998); Michael Ignatieff, *The Warrior's Honor: Ethnic War and the Modern Conscience*, London: Chatto & Windus, 1998.

3. Chris Hables Gray, *Post-Modern War: The New Politics of Conflicts*, London and New York: Routledge, 1997.

4. See, for example, the various chapters including my own chapter 'Elaborating the "new war" thesis', in Jan Angstrom and Isabelle Duyvesteyn, *Rethinking the Nature of War*, London and New York: Frank Cass, 2005; see also Errol A. Henderson and David Singer, '"New wars" and rumours of "new wars"', *International Interactions*, 7/2 (2002); Stathis N. Kalyvas, '"New" and "old" civil wars: a valid distinction?', *World Politics*, 54 (October 2001).

5. Martin Shaw, 'War and globality: the role and character of war in the global transition', in Ho-Won Jeong (ed.), *Peace and Conflict: A New Agenda*, Aldershot: Ashgate, 2000.

6. See David Jablonsky, *The Owl of Minerva Flies at Night: Doctrinal Change and Continuity and the Revolution in Military Affairs*, US Army War College, Carlisle Barracks, PA, 1994; Elliott Cohen, 'A revolution in warfare', *Foreign Affairs* (March/April 1996); Robert J. Bunker, 'Technology in a neo-Clausewitzen setting', in Gert de Nooy (ed.), *The Clausewitzean Dictum and the Future of Western Military Strategy*, The Hague and London: Kluwer Law International, 1997.

7. Jean Baudrillard, *The Gulf War*, London: Power Publishers, 1995.

8. George W. Bush, 'President Bush announces major combat operations in Iraq have ended: remarks by President Bush from the USS *Abraham Lincoln*', 1 May 2003.

9. Ibid.

10. Max Boot, 'The new American way of war', *Foreign Affairs* (July/August 2003).

51. The Social Movement Society?

David S. Meyer & Sidney Tarrow

Not long ago, one of us (Tarrow 1994, pp. 193–8) suggested that the social movement form of representing claims is becoming largely institutionalized in advanced industrial democracies – so much so that classical social movement modes of action may be becoming part of the conventional repertoire of participation.[1] The idea of a movement society advances three main hypotheses:

- First, social protest has moved from being a sporadic, if recurring feature of democratic politics, to become a perpetual element in modern life.
- Second, protest behavior is employed with greater frequency, by more diverse constituencies, and is used to represent a wider range of claims than ever before.
- Third, professionalization and institutionalization may be changing the major vehicle of contentious claims – the social movement – into an instrument within the realm of conventional politics.

To the extent that these three things are happening, the social movement may lose its power to inspire challengers and to impress antagonists and authorities; it may be moving from the edges of political legitimacy, where it has warranted special responses from the state and separate analytical treatment from social analysts, to become something more akin to interest groups and political parties. Before moving to any kind of grand generalization, however, we must examine the empirical facts of the frequency, diffusion, profes-

sionalization, and institutionalization of contentious politics and the social movement.

We begin from the assumption that the social movement is a *historical* and not a universal way of mounting collective claims. Movements, in our view, are best defined as *collective challenges to existing arrangements of power and distribution by people with common purposes and solidarity, in sustained interaction with elites, opponents, and authorities.* Movements became a viable way of making claims in national politics when the consolidated nation-state assured its citizens regular means of communication, created standard but fungible identities, and provided challengers with uniform targets and fulcra for acting collectively (Tarrow 1994; Tilly 1995b). But movements were never the only vehicles for contention; they acted in parallel and frequently intersected with other forms of collective action; with isolated incidents of collective violence; with strikes and campaigns mounted by unions or other institutional actors; and with the rebellions, insurgencies, and revolutions with which they have strong analogies (McAdam et al. 1997). Not only that, they often acted *within* institutional politics and movement activists learned to combine institutional modes of action with noninstitutional contention (Tilly 1978; Tarrow, 1996). Thus, if the definition of movements depends on a sustained, conflictual interaction with other actors, they have seldom been very far from institutional politics – especially in the pluralist democracies of the West.

If movements are historical phenomena and have always militated around the borders of the polity, it is surely a mistake to expect them to emerge and mobilize in characteristic forms as the world, around them changes. Although few basic changes marked the national social movement's trajectory after its appearance in the eighteenth century up until the Second World War, the processes that permitted movements to mobilize against powerful states have continued to evolve. New sets of claims and claimants have begun to emerge, even as the state's capacity to redress them has diminished (Ginsburg and Shefter 1990). Citizens with greater resources and increased skills have developed new capacities for action (McCarthy and Zald 1987). With increased travel, communication, and education, the potential networks of activism have broadened beyond the state (Keck and Sikkink 1998). States have to some extent been losing control over national life as international news services, television broadcasting, and even electronic mail allow news of claims and events to spread within and across countries with astonishing speed.[2] These changes have increased the ease with which contention can be mounted and have created at least imagined commonalities among challengers across social groups and national states.

The rapid spread of contention across the globe and the increased capacity of citizens to mount it have been seen by some to portend a new and more chaotic era of global turbulence (Rosenau 1990) and, by others, to represent direct challenges to state sovereignty (Badie 1995; Cerny 1995). This view is supported by the spread of such militant movements as Islamic fundamentalism transnationally from Iran to Afghanistan and to North Africa and by the more recent appearance of extremist groups like American militias and European naziskins.

The dramatic rise of potentially violent movements belies the fact that over the longer run in the history of Western Europe and North America, there is evidence of declining violence in the repertoire of contention (Tilly 1995a) and of a greater ease of ordinary citizens in mounting contention, which suggests its acceptability and even legitimation by elites and authorities. By accept-

ing and regulating contention, in this view, states may have learned to control it and, through this control, begun to domesticate the social movement within the political process.

[. . .]

Example of lighter, more decentralized collectivities abound in the activism of the post-1960s decades: in the American peace movement studied by one of us (Meyer 1990); in the temporary coalitions of Berlin-based groups organized for brief campaigns studied by Gerhards and Rucht (1992); in the spectacular recent successes of the anti-Walmart protests in the United States, largely diffused through electronic communication by people who had never met (Yin 1996); and in transnational environmental organizations like Greenpeace, which combine small groups of high-risk activists with literally millions of inactive supporters around the world (Wapner 1995).

Such movements are not 'new' in that they are 'spontaneous,' whereas their predecessors were 'organized'; or in that they put forward 'identity claims,' in contrast to the supposedly more 'instrumental' claims of 'old' social movements; or even in that they routinely use unconventional forms of action (Rucht 1990).[3] What is new is that they have greater discretionary resources, enjoy easier access to the media, and have cheaper and faster geographic mobility and cultural interaction. Among them, these features have made permanent, centralized, and bureaucratic organizations less important than they once were in attempts to advance effective challenges to elites or authorities. In the movement society, it is possible for lighter, more decentralized, and temporary collectivities to gain the logistical and financial advantages that formerly inhered only in bureaucratic mass organizations. Professionalization, then, needs to be conceptualized more broadly, as does the range of possible organizational forms dissidents may take.[4]

Unlike the stolid, bureaucratic organizations of the interwar period, contemporary activists possess what might be called 'moveable social capital': the capacity of transitory teams to assemble coalitions of local and translocal groups and to mount collective action after relatively brief preparation in a variety of venues. Rather than declining in the age of the mass media as some have hypothesized (Putnam 1995), social capital may have simply become more mobile; though losing ground in the permanent associations of local life, it may be growing in the capacity of citizens to put together temporary coalitions for contentious politics. Hanspeter Kriesi's team's (1995) work on new social movement organizations takes us a step toward formalizing this insight.

The growth and differentiation of movement-related organizations

Movements are generally composed of a number of organizations and affiliated organizations cooperating – to some degree – to advance political claims.[5] The form, organization, and relative prominence of movement organizations change over the course of a protest cycle. Key movement organizations are very seldom well structured during a movement's early phases. By using the term *well structured,* we follow Kriesi et al. (1995) in referring to their formalization, professionalization, centralized control, well-financed operations, and large number of supportive members. During their most protest-oriented phases, such organizations are usually in an emergent phase and depend more on protest as a resource with which to mobilize supporters than on more conventional internal or external resources (Lipsky 1968; Tarrow 1994). This finding has been confirmed in diverse contexts, including the American civil rights movement (Jenkins and Eckert 1986), the 1960s–1970s protest cycle in Italy (Tarrow 1989), and the new social movements in Western Europe in the 1980s (Kriesi et al. 1995). The major growth in movement organizations came *after* the height of both protest cycles.

Second, the strength of movement-related organizations cannot be measured simply by mass memberships. Social movements do not only produce organizations that aim at political mobi-

lization toward authorities or others (SMOs); in fact, as we have just argued, such organizations are more likely to mature after the height of mobilization has passed. They can also turn into indirect forms of political representation, like parties or interest groups, or take on constituency/client-oriented activities that produce *non*-political organizations, for either service or self-help purposes (Kriesi et al. 1995, p. 152 ff). This point suggests that movement organizations not only develop internally (e.g., greater formalization, bureaucratization, professionalization, and membership growth) but also put their energies into building other kinds of movement-related organizations – usually after their protest-related activities decline. As Kriesi et al. (1995, p. 156) note:

An SMO can become more like a party or an interest group; it can take on characteristics of a supportive service organization; it can develop in the direction of a self-help group, a voluntary association or a club; or it can radicalize, that is, become an ever more exclusive organization for the mobilization for collective action.

More important here than the various trajectories, or their importance to different types of movements, is the recognition that the variety of organizational outcomes provides social movements with a wider range of possibilities for subsequent action than previous theories of social movements acknowledged. To the extent that a movement expands into other forms of movement-related organizations, it develops lateral constituencies and cadres of activists whose numbers or potential commitment will not be evident by looking at the figures for SMO membership. This is a crucial point that may help to interpret the fact that recent 'new' SMOs tend to be more streamlined than older ones, in terms of both membership[6] and the number of their permanent organizational cadres. Roughly one-half of the groups Kriesi et al. examined had no paid staff at all; only in the German and Dutch SMOs was there more than an average of eighteen paid staff per organization; in France and Switzerland, the average was fewer than ten. But with affiliated self-help service, and party/political movement-related organizations, they may have a much larger activist cadre to draw on than appears evident from their number of members or permanent staff.

But there is another reason that the organizational diffusion described by Kriesi et al. is important for the movement society thesis: it suggests ways in which movement-originated identities, goals, and personnel may be blending into the structures of civil society without necessarily producing a higher visible level of protest, violence, or contention. Movement organizations need not be defined exclusively by the organization of protest campaigns, and more conventional political organizations may organize such campaigns (Burstein 1997). Indeed, much of the contention in contemporary societies does not come from movement organizations as such but from campaigns organized by parties, interest groups, professional associations, citizens' groups, and public servants. And this point takes us directly to the problem of institutionalization.

The institutionalization of movements

If social protest has become more common, more easily diffused and sponsored by increasing numbers and types of organizations, we must then ask, What sorts of protest? And what do they mean for the future of the social movement? Within the wide range of collective action forms in democratic states today, we find an apparent paradox: although disruption appears to be the most effective political tool of the disadvantaged (Lipsky 1968; Piven and Cloward 1979), the majority of episodes of movement activity we see today disrupt few routines, save perhaps those in the everyday lives of the protesters. As noted earlier, most contentious actions in Western industrial societies take the form of peaceful, orderly routines that break no laws and violate no spaces.

Why are conventional forms of collective action the ones most commonly employed, even in a tumultuous period of contention? Of course, part of the answer is tautological: what is conventional becomes so because it is commonly used, and the boundaries of acceptable conduct and claims are changed by social protest movements. Demonstrations and petitions – once contentious, unpredictable, and disruptive – are now less so. To understand what this means, we need to look at the interests of both the state and dissidents in negotiating means of claims making that are repeatable and routinized, regardless of outcome.

For us, institutionalization is defined by the creation of a repeatable process that is essentially self-sustaining (Jepperson 1991); it is one in which all the relevant actors can resort to well-established and familiar routines. For political movements, institutionalization denotes the end of the sense of unlimited possibility of the kind we saw in Berkeley, which paralyzed police and university administrators; for authorities, it means the ending of the uncertainty and instability that can result when unknown actors engage in uncontrollable forms of action. Institutionalization, in this view, is composed of three main components:

- First, the *routinization* of collective action, such that challengers and authorities can both adhere to a common script, recognizing familiar patterns as well as potentially dangerous deviations.[7]
- Second, *inclusion* and *marginalization*, whereby challengers who are willing to adhere to established routines will be granted access to political exchanges in mainstream institutions, while those who refuse to accept them can be shut out of conversations through either repression or neglect.
- Third, cooptation, which means that challengers alter their claims and tactics to ones that can be pursued without disrupting the normal practice of politics.[8]

These processes of routinization, inclusion/marginalization, and co-optation are distinct but complementary aspects of institutionalization (Meyer 1993), which allow dissidents to continue to lodge claims *and* permit states to manage dissent without stifling it.

Authorities manage dissent by insisting clearly and acting consistently on a spectrum of behaviors, some of which will be tolerated while others are either repressed or ignored. This has the effect of not only enticing some actors to embrace institutional politics but also inducing others to reject it, thus separating more radical activists from their more moderate allies, fragmenting coalitions of challengers, and weakening opposition overall. Institutionally oriented challengers are rewarded for their choice by the prospect of meaningful political access, whereas those determined to make more comprehensive challenges avoid the compromises inherent in institutional politics but risk repression or simply irrelevance.

We can usefully think about this equation by starting from the activists' perspective. Challengers will adopt the form of claims making that they believe to be most effective and least costly. Most activists will abandon forms that seem unduly costly, eschewing actions that invite repression when meaningful alternatives seem available. For example, activists learn that they can march and offer even the most radical claims, provided they stay on negotiated parade routes. They learn to control extremist elements within their ranks and on their fringes, whose actions risk turning police cooperation into conflict. [. . .]

Just as pursuing strategies that invite repression can destroy movement organizations, adapting routinized forms of action is also costly. By reducing the uncertainty in their tactics and accepting compromises in their claims, challengers reduce their capacity to inspire supporters and to hold the attention of elites. At the same time, groups who choose the institutional path can gain compensations – which is why many often do. Ordinary people are more likely to want to participate in forms of collective action they know and understand than risk the uncertainty, particularly potential violence, of radical direct action. As a movement's chosen form of action crystallizes into convention, it becomes a known part of the repertoire and lowers the social transaction costs for organizers and their supporters (Tarrow 1994, chap. 2). Once learned, these practices can be redeployed, tinkered with, and combined with other forms, just as a jazz group improvises around a central theme (Tilly 1978). Perhaps most significantly, adopting routinized forms can lead to influence on public policy; challengers can win victories, even if often uncredited and more modest than activists might wish.

In the long run, the evolution of the repertoire results from the absorption of the innovations that work and the rejection of ones that fail. Over time, originally disruptive forms like the strike and the demonstration have become conventional because they presented effective challenges, maintained and built solidarity, and usually avoided repression by controlling uncertainty. In the early twentieth century, the invention of the institution of parade marshals in France and elsewhere showed how uncertainty could be controlled (Favre 1990). In the last thirty years of our century, once-disruptive forms like nonviolent collective action, sit-ins, and building occupations have begun to produce less disruptive equivalents.

How do ongoing changes in contemporary institutions affect the process of institutionalizing dissent? Three notable developments in contemporary protest politics seem to be particularly important.

First, social movement activists have learned how to move between conventional and unconventional collective actions, and even to employ both sorts of strategies in combination. As example, the civil rights movement in the United States began with legislative efforts and legal challenges and moved to mass marches and sit-ins in the next phase of its efforts. Similarly, European antinuclear groups deployed a panoply of tactics ranging from the high-risk blockades of nuclear energy facilities all the way to educational efforts and lobbying local politicians. While some organizations specialize in a particular set of tactics, they can work in combination with both other specialists and organizations that deploy diverse methods. Activists can thus adapt strategies to the targets, claims, opportunities, and constraints of the historical moment.

Entering mainstream politics or other well-established nonstate institutions does not mean eschewing challenging claims. In chapter 9, Mary Katzenstein examines two institutions that we would expect to be rather insulated from the effects of dissidents within them – the army and the Catholic Church – and finds that these institutions *sometimes* reformed and restructured themselves in response to new claims and constituents. To some extent, bringing new practices and even a new language to the heart of establishments like the armed forces or the Church may have had greater long-term effects than even the most dramatic mass protest does on the streets.

Second, police practices increasingly encourage the routinization of contention by cooperating with protesters in planning their events, avoiding provocations, and allowing them a public but circumscribed hearing. These practices vary among Western democracies, as the comparison of France and Italy in chapter 5 by della Porta, Fillieule, and Reiter shows. But they have consistently shifted in the direction of the apolitical management of protest, despite occasional outcroppings of politics or police-inspired violence. Police images of 'good' and 'bad' protesters are dependent not on dissident claims or ideology but on conduct. And police practices have diffused transnationally over time, just as activist strategies and claims have.

Police practice illustrates the process of institutionalization in microcosm. Demonstrators negotiate the date and physical boundaries of their challenges. Police, representing the state, agree not only to tolerate them but to protect them against countermovements. Demonstrators can even escalate the challenge by adding 'civil disobedience' to their demonstration – as McCarthy and McPhail show in their discussion of the Justice for Janitors campaign. By informing police of planned challenges to the law – even asking lawbreakers to identify themselves with armbands – and agreeing to eschew violence, activists can make the experience of breaking the law safe and predictable. Police know what to expect, lay on stretchers and buses, and inform demonstrators how to avoid being hurt while they are carried off to be booked. Everyone can get home by the end of the day to observe the event on the evening news.

Do movements that routinize their practices in cooperation with the police eventually have to accept the other two aspects of institutionalization – inclusion and cooptation? Although this progress seems to have an inexorable logic, this is not necessarily the case. If we accept that movements can pursue system-challenging claims even *within* the institutions of the state, we have no reason to believe that routinized forms of contention are necessarily less challenging than their unruly cousins or that they determine other aspects of movement/state relations. In fact, putting half a million people in the streets for an orderly demonstration may push policies in activists' preferred direction more than the more dramatic and disruptive efforts of a few militants who firebomb opponents' offices or turn over cars.[9]

Third, the tactics used by movement organizations and those used by more institutionalized groups increasingly overlap. Just as movement leaders have become skilled at using the law, legislation, and the media, interest groups and parties frequently resort to the kinds of public performances that used to be identified exclusively with social movements. When Democratic members of Congress hold mock hearings on the steps of the Capitol to demonstrate their being shut out by the Republican majority or get arrested outside the South African consulate to protest apartheid, when members of a representational artists' association demonstrate outside the Museum of Modern Art in New York to protest their exclusion from the museum's exhibits, and when members of the Royal Association for the Prevention of Cruelty to Animals block calf-carrying trucks in British ferry ports, the instruments of social protests have indeed become modular. We now reach our final concern: a reflection on how social movements are conceived, operationalized, and how they relate to conventional politics.

NOTES

1. Although the first statements of the 'movement society' idea were proffered as possibilities rather than as explicit hypotheses, in this fragmentary treatment, Tarrow tried to distill a few key issues which recur in the literature. For other attempts to do the same, see Neidhart and Rucht (1993), where the term first appears; Fish (1995), where it is used somewhat differently; Minkoff (1994); and Meyer and Staggenborg (1996).
2. For a sampling of the rapidly growing literature on transnationalization of movements, see Keck and Sikkink (1998), Rucht (1996), Sikkink (1993), Smith et al. (1997), and Wapner (1995).
3. For the archetypical 'new' social movement claim, see Cohen (1985) and Cohen and Arato (1992). For a more historically based view that finds both instrumental and identity claims in previous waves of movement, see D'Anieri et al. (1990), and Calhoun (1995).
4. Scholars have lately examined the 'organizational repertoire' from which dissidents can choose; see Clemens (1993) and Minkoff (1994).
5. For a more developed statement of the coalitional aspects of social protest movements, see Meyer and Rochon (1997).
6. For example, Kriesi et al.'s (1995, p. 172) data on the most important SMOs in the four European countries he examined show clearly that, with the exception of Greenpeace, average membership is much lower for those organizations created after 1965 than those already on the scene in that year.
7. For example, so routinized has the *manifestation* become in France that political scientist Pierre Favre (1990) is able to chart a schema of its constituent elements graphically.
8. We follow Selznick (1949) here, rejecting the narrower definition of cooptation of some analysts that implies the abandonment of political goals.
9. The trade-off between numbers and intensity of participation required presents an intriguing puzzle that activists confront regularly but in scholarly research has been addressed only at a formal theoretical level (De Nardo 1985). Although we might assume an inverse relationship between numbers participating and the risk and cost of participation, we need empirical research to confirm this assumption and to examine the relative influence of different tactics on public policy.

REFERENCES

Badie, Betrand. 1995. *La fin des territoires: Essai sur le désordre international et sur l'utilité sociale du respect.* Paris: Fayard.

Burstein, Paul. 1997. 'Political Organizations: Interest Groups, Social Movements, and Political Parties.' In Andrew McFarland and Anne Costain, eds., *Social Movements and the American Political Process.* Boulder, CO: Rowman & Littlefield.

Calhoun, Craig. 1995. 'New Social Movements of the Early Nineteenth Century.' Pp. 173–215 in Mark Traugott, ed., *Repertoires and Cycles of Collective Action.* Durham, NC: Duke University Press.

Cerny, Philip G. 1995. 'Globalization and the Changing Logic of Collective Action.' *International Organization* 49: 595–625.

Clemens, Elisabeth S. 1993. 'Organizational Repertoires and Institutional Change: Women's Groups and the Transformation of American Politics, 1890–1920.' *American Journal of Sociology* 98 (4): 755–98.

Cohen, Jean. 1985. 'Strategy or Identity: New Theoretical Paradigms and Contemporary Social Movements.' *Social Research* 52: 663–716.

Cohen, Jean, and Andrew Arato. 1992. *Civil Society and Political Theory.* Cambridge, MA: MIT Press.

D'Anieri, Paul, Claire Ernst, and Elizabeth Kier. 1990. 'New Social Movements in Historical Perspective.' *Comparative Politics* 22: 445–58.

De Nardo, James. 1985. *Power in Numbers: The Political Strategy of Protest and Rebellion.* Princeton, NJ: Princeton University Press.

Favre, Pierre, ed. 1990. *La manifestation.* Paris: Presses de la Fondation Nationale des Sciences Politiques.

Fish, Steven. 1995. *Democracy from Scratch: Opposition and Regime in the New Russian Revolution.* Princeton, NJ: Princeton University Press.

Gerhards, Jürgen, and Dieter Rucht. 1992. 'Mesomobilization: Organizing and Framing in Two Protest Campaigns in West Germany.' *American Journal of Sociology* 98(3): 555–95.

Ginsburg, Benjamin, and Martin Shefter. 1990. *Politics by Other Means.* New York: Norton.

Jenkins, J. Craig, and Craig Eckert. 1986. 'Elite Patronage and the Channeling of Social Protest.' *American Sociological Review* 51 (December): 812–29.

Jepperson, Ronald L. 1991. 'Institutions, Institutional Effects, and Institutionalism.' Pp. 143–63 in Walter W. Powell and Paul J. DiMaggio, eds., *The New Institutionalism in Organizational Analysis.* Chicago: University of Chicago Press.

Keck, Margaret, and Kathryn Sikkink. 1998. *Activists beyond Borders: Advocacy Networks in International Politics.* Ithaca, NY: Cornell University Press.

Kriesi, Hanspeter, Ruud Koopmans, Jan W. Duyvendak, and Marco G. Giugni. 1995. *The Politics of New Social Movements in Western Europe: A Comparative Analysis.* Minneapolis/London: University of Minnesota Press/University College of London Press.

Lipsky, Michael. 1968. 'Protest as a Political Resource.' *American Political Science Review* 62: 1144–58.

McAdam, Doug, Sidney Tarrow, and Charles Tilly. 1997. 'Towards a Comparative Synthesis of Social Movements and Revolutions.' Paper presented at the Annual Meeting of the American Political Science Association, San Francisco, CA.

McCarthy, John D., and Mayer N. Zald. 1987. *Social Movements in an Organizational Society.* New Brunswick, NJ: Transaction.

Meyer, David S. 1990. *A Winter of Discontent: The Nuclear Freeze and American Politics.* New York: Praeger.

Meyer, David S. 1993. 'Institutionalizing Dissent: The United States Structure of Political Opportunity and the End of the Nuclear Freeze Movement.' *Sociological Forum* 8: 157–79.

Meyer, David S., and Thomas R. Rochon. 1997. 'Toward a Coalitional Theory of Social and Political Movement.' Pp. 237–251 in Thomas R. Rochon and David S. Meyer, eds., *Coalitions and Political Movements: The Lessons of the Nuclear Freeze.* Boulder, CO: Lynne Rienner.

Meyer, David S., and Suzanne Staggenborg. 1996. 'Movements, Countermovements, and the Structures of Political Opportunity.' *American Journal of Sociology* 101: 1628–60.

Minkoff, Debra C. 1994. 'From Service Provision to Institutional Advocacy: The Shifting Legitimacy of Organizational Forms.' *Social Forces* 72: 943–69.

Neidhardt, Friedhelm, and Dieter Rucht. 1993. 'Auf dem Weg in die 'Bewegungsgesellschaft'? Über die Stabilisierbarkeit sozialer Bewegungen.' *Soziale Welt* 44 (3): 305–26.

Piven, Frances Fox, and Richard Cloward. 1979. *Poor People's Movements.* New York: Vintage.

Putnam, Robert. 1995. 'Bowling Alone: America's Declining Social Capital.' *Journal of Democracy* 6: 65–78.

Rosenau, James. 1990. *Turbulence in World Politics: A Theory of Change and Continuity.* Princeton, NJ: Princeton University Press.

Rucht, Dieter. 1990. 'Campaigns, Skirmishes, and Battles: Antinuclear Movements in the U.S.A., France, and West Germany.' *Industrial Crisis Quarterly* 4: 193–222.

Rucht, Dieter. 1996. 'Mobilizing for "Distant Issues": German Solidarity Groups in Non-Democratic Issue Areas.' Unpublished manuscript, Wissenschaftszentrum Berlin.

Selznick, Philip. 1949. *TVA and the Grassroots.* Berkeley: University of California Press.

Sikkink, Kathryn. 1993. 'Human Rights, Principled Issue-Networks, and Sovereignty in Latin America.' *International Organization* 47: 411–41.

Smith, Jackie, Ron Pagnucco, and Charles Chatfield, eds. 1997. *Solidarity beyond the State. The Dynamics of Transnational Social Movements.* Syracuse, NY: Syracuse University Press.

Tarrow, Sidney. 1989. *Democracy and Disorder: Protest and Politics in Italy, 1965–1975.* Oxford: Clarendon.

Tarrow, Sidney. 1994. *Power in Movement: Collective Action, Social Movements and Politics.* Cambridge: Cambridge University Press.

Tarrow, Sidney. 1996. 'Fishnets, Internets and Catnets: Globalization and Transnational Collective Action.' Working Paper 78 (March).

Madrid; Instituto Juan March de Estudios e Investigaciones.

Tilly, Charles. 1978. *From Mobilization to Revolution.* New York: McGraw-Hill.

Tilly, Charles. 1995a. 'Contentious Repertoires in Great Britain, 1758–1834.' Pp. 12–42 in Mark Traugott, ed., *Repertoires and Cycles of Collective Action.* Durham, NC: Duke University Press.

Tilly, Charles. 1995b. *Popular Contention in Great Britain 1758–1834.* Cambridge, MA: Harvard University Press.

Wapner, Paul. 1995. 'Politics beyond the State: Environmental Activism and World Civic Politics.' *World Politics* 47: 311–40.

Yin, Jordan. 1996. 'The Role of Master Frames in the Sprawl-Busters Movement.' Unpublished manuscript, Cornell University, Ithaca, NY.

52. The New Terrorism

Walter Laqueur

Four hundred twelve men, women, and children were hacked to death by terrorists on the night of December 29, 1997, in three isolated villages in Algeria's Elizane region. Four hundred perished when a group of the Shah's opponents burned a cinema in Abadan during the last phase of the monarchy in Iran. There were 328 victims when an Air India aircraft was exploded by Sikh terrorists in 1985, and 278 were killed in the Lockerbie disaster in Scotland in 1988 which was commissioned by Libya's Colonel Khadafi and carried out by terrorists. Two hundred forty-one U.S. marines lost their lives when thee barracks were attacked by suicide bombers in Beirut in 1983, 171 were killed when Libyan emissaries put a bomb on a French UIA plane in 1985. The largest toll in human life on American soil was paid when 169 men, women, and children died in the bombing of the Alfred P. Murrah building Oklahoma City in 1995.

Terrorism has been with us for centuries and it has always attracted inordinate attention because of its dramatic character and its sudden, often wholly unexpected, occurrence. It has been a tragedy for the victims, but seen in historical perspective it seldom has been more than a nuisance.

Even the bloodiest terrorist incidents in the past, such as those just recounted, affected only a relatively few people. This is no longer true today, and may be even less so in the future. Yesterday's nuisance has become one of the gravest dangers facing mankind. For the first time in history, weapons of enormous destructive power are both readily acquired and harder to track. In this new age, even the cost of hundreds of lives may appear small in retrospect. Science and technology have made enormous progress, but human nature, alas, has not changed. There is as much fanaticism and madness as there ever was, and there are now very powerful weapons of mass destruction available to the terrorist. A hundred years ago a leading interpreter of international law, T. J. Lawrence, wrote that attempts made to 'prevent the use of instruments that cause destruction on a large scale are doomed to failure. Man has always improved his weaponry, and always will as long as he has need for them.' What Lawrence said then about warfare is *a fortiori* true with regard to terrorism.

In the near future it will be technologically possible to kill thousands, perhaps hundreds of thousands, not to mention the toll the panic that is likely to ensue may take. In brief, there has been a radical transformation, if not a revolution, in the character of terrorism, a fact we are still reluctant to accept. Even though Algerian terrorists never made a secret of their operations, there was disbelief in Europe that such atrocities as the Algerians committed were possible, and many thought some mysterious force was responsible for the mass slaughter.

There is public reluctance to accept the possibility that a few individuals could make use of the tremendous destructive power developed recently. It is the story of Prometheus and Epimetheus all over again: Prometheus tricked Zeus into giving him fire. But Zeus got his revenge; he sent to Epimetheus, Prometheus' less clever brother, Pandora's box, which he opened despite instructions not to do so under any circumstances. Out fluttered a host of calamities which have afflicted humankind ever since.

I do not suggest that most terrorist groups will use weapons of mass destruction in the near future; most of them probably will not. It is also quite possible that access to and the use of these weapons will not take a year or two but ten or fifteen. The technical difficulties standing in the way of effective use of the arms of mass destruction are still considerable. But the danger is so great, the consequences so incalculable, that even the occurrence of a few such attacks may have devastating consequences.

The traditional, 'nuisance' terrorism will continue. But fanaticism inspired by all kinds of religious-sectarian-nationalist convictions is now taking on a millenarian and apocalyptic tone. We are confronting the emergence of new kinds of terrorist violence, some based on ecological and quasireligious concerns, others basically criminal in character, and still others mixtures of these and other influences. We also are witnessing the rise of small sectarian groups that lack clear political or social agendas other than destroying civilization, and in some cases humankind. There was once a relatively clear dividing line between terrorists and guerrillas, between political terrorists and criminal gangs, and between genuine homegrown terrorism and state sponsored terrorism. Today these lines have become blurred, and the situation is even more confused than it used to be.

While the traditional terrorist movements historically consisted of hundreds, sometimes even thousands of members, the new terrorist groups can be very small, consisting of a few people or sometimes even one individual. The smaller the group, the more radical it is likely to be, the more divorced from rational thought, and the more difficult to detect. A sizable terrorist movement can be infiltrated by informers, but it is nearly impossible to infiltrate a small, closely knit group, perhaps composed of members of the same family or clan, let alone a single human being.

Some believe it is unlikely that extremists or fanatics possess the technological know-how and the resources to make use of weapons of mass destruction. But the technological skill, as will be shown, is not that complex, and the resources needed, not that rare or expensive. It is also possible that rogue governments, which may themselves not use these weapons for fear of retaliation, can readily supply the raw materials or the finished product to terrorists either by political design or for commercial gain.

Some believe that the horrific consequences of using weapons of mass destruction will deter even fanatics from using them. But this underrates the element of blind aggression, of rage, of suicidal impulses, of sheer madness, which unfortunately has always been part of human nature. Emperor Caligula reportedly said that he wished the Roman people had but one neck, so that it could be easily cut. Caligula was not a unique case.

[. . .]

The ready availability of weapons of mass destruction has now come to pass, and much of what has been thought about terrorism, including some of our most basic assumptions, must be reconsidered. The character of terrorism is changing, any restraints that existed are disappearing, and above all, the threat to human life has become infinitely greater than it was in the past.

[. . .]

Terrorism involves careful planning. The habits and movements of the targets have to be watched, weapons have to be procured, and transport as well as safe houses have to be provided. To make the most of their operations, terrorists need publicity, ideally even a public relations department. All major terrorist groups have a central command, sometimes a highly professional one. Decisions among the Russian terrorists were often made in committee meetings, but this was not a very effective approach. Sometimes the central command has been located outside the country, and this is now the case in the Middle East. This gives the leaders freedom of maneuver and freedom from fear of arrest. But the drawbacks of remoteness from the scene of terrorist action are serious.

The general tendency among terrorists has embraced centralization and the leadership principle. But this trend has its dangers, for terrorism always involves a great deal of improvisation, and even the best-laid plans may go wrong. If elaborate planning sacrifices the element of improvisation, this may rebound to the disadvantage of the terrorists.

Ideally, terrorist units should be small, because the bigger they are, the more open to infiltration they are. But very small units often have not had the resources and the know-how to carry out major operations. Many terrorist groups in the past were very small; they include the Japanese Red Army, Baader Meinhof, and the Symbionese Liberation Army, with its eight members. But others were large, including the Russian terrorists, Irgun, the IRA and the Argentinian and Uruguayan groups.

To be effective, terrorists need the anonymity of a big city for their operations; in a small town people know each other, and new faces attract attention and suspicion. Separatist religious movements are sometimes based in refugee camps, in certain quarters of a big city (as in Belfast), or in small cities where it is known that police control is less than perfect.

Small groups of terrorists usually develop a certain mind-set, an esprit de corps, but they exhibit also a tendency to isolate themselves from the political movement of which they are frequently a part. In larger units, on the other hand, there are often clashes between personalities and a tendency toward splits. Internal dissent is most likely to be a reaction to setbacks. Dissent also occurs amid success when the struggle becomes more important than the attainment of the goal for some of the militants.

Modern terrorists need money to finance their operations, whereas nineteenth-century terrorism could be run on a shoestring. The money needed is obtained from wealthy well-wishers at home or abroad, through robbing banks, or from foreign governments that, for reasons of their own, support terrorist groups as surrogates in the struggle against a common enemy. Some terrorist groups forge money, others engage in kidnapping and other forms of blackmail, including protection money, and others, such as the IRA, run legitimate businesses. The sums obtained through ransom have been impressive; the Argentinian Montoneros received 60 million dollars for releasing Jorge and Juan Born, the sons of the owner of one of the country's largest corporations. Of late, some terrorist money has come from drug dealers and cartels. Obtaining significant funds has been necessary to the terrorists, but it has also made it possible for the recipients to live a lifestyle to which they were not accustomed. Ideally, terrorists should be lean, hungry, and unspoiled by the temptations of the high life; when the infamous Carlos the Jackal grew fat and spent much of his time in nightclubs, his terrorist days were over.

Tools of the trade

Originally the dagger and later the pistol were the favored weapons of terrorists. The bomb we associate with the activity was first used in the Napoleonic age, and extended damage well beyond the intended target. In Orsini's attempt on the life of Napoleon III in 1858, eight people were killed; in the Fenian attack on Clerkenwell Prison in 1867, there were twelve killed and 120 injured. But the quantities of explosive used were considerable – five hundred pounds of black powder in the case of Clerkenwell. The Russian terrorists of Narodnaya Volya, which included some accomplished scientists, were the first to use dynamite, which had recently been discovered. But even then, the quantities needed were substantial and the terrorist attempts frequently failed, including one at the tsar's winter palace, because the perpetrators did not have sufficient explosives. When Johann Most predicted that a ten-pound bomb could destroy a warship, he was right, but he was off by a hundred years. The Irish militants in

America in the last century had many innovative ideas, including a type of Molotov cocktail, poison gas, and a submarine, but nothing came of these schemes at the time. The first letter bombs – parcel bombs, to be precise – were used on the eve of the First World War. At the same time, Russian and some of the French terrorists played with the idea of using motorcars, and the Russians invested money in the construction of an airplane. These schemes did not materialize, but they did presage the future.

Explosives were perfected during the First and Second World Wars, and these innovations soon reached the hands of terrorists. TNT was the explosive of choice after World War I, and plastic explosives such as Semtex became the favorite material after World War II. Automatic rifles and pistols replaced the old revolvers and guns, and RPGs (rocket-propelled grenades) were first used in Ireland, France, Germany, and Italy in the 1970s. Another favorite weapon was the car bomb, first used by Al Capone and his gang in Chicago. Limpet mines of various sorts were also used, sometimes exploded by remote control. While a small quantity of explosives sufficed to bring down an aircraft, much more substantial quantities were needed for attacks on land. It is estimated that one ton of explosives was needed for the bombing of the U.S. embassy in Beirut in April 1983, two tons for the bombing of the U.S. embassy in Kuwait, and up to six tons for blowing up the U.S. Marine headquarters in Beirut in October 1983. Preventive measures were taken to safeguard military installations, and few such attacks succeeded after 1983, but it was difficult to protect against attacks in civilian settings, such as the bombing of the World Trade Center in New York and the attack on Argentine Jewish institutions.

The old terrorist movements and many of the more recent ones have employed intelligence officers who penetrate 'enemy' installations and provide maps and timetables. This was of great importance as long as the attacks were directed against specific individuals. Once terrorism became more indiscriminate, intelligence became less important, as a bomb could be put in any supermarket or bus.

Nineteenth-century terrorist groups, as well as the IRA and Irgun, invested much effort in liberating from prison comrades-in-arms who had been captured. More recently, such operations have become rare because they involve too many risks.

Kidnapping was frequently used in Latin America as well as in other parts of the world. In many cases, ransom was demanded; in others, the victim was killed after a few hours or days.

One of the most dramatic kinds of terrorist action is the hijacking of airplanes. The first known case occurred in Peru in the 1930s, and there were a few more in the years immediately after World War II. In the 1960s, a great many U.S., planes were forced to fly to Cuba, although not always by terrorists, and there were dozens of other such attempts all over the world – sixty-four in 1971. Toward the end of the decade, this figure declined and has remained relatively low ever since. Airplanes are still hijacked, but usually by criminals or lunatics or people trying to escape from dictatorial regimes. What deters terrorists is probably not so much the controls at airports, which are often lax and superficial, but the fact that fewer and fewer countries are willing to listen to any demands from terrorists.

Some terrorist groups have tried to cause economic damage to their enemies. ETA conducted a campaign directed against tourist sites; since Spain accommodated more tourists than any other European country, it was hoped that the damage caused would be substantial. Similar tactics were used at one time or another by Arab terrorists against Israel and by Muslim fundamentalists against Egypt.

To be effective, terrorist movements depend on popular support, or at least support by a certain segment of society. Nationalist-separatist groups usually have had a broad base of sympathizers; the extremists of the left and right much less so. Aware of the fact that they have some such support, terrorist leaders have often come to over-rate the extent of their political influence. The moment they have decided to take part in parliamentary elections, they have hardly ever done well, as the results in Ireland and in the Basque region of Spain have shown. Nor did Irgun do well when it contested the elections after the establishment of the state of Israel; more than thirty years were to pass before they became a major force in Israeli politics. This pattern has repeated itself in Uruguay, Colombia, and other countries.

Terrorism and publicity

Classic terrorism is propaganda by deed, and propaganda is impossible without the use of the media. The alternative is the massive elimination of rivals or potential political rivals, such as the killing of the village elders in Vietnam and the Messalists in Algeria.

It has been said that journalists are terrorists' best friends, because they are willing to give terrorist operations maximum exposure. This is not to say that journalists as a group are sympathetic to terrorists, although it may appear so. It simply means that violence is news, whereas peace and harmony are not. The terrorists need the media, and the media find in terrorism all the ingredients of an exciting story. Their attitude toward terrorism has run the gamut from exaggerated respect to sycophancy (such as calling a terrorist a freedom fighter, an activist, a patriot, a militant, or a revolutionary). Media coverage has supplied constant grist to the terrorist mill; it has magnified the political importance of many terrorist acts out of all proportion. In some cases it has even been responsible for the murder of innocents and obstructed complicated rescue missions. The media cannot ignore terrorism, but society would certainly be better off if the media were not driven by sensationalism.

Terrorists have always recognized the importance of manipulating the media. The British War Office noted in 1922 that Sinn Fein's mastery of publicity was unrivaled. 'Its publicity department was energetic, subtle and exceptionally skillful in mixing truth, falsehood and exaggeration.' Irgun and the Stern Gang in Palestine had excellent relations with journalists, who helped magnify their strength and thus aided their cause. The shift in Latin America from guerrilla warfare to urban terrorism was motivated at least in part by the hope of gaining greater media attention. As one terrorist leader put it at the time: 'If we put even a small bomb in a house in town, we could be certain of making the headlines in the press. But if the rural guerrilleros liquidated thirty soldiers in some village, there was just a small news item on the last page.' Guerrilla warfare can exist without publicity, but urban terrorism cannot, and the smaller the group, the more it needs publicity. One of the reasons for the virtual absence of terrorism in totalitarian regimes and other effective dictatorships, besides the efficacy of the police forces, is the suppression of publicity. Unless the terrorists succeed in killing the dictator, which would be impossible to ignore, their deeds will pass unheralded.

It is also true that the media are mainly interested in some countries and not in others. Twelve people fell victim to terrorist attacks in Israel in 1985, two British soldiers were killed in Northern Ireland the same year, and the number of Americans killed by terrorists in 1982 was seven. There was great publicity in all these cases, whereas the tens of thousands killed in Iran and Iraq, in the Ugandan civil war, and in Cambodia (where hundreds of thousands were killed) went virtually unreported, because Western media either had no access or were not interested. This preoccupation of the media with some countries and with big cities rather than the countryside has on occasion induced terrorist groups to change their tactics in order to gain maximum exposure. Guerrillas, on the other hand, have no such interest in publicity, which would only harm them in their efforts to establish bases in the countryside without attracting the attention of the authorities. Mao's Long March and Tito's partisans were not covered by film crews, but in the end they were far more successful than any terrorist group. These are two examples of the difference between terrorism and guerrilla warfare.

[. . .]

Types of terrorists

What kind of group or individual would want to use weapons of mass destruction? The first category consists of deranged individuals. It should be recalled that most U.S. presidents who were assassinated (Garfield, McKinley, and Kennedy) were killed by individuals rather than political or terrorist groups. John Schrank, who shot and injured Teddy Roosevelt in 1912, was mentally unbalanced, and so was Zangara, who tried to kill Franklin Roosevelt but instead assassinated Mayor Cermak of Chicago. (Zangara thought that Roosevelt was somehow responsible for the stomach complaint from which he, Zangara, had suffered as a boy.) John Hinckley, who shot President Ronald Reagan, was mentally ill, as were several other assassins of political leaders in the nineteenth and twentieth centuries.

In some of these cases, the killers were driven by hate against their victims or wanted to draw attention to themselves, but in many other instances the act involved symbolism. The man suspected of having killed Swedish prime minister Olof Palme hated Sweden and Swedish society, not the prime minister himself. The same was true with regard to the assassination in 1966 of Henrik Verwoerd, the South African prime minister. The assassins wanted to register a protest against the system rather than just eliminate a single person.

In one of its rare publications of statistics, the academy of the Russian security forces asserted in 1997, that of all attempted aircraft hijackings they had tracked, 52 percent had been committed by mentally unbalanced people.

Many terrorist acts are committed by individuals following in the footsteps of Herostrat, the citizen of Ephesus in ancient times who burned the local temple simply so that his name would be remembered forever.

The second category consists of apocalyptic religious or religious-nationalist groups who believe the end is near for a sinful world. Members of a small Jewish sect in the early 1980s believed that it was their duty to create a catastrophe to force the hand of the 'Master of the Universe,' who would then wage a great and terrible campaign on their behalf. This led to the conspiracy of a few fanatics to explode the Mosque on Temple Mount in Jerusalem to start the third and final world war.

Retaliation will not deter those who believe the end of the world is already at hand. For some sectarians and millenarians, the ultimate disaster is a joyful prospect rather than something to be dreaded. Rational calculations, such as the likelihood of doing damage to themselves, do not apply. Sheikhs acting as gurus for extreme Muslim or Arab groups, and who declare that they love death and welcome it with the joy of a bride at the arrival of the bridegroom, will not be deterred, nor will sectarians convinced that a saving remnant will survive. The fallen will be taken to heaven in a *markabah*, or by special messengers sent by Allah, or in a spaceship. A few deranged individuals can be found in many religions, and while in the past they may have engaged in group suicide, they could, if they had access to weapons of mass destruction, prefer a deed aimed at others.

Third, fanatical nationalist groups, consumed by hatred against another national group in their midst or in a neighboring country, could opt to use weapons of mass destruction. This is especially likely in non-Western countries, where human lives count for less and humanitarian considerations seldom apply. These groups might believe that such desperate actions could at long last achieve their aim, by destroying the hated enemy or at least decisively weakening him. But evidence also tends to show that Western terrorist groups, including the IRA and ETA, and various factions in the former Yugoslavia, have shown greater cruelty in their attacks than European terrorist groups did in an earlier age.

Fourth, weapons of mass destruction could be used by various terrorist groups engaged in a long struggle without evident success and without much hope for success in the future. They may ask themselves: Why should our fight have been all in vain? We made many sacrifices and many of our best comrades fell in the struggle. Is it not our sacred duty to avenge the martyrs by engaging in one last desperate effort before admitting defeat?

Fifth, weapons of mass destruction could be used by terrorists acting on behalf of a state or even criminal-terrorist groups, who may calculate that the damage caused and the number of victims would be devastating but still limited. This could involve the use, for instance, of small nuclear devices or chemical substances to be sprayed over a limited area. (Some of the most deadly biological-warfare agents mentioned earlier, such as anthrax, would kill but would not cause an epidemic.) The intention might be to use such weapons to inflict dramatic but limited damage for the purposes of, say, threat and blackmail. One might argue that there is only a quantitative difference between such a biological weapon and a powerful bomb. However, most would conclude that the use of such weapons would cross a hitherto uncrossed barrier, and would lead to a war in which weapons that cause epidemics may be used.

Last, weapons of mass destruction could be used by small groups of individuals who suffer from one delusion or another and have personal grievances rather than political ones. This category is similar but not identical to the first category, because more than one person would be involved. These could be homicidal characters, or paranoiacs who believe the whole world is conspiring against them, or mad geniuses with unlimited ambitions (the mad scientist and the master from the world of science fiction). Unfortunately, there is almost an unlimited variety of this type. In the past, the damage they could inflict on the rest of the world was of necessity limited, but in the future this may no longer be the case. A single fanatic might be able to infect others who are in search of a message and a leader with his brand of madness.

53. Cosmopolitan Democracy

Daniele Archibugi

We live in a highly fragmented world that is, however, dominated by a small group of countries that, using a loose but readily understandable term, is defined as the West. The West is an entity composed of countries that have a market economy and consolidated democratic institutions. With the sole exception of Japan, the West involves Europe and its ancient settlements. Too often it is forgotten that this past of the world comprises at most one sixth of the world population. Within the West a single country, the United States, has today emerged as dominant. Never before has such a vast and profound hegemony been witnessed. Suffice it to observe the distribution of resources – production, consumption, knowledge, military capacity – to see how a relatively small part of the world became powerful. This power is not only material; its ideology is equally dominating. Cinema and science, literature and technology, music and mass communications are all in the hands of the West. The principles of political organization that prevail today were also produced by the West: the western visions of freedom and democracy have become increasingly universal values, and there is no reason to regret this.[1] The West has no cause to be ashamed of having proposed and developed forms of government that have gradually also spread to other parts of the world. The peoples of the five continents have taken to the streets to demand them, often against their own rulers, because they have fully understood that freedom and democracy not only guarantee greater personal dignity but also allow more material benefits to be distributed.

The West, for its part, has endeavored to make converts. Yet these efforts have proved incoherent and ambiguous. Freedom and democracy have been turned into ideological screens to defend vested interests and attack enemies. The vicissitudes of colonialism and then of imperialism show that only too often has the West claimed these values for itself and denied them to others. Can the power that the West wields today be used to involve and include rather than to dominate and subjugate? Is it possible to enlarge the number of subjects among whom to distribute the benefits? Cosmopolitan democracy has the objective of representing an intellectual contribution to the attainment of these objectives.

Cosmopolitan democracy opposes the idea of constructing a fortress in the western area and excluding all those who do not passively accept the new hegemonies. A strategy of this kind cannot but stir up new enemies and lead to futile crusades. Such a vision of the cosmopolitan project is also based on the factual observation that it is impossible to draw a dividing line between 'us' and 'them,' between 'friends' and 'enemies.' The planet is made up of 'overlapping communities of fate,'[2] to use the apt phrase coined by David Held, and it is a difficult, and often impossible, task to mark the confines between one and the other. What is the most suitable political community[3] to democratically decide on navigation on the Danube? Does not the spread of contagious diseases affect all the inhabitants of the Earth? And what must be said about issues concerning not only all the present inhabitants of the Earth but also those of the future, such as nuclear waste management or the ozone hole?

There is no obvious, easy answer to these questions. Nevertheless, the modern state – one of the West's favorite offspring – based on the assumption of sure frontiers and rigid criteria of membership continues to be the main political subject in international relations. In just a few centuries, the territorial state has spread over the entire land surface of the planet. With the sole exception of Antarctica, there is no longer a strip of land that does not belong to or is not claimed by a territorial state. In order to participate in world political life, each individual is obliged to become a member of a state, and each community must contrive to speak with a single voice, that of a monocratic government. World politics is therefore practiced by a small group of actors that have set up a directorate, giving rise to what may be defined as an intergovernmental oligarchy. It cannot be denied that the state plays an essential role in nourishing democracy: without actually deciding, often arbitrarily, who is in and who is out, it would not have been possible to develop self-government. The intensification of the processes of economic, social, political, and cultural globalization, however, has rendered traditional boundaries increasingly vague and uncertain, undermining the capacity for certain political communities to make decisions autonomously. The key principle of democracy, according to which decisions must be taken, only after discussion among all those affected by the decisions, is increasingly being questioned.

Today it must be acknowledged that the situation has changed. The rigidity of the frontiers of the political communities, an element that historically enabled self-government to be born and prosper, now stands in the way of democracy's evolving and even surviving. As soon as each political community receives and transmits the echo of its actions from and to the exterior, the state-based democratic procedure is eroded. In order to survive, democracy must undergo a radical transformation comparable to that experienced in the transition from direct to representative democracy. Democracy must be able to create new forms of management of public matters that are also open toward the exterior and to include in the decision-making process those who are affected by certain decisions.

Many attempts have already been made to increase participation and inclusion. International organizations, for example, have increased in number and functions, and almost every country in the world is now a member of the UN. In the so-called Old Continent, a mighty effort is being made to create common institutions, and the European Union has been extended southward, northward, and eastward. Half a century ago, the EU was concerned solely with coal and steel, while today it is competent in all aspects of public policy. Other regional organizations are developing on the other continents. World political life is beginning to assign jurisdiction and legitimacy to subjects other than state representatives, such as nongovernmental organizations, multinational corporations, cultural associations, and transnational pressure groups. This process of institutional integration is still only partial and unsatisfactory, however, compared with the intensity and rapidity of the changes occurring in the global process.

[. . .]

The key terms of the project illustrated herein – democracy and cosmopolitanism – encapsulate two of the loftiest ideals of political thought. Yet as is often the case with good intentions, both these concepts conceal insidious perils. The democratic idea – based on the principle that power belongs to the multitude – was established by drawing dividing lines between the persons to include and those to exclude. Power may be shared by the whole people but only on condition that we know who is being excluded. Paradoxically, the all-time enemy of democracy, despotism, has not had to face the problem of whom to include: obedience is expected from all individuals.

Throughout their journey, the democracies have gradually increased the number of citizens endowed with political rights: those rights have been extended from exclusively the free males of the polis to all adults. But even though the barriers have been whittled down, perhaps the most decisive one has remained standing: those who are in and those who are out. Extraneous peoples and individuals wishing to be included have been the most frequent victims of exclusion. The need to homogenize those who are different by means of assimilation, expulsion, or even elimination has brought out the dark side of democracy, transforming it into ethnocracy.[4] This dark side has dominated the process of nation building, but it would be wrong to consider this dark side solely as a problem of the past. In a world in which populations are subjected to great migrations, in which natural resources are scarce, and in which the processes of globalization, whether we like it or not, throw together different individuals, this dark side is always liable to re-emerge. The clashes of civilizations are nothing but the latest version of the deviation that can affect democracies at any moment. Cosmopolitanism as a school of tolerance would mitigate this genetic flaw in democracy and should prevent democracy from withdrawing into itself and allow democracy to continue to be a perpetually open and inclusive political system.

The vicissitudes of cosmopolitanism are equally turbulent.[5] In the course of the centuries, cosmopolitanism has cast off its ideal dimension and become a reality. The number of persons – merchants, explorers, writers, intellectuals, and the ever-increasing hordes of tourists – who have been able to travel and get to know the world has grown in parallel with prosperity and the development of mass society. Those who have become familiar with diversity have developed two different attitudes to it. The first is the curiosity (which, as Giovanbattista Vico tells us, is the daughter of ignorance and the mother of science) aroused by the customs of different societies. The second, parallel attitude is the idea that the various civilizations would ultimately converge toward common customs. Cosmopolitanism thus signifies not only knowing but also assessing, comparing, judging, selecting, and ultimately, wherever possible, actually applying the practices and customs deemed to be more valid. Only too often, however, the cosmopolitans have spread the conviction that, by pure chance, the best practices and customs are those of their own civilization.

The cosmopolitanism born as a school of tolerance can thus rapidly turn into its opposite. With the force of its convictions, cosmopolitanism does not fail to desire the assimilation of those who are different, sometimes through persuasion, other times by using violence. The question is whether this can still be considered cosmopolitanism. It is doubtful. The etymology of the word contains a reference to the citizen, a notion that implies equality and participation. The genes of the cosmopolitan should therefore contain the will to consult those who are different before making any decision. When cosmopolitanism becomes intolerant it is because it has swallowed a dangerous poison, that is intolerance, that has transformed it into fundamentalism. Unlike cosmopolitanism, fundamentalism no longer feels any doubt, wants to impose its view on all and sundry, and does not shrink from using violent and coercive methods. An antidote may be found by marrying cosmopolitanism with democracy: it is not enough for an idea to be a good one in order to be imposed; it is also necessary for that idea to be shared through the required procedures by means of persuasion, not force.

[. . .]

A project as ambitious as that of cosmopolitan democracy also requires the availability of an innovative legal apparatus. Here we focus on two crucial aspects: citizenship and, in the next section, the global legal system.

The desire for a citizenship accommodating all human beings, such as to allow them to travel to, visit, and live in any corner of the earth, is an old and never satisfied one.[6] In recent times, this desire has taken on much more concrete features for increasingly large groups of individuals. Managers, rock stars, and football idols have become the symbols of a nonterritorial citizenship, but less privileged groups of individuals, whether they are immigrants, refugees, or tourists, also discover they are living in a metanational space. In the abundant recent literature on the subject, cosmopolitan citizenship is often interpreted more in a sociological than legal sense.[7] Cosmopolitan democracy is therefore aimed at representing the condition of the inhabitants of the Earth in the present era, marked by problems and interactions that transcend one's own local community.[8] One characteristic of this sociological dimension is the extent to which it varies among different groups of persons: each individual makes use of and consumes global space in a different way. Significant studies have focused specifically on particular groups that, because of their own personal and collective history, have in identity and membership status that coincide only partly or not at all with a specific territorial state. Ethnic minorities, refugees, and immigrants are but several examples of this.[9] In these cases, the specific social condition has drawn attention to the need for institutional instruments other than those made available by the more conventional forms of citizenship.

However, when speaking of citizenship it is useful to separate the sociological problem from the legal one, the analysis of the ongoing processes from the type of regulatory and institutional response required. This distinction, which would facilitate all studies on citizenship – even those addressing a single country – becomes essential when dealing with the transnational sphere. From the sociological point of view, we are all more or less, directly or indirectly, willy nilly, citizens of the world. The evidence outlined above shows how a significant and growing percentage of the world population no longer perceive as their principal identity that corresponding to their own nation-state [. . .]. However, this social feeling in no way shows that the rights and duties of world citizenship already exist.

The distinction between the sociological and the legal dimension could not actually be more clear-cut: while individual participation in global processes increases, legal rules still link rights and duties to the territorial states. These are not abstract problems: public administrations have to cope daily with controversial issues. Let us take, for example, e-business, which accounts for a significant and increasing proportion of business transactions. There is no longer a clear link between the place in which the service is performed and the place in which taxes are levied on the service (where paying taxes is considered one of the citizens' duties). Similar problems arise in the case of different rights of citizenship: a growing number of persons, for instance, are entitled to or are denied health care in countries other than their own. In fields such as these, there is ample scope for IGO actions directed toward harmonization.[10]

Can the existing gap between social and legal conditions be bridged? What are the conditions to generating a global commonwealth in which citizens would have explicit rights and duties? Cosmopolitan citizenship is appealed to as an instrument or participation in and of safeguarding human rights. By virtue of the Universal Declaration of Human Rights and the subsequent pacts, individuals have been endowed with positive rights that they can claim from their own states. In addition, the states have accepted to be mutually accountable for these rights. However, despite the complexity of the international regulations governing human rights, in which governments, IGOs, and NGOs are involved, the effectiveness of those regulations has so far been very modest. Ever since its inception, the UN and the other IOs have failed both to safeguard individuals and to mete out effective sanctions against states that violate human rights despite the frequency and extreme intensity of the abuses committed. This failure has opened up a chasm between recognized rights and enforcement. This situation is closely linked to the very nature of the current regime of human rights, which is only partially able to offset the principle of noninterference and the dogma of sovereignty. One reason why the regime of human rights is so weak is linked to the fact that this regime has been managed mainly within the framework of intergovernmental relations. Condemnation and acquittal have thus often become negotiating tools in the diplomatic contest, while the most effective sanctions are still found to be those applied through denunciation to public opinion. Individuals find themselves in a hybrid situation: they possess certain rights but have no direct extrastate access channels through which to exercise those rights. The projection of individuals into a global sphere has taken place without any adjustment being made to their legal status.

The concept of world citizenship may hopefully help to close the existing gaps by obliging states to observe transparency and accountability in their actions vis-à-vis nonstate institutions. Cosmopolitan democracy is not intended to replace national citizenship with world citizenship. Such a replacement would lead back to the federalist option. World citizenship should not take on all the values of nation-state citizenship but rather be restricted to several fundamental rights. This would further mean that it is necessary to identify the areas in which individuals must have certain rights and duties insofar as those individuals are world citizens in addition to their rights and duties as citizens of secular states. In some cases the areas of competence may overlap and in others those areas may be complementary. The EU has shown that it is possible to accompany the citizenship existing inside the states with some form of transnational citizenship, and this experience is becoming an example for several other regional organizations.[11]

What spheres should world citizenship be invoked for? Let us take as our point of reference the Universal Declaration of Human Rights and the associated pacts. However sacred the principles enshrined in them are, they are so wide-ranging that it is impossible to imagine that the global institutions now being set up can manage to enforce them. Since they are not binding for anyone, the Universal Declaration has indicated such a vast array of principles that it may be considered a 'book of dreams.' It will be helpful to establish priorities on which world citizens hammer out an agreement to ensure that some core rights are enforced.[12] The first priority involves the sphere of survival. The second regards the respect of fundamental human rights and the possibility of each political community to govern itself and to share in the management of global problems.

Institutions and resources are required in order to achieve these goals. As far as institutions are concerned, these tasks should be entrusted to bodies that represent a direct expression of the citizens, regardless of and parallel to the institutions of their respective states. It is possible to envisage a world parliament expressing a secretariat that is called upon to act directly in cases of glaring need.[13] These cases would consist of natural disasters, famine, and any of the areas touching on survival. These institutions should be backed up by autonomous, albeit limited, resources that are not dependent on the member states. These resources could be funded by a small tax levy, for which numerous technical devices have been suggested, for instance, international taxes such as a surcharge on air tickets and financial transactions.[14] Only when survival is at risk because of conflicts would these institutions be entitled to request the intervention of the states, as the states have a much more powerful secular arm [. . .]. However, in addition to direct intervention, world citizenship should imply a political role of intervention in global affairs backed up by a mandate adequately covering the whole range of the Universal Declaration. A world parliament would have the authority to perform these tasks. Although lacking any concrete means for carrying out direct intervention, a world parliament would still be performing a politically burdensome role, particularly for the more democratic states. These interventions would actually no longer be bound by the principle of noninterference, as they would not now be promoted by a state but by a body representing world citizens.

A contract of citizenship characterized by basic rights and minimum duties opens up the way to a global commonwealth of citizens, which could take thicker forms for certain groups of persons in conditions of extreme need. Groups of persons deprived of their national citizenship rights could find protection in a more comprehensive world citizenship in which the institutions in charge perform several administrative functions such as the issue of passports, hitherto the exclusive competence of the states.[15] Refugees often live in conditions of extreme poverty and are certainly not members of any elite. Today they number about twenty million, often living in makeshift camps, who have to fight to survive. If these persons were provided with the status of world citizenship, they could become the first group to benefit from the 'right to have rights' ensured by cosmopolitan and denied them by their states of origin [. . .]. If refugees were granted certain rights associated with world citizenship, such as a guaranteed income and a chance to stay in a free port while awaiting repatriation, a significant discrepancy would arise between the social group to which the rights were granted and the social group having the duties. If the contributions needed to fund world citizenship were to come, as some have suggested, from taxes levied on air travel or financial transfers, it would be the elites who bore the brunt, while the beneficiaries of the rights would be groups, such as refugees, in conditions of extreme hardship.[16]

Another significant case is that of immigrants, although thus case leads to the opposite prescription. Immigrants have to live and work in countries different from their original one; they pay taxes but have fewer rights than members of the state in which they now live (for example, immigrants do not have the right to vote). If it is considered that the vast majority of immigrants gravitate toward the richer and more developed countries, it would be counterproductive to safeguard immigrants by means of a world citizenship, the legal and political strength of which would inevitably be weaker than that of the nation-state. It would seem in this case that the idea of world citizenship is more useful if used to request that the host states incorporate into their own system the extension to aliens of rights hitherto reserved to natives of these countries. In this sense, world citizenship would become an instrument for exerting pressure on the states to convince them to become champions of cosmopolitanism in their own territorial area by granting rights and duties to those who de facto participate in the life of their community.

NOTES

1. Amartya Sen, among others, usefully reminds us that westerners are too often not knowledgeable enough on similar principles developed by other civilizations. See Amartya Sen, 'Democracy Isn't "Western,"' *Wall Street Journal*, March 24, 2006.
2. David Held, *Global Covenant* (Cambridge: Polity Press, 2005), pp. x and 168.
3. I use *political community* to translate the Latin expression *res publica*.
4. The impressive and often disturbing research by Michael Mann, *The Dark Side of Democracy: Explaining Ethnic Cleansing* (Cambridge: Cambridge University Press, 2005) and, before him, the theses of Elias Canetti, *Crowds and Power* (New York: Viking, 1963) have not yet been properly digested by democratic theory.
5. For two recent narratives of cosmopolitanism, see Kwame Anthony Appiah, *Cosmopolitanism: Ethics in a World of Strangers* (New York: Norton, 2007) and Robert Fine, *Cosmopolitanism* (London: Routledge, 2007).
6. Its vicissitudes are described in Derek Heater, *World Citizenship and Government* (Basingstoke: Macmillan, 1996) and April Carter, *The Political Theory of Global Citizenship* (London: Routledge, 2001).
7. See, for example, Kimberly Hutchings and Roland Dannreuther, eds, *Cosmopolitan Citizenship* (Houndmills: Macmillan, 1999) and Nigel Dower and John Williams, eds, *Global Citizenship: A Critical Reader* (Edinburgh: Edinburgh University Press, 2002).
8. Saskia Sassen, 'The Repositioning of Citizenship: Emergent Subjects and Spaces for

Politics,' *New Centennial Review* vol. 3, no. 2 (2003): 41–66.

9. The problem has been stressed, among others, in Hannah Arendt, *The Origins of Totalitarianism* (London: André Deutsch, [1950] 1986); Will Kymlicka, *Multicultural Citizenship* (Oxford: Clarendon Press, 1996); Seyla Benhabib, *The Rights of Others: Aliens, Citizens and Residents* (Cambridge: Cambridge University Press, 2004) and Rainer Bauböck, *Transnational Citizenship* (Cheltenham: Edward Elgar, 1995).

10. For a wide-ranging analysis of changes occurring in the traditional interstate system, see Andrew Linklater, *The Transformation of Political Community* (Cambridge: Polity Press, 1998).

11. Ulrich Preuss, 'Citizenship in the European Union: A Paradigm for Transnational Democracy?', in Archibugi, D., Held, D., and Köhler, M., eds, *Re-imagining Political Community* (Cambridge: Polity, 1998), pp. 138–51.

12. For an attempt in this direction, see Alessandro Ferrara, 'Per una seconda dichiarazione dei diritti,' *Filosofia e questioni pubbliche* vol. 9, no. 2 (2004): 33–45.

13. The possibility of setting up a world parliament will be discussed in chapter 6. The proposal has now been put forward by a growing number of persons – cf., for instance, Richard Falk and Andrew Strauss, 'Toward Global Parliament,' *Foreign Affairs* vol. 80, no. 1 (January–February 2001): 212–20 and George Monbiot, *The Age of Consent: A Manifesto for a New World Order* (London: Harper Perennial, 2003).

14. See Inge Kaul and Pedro Conceiçao, eds, *The New Public Finance: Responding to Global Challenges* (Oxford: Oxford University Press, 2006).

15. As is the case, de facto, for refugees, cf. Pierre Hassner, 'Refugees: a Special Case for Cosmopolitan Citizenship?' pp. 273–86 in *Re-imagining Political Community*, ed. Archibugi et al.

16. Also in a national context there are often discrepancies between the communities of duty-holders and right-holders (for example, very affluent groups may pay with their taxes a substantial part of welfare benefit to groups with a high unemployment rate). Within a national context, a common identity makes the two groups permeable, also because, at least in principle, any individual can potentially move from one group to the other. The rights and duties associated with a world citizenship are more likely to belong to separate groups. Obligations will therefore need to be based on solidarity rather than on identity.

Theme 10 – Further Reading

A good introductory text is always a good place to start, so Keith Faulks's (2000) *Political Sociology: A Critical Introduction* (New York: New York University Press) covers the field and is up to date. David Held's (2006) *Models of Democracy*, 3rd Edition (Cambridge: Polity) explores the concept and varied practices of democracy around the world. On social movements, try Donatella Della Porta and Mario Diani's (2005) *Social Movements: An Introduction*, 2nd Edition (Oxford: Blackwell Publishing). Martin Shaw's (2003) *War and Genocide: Organized Killing in Modern Societies* (Cambridge: Polity) is an excellent account of modern warfare and its changing forms. Finally, anyone looking to understand terrorism old and new should try Gus Martin's (2012) *Understanding Terrorism: Challenges, Perspectives and Issues*, 4th Edition (Thousand Oaks: Sage).

Giddens and Sutton *Sociology 7th Edition* (2013)

Sociology's introduction to political sociology can be found in Chapters 22 and 23. In addition, there are the following sections: Chapter 4 on political and social change, pages 125–7; Chapter 5 on environmental citizenship, pages 196–7; Chapter 6 on governing cities, pages 238–40; Chapter 11 on disability and public policy, pages 468–70; Chapter 13 on poverty and the welfare state, pages 553–63; Chapter 13 on global inequality and international institutions, pages 610–2 and Chapter 18 on the politics of the media, pages 805–6. Also search the Index for references to specific social movements mentioned across the book.

Index